Norman Backhaus

Tourism and Nature Conservation in Malaysian National Parks

Kultur, Gesellschaft, Umwelt
Band 6
Schriften zur Südasien- und Südostasien-Forschung
Culture, Society, Environment – South Asian and South East Asian Studies

Edited by / herausgegeben von

Ulrike Müller-Böker, Division of Human Geography,
Department of Geography, University of Zurich

Samuel Wälty, Swiss Agency for Development and Cooperation, Berne

Norman Backhaus

Tourism and Nature Conservation in Malaysian National Parks

Cover photo: Canopy walkway in Taman Negara (by Norman Backhaus)

Bibliographic information published by Die Deutsche Bibliothek
Die Deutsche Bibliothek lists this publication in
the Deutsche Nationalbibliographie; detailed bibligraphic data are available
in the internet at http://dnb.ddb.de.

Backhaus, Norman
Tourism and Nature Conservation in Malaysian National Parks /
Norman Backhaus – Münster : LIT, 2005
    (Kultur, Gesellschaft, Umwelt | Culture, Society, Environment; 6.)
    ISBN 3-8258-9037-6

NE: GT

Cover Design: Martin Steinmann, Zurich
Typeset: Syntax, Frutiger and Adobe Garamond

A catalogue record for this book is available from the British Library

©LIT VERLAG Münster 2005
Grevener Str/Fresnostr. 2   D-48159 Münster
Tel. +49/(0)251-62 03 20   Fax +49/(0)251-23 19 72
e-Mail: lit@lit-verlag.de   http://www.lit-verlag.de

Distributed in the UK by: Global Book Marketing, 38 King Street, London WC 2E 8JT
Phone: +44 (0) 207 240 6649 – Fax: +44 (0) 20 7497 0309, http://www.globalbookmarketing.co.uk

Distributed in North America by:

Transaction Publishers
New Brunswick (U.S.A.) and London (U.K.)

Transaction Publishers
Rutgers University
35 Berrue Circle
Piscataway, NJ 08854

Tel.: (732) 445–2280
Fax: (732) 445–3138
for orders (U.S. only):
toll free 888-999-6778

Acknowledgements

This study would not have been possible without the help and support of the following persons: Patricia Anak Anoy, Balvinder Kaur Kler, Dr. Urs Geiser, Dr. Andreas Huber, Dr. Michael Kollmair, Regina Kohler, Prof. Dr. Lee Boon Thong, Sara Landolt, Lee Hui Min, Urs Müller, Prof. Dr. Ulrike Müller-Böker, Munirah Abd. Manan, Ng Wang Ching, Nicole North, Ooi Chew Bee, Marco Pronk, Andrea Scheller, Siow Soo Fei, Dr. Susan Thieme, Dr. Tan Wan Hin, Samuel Wälty, Won Siew Foong, Ingrid Wyss, Yee Mei Ling, Dr. Marc Zaugg, and all my interview partners.

The field work was supported by the Swiss Academy of Sciences (SCNAT) and the University of Zürich.

Thank you all!

Content

Introduction

I   Focus and aim 1
    1 Introduction 2
    2 Aim and research questions 6
    3 Triangulation of methods 9
    4 Overview 10

II   Context and theory 13
    1 Theoretical framework 14
    2 Risk, control and tourism 18
    3 Tourism and modernity 25
    4 Authenticity and non-places 43
    5 Ecotourism and nature conservation 51

III   Nature conservation and national parks in Malaysia 79
    1 (Eco)tourism in Malaysian conservation areas and national parks 80
    2 Most important parks and reserves in Malaysia 93

Analysis

IV   Malaysian urbanites and their national parks 115
    1 Introduction 116
    2 Methods 117
    3 Connotations of nature 125
    4 Visited parks and recreation areas 128
    5 Opinions about nature protection and tourism 144
    6 Recreation and theme parks 164
    7 Summary 168

V   The experts' discourse about nature conservation in Malaysia ... 171
    1 Introduction 172
    2 Method 173
    3 Important topics of nature conservation 175
    4 Summary 201

VI   Tourists in Gunung Mulu National Park 203
    1 Introducing Gunung Mulu National Park 204
    2 Methods 208
    3 Tourism and its potential in Gunung Mulu 211
    4 Summary 243

Conclusion

VII Regionalising conservation areas 245
   1 Conservation areas: a consequence of aggregated actions 246
   2 Urban Malaysians are discovering conservation areas 247
   3 The experts' biggest concerns 249
   4 Types of tourists become forms of tourism 255
   5 Creating the potential to have authentic experiences 258
   6 Important issues of the National Ecotourism Plan 260
   7 Final remarks on theory, methods and future prospects 264

VIII Index and Bibliography 267
   Index of authors 268
   Bibliography 271

Table of Figures

1: Development of world protected areas in the 20th century 3
2: Development of protected areas of Malaysia in the 20th century 4
3: Protected area and its percentage in Southeast Asian countries 5
4: Foreign tourist arrivals to Malaysia 6
5: Conservation management and the focus of the study (highlighted) 8
6: Stratification model of consciousness and action 17
7: Countries with more than 5 million foreign visitors 29
8: Backpackers and local development 38
9: Selected definitions of ecotourism 53
10: Hard and soft ecotourism 55
11: Humans: part of nature or not 56
12: Exploitive, passive and active ecotourism 56
13: Ecotourism in the context of other tourism types 58
14: Preferred destinations by ecotourists of selected countries 61
15: The conflict triangle in a conservation area 72
16: Main issues of the National Ecotourism Plan 90
17: Location of Malaysian national parks 94
18: Visitors of Taman Negara National Park 96
19: Visitors to Bako National Park 100
20: Visitors to Gunung Gading 101
21: Visitors to Kubah National Park 103
22: Visitors to Niah National Park 104
23: Visitors to Lambir Hills National Park 105
24: Visitors to Gunung Mulu National Park 106
25: Visitors to Gunung Kinabalu National Park 108
26: Climbers of Gunung Kinabalu 109
27: Visitors to Tunku Abdul Rahman National Park 111
28: Visitors to Pulau Penyu National Park 113
29: Indexed development of selected parks 114
30: Places, where the interviews were conducted 118
31: The sample compared with Kuala Lumpur and Malaysia 120
32: Ethnicity and religion of the sample 121
33: Place of residence of the respondents 122
34: Occupation of the sample 123
35: Reasons for approval and disapproval of the place of residence 124
36: 'Nature' and the 'opposite of nature' according to the respondents ... 125
37: Location of Malaysian national parks and visits by the respondents ... 129
38: Expectations about a future visit to a conservation area 130
39: Most favoured recreation areas (excl. national parks) 131

40: Favoured parks (conservation and recreation; ranked by number of visits) 132
41: Visited Malaysian national parks (by number of visiting respondents) 133
42: Visited national parks and percentage of domestic visitors 134
43: Categorisation of parks and recreation areas: length of stay 136
44: Parks and reasons for visiting them 142
45: Reasons for the establishment of new conservation areas 145
46: Reasons against the establishment of new conservation areas 146
47: Statements the respondents are confronted with 147
48: Average score to each statement (including standard deviation) 148
49: Age, nature and tourism 154
50: Education, nature and tourism 155
51: Ethnicity, nature and tourism 156
52: Religion, nature and tourism 158
53: Gender, nature and tourism 159
54: Scores of aggregated answers about nature conservation 161
55: Differences between specific groups of respondents 163
56: Map of most visited theme parks 166
57: Most visited theme parks 167
58: Most favoured theme parks 167
59: The analysed discourse threads and the respondent categories 175
60: Visitors to national parks in Sarawak 2000 (monthly) 204
61: Climate data of three stations near Mulu in East Malaysia 205
62: Sketch of the Gunung Mulu headquarters 206
63: Gunung Mulu National Park 207
64: Respondents' origin and all visitors of Mulu during interview period 209
65: Checklist on tourism potential of Gunung Mulu 211
66: Evaluation of transport 213
67: The main reasons for visitors to come to Mulu 216
68: Visited attractions by individual and group travellers 222
69: Length of stay 223
70: Length of stay and visited attractions 224
71: Evaluation of the attractions by the visitors 225
72: Costs for various activities and attractions in Mulu 226
73: Evaluation of the entrance fee 228
74: How much the respondents are prepared to pay 229
75: Accommodation used by the respondents 231
76: Evaluation of specific accommodation 232
77: Evaluation of the restaurant and the canteen near the headquarters 235
78: Visit and evaluation of the interpretation centre and its information 239
79: Information media used before the visit to Mulu 240

Introduction

1 Focus and aim

1 Introduction

The systematic protection of nature has become a global phenomenon in the 20th century. Starting in the "new" nations of Australia, Canada, New Zealand, South Africa and the USA, the modern protected area movement has spread around the world. Since 1900, when the idea of nature conservation slowly began to become globalized, the number of protected areas, as well as their size has increased considerably. Between 1960 and 1990, the area protected worldwide increased by a factor of 6. The number of sites increased by a factor of 4. In 2002, some 44,000 sites, covering 10% of the world's surface, meet the IUCN definition of a protected area.[1] The highest rates of newly documented national parks and other conservation areas can be found in so-called developing or newly industrializing countries.[2] The purpose of conservation has changed considerably since the first parks were set aside for protection.[3] The internationally acknowledged management categories of protected areas by the IUCN differentiates between different management purposes. All but one, the Strict Nature Reserve/Wilderness area (Ia), serve recreation and tourism purposes to a varying degree. Tourism and recreation are primary objectives, especially for categories II and III, National Parks and National Monuments. Other vital objectives are the preservation of species, biodiversity and landmarks.[4]

Tourism has become the world's number one industry.[5] The total number of tourists (domestic and foreign) was estimated as 5.4 to 5.5 billion, for the year 2000. International tourists were estimated as 702 million.[6] International tourism created revenues of over US$ 455 billion in 1999 and an estimated 462 billion in 2000. Domestic tourism totalled US$ 3,395 billions, for the same period.[7] It is estimated that there will be a continuation of the exponential growth of international tourism during the next decades. Expanding networks of international air travel, rising educational levels, the growing importance of being able to travel abroad, as part of people's cultural capital (in the sense of Bourdieu[8]), are important factors for the future development of tourism, not only in the so-called industrialized countries.

---

1 Eagles, P.F.J., McCool, S.F. & Haynes, C.D. 2002, p. 8.
2 World Conservation Monitoring Centre & IUCN 1998.
3 See Soliva, R. 2002.
4 Eagles, P.F.J., McCool, S.F. & Haynes, C.D. 2002; IUCN 1994.
5 Eagles, P.F.J., McCool, S.F. & Haynes, C.D. 2002.
6 World Tourism Organisation (WTO) 1997 in: Eagles, P.F.J., McCool, S.F. & Haynes, C.D. 2002, p. 18.
7 Fischer Weltalmanach 2002, p. 1247.
8 See Jenkins, R. 1993.

In conservation areas, we must count on a more than proportional increase of demand by tourists, mainly because of four factors, according to the IUCN[9]. First, a rising educational level increases the demand for outdoor activities, because more people are working indoors. At the same time, the awareness of the fragility of the earth's ecosystems increases and people want to see and feel pristine, unpolluted and authentic environments. Second, for a certain group of people, leisure time will increase, due to shorter working hours and more automation in housework. For many, i.e. single parents, women who work and have to do housework, students who have to work besides their studies, the amount of available leisure time has decreased. Third, an ageing population that is also fitter, demands moderate outdoor activities such as walking, nature study, fishing or wildlife observation. Fourth, the decreasing gap between the genders results in an increasing demand of nature tourism by women. Women with children, especially, often decide to visit a national park as child-centered leisure. In addition, their increasing presence in park management and nature related NGOs, makes women visible in the context of nature conservation. They may serve as role models for other women and therefore attract more women to conservation areas.

Figure 1: Development of world protected areas in the 20th century

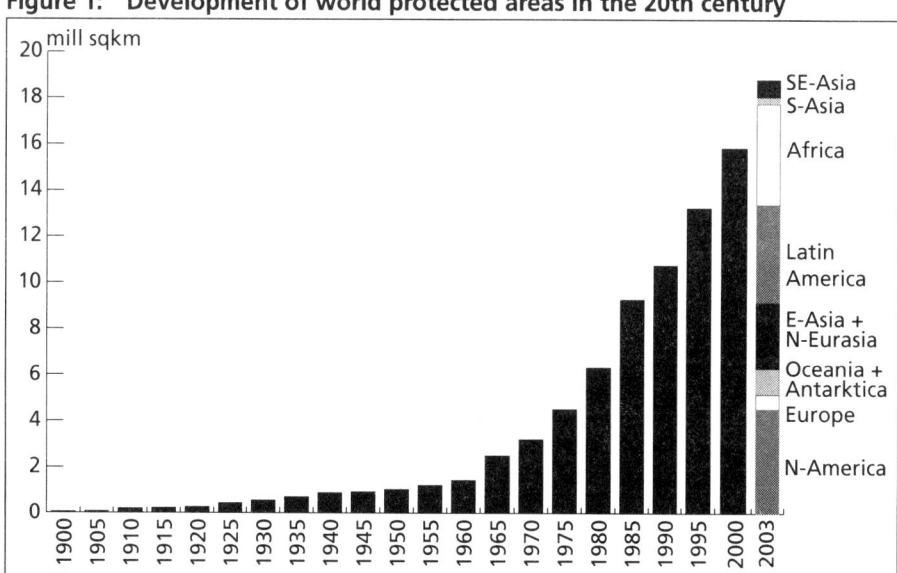

Source: own draft; data: World Conservation Monitoring Centre & IUCN 1998.

---

9   Eagles, P.F.J., McCool, S.F. & Haynes, C.D. 2002, p. 14-16.

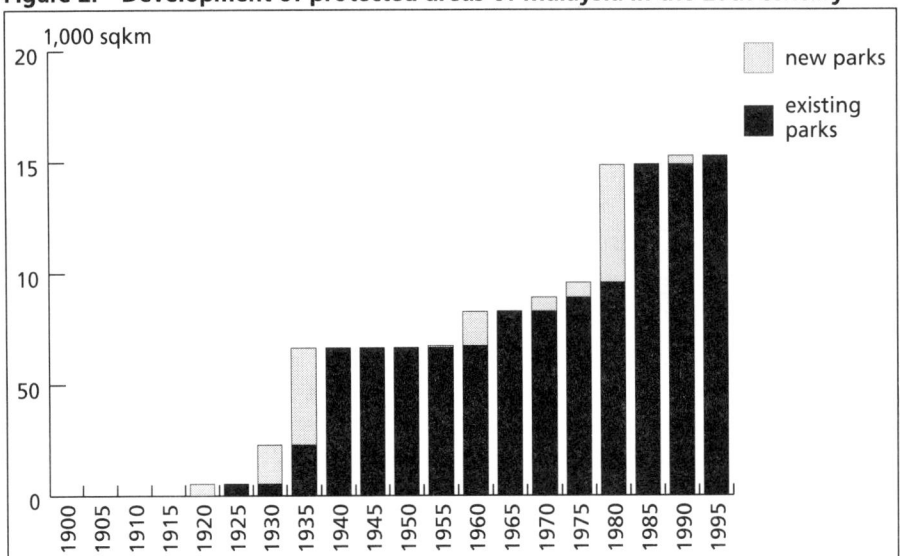

Figure 2: Development of protected areas of Malaysia in the 20th century

Source: own draft; data: World Conservation Monitoring Centre 2002; World Conservation Monitoring Centre & IUCN 1998.

A globally heightened awareness of ecological problems, combined with cheaper and easier long haul flights, and a greater demand for tourist destinations have the potential for developing newly industrialized countries. Countries with a high degree of biodiversity, charismatic or flagship species and/or spectacular ecosystems, i.e. Malaysia[10], can benefit, especially, from the increasing demand for nature based tourism. The label 'national park' plays an important role as an attraction, for it serves as a guarantee of an unspoiled, pristine environment and therefore for authentic experiences. Most countries vie for a share of the immense tourist market. Malaysia has advanced to one of the top twenty[11], ranking 18 just after Switzerland and before the Netherlands. Malaysia has also just recently overtaken rivalling Thailand in terms of international tourist arrivals. Although Malaysia does not exclusively advertise its natural attractions, they play an important role. The flagships of Malaysia include the World Heritage Sites of Kinabalu, which is a biodiversity hotspot with the highest mountain of Southeast Asia, and Gunung Mulu, with the biggest cave chamber and cave

---

10 Malaysia is a 'megadiversity' country (together with Australia, Brazil, China, Colombia, the Democratic Republic of the Congo, Ecuador, India, Indonesia, Madagascar, Mexico, Papua New Guinea, Peru, the Philippines, South Africa, Venezuela and the United States) that together contain sixty percent of earth's species (Ministry of Science Environment and Technology Malaysia 1998. p. 7).
11 Bundesamt für Statistik Schweiz 2002.

mouth in the world. These sites, along with Taman Negara, the world's oldest rainforest, attract an increasing number of foreign and domestic tourists (see figure 24 on page 210). Moreover, its political stability and good transportation and infrastructure, make Malaysian parks easily accessible for a wide range of tourists. It has therefore become one of the prime destinations for nature based tourism, in the world.

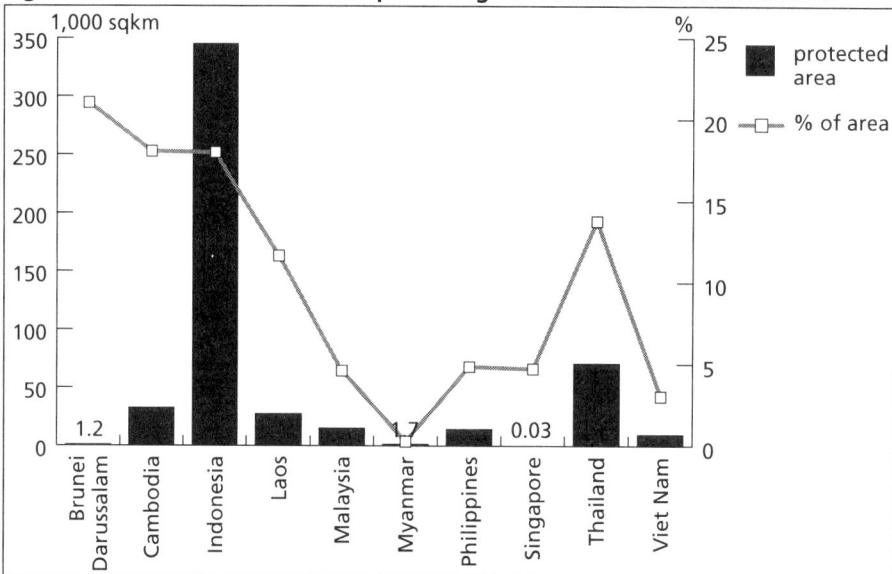

Figure 3: Protected area and its percentage in Southeast Asian countries

Source: own draft, data: World Conservation Monitoring Centre 2002

Compared to its neighbours Indonesia and Thailand, Malaysia has considerably less area under protection, in absolute as well as in relative terms. Nevertheless, because of their accessibility, Malaysian national parks have become an important factor in the tourist industry. Along with other Southeast Asian countries Malaysia had a steady growth of tourist arrivals during the last twenty years. There was a first peak in 1990 and a sudden plunge in 1991, due to the 2nd Gulf war, which affected most Asian countries, especially those with a Muslim majority. In 1995 the total for 1990 (7.5 million) was reached again. The recession in Europe, and subsequently the Asian currency crisis and 'the haze' in 1997/98 led to another decrease. From then on, there was considerable growth, until 2001 when Malaysia was visited by more tourists than Thailand. In 2002, the number of tourists increased slightly (4%) and amounted to more than 12 million visitors[12] (a number that was estimated to have been reached already in the year 2000[13]). This was probably due to the events of September 11th, which made people more cautious about travelling by air. It remains to be seen what consequences the war in Iraq will have on the tourist numbers in 2003.

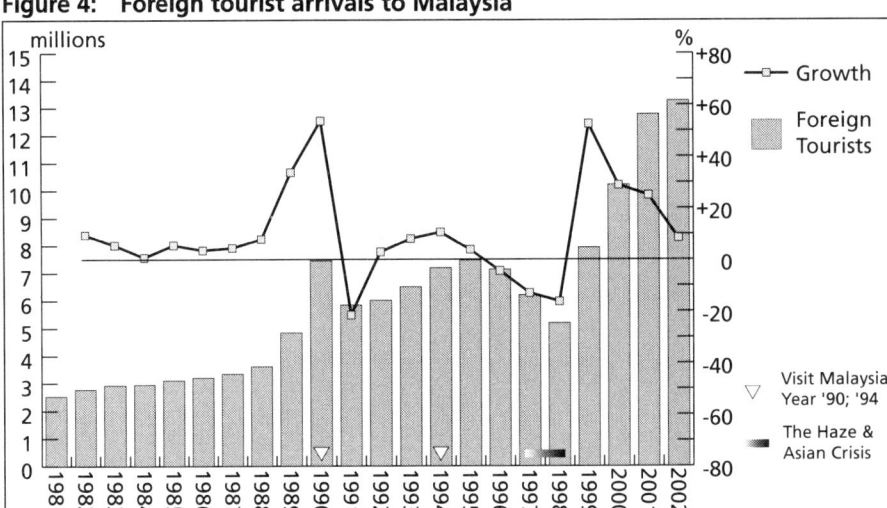

Figure 4: Foreign tourist arrivals to Malaysia

Source: own draft; data: Immigration Department of Malaysia 2002/2003.

2 Aim and research questions

Nature conservation and tourism are not mutually exclusive. Tourism creates such opportunities as the financing of conservation, and income generation for local people. However, an increasing number of visitors can cause many problems in these areas, especially in parks which are understaffed. If current trends continue, Malaysian parks will face tourism related problems in the coming years, due to an increasing demand in general, and due to a growing heterogeneity of visitors (i.e. foreign and domestic visitors) and their demands. If their budgets remain the same, they have to meet these problems, generally, with a minimum of staff and little financial means. It is therefore the aim of this study to analyse the relation of different forms of tourism and nature conservation in Malaysia in order to contribute not only to scientific discourse but also to the knowledge base of people and organizations concerned with nature conservation and ecotourism and, ultimately, to better planning and implementation.

---

12 The slight increase of 4% is mostly due to visitors from other ASEAN countries (especially from Singapore and Thailand; figure 7 on page 29). From almost all other countries, the number of visitors decreased. The reasons can probably be found in the general economic situation and the aftermath of the terror acts of September 11th, 2001.
13 WWF Malaysia 1996, p. 62.

The topic is approached from three different angles that influence the management of conservation areas: the point of view of Malaysian urbanites, experts and different tourist types, i.e. domestic tourists, international tourists (see figure 5 on page 8). This shall be elaborated as follows:

- The concept of modern national parks is a generally a western concept that has been globalized. Therefore, most national parks in nonwestern countries were designed to cater to the needs of foreign (western) tourists, rather than to those of the growing number of domestic visitors. Therefore, knowledge of the opinions of potential Malaysian visitors, who come mostly from urban areas, about nature conservation and ecotourism serves is important for the management of Malaysian national parks. Tourism is a relatively new phenomenon in Malaysia, and Malaysians have only recently become aware of sustainable development. It is, therefore, expected that urban Malaysians are not well acquainted with the principles of ecotourism and have diverse desires and demands when they visit a conservation area. The question that arises is: What are urban Malaysians' opinions about nature conservation and ecotourism?

- Malaysia has a long and successful tradition of establishing, managing, and maintaining conservation areas and there are many experts with specific knowledge in their respective fields. However, this knowledge is not a generally shared knowledge. One reason for this is the distance (spatial, topical, ideological, and political), another the lack of opportunities for exchange. This study's aim is to present an outsider's view of the Malaysian experts' discourse. For these experts it can be useful to have an outside view comprised of a wide range of topics and relevant discussions. Hence, the question: How do Malaysian experts perceive the tourism-nature conservation nexus?
Most experts working in the field of tourism and nature conservation received training influenced by essentially western notions Tourism in conservation areas was initially set up for middle to upper class, mostly western tourists. We would expect, therefore, that one of the most important problems is the integration of the needs of domestic tourists into conservation.

- There is an important difference between the groups of foreign and domestic visitors. There is also a much discussed difference between individual and group travellers. The differences in their evaluations, and their behaviours were analysed in a selected Malaysian national park, Gunung Mulu National Park in Sarawak. What are the needs of different groups of tourists (i.e. individual and group travellers and domestic and foreign travellers) and how can they be balanced in conservation areas?

The range of groups with different social, cultural and economic backgrounds, who visit conservation areas in Malaysia, is growing. The needs of the tourists are also increasingly diverse. With good interpretation and information, their needs can hopefully be reconciled with each other, and with conservation.

- How can an increasing number of tourists be guided through a park with limited personnel, without causing harm to the environment? Can authenticity be constructed or staged in a way that enhances the experiences of the visitors without compromising nature conservation?

Tourists want to have fun and enjoy themselves in conservation areas, like they do, for example, in theme parks (which can be regarded as 'non-places'). Therefore, certain aspects of theme parks could be used in order to guide increasing numbers of people through a park and to meet their recreational needs without inhibiting the protection of nature.

Figure 5: Conservation management and the focus of the study (highlighted)

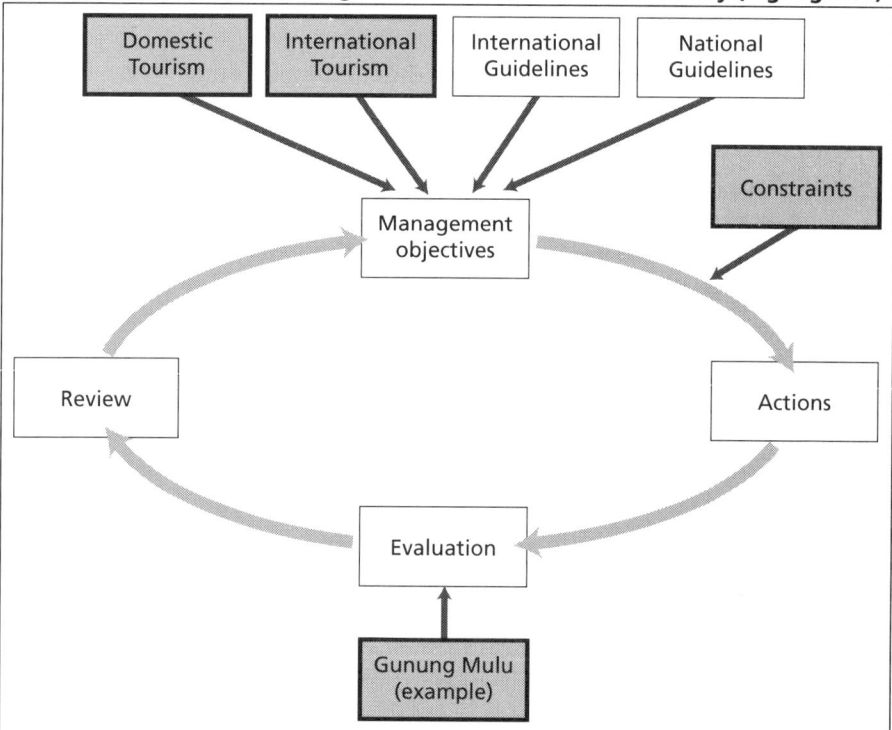

Source: own draft, adapted after Eagles, P.F.J., McCool, S.F. & Haynes, C.D. 2002, p. 42.

The above become a mosaic of the management process of a conservation area, and serve as a basis for planning and orientation. Tesserae of this mosaic that are not further analysed are different ecological systems and environmental impacts. The interpretation of the results will be based on the theory of structuration, and more specifically its concept of ontological security, which will be applied and adapted to (eco)tourism. Moreover, the question of a paradoxical juxtaposition will be raised: can pristine, and therefore authentic environments, such as rainforests be combined with the concept of 'non-places' (places that are not spatially and temporally embedded, such as airports, railway stations or fast food restaurants)?

3 Triangulation of methods

In traditional geographical studies, research focused on an area, or space, a unique section of the earth's surface. Geographers then used a holistic approach, in order to grasp the area's characteristics in their totality, including physical, biological and human factors. Space was thus perceived as a container of all these elements. For various reasons, this approach proved to be problematic and analytically unsatisfying.[14] Modern geography tries to understand social geographical realities, starting where they are constructed. They consider the human actors who structure and regionalise their environment with their perceptions and actions. The space which is thus structured or regionalised is also part of the framework or context for our actions. 'Context'[15], remains an important factor of geographical studies, because actions refer to it and reproduce or change it, at the same time. Hence, tourists visit an area, *because* it was advertised as a national park. Their actions within a specific park can contribute to the protection of the ecosystem or can be detrimental to it. The context, however, is not one-dimensional but multilayered. Therefore, the issue of ecotourism in Malaysian national parks has to be analysed regarding different view points. The triangulation of methods, which is often used in geographical studies, serves as a good – if not unproblematic – tool for that purpose. As the expression 'triangulation' indicates, the idea behind this methodological concept was borrowed from geometry. Accordingly, the aim is to precisely locate an inaccessible point (insights, knowledge) with known methods, like the gaugers could precisely calculate the height of Mt. Everest without having climbed it, because they took measurements from different angles. If we, therefore, apply different methods to a research subject, we receive results that allow us to view the subject from

---

14 For a discussion of landscape geography see Werlen, B. 1995, 1997 and 2000.
15 For an elaborate discussion of 'context' see Thrift, N. 1996.

different angles. The picture that emerges from this triangulation of methods is generally regarded as more precise and adequate. However, often the facts are disregarded that all methods have advantages and disadvantages and that their cumulation does not necessarily lead to a better understanding of the research topic.[16] There are advantages of this triangulation, not the least of which is the realization that the results of different methods do not always fit together. If we can keep various methods and subjects separate from each other, we can hope to maintain impartiality, be able to see agreements and discrepancies between different aspects of the research topic.

In this study, the following methods are applied. Besides observations (participatory and non-participatory) I use secondary data, mostly statistics on park visitors. I conducted two types of standardised interviews (in Kuala Lumpur and Gunung Mulu National Park) and held qualitative interviews with experts in all parts of the country. The methods[17] and results of these different 'sub-studies' are presented. In chapter IV "Malaysian urbanites and their national parks", p. 115, are discussed, in chapter V "The experts' discourse about nature conservation in Malaysia", p. 171, is addressed. In chapter VI "Tourists in Gunung Mulu National Park", p. 203, are discussed. Results from observations and preliminary talks area also in chapter II "Context and theory", p. 13.

4 Overview

Having introduced the aims, research questions and methods of the study, I want to give a brief overview of the chapters that follow. In chapter II "Context and theory", p. 13 the theoretical framework and the context of the study will be explained. Social geography and how it is conducted will be briefly explained. Some basic principles of the theory of structuration, of Anthony Giddens, which serves as background theory for the research, will be highlighted. Important aspects of this theory are 'ontological security' and 'critical situations'. In the field of tourism, risk and control are important topics. These are examined with respect to the contrasting concepts of ontological security and critical situations. The latter two terms encompass much more than feeling well and secure, or uncomfortable and insecure during a journey. In order not to unduly stress these umbrella terms, this study uses the terms 'safeness' and 'adventure'. In order to better understand how tourists travel and why, a short excursus about the concept of 'habitus' of Pierre Bourdieu is inserted. After these more general theoretical deliberations, the development of tourism, starting with the Grand

---

16 Reichertz, J. 2000.
17 More elaborate explanations about the applied methods are given in the respective chapters.

Tour and ending with the "end of tourism", is outlined. An important aim of tourism and travelling is to see authentic things or to have authentic experiences. Therefore, it is explained what authenticity means and how it can be interpreted. The last section of the theoretical background is devoted to the concept of ecotourism and the situation in Malaysia.

In chapter III "Nature conservation and national parks in Malaysia", p. 79 they most important parks of Malaysia and the National Ecotourism Plan (NEP) are presented.

In chapter IV "Malaysian urbanites and their national parks", p. 115, I outline methods and display the results of a survey done with 500 people from the Kuala Lumpur area. After explaining the methods that were used, the key characteristics of the sample are compared with key statistics of Kuala Lumpur and Malaysia, and are explained. The respondents' perceptions of nature are presented. The next section describes which parks and recreation areas were visited by the respondents, what they think about them and what expectations they have about future visits. I was also interested in their general opinion about nature protection and tourism in Malaysia, and whether it differs from the views of western tourists. The respondents' opinions of theme parks was also interesting, because theme parks are often seen as the opposite of authentic, and therefore, probably the opposite of conservation areas. Theme parks are booming in urban areas of Malaysia. Many people frequent them for recreation and to relax with their family and friends. They want the same experiences in conservation areas.

What Malaysian experts think about tourism and nature conservation is the subject of chapter V "The experts' discourse about nature conservation in Malaysia", p. 171. The most important topics of this qualitative study, concern park management and the publicizing of parks, the participation of local communities, privatisation, and tourism in general. The experts were selected according to their affiliation to the 'administration', 'NGOs', 'science' and the private sector of 'tour operators', in order to get a wide field of expert opinions.

Another quantitative survey with the focus on tourists who visited a specific national park (Gunung Mulu National Park in Sarawak) is subject of chapter VI "Tourists in Gunung Mulu National Park", p. 203. Using a checklist of the World Tourism Organisation (WTO)[18] about the attractiveness of the park, the findings of the survey are relayed along with recommendations for the park management.

In the last chapter (VII "Regionalising conservation areas", p. 245) I draw conclusions from the study. First, I explain how national parks are regionalised. Second, the conclusions of the survey in Kuala Lumpur, the expert interviews

---

18 WTO/UNEP 1992, p. 17.

and the survey in Mulu are presented. Third, the potential for authentic experiences for tourists, is discussed. Fourth, the most important issues of the National Ecotourism Plan of Malaysia (NEP) are examined in the light of the findings of the surveys and interviews. Last, an evaluation of the methods is made with remarks about future prospects.

II Context and theory

1 Theoretical framework

1.1 Social geography

In this study I frequently use terms such as "space", "regions", "context", and specific "areas", which could suggest that they have a distinct manifestation, per se. However, in modern social geography they are not perceived in that way. Rather they are seen as social constructions relating to the perceptions and actions of individuals. Thus, a specific region such as a conservation area is constructed, in the sense of Giddens theory of structuration,[19] by the application of rules and regulations and the practice of this application. Therefore, the point taken here is constructivistic, based on actions of individuals and their (intended and unintended) consequences. Moreover, actions are seen as interrelated in the sense of a structuration process[20], where consequences of actions serve as frameworks for future actions. Consequently, (eco)tourists visiting a Malaysian national park are not merely entering a location on the surface of the globe, where specific things (e.g. vegetation, animals, climatic and geological conditions) can be found. Rather, their immediate experiences are based on what they have learned about the area before their visit, on their social background and on the way they refer to their knowledge and perceptions.

Regions do not exist per se, they are made, in other words they are a consequence of human action. Regions resulting from every day actions, including perceptions, are therefore also social constructs. Regionalisation can be understood as the practice of being "tied to the world".[21] This comprises social control of spatial relations in order to regulate one's own actions and the practices of others. Moreover, 'regionalisations' as appropriations of the "world" are specific forms of re-embedding things that have been removed in the process of modernisation and globalization[22]. Regionalisation can also be regarded as a way in which we relate to the world and try to make sense of it. Consequently, there are regions that only have special meaning for specific individuals or groups, and others that are more or less of common knowledge such as the classification of a specific area as a national park. Therefore, we move through a great number of regions during our daily activities, through which we orientate ourselves and which we reproduce and change. Although the concept of nature conservation and its manifestation as a national park is widely known and accepted and the rules are more or less clearly defined, we do not all perceive it in

---

19 Giddens, A. 1995.
20 Giddens, A. 1995.
21 Werlen, B. 1999, p. 264.
22 Werlen, B. 1999.

the same way. Hence, the visitors' perceptions and notions about a specific national park comprise a wide range of different 'regionalisations'. In addition to that, other stakeholders such as park administration, tour operators or the local people have their own perceptions and notions. We can consequently perceive – or regionalise – a national park as an "arena" of interrelating actions and perceptions of different groups of actors. The "grouping" serves only as a tool to reduce complexity. When individuals interact with other people or when they have to relate to results of their actions, they rarely do this in a neutral mode, meaning that there are almost always power relations involved. People and groups who appropriate an area by physically entering it or by producing and reproducing rules and regulations that apply to it, are engaged, knowingly or unwittingly, in power relations with others. People or groups who have control over 'allocative' and 'authoritative'[23] resources can also define the rules and regulations applying to a certain area. This is also true for conservation areas. Once gazetted[24], new rules are made and people's rights to appropriate the area change considerably.

1.2 Theory of 'structuration'

In his theory of 'structuration' Anthony Giddens[25] tries to overcome the difference between structure and action or between society and the individual. The theory wants to bridge the gap between the macro level (e.g. structuralism, functionalism) and the micro level (e.g. action theory, symbolic 'interactionism') and solve the following dilemma: should we regard people as creative human actors, actively controlling the conditions of their own lives, or is what they do the result of general social forces outside their control?[26] Giddens proposes to concentrate on social practices which form us as actors, and which also embody or realise structures.[27]

I will not fully outline the whole theory[28], rather I want to explain its basic principles and their importance for this study. In the centre of the sociological concern is action or agency which is not determined; thus it is implied that it is

---

23 According to Giddens (1995) a person disposes of allocative resources, if she/he has control over material things. Authoritative resources comprise control over people and information.
24 'To gazette' as a verb is rarely used. However, in Malaysia it is often used for newly advertising or installing a park. Therefore, I will also use this term, although it is a bit unfamiliar.
25 Giddens, A. 1995.
26 Giddens, A. 1993, p. 718.
27 Craib, I. 1992, p. 34.
28 For a more in depth description and analysis of the theory of structuration see for example: Giddens, A. 1991; Giddens, A. 1992; Giddens, A. 1995; Bryant, C.G.A. & Jary, D. (eds.) 1991; Craib, I. 1992; Werlen, B. 1995.

always possible to act differently. However, our actions are not consequences of pure ad hoc creation, which is why we cannot abandon the idea of structure. In the centre of structuration theory therefore, is the 'duality of structure', which refers to the fact that structures are both produced by human action and are the medium of human action. Structures are not external to us and they do not exist per se. Rather, they exist as traces in our memory and in the moment we act[29]. It is also important to note that structures are not only constraining or limiting the range of our actions, but that they are enabling us to act in the first place.

Structures are basically rules and resources. Rules of social practice are like the rules of a game. In most cases they are not as clearly defined as the rules of a football match; there are even cases where we cannot formulate a rule (or a set of rules) but still adhere to it. Moreover, the fact that there are rules does not mean that we follow them by the letter. We always interpret rules according to a given situation and usually there is an 'etcetera clause' at work enabling us to vary our interpretation of the rule.[30] In some cases we can discursively explain why we applied a certain rule in a specific way, in other cases we may have difficulty formulating the rule, because many rules we follow are routine practical knowledge.

Figure 6 on page 17 shows the different levels of consciousness that are involved in our actions. Actions have intended and unintended consequences. The latter occur when we either do not acknowledge all the conditions of the context of our actions and/or all possible outcomes (which is virtually impossible). With the control of resources, which is regulated by rules, power relations enter the equation.

Applied to the gazetting of a national park, this means that there are (international) rules stating that areas with a high degree of biodiversity should, for example, be protected. International and national organisations concerned with nature protection (e.g. IUCN, WWF, Malaysian Nature Society etc.) try to spread and enforce that rule and they have (limited) resources (i.e. money, manpower, infrastructure, skills, knowledge, contacts to people and other organisations etc.) they can make use of in order to achieve their goals. Moreover, there

---

29 Giddens (1976, p. 121-122 in Craib, I. 1992, p. 43) uses the example of language: "Language exists as a 'structure', syntactical and semantic, only insofar as there are some kind of traceable consistencies in what people say, in the speech acts which they perform. From this aspect, to refer to rules of *syntax*, for example, is to refer to the reproduction of 'like elements'; on the other hand, such rules also *generate* the totality of speech-acts which is the spoken language. It is this dual aspect of structure, as both inferred from observation of human doings, yet also operating as a medium whereby those doings are made possible, that has to be grasped through the notions of structuration and reproduction." (Emphasis in the original).
30 Craib, I. 1992, p. 45.

are rules on the governmental (national, regional and local) level that make it possible for politicians to propose and enforce, or to prohibit the gazetting of an area as a national park. The controls over resources they can use to achieve their goals are granted to them by other rules such as the constitution which again is a result of an aggregate of individual actions, e.g. the vote of the people, etc. Once an area is protected more rules are applied regulating the use of a park's natural resources, which can result in conflicts, for example when local people had been applying other rules of natural resource use before the establishment of a park, such as hunting animals or felling trees which are widely prohibited by most park rules. The park administration makes use of resources (i.e. rangers) to enforce the new rules. Since rules are generally not followed or carried out to the letter, but interpreted and applied by individuals to the specific circumstances, there is room for social change, meaning that structures can change too.

In the following, I want to view tourism and nature conservation in the light of the theory of 'structuration' and use its terminology. In the chapter, "2 Risk, control and tourism" on page 18 I want to focus on 'ontological security' and 'critical situations', which are important aspects of the theory explaining why and when we can feel safe and in control of our everyday lives.

Figure 6: Stratification model of consciousness and action

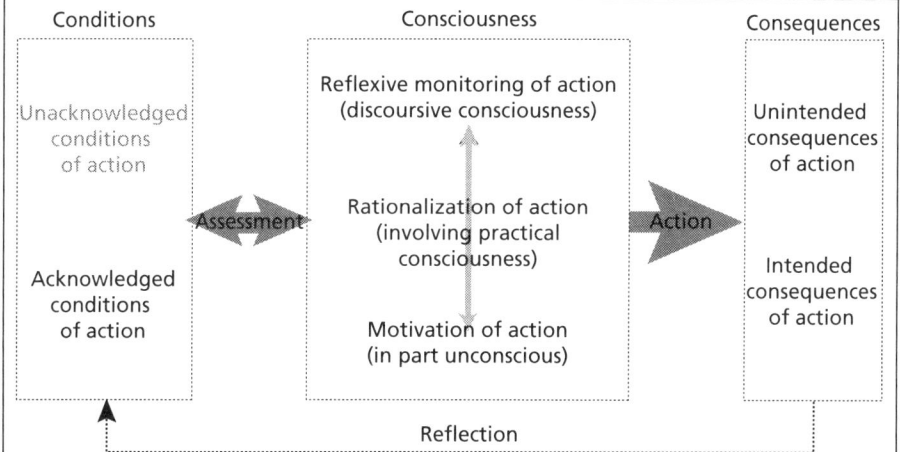

Source: own draft and complementing, adapted from Bryant, C.G.A. & Jary, D. 1991, p. 9.

2 Risk, control and tourism

2.1 Controlling risks in tourism

If we agree with Urry's[31] statement that tourism is demarcated from work and every day life and that tourists draw a line between leisure and their "ordinary life", then often they enter a realm of uncertainty when they travel. At least to a certain extent they take the risk that unknown environments may bear. However, this is only true to a certain extent. Especially 'fordist' mass tourism that is highly efficient, predictable and controlled seems to do everything to remove uncertainty from tourists' itineraries.[32] There seems to be a great difference in tourists' risk taking and their perception of uncertainty between adventurers who seek risks, and the package tourists who book an all-inclusive arrangement. Consequently, Meethan[33] argues that we have to deal with different tourisms rather than with tourism as a single category. From his point of view this certainly makes sense. However, I propose to look at the issue from a different angle, because we do not have an objective position from which we can assess the degree of risk and uncertainty a person experiences when travelling. Thus, the seasoned adventurer might perceive the un-guided trek through the jungle as much less risky as a group tourist perceives eating at a hawker's food stall. In other words, it depends on the tourist how he/she experiences a journey. Therefore, I want to apply and adapt Giddens' concept of 'ontological security' and 'critical situations'[34] to tourism. In order to better understand the individual tourist and his background I will draw upon the concept of 'habitus' by Bourdieu[35], knowing well that with this eclecticism I might mix oil with water. However, it is not my aim to develop a theory of tourism, rather I want to be able to describe the things people encounter during the process of taking part in (eco)tourism in a comprehensible way, thus drawing upon different theories.

Another consequence of tourism are risks which have not yet been mentioned, namely those experienced by the visited, the so called 'local people'. Especially in developing countries they are often in an economically vulnerable position and changes to their livelihood can pose serious risks for them. Tourism generally involves such changes, and the visited are – due to a lack of adequate resources –, not always in a position to benefit from these changes.[36] It is not the

---

31 Urry, J. 2002.
32 Ritzer, J. & Liska, A. 1997 in: Meethan, K. 2001, p. 75.
33 Meethan, K. 2001, p. 75.
34 Giddens, A. 1995 and 1996.
35 Krais, B. & Gebauer, G. 2002.
36 For examples of such problems see for example Grütter, K. & Plüss, C. 1996; Plüss, C. 1999.

primary aim of this study to analyse the risks local people are confronted with when they come into contact with tourism. Nevertheless, the perception of their situation by experts and urban Malaysians will be addressed and analysed.

2.2 Excursus: 'Habitus' and the field of tourism

2.2.1 The concept of 'habitus'

The term 'habitus' is central to Pierre Bourdieu's sociology. With the 'habitus' concept Bourdieu tries to bridge the explanatory gap between individualism which explains society as an aggregation of (only) individual actions, and supra-individual structures, as system theories would have it. 'Habitus' is thus a "structured and structuring structure"[37] incorporated in our heads as well as in the rest of our bodies[38]. Like language enables us to speak and make sense for others, our habitus enables us to act as a member of a society. Through practices of actors and their interaction with each other and their environment, habitus becomes manifest to others. However, Bourdieu emphasises that habitus is not only manifest in behaviour[39] but an integral part of it. Moreover, habitus is not determining our actions in a behaviouristic sense; rather it enables us to act according to our possibilities. It is like knowing a language to a certain extent and thus being able to construct an almost unlimited number of different sentences out of it. For Bourdieu it is impossible not to have a habitus. Consequently we are born with a habitus, because as soon as we are here, we interact (using our body) with our social environment. Through this interaction – practice – we develop, adapt and also change our habitus. It is thus not an unchangeable given but it is also not changed easily. We can understand habitus as not only a mental disposition; it is part of our body. The way we walk, talk and bear ourselves is dependent on our habitus.[40] Members of different social classes have different habitus[41], which means that it is not easy to enter the social field of the members of the other classes, however not impossible. Habitus is also gender related and

---

37 Krais, B. & Gebauer, G. 2002, p. 34.
38 Jenkins, R. 1993, p 75.
39 I use the term 'behaviour' as synonym to 'action' or 'agency' and therefore not in a behaviouristic sense.
40 In a scene of Tom Wolfe's "Bonfire of the Vanities" (Wolfe, T. 1990) an attorney not very successfully tries to "get the pimp roll out of a client" charged with a drug related crime. The "pimp roll" is certain way of walking that is associated with gangs in Brooklyn and therefore does not make a good impression on judges and juries in a court. The client has incorporated this walk into his habitus and it is a part of his personality that it is almost impossible for him not to walk the roll. But it also brands him as a gang member or at least as somebody who is a part of their social field.
41 I am using the Latin plural of habitus which is written like the singular but spoken with a long u.

it is much more difficult to change the gender aspect of one's habitus.[42] If people find a point of contact with habitus of other classes, they can enter their realm and also are able to alter their habitus to a certain extent.

2.2.2 Similarities and differences to the theory of structuration

Bourdieu's theory of social practice is in many aspects very similar to Giddens' theory of structuration. One main difference is that Giddens assumes that an individual is more or less free in his or her decisions and that structuration occurs by relating to other peoples' actions as well as to structures embedded in our heads as memory traces from past practices.[43] He probably agrees with Bourdieu that structures are a product of social practice and that they do not exist by themselves. In Giddens' theory individuals seem to be more flexible and better able to change or influence their lives. The individual in Bourdieu's theory seems to be more restrained by its habitus and thus less flexible and able to change and influence his or her livelihood. He says: "We can always say that individuals make choices, as long as we do not forget that they do not choose the principles of these choices."[44] I am well aware that I am simplifying these differences but I hope the explanations serve the purpose of clarifying my position. I furthermore do not attempt to operationalise Bourdieu's concept for this study[45], rather I want to address the differences with which societies (including tourists or tourist groups) can be looked at and point out that there are alternative views to the one proposed by Giddens.

2.2.3 The social field

Bourdieu uses another important concept: the 'social field' or 'fields' with which he accounts for our modern society that is characterised by the division of labour. In other words social systems – the consequences of social practices are differentiated. Bourdieu understands the emerging fields as structured systems of social positions, the nature of which defines the situation for their occupants.[46] It is also a system of power relations between these positions[47]. The actions of subjects follow a logic that is specific to or characteristic for the field in question, meaning that a farmer is moving around in another world (field) than a park

---

42 It is difficult to change gender related habitus but not impossible which shows the example of transsexuals. Interestingly, studies show that for them it is easier to "unlearn" their old habitus than to acquire a new habitus (Krais, B. & Gebauer, G. 2002, p. 51-52).
43 This is more emphasised in Giddens' political work (Giddens, A. 1999; 2000).
44 Bourdieu, P. 1977 in Jenkins, R. 1993, p 77.
45 For the difficulties and advantages to work with Bourdieu's concept see Dörfler, T., Graefe, O. & Müller-Mahn, D. 2003.
46 Jenkins, R. 1993, p 85.
47 Krais, B. & Gebauer, G. 2002, p. 57.

ranger or a scientist. The field is therefore a "game" about power and influence. The farmer must know something about sowing and ploughing and the rules of competition within agribusiness, the park ranger must know about the dangers of the forest and how to apprehend poachers from hunting protected species and the scientist must be knowledgeable in his subject and know the rules of "publish or perish", for example. "Players" within a field must have a professional knowledge about it. Of course these fields are not hermetically protected and outsiders can also enter them, if they have a disposition to. The field opens a room of possibilities or an "amount of probable constraints as well as condition and complement of a limited amount of possible uses"[48].

According to my opinion it is not so important that players vie for better positions within a field as that these fields have different sets of rules or institutions[49] and those actions of individuals have to be seen within the context of the respective fields. This helps to explain why people act differently in different contexts, settings or fields. Outlining the field of tourism is not easy, because most participants lack the requirement of professionalism, moreover the struggle for positions is not very pronounced. However, tourism and leisure activities in general are distinct from our every day life and therefore also distinct from other fields in which we move about. Tourists enter the field of tourism with their habitus, which makes them choose specific destinations and the kind of journey they embark on. According to their respective habitus tourists enhance their social capital when they visit the "right" destinations. For example a honeymoon trip to Switzerland awards Indian couples with high esteem when they return back home. Here, the other social fields in which the tourists move around during their every day life play an important role. Therefore, not only the tourists' social statuses are important but also their cultural background. Therefore, it cannot be assumed that tourists with a western middle-class background travel in the same way as Asian middle-class members. With the concepts of habitus and field we can thus better explain why the latent motives of tourists often remain un-expressed, when they are asked the reasons why they travel.

One might think that it would be easy to form (tourist) groups according to people's different habitus. To a certain extent this is certainly possible; however, I do not propose such a grouping because habitus does not consist of a few easily discernible categories. I rather want to focus on the different activities of tourists which then can be related to certain habitus, but not the other way round.

---

[48] Bourdieu, P. 1999 in Krais, B. & Gebauer, G. 2002, p. 58.
[49] Institutions are here regarded as "rules of the game" in the sense of rules in the theory of structuration (see North, D.C. 1990; Leach, M., Mearns, R. & Scoones, I. 1999).

2.3 Risk and ontological security or rather adventure and 'safeness'

2.3.1 Living in a 'risk-society'

According to Beck[50] the production of wealth goes hand in hand with the production of risks in the era of late modernity. We are currently living in a 'risk-society' in which global risks such as atomic war, environmental pollution, and global warming can be considered as common threats. Damage resulting from those risks has lost any spatial and temporal limitations and cannot be attributed to specific causes anymore. Rather, (almost) everybody somehow contributes to these (global) risks to a certain extent.[51] To cope with risks has therefore become a central mode of life. To live with risks means to live with uncertainty. Nevertheless, we do not live in constant distress because of all the risks we face. This has to do with the routines with which we regain a sense of feeling in control of our surroundings. Giddens[52] uses the term 'ontological security' to describe this feeling of being able to make sense of one's environment and to act appropriately. In our day-to-day activities we have achieved a high level of reliability in assessing situations adequately in order to act "acceptably". In Bourdieu's terms we could say that our habitus is our tool to act adequately within the social fields in which we move. Due to the constant reproduction and application of social practices, the framework giving us ontological security has become rather robust.

Ontological security breaks down when we cannot assess a situation (e.g. the actions of other people and/or our environment) adequately, and/or when we do not have the means to act in an appropriate way. These 'critical situations' can vary in degree and their perception again varies according to the disposition (or the habitus) of each individual. Entering a context (or a social field) that is unfamiliar can already be perceived as a critical situation, because the individual does not know how to behave appropriately. More severe forms of a breakdown of ontological security are, for example, wars or natural disasters, when there is nothing stable enough to hold on to. However, Rojek argues that ontological insecurity (or critical situation)[53] is increasing in the risk-society, which has consequences for leisure activities. People living in a certain degree of ontological insecurity thus yearn for stability and seek symbolic continuity in fixed horizons and stable spaces. Consequently, the desire to preserve places of outstanding beauty from industrial and commercial development can be interpreted as

---

50 Beck, U. 1986.
51 See Backhaus, N. 1999.
52 Giddens, A. 1991, p. 36-38.
53 Rojek terms critical situations as ontological insecurity (2000, p. 172).

an expression of the modern desire for stability.[54] This, however, mostly applies to western or urban people who have the resources to travel to protected areas. Underprivileged people in developing countries who are also confronted with global (and local) risks but who do not have the resources to travel may also have the desire to protect places of outstanding beauty. However, such places are often needed as resources to survive and are consequently overused and degraded. Since ontological security encompasses many aspects of life and moreover, goes deep into the realms of the unconscious, I do not want to use the term for things that are only aspects of ontological security. Although tourism has to do with losing and gaining ontological security a little bit, it is rarely threatened or broken down entirely. Therefore, for the (slightly) critical situations that tourists encounter I would rather use the expressions 'safeness'[55] and 'adventure'. Thus, I am using terms that do not go as deep and that are not as all-encompassing as the terms coined by Giddens, in order to explain very vital aspects of our lives.

2.3.2 Tourism between adventure and safeness

I want to argue that tourism is a context in which the tourists in a way oscillate between safeness and adventure. If we listen to the stories people tell coming back from their holidays, we often hear about the things that did not go smoothly, the little adventures they had to "survive" or an unplanned walk on the wild side. Thus, those kinds of adventures can be seen as the salt in one's journey. Like critical situations, adventures can also be perceived quite differently. An adventure can be getting lost in the Taman Negara of Malaysia Peninsula at dusk without adequate equipment and knowledge about where the headquarters are or about whether tigers are deterred or attracted by loud singing. But an adventure can be much less dangerous and frightening, such as having an argument with a Kota Kinabalu taxi driver about his refusal to use the meter, not knowing whether he wants to cheat or if this is the local custom. Consequently, for the European package tourist it might be enough adventure to bargain for a souvenir, whereas others are only satisfied when they can (coolly) tell about how they "almost died" struggling with a twenty-foot python in the jungle of Borneo. Moreover, we can perceive it as an adventure when we enter a social field with a habitus that we are not conversant with.

Although adventures are important for many tourist undertakings, safeness is still what people seek most when travelling. Tour operators provide tourists with safeness in unknown contexts. In fact the whole tourist industry takes great expense to provide for tourists' safeness. Doing that during the high time of

---

54 Rojek, C. 2000, p. 172.
55 Safeness comes from the Latin *salvus* safe, healthy and means to be free from harm or risk and secure from threat of danger, harm, or loss.

fordist mass production and mass tourism resulted in a standardisation of tourist infrastructure. Sometimes this lead to the development of tourist enclaves that are interchangeable and have almost no connection to their spatial context – or in other words they became non-places (see "4.2 Perceiving authenticity" on page 45). Extreme examples of such tourist non-places are theme parks such as Disneyland or the Sunway Lagoon Park near Kuala Lumpur. It has also had the consequence that (individual) travellers can today venture much further into realms unknown to them, than before. Due to the existence of a tourist industry in a country, (local) people get used to accommodating tourists, transport systems become adapted to tourists and hotels and guest houses acquire an international standard. Tourists want to know what they get when travelling somewhere in order to feel comfortable or safe. Moreover, they not only want to experience (certain) stability and safeness during their journey but they also seek stability in their fantasies about distant locations. Since work and every day life are often perceived as stressful, unfulfilling and more and more insecure, many people dream of great experiences in their leisure time onto which they project the feeling of stability[56].

In order to find their way around quickly, in contrast to Goethe who travelled for months through Italy, (post-)modern travellers can only afford one or two weeks of vacation a year. In different and unknown contexts, tourists need clear and reliable information. It has to be provided in an understandable and easily accessible way, since they often do not want to prepare themselves months in advance in order to have adequate knowledge about the place they visit. Such information is provided by an ever-increasing number of guidebooks, television broadcasts, travel magazines or tour operators. Even people sitting in an aircraft heading for their holiday destination, learn for example from an information sheet, that they are bound for Haiti, a former French colony in the Caribbean, and not for Tahiti, Gaugin's refuge in the South Seas. By reading magazines, books, or watching television broadcasts they create a certain anticipation for the kind of places they later choose to visit. As a consequence, they know what to look for, or how to gaze at or read landscapes, landmarks and cultural features[57]. Tourists do not only read about the context of their destination, they also read the context of the destination itself.

The increasing market of travel guide-books helps to provide this feeling. People know what to look for and to look at, what customs to expect and (respect) and how much they have to pay for accommodation, transport, etc., before they embark on their journey. A very important aspect of safeness is the feel-

---

56 Rojek, C. 2000, p. 171.
57 Urry, J., 2002, p. 3; Schurian-Bremecker, C. 2001, p. 200; 2002, p. 179-185.

ing of not being cheated. It is not only that people fear being cheated out of money but also out of experiences. Thus the feeling of being cheated has to be avoided, because it is embarrassing and a sign of one's insecurity. If tourists look for authentic experiences (e.g. to see rare animals in a pristine jungle), they feel cheated if they perceive it as artificial (e.g. not being able to see the animals).

3 Tourism and modernity

Since tourism has become the most important industry in the world, it can be seen as the emblem of reflexive or (post-)modern society. According to Lash & Urry[58], mobility is central to a modern world that is characterised by 'time-space distanciation'. Life and social order are disembedded from the local context as a result of a combination of rapidly changing transport technology and organisational transformation. Thus, people are enabled both to act at a distance and to cover great distances quickly. Long distance travel has become an integral part of western culture and increasingly of primarily urban people in industrialising and developing countries. How travel became such an important part first in western countries but increasingly in almost all societies of the world, will be sketched in the following chapters.

3.1 Pilgrimages and the Grand Tour[59]

In traditional or pre-capitalistic societies, social life was deeply embedded into the location where people lived. Only few, the affluent and some members of the clergy, had the means and reason to travel frequently. Most people, except nomads who travelled over great distances, could only afford a pilgrimage once or twice in their lives. Since the range of activities was very limited for most people, they knew their own vicinity very well and could rely on that experience when roaming through their area. Places, people and locations outside this range of known context therefore bore risks, uncertainties or even danger. For them ontological security was therefore also limited to the place where they lived. Reasons for travel were business, pilgrimages and explorations. Pilgrims wandered on well defined routes, that were widely known and the risk to get lost was small.[60] Although the pilgrimage was a prequel to modern tourism, the rea-

---

58 Lash, S. & Urry, J. 1994, p. 252-254.
59 Where not indicated otherwise the elaborations in this chapter derive from Brilli, A. 1997, a very comprehensive account on the early stages of tourism.
60 In earlier forms of the Christian pilgrimage the believers were looking for salvation travelling around as *peregrini* (lat. for foreigners) without a concrete aim (*peregrinationes pro Christo*). Later these travels were superseded by pilgrimages to holy places (*ad loca sancta*) on pre defined routes (Herbers, K. 1991).

sons for travelling were quite different. To see different landscapes and to meet other people was not why most pilgrims were on their journey. They wanted and still want to visit holy places, and their arduous journey was often seen as a part of doing penance for sins committed in the past or to come closer to salvation (paradise or nirvana). The explorations of seafarers and merchants lead them into new and unknown places. However, their main goal was to establish business relations and to discover new products to trade. Nonetheless, they also brought home tales and descriptions of other peoples and localities that aroused wonder and curiosity in others.

The first tourists in the modern sense were probably European aristocrats who went on a Grand Tour preferably to and through Italy.[61] It developed from the custom of British, German and French members of the upper class of sending their sons to study at universities in Italy. Their importance as educational institutions declined due to the establishment of more universities in northern Europe in the 17th and 18th centuries. At the same time the concept of the Grand Tour developed as a means to quench the curiosity of the classically educated and universally interested aristocrat. The traveller of the Grand Tour is driven by curiosity and the wish to have a complete experience. He gathers specimens, indexes them and writes down his experiences while travelling through different landscapes and cultural settings. These experiences were then more and more seen as an integral part of any (affluent) man's education and hence adolescents were sent on their own Grand Tour to gather experiences of a great variety. Italy was still the main focus of the grand tourists for its rich classic heritage that manifests itself in ancient buildings and ruins. Therefore, the Grand Tour became synonymous with the 'Italienreise' which was subsequently even the title of one of Goethe's works. This increase of travel activity was accompanied by the establishment of guesthouses and inns that catered for the travellers.

During the 18th and 19th century travellers developed a specific way to gaze at landscapes and thus became "picturesque travellers". While first seeking the grand and beautiful in a landscape they now were eager to see compositions in nature, often involving ruins of antique buildings. They even used a device, the Claude glass, which worked like a camera obscura with a tinted mirror that rendered the landscape in colours resembling picturesque paintings and sketches. The travellers started to actively compose what they saw and thus developed a specific gaze that could be seen as a predecessor of the gaze through the lens of a modern camera.

---

61 Siebers, W. 1991.

3.2 Mass tourism, fordism and the tourist gaze

3.2.1 Fordist tourism

The journeys of early travellers have little in common with the mass phenomenon that started after the Second World War in a few western countries, along with the concept of free or leisure time, and which was a consequence of the industrial division of labour and Fordism. Social change and the fact that transportation costs decreased rapidly during the 20th century made the mass tourism as we know it today, possible. Mass tourism is characterized by a small number of producers – mostly transnational corporations which dominate the world market – who offer highly standardised products using the benefit of economies of scale. A common manifestation of this rigid tourism industry is the package tour. The industry offers structured package tours at bargain prices to large numbers of middle-class consumers. In order to generate profits with low margins, which allow the bargain prices in the first place, high numbers of visitors are needed. This standardisation leads to a proliferation of quite similar architecture, facilities, and entertainment in mass tourist destinations. Often this results in resorts that are 'enclavic' spaces where tourists are spatially segregated from the local context.[62] Therefore, the package tours ensure highly predictable, efficient, calculable and controlled vacations and thus reduce uncertainty and risk. Subsequently, holidays of package tourists become as standardised or McDonaldised[63] as their day-to-day lives. With their rigidity and inflexibility, resorts do not adapt well to the conditions of their surroundings and often they pose an environmental problem.[64]

In order to safely travel to distant localities tourists cannot rely on their knowledge of the immediate surroundings anymore. Rather, they have to trust other people (and organisations) to guide them through different contexts. Without this trust they lose their safeness, which might inhibit them in the enjoyment of their journeys, or in being able to move freely about. In modern societies people trust experts with professional knowledge. If they feel that they can rely on others' expertise while travelling, they can minimise risk, although they are moving in contexts which they did not know before. This trust is not automatically given; it has to be learned, best by experience with travelling. Experienced tourists or travellers develop a cosmopolitan attitude that lets them

---

62 In some areas these enclaves were also built in order to shelter the local population from detrimental (Western) cultural influences. An example is the resort Nusa Dua on the Southern tip of Bali, that was built during the 1970ies in a remote and scarcely inhabited part of the island.
63 Geisel, S. 2002.
64 Torres, R. 2002, p. 90-91.

feel safe in distant places. Trust-giving experts are tour operators, railway and flight companies, hotel managers etc. One of the first of such travel experts was Thomas Cook, who in 1841 started his business by issuing return railway tickets to people of the lower classes who were not used to travelling far from their homes. He was soon able to provide them with packages including accommodation, meals and guidance, thus giving the initial spark to what later became mass tourism in the 20th century.[65]

In (late or post-)modern societies tourism has become a part of almost every person's life at least in western countries, from where 80 % of outbound tourism originates (see figure 7 on page 29). Not to be able to travel for economic reasons is regarded as a stigma and during economic recessions people tend rather to cut down other expenses instead of foregoing travelling during their holidays.[66] Being able to travel and to subsequently talk about one's experiences is a part of people's social capital. Social capital is part of a person's 'habitus'[67] according to which certain destination and travel arrangements are regarded as favourable. Therefore, package tourism is targeting people from the middle-class among whom this travel form is acknowledged as the 'right way to travel'.

3.2.2 Motives of modern tourists

We have not yet addressed the reasons why people travel in the first place. When asked in surveys in western societies the answers to this question often cover the following topics[68] people say they travel in order...

... to relax and unwind
... to be active
... to experience new things and change
... to seek out authenticity and exotic places
... to widen their horizon
... to get to know foreign cultures and understand other mentalities
... to contribute to international understanding

---

65 Lash, S. & Urry, J. 1994, p. 255-256.
66 Of course tourists also cut down their travel expenses in times of economic problems, but they nevertheless go on vacations (Bieger, T. & Laesser, C. 2002).
67 Jenkins, R. 1993.
68 Kiefl, W. 1997.

Figure 7: Countries with more than 5 million foreign visitors

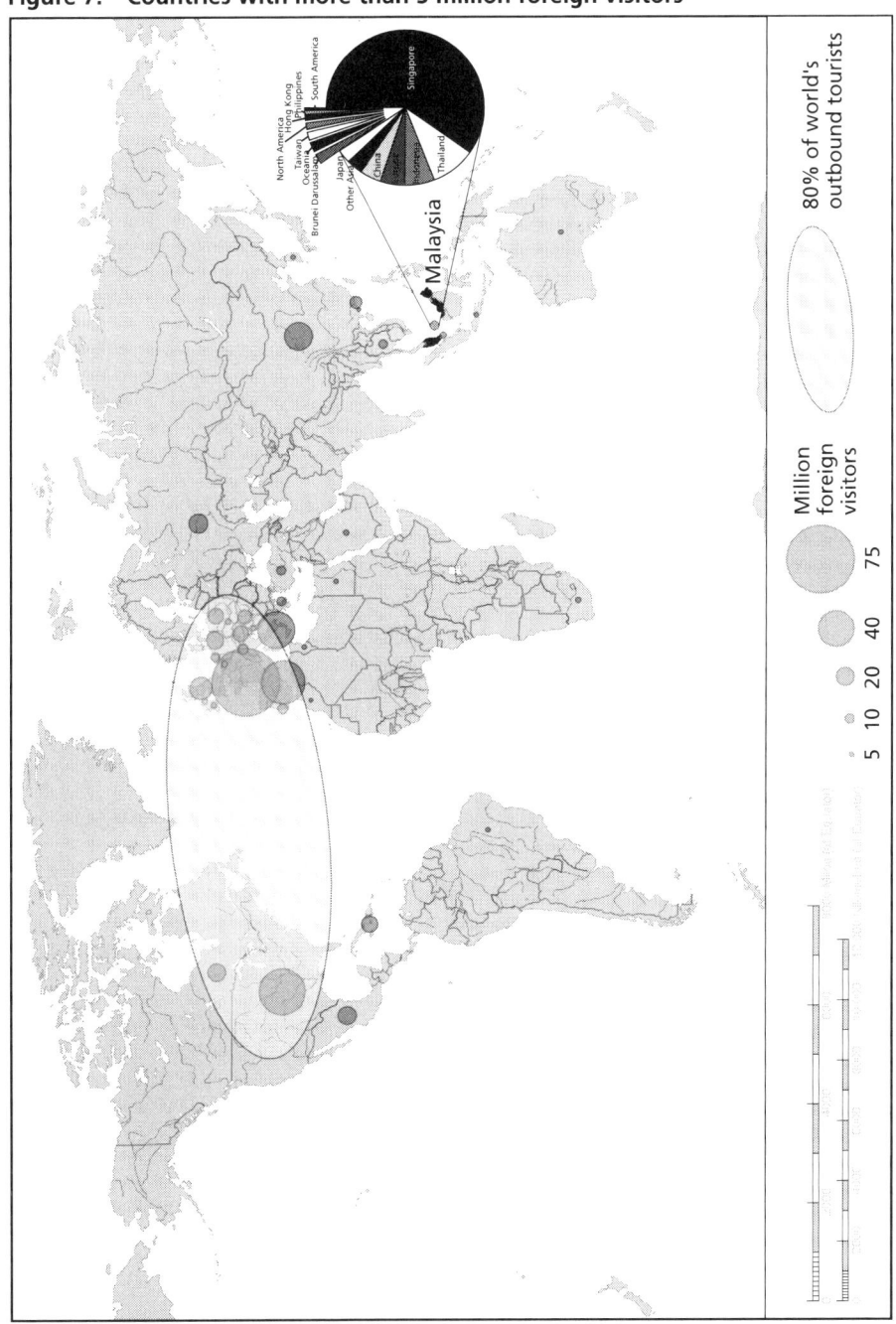

Source: Own draft; data (for 2000) Tourism Malaysia 2003; World Tourism Organisation 2003; Le Monde diplomatique 2003.

When tourists from other cultural contexts, with different habitus, are asked the same questions, the answers are not always the same. According to our study about the motives of Indian tourists[69] in Switzerland, Indian tourists came to Switzerland in order to see or experience…

… beautiful landscapes
… snow and ice
… 'paradise'
… to honeymoon
… the cool climate
… the famous country
… recreation
… shopping
… cleanliness

These reasons, whether in a western or Indian context, are the ones that are consciously admitted and deemed socially accepted in their respective contexts. However, often they differ quite a lot from what people actually do when on holiday. Kiefl[70] argues that these manifest and socially accepted motives are not the most important ones in order to understand and plan for tourism. He stresses that if the tourist industry bases their offers solely on these motives (mostly uttered in short quantitative surveys), they are not planning adequately. In longer and unstructured qualitative interviews, Kiefl tried to find out other – socially un-accepted or repressed – motives of tourists. Hence, people also travel in order…

… to temporarily escape from job-related and other social obligations
… to satisfy their need to prove themselves (in physical activities)
… to satisfy their need for prestige (being able to travel to exotic destinations)
… to experience "rituals" of esteem (even if they are "bought")
… to have new (and not to close) contacts to other people (mostly other tourists)
… to experience erotic adventures (either with other tourists or local people)
… to temporarily get rid of the constraints of every day life
… to play a different role
… even to "confirm" one's superiority over people from another cultural background.

Because most of these motives are not socially accepted, or may even be repressed, the tourism industry cannot openly advertise destinations where these needs can be fulfilled. Therefore, a dilemma between the tourists' (latent) needs

---

69   Keller, U., Backhaus, N. & Elsasser, H. 2002.
70   Kiefl, W. 1997, p. 216.

and the reality of tourism arises. The dilemma is emphasised by studies about tourism that structure tourist types according to the first mentioned manifest travel motives. Indeed, it may be useful for tourism managers to know the socioeconomic attributes of their customers. However, the creation of tourist types from a combination of their manifest motives such as "cultural hedonists", "family oriented" or "to see and to be seen"[71] says more about the authors of those studies than about the tourists themselves. Of course it is important to know more about the motives for travel, but most motives (both manifest and latent) are not permanently intrinsic to the individual that utters them. Moreover, the motives can change during a trip or even within a day. IT is better to talk about different needs that tourist destinations are confronted with, regardless of the "type" of individuals that have these needs. Subsequently, for the purposes of the management of tourist destinations (or for travel agents) it can be useful to look for socio-economic patterns – as part of people's habitus – behind these needs, but not the other way round. Therefore, when in the following chapters I will address "individual" and "group travellers", or "domestic" and "foreign" tourists, it is because in interviews with experts of tourism and nature conservation, specific needs have been attributed to these groups of tourists. It does not, however, mean that tourists cannot "change" categories during their tourist career or that all people subsumed under one category necessarily behave the same way.

3.2.3 Modernity and the tourist gaze

Increased mobility is also responsible for altering one's experience of the world. While travelling by train, car or air plane, tourists perceive their surroundings through a window, an unchanging frame, through which the landscape panorama is changing. The ways in which people view landscapes have changed, and according to Sontag[72] this is responsible for the increasing importance of camera use to capture what people see during their travels.[73] Their experience in the modern world has taught them to doubt what they see or hear and to question and judge what they experience.[74] In other words, they are much more careful about what they see and do. Hand in hand with the increasing importance of taking photographs, is the proliferation of images and other information that is readily available for potential tourists before they embark upon a journey. The

---

71 Bundesamt für Statistik Schweiz 2002.
72 Sontag 1979, in Lash, S. & Urry, J. 1994, p. 255.
73 Sontag moreover postulates that the view of the scenery through the lens of a camera is an appropriation of the scene that helps to reduce uncertainty and therefore the fear of the unknown.
74 Smart, B. 1999, p. 68.

perception of these images structures the mental images of the tourists.[75] Hence, tourism starts much earlier than the first day of one's vacation. While travelling and thus developing a cosmopolitan attitude, they both get used to being in places foreign to them. They not only change their image of the place they visit, but they change the place they visit, as well. Through the process of globalization, cosmopolitan aesthetics of viewing things or gazing at them (while travelling) have developed. However, as with many processes of globalization how one perceives ('gazes at') things is not universal, but adapted locally according to the context or habitus of an individual. Hence, viewing (and photographing) habits can differ between tourists from different provenances.

Experienced, mobile and reflective tourists who are open to others and willing to take risks (to a certain extent), are able to reflect on and judge different regions, landscapes societies and times they experience. This explains the growing importance of the cultural heritage industry. Locations thus become comparable with each other.[76] Tourists read the landscapes and destinations they travel through, and they gaze at them through a filter that is influenced by their own individual habitus and experiences. Since many tourists have the same experiences during their travels, they adopt a common cosmopolitan attitude. Although nowadays, many people have travel experiences, or meet experienced travellers during their early travels, and have therefore learned how to move within tourist contexts, not all tourists have the same needs and expectations when they travel. The fact that tourism and travel have become the most important industry in the world has provided a very large number of people with the necessary knowledge and experience to become cosmopolitan travellers. This knowledge comes from a structuration process between the tourism industry which provides infrastructure, and the tourists who have certain expectations about their destinations. In mass tourism these expectation are channelled for the package or group tourist. Tour operators, guides and other travel experts present tourists with sites and even tell them where to take the best photographs, where to look and how to look. Thus, the majority of tourists could be grouped according to their specific motives and interests[77] and then each group as a whole can be treated and provided for in the same way. Yet the tourism industry is not merely reacting on the different groups' needs and wishes. It is actively offering things to see and do for specific groups and thus it is also creating groups of tourists. Mass tourism is therefore a rather thoroughly organised phenomenon.

---

75 See for example Luger, K. 1995.
76 Lash, S. & Urry, J. 1994, p. 260.
77 An extensive list can be studied in Vorlaufer, K. 1996, p. 46-48.

John Urry[78] outlines the historical and social background that characterises modern tourism, including mass tourism:
- "Tourism is a leisure activity which presupposes its opposite, namely regulated and organised work. It is one manifestation of how work and leisure are organised as separate and regulated spheres of social practice in 'modern' societies. Indeed acting as a tourist is one of the defining characteristics of being 'modern' and is bound up with major transformations in paid work. This has come to be organised within particular places and to occur for regularised periods of time.
- Tourist relationships arise from a movement of people to, and their stay in, various destinations. This necessarily involves some movement through space, that is the journeys, and periods of stay in a new place or places.
- The journey and stay are to, and in, sites outside the normal places of residence and work. Periods of residence elsewhere are of a short-term and temporary nature. There is a clear intention to return 'home' within a relatively short period of time.
- The places gazed upon are for purposes not directly connected with paid work and they normally offer some distinctive contrasts with work (both paid and unpaid).
- A substantial proportion of the population of modern societies engages in such tourist practices; new socialised forms of provision are developed in order to cope with the mass character of the gaze of tourists (as opposed to the individual character of 'travel').
- Places are chosen to be gazed upon because there is an anticipation, especially through daydreaming and fantasy, of intense pleasures, either on a different scale or involving different senses from those customarily encountered. Such anticipation is constructed and sustained through a variety of non-tourist practices, such as film, TV, literature, magazines, records and videos, which construct and reinforce that gaze.
- The tourist gaze is directed to features of landscapes and townscape which separate them off from everyday experience. Such aspects are viewed because they are taken to be in some sense out of the ordinary. The viewing of such tourist sites often involves different forms of social patterning, with a much greater sensitivity to visual elements of landscape and townscape than normally found in everyday life. People linger through photographs, postcards, films, models and so on. These enable the gaze to be endlessly reproduced and recaptured.

---

78 Urry, J. 2002, p. 2-3.

- The gaze is constructed through signs, and tourism involves the collection of signs. When tourists see two people kissing in Paris what they capture in the gaze is 'timeless romantic Paris'. When a small village in England is seen, what they gaze upon is the 'real olde England'. (...).
- An array of tourist professionals develop who attempt to reproduce ever new objects of the tourist gaze. These objects are located in a complex and changing hierarchy. This depends upon the interplay between, on the one hand, competition between interests involved in the provision of such objects and, on the other hand, changing class, gender, generational distinctions of taste within the potential population of visitors."

For Urry the gaze of tourists is the most important feature of modern tourism. It manifests itself in the need of most tourists to take photographs during their journey. While taking photographs they gaze upon their surroundings in a special way that includes and excludes specific things. The way this is done – from taking a picture of his or her mate in front of tourist objects with a one-way camera, to the hobby "Ansel Adams" who only shoots landscapes – highly depends on the habitus of the tourist. Markwell[79] demonstrated this in a study where he analysed photographs taken by a group of young Australian tourists in Malaysia. One subject was a cabin in a national park that was photographed by the tourists exclusively without including the adjacent satellite dish in the frame. Back home the tourists remember their trip by gazing at the pictures and at the same time have proof of the fact that they have been "there". In addition they can show others but also remind themselves that the trip was worthwhile and a success, when they select pictures to be shown, to be looked at and to be remembered.

Although his work has become a classic of tourism theory, there are also critics who say that Urry ignores the physical experiences of tourists when concentrating on their gaze. Perkins and Thorns[80] as well as Wöhler[81], therefore propose to put the term "performing" beside the "gazing", in order to be able to grasp the physical and cognitive sensations of tourists. The concept of the gaze leaves little room for an engagement between the tourists and the places they visit. Especially for nature based tourism this engagement is an important factor for the tourists. They not only want to see the rainforests – which is still probably the most important reason to visit them – they want to hear its animals' noise, smell its odours, feel the moisture and feel themselves hiking beneath the forests' canopy. This criticism is certainly appropriate, although I think that the gaze – even if there are cultural differences – is still a very important reason for

---

79 Markwell, K.W. 1997.
80 Perkins, H.C. & Thorns, D.C. 2001.
81 Wöhler, K. 2003.

tourists to go somewhere in the first place. Moreover, if we extend the gaze on landscapes to the gaze on images, it encompasses a lot more than a somewhat passive looking at things. If people think about travelling to certain areas they probably have already gazed upon a variety of pictures of potential destinations. Subsequently, they create a mental image of how travelling to this or that destination will be. This mental image includes gazes at land-, sea- or cityscapes but it is much more. It also consists of the vision of the tourists themselves. They mentally "see" themselves at that place which includes experiencing the place, too. Even when they are actually at their chosen destination, the imagination continues. The experiences are embedded in these imaginations. This means that tourists not merely lie on a beach in the sun or hike up a steep mountain, they have an image of themselves lying on the beach or hiking. They are probably not constantly monitoring themselves in that manner but in a reflective society they are increasingly doing so. Therefore, the gaze can be extended to the imagination of being at a certain place which includes performing.

3.2.4 Individual travellers vs. group travellers

Not all tourists travel in groups or book package arrangements. There are a great number of individual tourists – or non-institutionalized travellers.[82] The relationship of individual tourists and group or mass tourists is ambivalent. Often, individual travellers (or backpackers as they are also called) are seen as the precursors of mass tourism development, because they "discover" new and unspoilt destinations that subsequently develop into mass tourism destinations.[83] A motivation for this development is the individual traveller's aversion to "mass tourist destinations" – or even mass tourists themselves – which impels them to seek out less crowded or less organized methods of travel[84]. This results in a denser net of locations that are visited by individual travellers.[85] Nevertheless, they also profit from certain consequences of mass tourism, such as cheap air fares, unproblematic visa regulations etc.

Travel books play an important role for the individual traveller's image of a destination. Although, guidebooks, whose function is to reduce risk and provide

---

82 See Elsrud, T. 2001, p. 601.
83 See Vorlaufer, K. 1996, p. 45. A study by Roger Schwegler (2002) on tourism in South Thailand however, shows that not all destinations go through the "life cycle" of being discovered by backpackers and changing into mass tourism destinations. Some destinations remain backwaters and some are straight away developed as mass tourism destinations without having been a backpackers' destination first.
84 Uriely, N., Yonay, Y. & Simchai, D. (2002) discovered that backpackers indeed visit destinations that are visited by package or mass tourists too, however, they often downplay the fact that they have been there or describe it as accidental.
85 Oppermann, M. 1992, p. 152-153.

a trustworthy resource for tourists, have existed for a long time, so called "alternative guidebooks" emerged at the end of the 1970's and in the 1980's. They give information about where backpackers can travel cheaply and about how not to get cheated or mistreated by the "locals"[86]. Some authors of these travel-books were able to build a still growing publishing empire covering virtually every corner of this ('lonely') planet. In the English speaking world, the 'Lonely Planet' travel-books are leaders in their field. Since they are updated frequently, they contain useful information about prices and destinations and are therefore bought by many travellers who can read English. As a consequence, they shape the landscape of individual tourism (and increasingly of group tourism too). Hotels that are not listed in these guidebooks are often not considered by travellers, because the very fact of their absence in the book makes them suspicious or risky. If a destination is labelled as crowded with package tourists it is visited less often by individual travellers who may seek out the "insider's tip" in the book and perhaps go a bit further afield. Thus, the title of the first Lonely Planet guide 'Southeast Asia on a Shoestring' can serve as an emblem for this kind of guidebook. The double meaning in the title implies both the fact that backpackers want to travel cheaply and that they follow strings of destinations that are laid out for them by the guide.

The content and quality of travel books have improved since their first emergence in the wake of growing concerns about sustainable or ecotourism. They now often include an extended section about a people and their culture and have omitted the worst transgressions such as advertising certain temples in Thailand as places where the traveller could get a meal for free because the monks there believe in selfless charity, etc. It was probably also an economic decision by the publishers to make the contents of their guidebooks acceptable for a wider range of people who are willing to (sometimes) pay more for accommodation than just the minimum. Moreover, the individual travellers of the 1980's became the tourists of the late 1990's, who were used to the guidebooks, but developed different wishes, needs and tastes when they grew older. Some authors regard this "softening" of travel books just as a fig-leaf[87], because they still provide information about how to be on the road as long as possible using as little money as possible without concerns about the cultural (and natural) environment.

The "versus" in the title of this section is not unidirectional. Often group travellers or package tourists look with disdain upon the (mostly young) backpackers when their paths cross (which happens not too often), perceiving them as hippies or bums who are just lazing around.[88] An important factor for this is

---

86 Trojanow, I. 2002; Elsrud, T. 2001.
87 See Trojanow, I. 2002.

that these (mostly young) travellers are dressed in well worn semi-traditional clothes. This attire is often considered by the package tourists (and others) as a sign of laziness, drug abuse or anti-capitalism. Among the travellers, however, their tattered T-shirts and trousers are proof of their adventurous spirit – and less often for their anti-capitalistic position – and thus enhance their social capital within their group[89].

The tourist industry that is used by group travellers caters mostly for this specific segment of tourists. Tourism promoters from the governments of host countries tend to stress the importance of revenue generation by mass tourism; individual tourists are mostly neglected or even actively discouraged[90]. Nevertheless, they have the potential of promoting development in remote or underdeveloped areas. In contrast to the opinions of many governmental tourism agencies, individual travellers spend even more money on their journeys than mass or package tourists, because they stay longer in a country.[91] Moreover, the money backpackers spend stays within the domestic economy, whereas the 'leakage' of money spent by mass tourists to the tourists' home countries is much greater[92]. However, the reservations against backpackers or individual tourists are not all based on misperception. It often occurs that they haggle fiercely and thus cause local entrepreneurs to sell without profit.[93] Sometimes

---

88 The novel 'The Beach' by Alex Garland (1997), that was subsequently adapted for the movie of the same name starring Leonardo di Caprio, brought some insights of the backpackers' scene to a broader public.
89 According to Torun Elsrud (2001) well worn Indian clothes signify high social capital within the group of backpackers travelling through southeast Asia. Having "survived" India – and looking like it – is regarded as a great feat among them.
90 Little 1991 in: Scheyvens, R. 2002, p. 146.
91 A study on the expenditure of backpackers in Australia in 1992 revealed that each backpacker spent more than twice as much as a mass tourist (US$ 2,667 vs. US$ 1,272) on his or her trip (Haigh R. 1995 in Scheyvens R. 2002, p. 151).
92 Hampton, M.P. 1998, p. 649. Another study by M. Pobocik and C. Butalla (1998, in Scheyvens, R. 2002, p. 153) in the Annapurna area of Nepal showed that group travellers spend US$ 31 per day in Nepal compared to only US$ 6.50 that independent trekkers spend. However, with their smaller contribution they contributed much more to the local development than the group travellers. However, Gäth in his study about tourism in the Langtang National Park in Nepal (Gäth, P. 1999) argued that many individual tourists engage porters and that they therefore spend (US$ 22) more or less the same amount as group tourists (US$ 25).
93 When I was considerably younger I did my share of backpacking in Southeast Asia. I hope not to have stressed my hosts' tolerance in a way some backpackers do and did then. I remember an occurrence that is symptomatic for many backpackers' attitude. Staying on the island of Nias where prices were incredibly low, I had may hair cut short by a local barber. Coming back to the guesthouse a traveller asked how much I paid. I said 1,000 Rupiah (then approximately half a US-dollar). He answered ironically: "I know a guy who had it done for 700 and he had cut his hair shorter and he had a bigger head than you."

they do not show the proper respect to their host communities probably due to a lack of self-reflexivity. Figure 8 on page 38 shows some of the positive and negative aspects that backpackers can have on the development of remote areas.

Figure 8: Backpackers and local development

Positive aspects	Negative aspects
• Spend more money than other tourists because of longer duration of their visit	• The total amount spent per day is still smaller compared with mass tourists
• Money is spread over wider geographical areas due to adventuresome nature of travel and longer duration	• The flow of money is much less controllable, which can also lead to its asymmetric allocation
• Greater demand for locally produced goods and services and less luxury consumption	• The marketing of locally produced luxury goods is difficult, therefore, an upgrading of goods is not easy
• Individuals with little capital or training can provide desired products and services, and skills can be learned on the job	• The possibility of starting an enterprise with only little capital or training can lead people to take unknown risks and to prohibit them to get proper training
• Basic infrastructure is required which can be locally and cheaply produced, thus ensuring low overhead costs	• To build the infrastructure that is needed for tourism enterprises can be a strain on the local environment
• Multiple effects from drawing on local skills and resources	• The urge of backpackers to travel as cheaply as possible can lead to local peoples' self-exploitation
• Ownership and control over the small enterprises catering for backpackers can be retained locally	• The proliferation of backpackers in a certain area can lead to cultural problems
• Local people can gain better self-fulfilment running own tourist operations instead of filling menial positions in enterprises run by outside operators	• Working within a family enterprise can lead to the exploitation of certain family members
• Local business owners can form organizations which promote but also control local tourism, upholding their interests	• Alternative tourism can foster local disparities
• The interest of backpackers in traditional skills and local customs can lead to a revitalisation of local culture	• This interest can lead to a "musealization" of traditions and inhibit their development
• Backpackers use fewer resources and are therefore kinder to the environment[a]	• Economies of scale of mass tourism can better facilitate environmentally friendly systems
• Local servicing of the tourism market challenges foreign domination of tourism enterprises	• The "life cycle" of tourist destinations can lead to the encroachment of international enterprises replacing local ones

a. This is not automatically so; rather the backpackers' need to have the opportunity to act environmentally friendly should be supported (Firth, T. & Hing, N. 1999).
Source: Scheyvens, R. 2002, p. 152 (extended).

We can thus conclude that backpackers or individual travellers make a contribution to the development of the areas they visit, that should not be neglected.

Their impact is more local and not as easily measurable as the expenditures of mass tourists who because of their larger number contribute a bigger share to the tourist income of a country.

3.2.5 Domestic tourism in developing countries

Although domestic tourism accounts for almost 70 % of the tourism in ASEAN countries[94], the topic is not very well researched.[95] Moreover, most government agencies concentrate on international (or more specifically overseas) tourism within their policies. It is often overlooked that domestic tourists contribute more money to the tourist industry than foreigners, not per person but as a whole[96], and that they are growing in importance and number.[97] The reason for the disregard of domestic tourism can be found in the difficulty of defining a domestic tourist and therefore to find adequate statistical data on their numbers, etc. Domestic tourism in the South (or 'Third World') developed mostly from visiting relatives, religious pilgrimages and business travels. These modes of travel are still quite important, but today the urban middle class mostly travels for leisure purposes – often combined with a visit to relatives, a religious shrine, a business meeting or shopping – within their home countries. The growing urban population along with an increasing differentiation of production and work and the globalization of modern ideals (with a western bias) leads many urbanites to travel from their cities into the countryside. Many of them have started to visit national parks or nature sites. Visitor statistics show that some Malaysian national parks are visited by considerably more domestic tourists than foreigners (see "2 Most important parks and reserves in Malaysia" on page 93).

In Malaysia, most urbanites or their parents have their roots in rural areas. Many came to the urban areas in order to find work during the boom time during the 1980's and 1990's and still do so. Most younger urbanites did not grow up in the countryside but many still have relatives in rural areas who they visit. They have a different attitude towards "nature" compared with their rural relatives because they have not experience the hardship and danger that is inherent

---

94 In 2003 87 % of all foreign visitors to Malaysia were from ASEAN countries. Over 56 % came from neighbouring Singapore (Tourism Malaysia 2003); see figure 7 on page 29.
95 A quick search with the keyword "domestic" within the *Annals of Tourism Research* from 1995 to 2002 listed 11 articles where the term appeared either in the title, in the abstract or in the keywords. From these 4 concerned countries in the south (Hong Kong, Tobago and Barbuda, Kenya, and Thailand). The same search within *Tourism Management* brought 21 hits, from which 5 concerned countries in the south (Korea, Turkey, India, China and Zimbabwe). Ghimire (2001a, p. 27-28) did the same for the years from 1990 to 1995. There was no hit with "domestic" within the *Annals of Tourism Research* and only one – concerning Great Britain – within the *Tourism Management*.
96 Ghimire, K.B. 2001a.
97 See for example Seckelmann, A. 2002, or Ghimire, K.B. 2001b.

in cultivating land especially if it is near a forest. Moreover, urban areas have experienced increasing pollution through traffic and industry. At the same time, ecological awareness has been heightened through education and campaigns by local and global NGOs. The Malaysian government addressed potential domestic tourists only during the Asian Currency Crisis in order to keep them from spending money outside the country. Subsequently, the beauty of Malaysia and especially its natural beauty were advertised for domestic tourism at this time.

For the management of national parks, this growing domestic clientele can be a challenge because they have different needs than foreigners who visit the same parks. It is a hypothesis of this study that needs such as "spending leisure time with friends in unpolluted surroundings" or "to have fun" are important for domestic travellers. If that is the case, park management need to meet and regulate these needs in adequate ways, which will not threaten the ecological balance of the park and that are able to accommodate the needs of a great number of domestic tourists.

3.3 Post(-fordist) tourists and the "end of tourism"

3.3.1 Post-fordist tourism: flexible and customized

In line with the shift from Fordist mass production of goods to more flexible, specialized and smaller-scale production (and consumption) modes, the modes of (mass) tourism have changed, too. Consumer tastes are rapidly changing and are more diversified which lead to the emergence of speciality niche markets. Middle class mass tourists have diversified their tastes. First, many of them have experienced the uniformity of package tours and want to see and do something new. Second, the standardisation that came with mass tourism has made individual travelling easier and safer for a wider range of tourists. Third, an increasing number of people started their own 'tourist career' with backpacking, which lets them seek out other forms of (mass) tourism when they grow older. Fourth, increasing flexibility in the working sphere has resulted in more frequent short-haul or interrupted holidays[98]. The tourism industry has changed, too. Although transnational corporations lead the tourist industry, they more and more out-source certain support activities (e.g. catering, laundry, guiding). This development results in the emergence of smaller-scale and customized tourism products. Low impact, green or ecotourism are among such small-scale products. Post-Fordist tourists are considered to be more responsible and to have greater interest in discovering new things (culture, nature). They seek out the untouched, the authentic, the pristine and the indigenous.[99] Here, potential

---
98 Torres, R. 2002, p. 92; Bieger, T. & Laesser, C. 2002.
99 Torres, R. 2002, p. 93.

mass tourists converge with the aims and goals of individual travellers or backpackers.

We can argue that the characteristics of post-Fordist tourism are not entirely new. There have been customized small-scale tourism productions operating at the fringes of mass tourism since its beginning. What is new is the scale of this type of tourism and the increasing need for flexibility. Tourists who seek out post-Fordist products are still more affluent than the average package tourist. The distinction between certain types of tourists according to their economic capital and their tastes and demands regarding tourism is increasingly difficult. Therefore, we cannot say that the Fordist mass tourist is now becoming the post-Fordist tourist seeking out customized tourism products. Both types of tourism exist. They do not exclude each other and the difference between them may be less than distinct. As a consequence, consumers have a wider diversity of choices within mass tourism. Ritzer suggests that we are experiencing a 'mass customization' that is oriented towards smaller-scale production of higher-end goods and that targets speciality market[100]. Therefore, Ioannides and Debbage[101] suggest that 'neo-Fordism' is a better term, because it more accurately describes the enhanced flexibility in Fordist sections of the tourism industry.

3.3.2 The "end of tourism"

Lash and Urry[102] also state that tourism has moved away from ordinary mass tourism towards a disorganised form of tourism that covers a larger sphere than traditional tourism. Therefore, they talk about the "end of tourism" because everything becomes touristic or can be the object of tourist appropriation. This also leads to the end of certainty that was inherent in the era of organised mass tourism, even for the individual tourist. An inroad of tourism into many people's everyday lives started with the things and habits that tourists brought back from their journeys. One important example is eating out in a restaurant, which most people previously did only rarely when at home. Tourists brought that habit back from their holidays which led to a proliferation of restaurants of a great variety of cuisines. This development is paralleled by the increasing number of pictures and images that came into their homes through different channels. Thus, the separation of leisure and work begins to cease to exist. It does not, however, mean that people stop travelling because they can experience foreign places from their home. On the contrary, the ever-present images of foreign places, combined with a well oiled infrastructure for the organisation of mass tourism and sinking transport costs, enable even more people to travel

---

100 Ritzer, G. 1998, in Torres, R. 2002, p. 94.
101 Ioannides, D. & Debbagge, K. J. 1998, in Torres, R. 2002, p. 94.
102 Lash, S. & Urry, J. 1994, p. 269-270.

than before. Post-tourists in the era of post modernity have a vision of their journey garnered through the internet, travel magazines, television or travel guides, and therefore are able to judge what they want to see and visit even before they start their journey. They want flexible and customized travel arrangements instead of standardized and packaged ones. The role of tour operators and other travel experts has also changed. They do not tell the travellers anymore what to look at, they are rather interpreters of what the travellers see and experience. The wish or need for interpretation also shows itself in the increasing number of museums[103] almost everywhere and about a great variety of topics.

The development from the early grand tourist to the Fordist mass tourist to the neo-Fordist or post-tourist is not an absolute change, for not all tourists today are post-tourists with a customized itinerary and there are even travellers who at least try to embark on something like a Grand Tour. Moreover, we have to bear in mind that pilgrimages are not only undertaken in many countries of the South, but that they have became increasingly popular in the rest of the world. All forms exist concurrently which is quite demanding for all people involved in the tourist business. Currently there is a trend of increased orientation toward special experiences. Tourists are more conscious of cost differences which can also be attributed to the global process of standardisation that made tourism products and even destinations exchangeable and thus comparable. Moreover, surveys show an inclination of tourists toward a higher ecological sensibility, especially if it is visible (e.g. pristine and untouched landscapes, clear water etc.).[104] For conservation areas, this development seems to be favourable.

---

103 This has the effect that tourists can now better judge the quality of museums which results in a stronger competition between different museums.
104 See Bieger, T. & Laesser, C. 2002.

4 Authenticity and non-places

> *"Authenticity will be the buzzword of the twenty-first century. And what is authentic? Anything that is not devised and structured to make a profit. Anything that is not controlled by corporations. Anything that exists for its own sake, that assumes its own shape. But, of course, nothing in the modern world is allowed to assume its own shape. The modern world is the corporate equivalent of a formal garden, where everything is planted and arranged for effect. Where nothing is untouched, where nothing is authentic."*[105]

4.1 Authenticity – a social construction

4.1.1 Authenticity – a consequence of modernity

According to Relph something that is authentic is "genuine, unadulterated, without hypocrisy, and honest to itself, not just in terms of superficial characteristics, but at depth."[106] It can be attributed to places and to people. It is most often used in the context of culture where questions arise as to whether cultural manifestations can be regarded as authentic or not.[107] Relph went on to discuss the authentic attitude to place which is "a direct and genuine experience of the entire complex of the identity of places – not mediated and distorted through a series of quite arbitrary social and intellectual fashions about how that experience should be, nor following stereotypical conventions."[108] The concept of authenticity was moreover regarded as a consequence of modernisation during which people became alienated from "reality" or dis-embedded from space and time. As a reaction to this, tourists were seen as being on a quest for authenticity, for the 'real' that is not part of their own every day life[109]. MacCannell[110] subsequently argues that the tourism industry started to stage authenticity in order to provide tourists with what they are looking for. This is necessary in order not to compromise the life – or the backstage, using a term coined by Goffman – of the visited, but also because tourists are outsiders and as such normally not entitled to look behind the facade of what they encounter.

---

105 Crichton, M. 1999, p. 444.
106 Relph, 1976, p. 64 in Peet, R. 1998, p. 50.
107 In discussions about the authenticity of specific cultures it is often overlooked that the taken-for-granted homogeneity of (pre-modern) cultures is often not more than a myth (see Ackermann, A. & Müller, K. E. (eds.) 2002.
108 Relph, 1976, p. 64 in Peet, R. 1998, p. 50.
109 MacCannell, D. 1989, p. 3.
110 MacCannell, D. 1989, p. 98-99.

4.1.2 Staging authenticity

If we look at these notions from a constructivistic perspective, we have to admit that there is no way not to look at places in an un-mediated way, because our perception is always influenced by social and cultural aspects (and by our habitus). Rather than perceiving authenticity in an absolute and objective manner, we should perceive it as a social construction, because there is no objective position that tells us what is authentic and what not. We could then argue that authenticity is very arbitrary and only dependent on the beholder's point of view and thus varies with different people, different times and different places[111]. This may be true in theory, but not in practice, because there is a common notion about what can be regarded as authentic and what not. Cohen[112], who considers the topic of authenticity and tourism, proposes a continuum between the authentic and the in-authentic rather than a dichotomy. Moreover, he calls the need for authentic experiences as a given part of every journey, into question. He argues that both the perception of authenticity as well as the wish to experience it, are variable. He also writes that tourists do not necessarily have to feel cheated when presented with staged 'authenticity', if this includes a proviso. I want to take the issue a little bit further and argue that we have to distinguish between authentic experiences of tourists and what we might be an authentic lifestyle or place within a region.

MacCannell[113] uses Erving Goffman's concept of front and back regions showing the social differentiation of modern society to explain what tourists want to see when they are looking for authenticity. The front region (in a tourist setting this could be a restaurant, a guided tour or an information centre of a park etc.) is the stage where people play a role which subsequently is perceived by the audience. The back region (e.g. the restaurant's kitchen, the tour guide's home or the warden's private office) is where people can be themselves – according to their habitus – and where they do not have to perform a role in front of an audience, spectators or customers. These regions are not fixed entities; rather, they depend highly on the context, the perception, function and habitus of the people involved. MacCannell argues that tourists who are looking for authenticity can only find it in the back regions, where people are themselves or in other words where they are authentic. It has often occurred (and probably still occurs) that tourists seeking authenticity have walked into the kitchens in order to have authentic experiences. In the Balinese village of Ubud for example tourists frequently stepped into Balinese homes and wanted to participate in an (authen-

---

111 Bruner, E. 1994, May, J. 1996 in DeLyser, D. 1999, p. 604.
112 Cohen, E. 1988.
113 MacCannell, D. 1989, p. 91-107.

tic) tooth filing ceremony, a very private occasion, until the villagers set up rules for the tourists that prohibited them from entering a compound without asking permission. Because of this quest for authenticity, tourist destinations have started to decorate their front regions with elements of back regions (e.g. with local objects of utility in a restaurant, ranger's uniforms in the style of local costume, maps carved into wood etc.). In doing so, they stage authenticity to a certain degree. The notion that front regions with staged authenticity are perceived as less authentic may be true for certain groups of tourists but not as a rule. Individual travellers often perceive the presence of other tourists as a threat to the authenticity of the place, and resent them. People decide individually – and again according to their habitus – whether to perceive something as authentic or not, even if they know that it is staged. Therefore, the label "authentic" cannot be regarded as an absolute. Consequently, a wide range of (staged) authentic experiences is possible. However, if the label "authentic" is used for tourist attractions it will be questioned by the tourists because they have individual notions about authenticity. Therefore, authenticity has to be staged in a way that does not need to be advertised as such. Then it opens a wide range of interpretations of authenticity for the visitor.

4.2 Perceiving authenticity

For many tourists a jungle is the epitome of authenticity, with its abundance of fauna and flora and that is what most tourists are looking for when visiting a national park.[114] Hence, a great biodiversity serves as a sign for intact and therefore authentic rainforests. Consequently, national parks are often advertised as having an abundance of numbers of species.[115] Since nature does not have front or back regions, a jungle is basically not perceived as staged. However, a jungle that carries the label of a national park is often regarded as more authentic than other forests with the same features that are not protected. Moreover, if these rainforests are advertised and promoted by the tourist industry, they are already staged. When tourists visit such (staged) national parks, they go there with expectations about what they are going to see and experience. Some of their expectations are connected to authenticity. If the tourists' expectations are met, they will perceive their experience as more authentic than if not. Authenticity can be perceived via relevant signs. These signs depend on the discourse about rainforests and jungles (see "5.2.6 Images about rainforests" on page 75) and how they are perceived by (potential) tourists. Different groups of tourists (e.g. foreigners and Malaysian locals) have different interests when they visit a na-

---

114 Vorlaufer, K. 1996, p. 208.
115 See Wong, K.M. & Phillipps, A. 1996 or Hutton, W. 1998.

tional park. They perceive (or 'read') the context of their destinations differently. Consequently, they are looking for different signs in this context. If they, for example, come to a national park in Borneo in order to see rare animals or plants, such signs could be the footprint or the sound of an animal or the animal itself. But it could also be a bus driver stating that in a specific park rafflesia are in bloom. If the travellers are interested in culture they are looking for people dressed in traditional attire or for traditional huts and villages, unaware that so-called traditional societies are changing, too[116].

If tourists do not find the relevant signs – proving great biodiversity for instance – they will probably be disappointed[117], which does not help in sustaining ecotourism. It is not possible to anticipate every expectation of tourists and provide them with relevant signs. This is not even necessary, rather, it is important to provide signs that tourists can relate to and that they can understand. If they do not find the animal or plant they came for, they may be directed to other interesting species, or a ranger could tell them why the hornbills hide and the rafflesia are not in bloom at the moment. To prevent the different interests of tourists from clashing and to co-ordinate them with the concept of ecotourism is a great challenge for the authorities and the park management. It is a difficult task for the park management to provide tourists with authentic experiences on the one hand and on the other hand to protect the source of authenticity. Consequently, we have to ask whether it is possible to guide tourists in an eco-friendly way through national parks and at the same time to enable them to experience authenticity. For, if the expectations of tourists can be met in an eco-friendly way, in the end it serves both conservation and the tourist economy. It is my hypothesis that this goal can be better achieved with the help of elements of so called 'non-places'[118], places of global 'understanding' (albeit with a western bias). These non-places (e.g. airports, shopping malls, turnpikes or theme parks) play an increasingly important role in everyday life and also while travelling.

4.2.1 Excursus: images of Borneo[119]

Since a substantial part of Malaysian conservation area is located in Sarawak and Sabah on the island of Borneo, it is useful to know something about the image of Borneo[120] especially because it still has the sound of adventure and something exotic. Rüegge made an analysis of the image of Borneo in newspapers (Frankfurter Allgemeine Zeitung, Neue Zürcher Zeitung) and magazines (Geo, National Geographic Magazine).

---

116 Lee, B.T. & Bahrin T. S. 1998.
117 See Hitchcock, M. & Jay, S. 1998.
118 Augé, M. 1995.
119 Information provided in this chapter are from Rüegge, B. (2003) if not stated otherwise.

The first images about Borneo in Europe were influenced by explorers and traders who visited the island. These images were dominated by 'noble savages' who were seen to roam the forests oblivious of morals and civilization. Moreover, people speculated as to whether the orang-utan was a human species with an accidental inability to speak. Later reports – mostly during the reign of James Brooke[121] – concentrated on some of the Dayak[122] people's habit of headhunting and thus emphasised Borneo's image as inhabited by savages. Along with the description of Mount Kinabalu by Hugh Low, who in 1852 climbed it as the first European, these images are still present in today's tourism brochures, where the west is depicted as civilized, modern, complex and developed and Borneo as wild, traditional, simple and backward.[123] This image is more or less in line with attributes of the rainforests that cover large tracts of the island and which are – together with the culture of the Dayak – the main tourist attractions of Borneo.

The image of Borneo's nature in magazines and newspapers does not differ from the above mentioned image. Usually, the abundant and lush wilderness with strange animals and huge plants is described. Some articles (fewer than half) also mention negative aspects – in newspapers more than in magazines – such as the deterioration of forested land. The Dayak are mentioned, in two threads of the discourse about Borneo. On the one hand the problems of the Penan, who are losing their habitat to logging, are depicted as peaceful victims who have never participated in head hunting. On the other hand, the conflicts of the Indonesian Dayak with immigrated Madurese were described, where the Dayak "picked up their old trade of head hunting" and killed the Madurese settlers. Hence, we find both the aspect of the threatened habitat (for people and other species) as well as the aspect of wild and savage tribes.

The focus on the Penan is most certainly the result of the activities of the Swiss environmentalist Bruno Manser. Manser grew up in Basel and spent some

---

120 The name 'Borneo' comes from the local word 'burni', the name for the powerful muslim state in the north-west of the island, that had its capital in present-day Bandar Seri Begawan. Due to a European malapropism burni became Borneo. Before, in the 16th century Borneo was called 'Java Major'. The Indonesians call the island Kalimantan (which means river of precious stones in Javanese). Outside Indonesia the expression Kalimantan is used for the Indonesian part of the island, the whole island is called Borneo. In Malaysia 'Borneo' is rarely used, either people speak about a specific state (i.e. Sabah, Sarawak, Brunei or Kalimantan) or more general about East Malaysia.
121 For a history of Borneo see for example King, V.T. 1993.
122 Dayak is a collective term for the non-Malay (and mostly non-muslim) people living on Borneo, consisting of Iban, Kayan, Kenyah, Bidayuh, Penan, Kadazaan-Dusun, Rungus, Ukit among others.
123 King, V.T. 1992.

summers as a herdsman in the Swiss Alps after graduating from high school. He soon yearned to learn about nature from a people that still live "close to its roots". After reading an article about the Penan of Sarawak, he decided to visit them, learned Malay and flew to Sarawak. He actually met Penans who took him to their camp and soon after accepted him as a member of their group. After 1984 the habitat of the Penan was more and more threatened by logging companies. In 1986 Manser helped the Penan to set up a roadblock, thus successfully preventing a bulldozer from clearing their forest. The police – and after further blockades, the government – accused Manser of being an insurgent and tried to arrest him. Twice he escaped the police just before they could catch him. Until 1990 he lived with his Penan group, and then he decided that he could help them better from the outside and returned to Switzerland. There he launched many campaigns in order to prevent European governments from importing wood from threatened rainforests. In 1998 he went back to Sarawak where he landed with a self-propelling parachute in the middle of Kuching, the capital of Sarawak, where he was instantly arrested and deported. In 2000 he embarked on a journey that would (probably) to be his last. He wanted to enter Sarawak from Kalimantan in order to visit his Penan friends, but he never arrived. His fate is still unknown and the speculation ranges from the notion that he was killed by logging companies or even government agents, or that he had an accident in the jungle and died, to that he is hiding with a remote group of Penans in the jungle and waiting for an appropriate moment to emerge. German and Swiss magazines and newspapers do mention him often – American National Geographic Magazine does not mention him at all – and most articles concern his disappearance and the fact that he was out of favour with the Malaysian authorities and that local NGOs do not want to be associated with him. Nevertheless, they also emphasise his courage and stamina and that he at least brought the problem of the Penans to the public arena.

In German speaking countries, tourists are familiar with the activities of Manser and are well aware of the problems he pointed out, when they travel to Borneo. Therefore, the notion that rainforests are threatened and thus have to be protected is probably prevalent among many western tourists travelling to Borneo.

4.2.2 Non-places: dis-embedded from their context

Augé[124] is concerned about the change of our experience of space. Due to processes of globalization (e.g. telecommunication and information technology) we live less in the "here and now" and in less well definable cultural contexts. We

---

124 Augé, M. 1995.

have access to a great variety of images of places that are far away which leads to a shrinking of the world or an expansion of our range of experience.[125] Thus, we know many places although we have never been there, through virtual experience. This experience is detached from "eye witnessing" and thus an "artificial authenticity" is created. Consequently, the "being there" at a concrete place is often regarded as authentic experience in contrast to the one that is mediated by television or magazines.[126] Along with the proliferation of images of other areas so called non-places have emerged. They do not have many specific characteristics and are not embedded in their context. They are sort of "immune" to cultural appropriation[127]. "If a place can be defined as relational, historical and concerned with identity, then a space which cannot be defined as relational, historical, or concerned with identity will be a non-place. […] [Non-places] are like palimpsests on which the scrambled game of identity and relations is ceaselessly rewritten."[128] Since even non-places are located somewhere they never exist in their pure form (except maybe in cyberspace). Moreover, there is no dichotomy between place and non-place, rather there is a gradual difference. Very often non-places are transit spaces, where people spend a limited time and are led to other places. Typical examples of such transit spaces are airports, train and petrol stations but also international hotels with interchangeable interiors. They are readable by the visitor through signs which are often standardised (e.g. pictograms at airports[129]). With their standardisation, non-places can provide islands within a foreign context. Thus, a simple bancomat (cash dispenser) can provide safeness in a place where one does not know how to deal with moneychangers. Since non-places are being globalized, travellers encounter them more and more. In addition to providing safeness in certain situations, they enable many tourists to travel into areas into which they would not have travelled before unless with a group or guide. The proliferation of non-places thus makes travelling easier but it also raises (more) questions about authenticity, which cannot be easily answered. For example, Disneyland can be regarded as a non-place with no connection to the local context. It could be anywhere, as could

---

125 Ahrens, D. 2001, p. 166-168.
126 In discussions we can often experience the authority of eyewitnesses. "I have been there and seen it" is often regarded as the better argument although an opinion based on mediated knowledge can sometimes be much more accurate.
127 Bormann, R. 2000, p. 226.
128 Augé, M. 1995, p. 78-79.
129 People who are used to pass through non-places and to read pictograms become able to even understand signs they have never seen before. For example the pictogram giving directions to the (islamic) prayer room in Kuala Lumpur International Airport (KLIA) is understandable by many Europeans who have never seen such a pictogram, because they are used to read and decipher pictograms.

Disney World in Florida and Euro Disney in Paris. However, it could also be regarded as a typical example of American culture and therefore as an authentic part of American lifestyle. It also means that within the discussion about non-places it is difficult to define what is authentic and what not.

4.2.3 Tourist spaces of experience and adventure

According to Wöhler[130], places become charged with notions and emotions, by tourist Presented in a fitting context they engrave themselves in the tourists' memories. The important things are not the places, but the emotions and experiences that tourists are looking for. The (post-)modern tourist industry can provide (or stage) these experiences in many different settings or contexts. Hence, the experiences that tourists have and seek to have do not depend on a specific place or location anymore. The location is replaced by the event or the experience, and thus the experience becomes atopic. Tourists do not ask for specific locations but for fulfilling experiences that are subsequently "re-embedded" or "territorialized" into certain locations. Tourists can have authentic experiences[131], because they (re-)connect their experiences with the context, the locations where they have had them. A precondition for this is that locations "talk" in a way that tourists are made aware that they will be able to have certain experiences. They have to be able to read the experience-related signs in a location. Wöhler argues that these places are not non-places, because tourists make a connection between experiences and place, for they not only gaze at them but also perform within them. I want to emphasize that the emergence and development of non-places is connected to the dis-embedding of experiences from places and their later re-embedding. Even if we do not perceive non-places as locations of authentic experiences, the readability of their signs can serve as a base for the readability of locations where "authentic" experiences can be made. Moreover, these experiences can be perceived as a contrast to the non-places that have become an integral part of our every-day life.

A national park is not a theme park and therefore not a non-place, at least that is how most people perceive it. However, if we assume that authenticity is a social construction, then the attractions of a national park and the experiences that can be connected to them are "staged" in one way or another. This staging can consist of small things such as putting up signs in front of trees with their

---

130 Wöhler, K. 2003.
131 It is debatable whether tourist experiences in the cyberspace can be regarded as authentic or not. An utopian vision of such experiences was displayed in the movie "Total Recall", where Arnold Schwarzenegger went to a cyberstation in order to have memories of a tourist journey implanted. Of course in the movie everything goes wrong and Schwarzenegger has to shoot his way out of difficult situations.

botanical names on them; but it can also comprise the deliberate planting of specific vegetation and species which may be attractive to people, and the introduction of rare animals.[132] Moreover, parks that can be visited need an infrastructure and a management, in order to be able to cope with visitors. This management has to satisfy the needs of the visitors, and provide relevant signs for the tourists' experiences. On the other hand, it has to protect the environment from the damaging influences of tourism. To combine both demands is quite difficult for the management, especially when understaffed. Therefore, I want to argue that elements which people know from non-places can be useful for that task.

5 Ecotourism and nature conservation

Ecotourism is most often associated with protected areas. However, ecotourism is not necessarily restricted to conservation areas. Depending on its definition, every mode or form of tourism can be (or eventually should be) transformed into ecotourism. In the following, I want to follow the mainstream of definitions of ecotourism that focus on natural features and concentrate on conservation areas, because the focus of this study is on Malaysian national parks and their tourism management.

5.1 Defining ecotourism

The term 'ecotourism' is not clearly defined, as we will see below, and there is a great range of definitions that comprise differing types of tourism. Because the term is relatively new, there are no comprehensive studies about ecotourism and 'ecotourists'. However, the World Tourism Organization has published a series of seven volumes[133] concerning the ecotourism market in the USA, Canada, Italy, France, Spain, Germany and the United Kingdom. Here we can find at least an estimate of the potential of ecotourism and the profile of 'ecotourists' in these countries, which are among the major countries of tourists' origin. Although difficult to compare – because of different data sources – the reports give us a rough idea of the significance of ecotourism. The most outstanding results of the seven studies are described at the beginning of each report[134]:

"1. The use of the term 'ecotourism' in the marketing and promotional tools and used by tour operators is still relatively limited. It would appear that this

---

132 See for example Selengut, S. 1995 or Masing, J.J. 1999.
133 World Tourism Organisation 2001a; 2001b; 2002a; 2002b; 2002c; 2002d; 2002e.
134 World Tourism Organisation 2001a; 2001b; 2002a; 2002b; 2002c; 2002d; 2002e, p. 5 (in every report).

term has not yet been integrated in the marketing strategies of the nature tourism sector.
2. Likewise, the tourism sector that most closely matches the concept of ecotourism represents a relatively small share of the market, an observation that is borne out by the small dimension of the tour operators that comprise this segment and the small number of tourists they cater for.
3. Conversely, these same tour operators apparently believe that the growth of ecotourism may out pace that of other tourism activities overall. Moreover, this growth appears to be consolidating irrespective of the destination considered. A priori, no world region appears to have a head-start although each region does have several landmark destinations.
4. The surveys conducted among the various audiences show that enthusiasm for nature tourism invariably goes hand-in-hand with a desire for meeting local communities and discovering different facets of their culture (gastronomy, handicraft, customs, etc.).
5. According to tour operators, ecotourism enthusiasts are mostly people from relatively high social brackets and with relatively high levels of education; they are over 35 and women slightly outnumber men.
6. These studies also show that environmental awareness, while still in its infancy, is clearly growing."

In the following chapters I will try to outline the concept of ecotourism and certain aspects of the ecotourists' habitus and what they expect at their destinations.

5.1.1 Ecotourism and its wide range of definitions

Usually after the question "what is ecotourism?" one expects a concise definition of the term ecotourism. However, Kurte[135] listed 40 different (English) definitions of ecotourism in her book discussing the concept. They range from tourism into ecologically interesting areas over adventure tourism, to environmentally and socially responsible travel.[136] Therefore, I will not present the 41st definition of ecotourism. Rather, I want to understand the discussion about ecotourism as a discourse with different threads. The origin of the term "ecotourism" goes back either to the late 1980's, when Hector Ceballos-Lascuráin used and distributed the concept or even to the late 1960's, when Hetzer proposed an "ecological tourism ('eco-tourism')" in the sense of soft or sustainable tourism. Whatever the source of the term is, Ceballos-Lascuráin certainly is cited most. He also continued to spread the word when he was working for the

---

135 Kurte, B. 2002, p. 141-147.
136 Kurte, B. 2002, p. 11-12.

IUCN.[137] The term entered the scientific discourse in the 1990's and is today often called a "buzzword", meaning that it is widely used without proper definition, and that it has entered mainstream discussion about tourism. The concept of ecotourism can be used in a descriptive (e.g. the evaluation of existing modes or forms of tourism) or normative way (e.g. how tourism should be conducted in order to be sustainable), thus covering a broad spectrum of interpretations. Many definitions of ecotourism all have the same thrust towards "sustainable tourism" but differ considerably in length and concreteness (see figure 9 on page 53). Kurte[138] defines three dimensions according to which the agents of (eco)tourism can be analysed: the destination, the tourist and the organisation of the journey. Not all definitions cover all three dimensions and according to Blamey[139] there is a debate about the perspective of ecotourism: does ecotourism only make sense if there is a demand by tourists for activities that can be attributed to ecotourism or should there also be an emphasis on the supply side, even if there is no specific demand for ecotourism in an area?

Figure 9: Selected definitions of ecotourism

Source	Definition
Ceballos-Lascuráin, H. (1987)*	Travelling to relatively undisturbed or uncontaminated natural areas with specific objective of studying, admiring, and enjoying the scenery and its cultural manifestations (both past and present) found in these areas.
Ziffer, K. (1989)**	A form of tourism inspired primarily by the natural history of an area, including its indigenous cultures. The ecotourist visits relatively undeveloped areas in the spirit of appreciation, participation, and sensitivity. The ecotourist practices a non-consumptive use of wildlife and natural resources and contributes to the visited area through labour or financial means aimed at directly benefiting the conservation of the site and the economic well-being of the local residents. Ecotourism also implies a management approach by the host country or region which commits itself to establishing and maintaining the sites with the participation of local residents, marketing the area appropriately, enforcing regulations, and using the proceeds of the enterprise to fund the area's land management as well as community development.
The Ecotourism Society (1991)*	Responsible travel to natural areas which conserves the environment and improves the well-being of local people.
Honey, M. (1999)**	Ecotourism is travel to fragile, pristine, and usually protected areas that strives to be low impact and (usually) small scale. It helps educate the traveller; provides funds for conservation; directly benefits the economic development of local communities; and fosters respect for different cultures and for human rights.

---

137 See Ceballos-Lascuráin, H. 1996.
138 Kurte, B. 2002, p. 22.
139 Blamey, R.K. 2001.

Source	Definition
Sirakaya, E. (1999)**	Ecotourism is a new form of nonconsumptive, educational, and romantic tourism to relatively undisturbed and undervisited areas of immense natural beauty, and cultural and historical importance for the purposes of understanding and appreciating the natural and sociocultural history of the host destination.
World Tourism Organization (2002)***	Ecotourism is a form of tourism with the following characteristics: i. All nature-based forms of tourism in which the main motivation is the observation and appreciation of nature as well as the traditional cultures prevailing in natural areas. ii. It contains educational and interpretation features. iii. It is generally, but not exclusively, organised for small groups by specialized and small locally-owned businesses. Foreign operators of varying sizes also organize, operate and/or market ecotourism tours, generally for small groups. iv. It minimizes negative impacts on the natural and socio-cultural environment. v. It supports the protection of natural areas by: - generating economic benefits for host communities, organizations and authorities that are responsible or conserving natural areas; - creating jobs and income opportunities for local communities; and - increasing awareness both among locals and tourists of the need to conserve natural and cultural assets.

Source: *Blamey, R.K. 2001, p. 6; **Kurte, B. 2002, p. 141; ***World Tourism Organisation 2002e

According to most definitions ecotourism is considered to share three basic characteristics[140]:
1. The natural environment or a specific natural feature is the prime attraction.
2. The basis of that attraction is an inherent appreciation or educational interest in that natural feature, which leads to specific kinds of activities (e.g. bird watching, stargazing, bush walking, nature photography etc.).
3. A management regime exists which is directed at the conservation of or sustainable use of that natural environment.

5.1.2 Analysing the concept of ecotourism

Although aimed at sustainability, the result of ecotourism is not always sustainable and is sometimes detrimental to the attractions visited. There are a great variety of tourism operators and agencies that use different meanings of the label 'ecotourism'. Therefore, it is useful to analyse roughly different types of ecotourism. Orams[141] lists three types of analysis that focus on characteristics of the tourists, the norms behind the specific concepts and the degree of exploitation of nature that comes from tourist activities. Together they provide a good framework for capturing the wide range of possible ecotourism. Of the increas-

---

140 Orams, M.B. 2001, p. 27.
141 Orams, M.B. 2001, p. 28-30.

ing number of tourists who travel in a way that could be called ecotourism, probably most are people who are not very dedicated or knowledgeable about their environment and that prefer a more or less comfortable way of travel (see figure 10 on page 55). Only a few have a specific dedication (e.g. climbers, trekkers) or knowledge (e.g. hobby ornithologists). This categorisation does not tell us anything about the eco-friendliness of these approaches. The most dedicated entomologist who lives in a tent in order to be able to study insects can do more harm than "unknowing" tourists, who like to sleep in clean beds after a visit to the jungle.

Figure 10: Hard and soft ecotourism

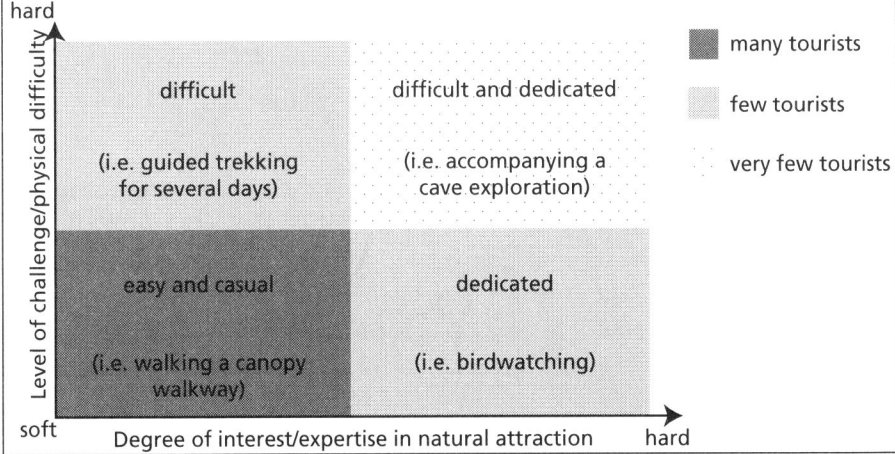

Source: own draft after Laarman, J.G. & Durst, P.B. 1987 in Orams, M.B. 2001, p. 28.

Regarding the question of whether humans are an inseparable part of nature or whether all human actions that have an impact on nature (see figure 11 on page 56) are a disturbance, I propose a relativistic point of view; relativistic in the sense that it depends on the spatial and temporal scales we consider. If we regard our whole planet as an ecological entity, humans have to be seen as an integral part of it and as powerful agents who cause an acceleration of the dynamics of this system. If we consider a national park and its development (or dynamics) for a few years we can separate humans from nature, because they have only limited and regulated access to the area. Thus, for this study I will regard humans – mostly tourists – as external to the natural environment of the research areas.

Regarding the degree of exploitation through ecotourism (see figure 12 on page 56), I hope that the results of this study will contribute to a minimisation of damage and to the sustaining "health" of the host environments.

Figure 11: Humans: part of nature or not

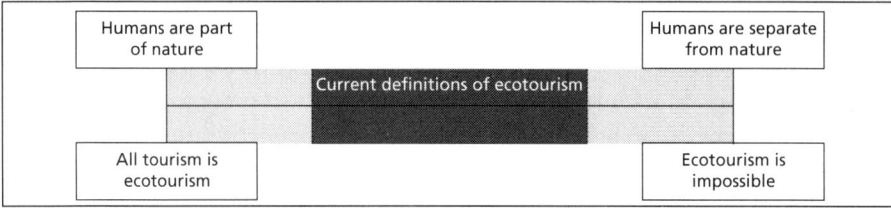

Source: own draft after Miller, M.L. & Kaae, B.C. 1993 in Orams, M.B. 2001, p. 29.

Figure 12: Exploitive, passive and active ecotourism

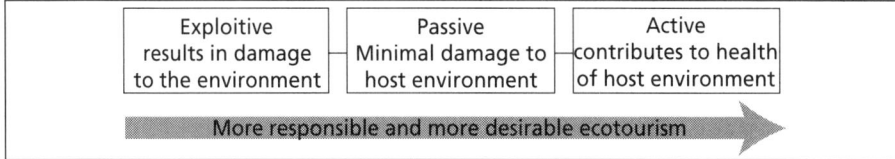

Source: own draft after Orams, M.B. 1995 in Orams, M.B. 2001, p. 30.

5.1.3 Ecotourism and other types of tourism

Weaver[142] tried to narrow the term ecotourism by putting it into relation to other types of tourism that are often associated with ecotourism. In Venn diagrams he visualized these relations (see figure 13 on page 58). In earlier stages of the discussion about ecotourism, it was often portrayed as indistinguishable from nature-based tourism. However, ecotourism with its emphasis on protection and sustainability is only a subgroup of nature-based tourism. But as the diagram (a) shows, not all ecotourism is also nature-based tourism, although that is usually the case. A small part of ecotourism is not nature-based but directed at cultural activities or urban settings. The overlap of ecotourism with adventure tourism in the diagram (b) is only small, if we keep in mind that most 'ecotourists' are engaging in soft ecotourism. If we were to apply a "hard" definition to adventure[143] tourism, it would require an element of risk, and higher levels of physical exertion and the need for specialized skills[144].

Therefore, most ecotourism cannot be regarded as adventure tourism (in a strict sense). Trekking – understood as hiking for a considerable length of time – can be regarded as a combination of adventure, cultural and ecotourism (c). However, even if nowadays most treks include these aspects, some forms do not include ecotourism. Therefore, the positioning of trekking in the middle of the

---

142 Weaver, D.B. 2001.
143 In chapter "2.3 Risk and ontological security or rather adventure and 'safeness'" on page 22 I use a broader and relational definition of adventure as a form of a critical situation. While the element of risk is part of that concept, physical exertion and special skills are not specifically included (neither are they excluded).
144 Weaver, D.B. 2001, p. 74.

three circles is idealistic and normative. The 3S (sea, sand, sun) tourism is commonly associated with mass tourism and therefore regarded as incompatible with ecotourism (d). The overlap occurs in the field of scuba diving and snorkelling which are often done in an ecologically sustainable way. Unlike Weaver I would not only attribute the overlap to diving activities, for beach tourism can also be organised in an eco friendly way, if it can cope with masses of tourism or if it can restrict them. Alternative tourism is commonly seen as the antagonist or alternative to mass tourism (e), especially since negative impacts of mass tourism are broadly discussed. Both forms are seen as incompatible with each other. Ecotourism is consequently regarded as a sub category to alternative tourism which focuses on nature-based activities. This perspective is increasingly being challenged and the antagonists are now seen as poles of a continuum, rather than as a dichotomy.

While small-scale tourist enterprises can more easily fulfil the requirements of ecotourism there is no inherent reason that it is not possible for large-scale tourism. The softer kind of ecotourism has already developed into a mass phenomenon in certain areas. Therefore, it is more appropriate to depict tourism as a gradient from mass tourism to alternative tourism, within which ecotourism is placed (f). Sustainable tourism is a norm that was introduced in the late 1980's after the release of the so called Brundtland report[145].

According to the Brundtland principles, ecotourism should be sustainable, therefore it can be seen as a subset of sustainable tourism. Alternative tourism is rather small-scale, but sustainable tourism extends into the realm of mass tourism, with a bias towards alternative tourism (g). Tourism can also be differentiated according to consumption (h). Non-consumptive tourism is regarded as focused on experiences rather than on goods. If we take a closer look at consumption by ecotourists, we see that they mainly consume fuel when travelling, buy souvenirs, contribute to a gradual and imperceptible degradation of walks etc. Therefore, according to a strict definition of consumptiveness, no type of tourism can be regarded as non-consumptive. However, if we set aside the consumption that occurs through almost any kind of tourism, ecotourism is not an "extractive" form of tourism, such as hunting or playing golf. In the continuum from consumptive to non-consumptive tourism, ecotourism has a bias towards the latter.

---

145 WCED 1987 in Weaver, D.B. 2001, p.80.

Figure 13: Ecotourism in the context of other tourism types

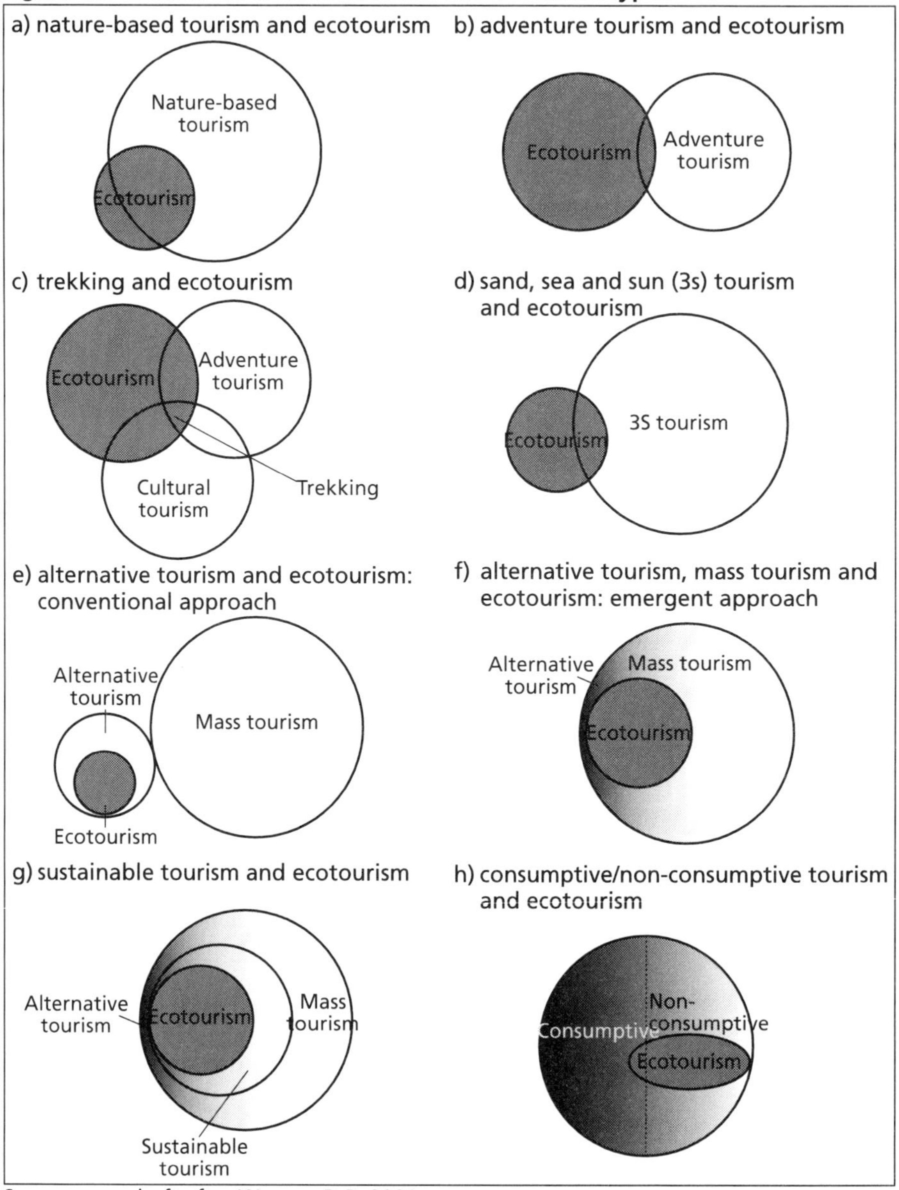
a) nature-based tourism and ecotourism
Nature-based tourism
Ecotourism
b) adventure tourism and ecotourism
Ecotourism
Adventure tourism
c) trekking and ecotourism
Ecotourism
Adventure tourism
Cultural tourism
Trekking
d) sand, sea and sun (3s) tourism and ecotourism
Ecotourism
3S tourism
e) alternative tourism and ecotourism: conventional approach
Alternative tourism
Mass tourism
Ecotourism
f) alternative tourism, mass tourism and ecotourism: emergent approach
Alternative tourism
Mass tourism
Ecotourism
g) sustainable tourism and ecotourism
Alternative tourism
Ecotourism
Mass tourism
Sustainable tourism
h) consumptive/non-consumptive tourism and ecotourism
Consumptive
Non-consumptive
Ecotourism

Source: own draft after Weaver, D.B. 2001.

5.1.4 Growth of ecotourism and potential demand

Nature-based tourism, and with that ecotourism, is a growing sector within the also growing tourism industry[146]. An increasing number of tourists include a visit to a park or a protected area when travelling. In addition, more people are indulging in nature-based activities such as hiking, diving, rafting etc. Along with the increasing demand for eco-activities the demand for travel professionals (e.g. travel agents, tour operators, guides etc.) increases.

Tourism thus becomes more and more segmented, which can be regarded as a chance for many destinations to promote ecotourism rather than less eco-friendly forms of mass tourism. Consequently, many countries – including Malaysia[147] – have introduced ecotourism plans in order to be able to profit from that growing sector, but also in order to counter the worst consequences of mass tourism. A milestone for the acknowledgement of ecotourism was the 'International Year of Ecotourism', which was declared by the UN in 2002. In the 'Québec Declaration on Ecotourism'[148] policies for future ecotourism ventures were articulated. It was emphasised that ecotourism should contribute to making the overall industry more sustainable and that (eco)tourism has to be planned and managed carefully in order to efficiently prevent threats to wildlife, biodiversity, water quality, livelihood of indigenous people etc. On the governmental level, the requirement for regular monitoring and for the introduction of eco labels was suggested. The labels however, should reflect regional and subregional criteria. Although such eco labels would be very useful, the non distinctive definition of ecotourism makes attempts to create labels based on such definitions futile. Although, the International Year of Ecotourism had certainly a mostly positive impact on the discussion and development of ecotourism, it was not much noticed in the (middle European) media. It was much less often covered in the press than the 'International Year of the Mountains 2002', which had a greater impact.

The demand for ecotourism varies among the countries that were included in the study by the WTO. The realised demand of ecotourism 1996 of all people over 15 years who were engaged in tourist activities ranges between 2 % in Italy[149], 5 % in Germany[150] and 6 % in Canada[151], Spain[152], and the USA[153]. The surprisingly high percentage of each of the latter three countries has to do with the great number of national parks in Canada and the USA that have been an attraction for domestic and foreign tourists for a long time. Moreover, in Spain, with a smaller tourist sector, but which is quickly growing, many national

---

146 Hawkins, D.E. & Lamoureux, K. 2001.
147 See WWF Malaysia 1996 and "1.2 The 'National Ecotourism Plan Malaysia' (NEP)" on page 86.
148 Ecotourism Society 2002.
149 World Tourism Organisation 2002a, p. 38.
150 World Tourism Organisation 2001b, p. 26.
151 World Tourism Organisation 2002c, p. 31.
152 World Tourism Organisation 2002b, p. 36.
153 World Tourism Organisation 2002e, p. 29.

parks that are now promoted as ecotourism destinations, the Spanish 'ecotourist' is likely to stay in his or her own country. The numbers of ecotourists differ even more: Spain has approximately 300,000 ecotourists, Canada 1.8 million and Germany between 1 and 3 million, (absolute numbers for the other countries are not available). The potential number of ecotourists in the near future is expected to be roughly between 20 % and 30 % of all tourists[154]. Based on interviews with experts, all studies conclude that the ecotourism market has a potential that exceeds[155] the estimated growth of tourism in general. The reasons given in favour of a growing ecotourism market are the increasing importance of ecological themes in general, that many children are more environmentally conscious than their parents, and the increasing efforts of many tourist attraction managements to become more environmentally friendly. However, the reports also mention reasons against a rapid increase of ecotourism: a decreasing willingness to behave ecologically, higher costs that people are not prepared to bear and that ecotourism is often regarded as a mere fashion that will vanish in a few years.[156]

5.1.5 The main ecotourism destinations

It is difficult to ascertain the preferred destinations of ecotourists. The surveys conducted by the WTO have different data bases and can therefore not be easily compared. The table of data, however, shows certain trends (see "Figure 14: Preferred destinations by ecotourists of selected countries" on page 61). It is not surprising that neighbouring countries (or their own countries) are preferred not only by tourists in general, but also by ecotourists. Malaysia is only mentioned by the Canadians. Surprisingly the Canadian survey additionally mentions Borneo which is also a part of Malaysia; moreover, the British survey mentions Borneo and Indonesia, but not Malaysia. This is a sign of the importance of the island of Borneo as an ecotourism destination. In addition, the label 'Borneo' (see "4.2.1 Excursus: images of Borneo" on page 46) is so important or well known that it is mentioned along with the countries that have territories on the island or even without them.

---

154 The values were derived from representative surveys and consist of the number of people who were saying that they would like to participate in nature-based and/or ecotourist activities.
155 The reports point out that their data was collected before the terrorist attacks of September 11th 2001 and that therefore the projections at least for the near future are probably too optimistic.
156 World Tourism Organisation 2001b, p. 28.

Ecotourism and nature conservation

Figure 14: Preferred destinations by ecotourists of selected countries

Destin. Origin	Europe	Africa	Asia	Latin America	N-America	Oceania
Canada	Scotland, France, Norway, Sweden, Finland, Denmark, Germany, Italy, Bulgaria, Romania, England		Nepal, Malaysia, **Borneo**, Thailand	Bolivia, Ecuador, Galapagos, Venezuela, Patagonia; Trinidad & Tobago, US Virgin Island, Bermuda, Cuba, British Virgin Islands	Canada, USA	New Zealand
USA[a]	UK (3.9), Germany (2.0), France (1.9), Eastern Europe (0.5): 16.7	Kenya (1.8), South Africa (1.7): 5.2	India (2.3): 9.6	Mexico (25.8), Jamaica (5.1), Costa Rica (4.0), Peru (3.9), Bahamas (2.3), Brazil (1.5), Chile (1.5), Ecuador (1.5), Argentina (1.2), Belize (0.8): 55.8		Australia (5.4), New Zealand (3.9): 10.0
France[b]	n.a.	34	25	30	6	2
UK[c]	Spain, Turkey, Iceland, Cyprus, Poland, Slovakia	South Africa, Tanzania, Botswana, Namibia, Madagascar, Morocco, Seychelles, Uganda	Nepal, India, **Borneo**, China, Vietnam, Bhutan, Indonesia, Iran, Mongolia, Pakistan, Siberia, Sri Lanka	Peru, Ecuador, Argentina, Chile, Costa Rica, Belize, Brazil, Mexico, Bolivia, Guyana, Nicaragua, Venezuela, Trinidad & Tobago, Cuba, Dominica, Haiti	Canada	Australia, New Zealand
Germany[d]	Italy, Poland, Greece, Spain, France, Norway, Switzerland, Ireland, Sweden, La Gomera, Romania, Turkey	n.a.	Nepal, Russian Federation, Oman, Kirgistan	Costa Rica, Peru, Bolivia	Canada	Australia
Italy[e]	Italy, Turkey, France, Spain, Russia, Croatia, UK, Ireland	Egypt, Tanzania, Botswana, Zimbabwe, Madagascar, Morocco, Namibia, Tunisia	India, Tibet, Thailand, Indonesia, China, Yemen, Nepal	Brazil, Ecuador, Peru, Mexico, Chile, Venezuela, Costa Rica, Colombia	USA, Canada, Alaska	Australia, New zealand
Spain[f]	Alps, Scandiavia, Portugal, UK, Bulgaria, Iceland, Romania	Egypt, Namibia, Tanzania, Botswana	n.a.	Brazil, Guatemala, Mexico, Cuba, Peru, Argentina	n.a	Australia

a. The survey in the USA excluded the destinations in Canada and the USA itself, which comprise the majority of the destinations. The numbers behind the countries represent the percentages of U.S. American ecotourists who visit that country, the numbers at the end of the list represent the percentages of the U.S. American ecotourists who visit the whole region.
b. Also the survey in France was conducted with tour operators. Europe was excluded and it is estimated to account for 10 to 40 % of the destinations sold by the tour operators. Therefore, the percentages in the table are excluding Europe (and 3 % of no responses).
c. The survey in the UK was conducted with tour operators who stated the favourite destinations of their ecotourist customers.
d. The survey in Germany was conducted with visitors of two tourist fairs.
e. The survey with Italian tour operators includes destinations in Italy.
f. Also the Spanish survey was conducted with tour operators.

Source: data: World Tourism Organisation 2001a; 2001b; 2002a; 2002b; 2002c; 2002d; 2002e.

5.1.6 Who are the ecotourists?

The question is difficult to answer, because there is no clear definition of ecotourism and because it is not clear whether ecotourists differ considerably from other types of tourists. No all tourists who engage in ecotourist activities perceive themselves as ecotourists. Hence, we cannot assume that ecotourists can be identified by their habitus. According to an Australian study, nearly half of the entire range of tourists has an interest in nature and learning as part of their vacation[157], and ecotourism is now seen as the fastest growing segment of tourism[158]. There are different hypotheses for this development:

- In western countries the older population is increasing, so there is a greater demand for less strenuous but more educational activities.
- Many ecotourist activities are becoming cheaper and more easily accessible, so that they are better accessible to a wider range of tourists – especially for individual travellers (or FITs: free individual travellers).
- A growing number of the urban middle class in the South have "discovered" nature-based tourist activities and visits national parks.
- There is a generally greater awareness of environmental problems – and of some of the negative consequences of mass tourism. Therefore, more people are seeking to visit places of unspoiled and pristine nature.

'Ecotourists' tend to be slightly better educated, higher earning and older than other tourists. The percentage of women in this group is increasing and has already surpassed the percentage of men.[159] These trends are diminishing with the increase in the number of ecotourists. If this development continues, many destinations that have catered to a small number of ecotourists (i.e. national parks in remote areas) could come under pressure because of an increasing overall demand, including tourists with different needs and demands. In addition,

---

[157] Wight, P.A. 2001, p. 38.
[158] Cook, S.D. et al. 1992; Laarman, J.G. & Durst, P.B. 1993; Parker, T. 1993; and WTO News 1997/98 in: Wight, P.A. 2001, p. 38-39.
[159] Wight, P.A. 2001, p. 40-43.

the focus on walking and wildlife viewing which are the greatest motivations of western tourists[160], will probably change when more 'general interest' tourists visit conservation areas. Since most parks are set up for the needs of western tourists, in some cases their management will have to change the infrastructure of these facilities.

The WTO report on the Canadian ecotourism market shows that while ecotourists come from all parts of the country they have a very high household income (over 70,000 Can$). The age varies quite considerably, but it is generally higher than the average age of all tourists and the most strongly represented group is between 40 and 65 years old (with 25 % of people over 55). However, there is a slight trend towards younger people in recent years and the most independent travellers among the ecotourists are between 25 and 54. The gender ratio is more or less balanced with more women booking a tour with a tour operator and more men travelling individually. 82 % of the ecotourists are couples (38 % with children), 14 % are singles and 4 % singles with children. Canadian ecotourists are a very highly educated group with only 9 % who have not completed high school and 37 % with a college or university degree. Ecotourists usually travel as couples (48 %) or singles (45 %) and spend more time than the average tourist at their destinations.[161]

U.S. ecotourists have a higher income than the average tourist but only slightly and only recently (before 1996 they had less than an average income). The mean age of 43.7 years indicates that U.S., American ecotourists are also generally older than the average tourist. 25 % are between 35 and 54 and there are many more male travellers (54 %) than female. Regarding their occupations, ecotourists do not differ from other tourists. More than half of them travel with their spouse and almost 10 % (vs. fewer than 7 %) travel with children, and they stay longer on their trips than typical U.S. travellers.[162] Most British ecotourists[163] are also in the range of 35 to 54 years old (46 %) and a considerable proportion are over 55 (36.4 %). They are also better educated than the average tourist and the survey indicates that they also stay longer at their destinations.[164]

The French ecotourist profile shows that 51 % are in the 35 to 50-age bracket and 30 % in the 50 to 65-age bracket, and that many more women (55 %)

---

160 Wight, P.A. 2001, p. 53.
161 World Tourism Organisation 2002c, p. 38-43.
162 The survey consists of clients of tour operators. Therefore, it is likely that the proportion of older people and of women is higher than if the individual ecotourists would have been included.
163 World Tourism Organisation 2002e, p. 39-45.
164 World Tourism Organisation 2001a, p. 52-54.

are ecotourists. They are also well educated (50 % hold managerial or professional positions). The ecotourists are average to high income earners.[165]

Most of the German ecotourists (24 %) are in the age group from 40 to 49 years and are mainly women. They are more affluent than other tourists and have a higher educational level, many of them are teachers.[166]

The Italian ecotourist is considerably younger than those of other countries, most of them are under forty (38 % of the package ecotourists are between 20 and 39 and 55 % of the individual ecotourists are between 25 and 34). Women make up 55 % of ecotourists and around a third are employed and/or professionals.[167]

Ecotourists from Spain are relatively young (59 % are between 20 and 39), which can be explained – by the fact that Spain, like Italy, does not have a long tradition of tourism and travel. Women make up the majority of the ecotourists (55 %) most of whom are in the middle income range, and have a good education (61 % studied at university). Most of them come from the metropolitan regions of Madrid and Barcelona.[168]

In general, the ecotourists of the countries included in the WTO study have more or less the same profile. The tendency is that the average age is decreasing (especially in countries without a long tradition of tourism and travel), probably because the younger generation is more environmentally conscious.

5.1.7 Expectations of ecotourists

We can assume that ecotourists have different expectations about their trips than ordinary tourists. One reason for this is that they have to spend more money compared to other kinds of tourists do and that they therefore want to get a "good return" on their investment.

The main reason given for Canadian ecotourists taking a nature or ecotourism trip is scenery, however, the desire to have new experiences is also rather high, followed by the familiarity with a place and the desire to return to it. The activities they prefer most include hiking (39 %), camping (30 %) and walking (21 %). Most choose hotels or motels as accommodation but there is a considerable number who sleep in tents, cabins and lodges. A small portion is interested in luxury accommodation, whereas others want it basic. The most important experiences sought by independent ecotourists are those involving wilderness and remote areas, interpretative and learning experiences and discovering local cultures and foods. The tour operators offering ecotourism experiences mention

---

165 World Tourism Organisation 2002d, p. 51.
166 World Tourism Organisation 2001b, 31-32.
167 World Tourism Organisation 2002a, p. 53.
168 World Tourism Organisation 2002b, p. 51-53.

that the features which appeal most to eco tourists are knowledgeable guides, interpretive and learning experiences and wildlife viewing.[169]

Because U.S. American ecotourists also seek leisure activities and often combine their trips with visiting relatives and doing business they can be considered 'casual' or 'soft', rather than 'dedicated' or 'hard' ecotourists (see figure 10 on page 55). They are engaged in multi-purpose vacations and are likely to engage in the same leisure activities as the average American tourist, including gambling and going to nightclubs, activities that normally are not associated with ecotourists. Nevertheless, they are six times more likely to go camping and hiking, five times more likely to visit a national park than an average tourist. Tour operators say that their clients put the highest priority on being in the wilderness and viewing wildlife, followed by visiting indigenous people and archaeological sights. 'Ecotourists' seek all kinds of accommodation, but they are more likely to spend their nights in cabins, lodges and inns than general tourists.[170]

According to British tour operators, their clientele puts the greatest priority on being in the wilderness, secondly they want to meet indigenous people and see their culture[171], after which they are interested in the spotting of rare species and education and learning.[172]

The French ecotourists' most important motivation is the discovery of protected natural areas (parks and reserves), then playing sports, observing fauna and flora and discovering civilisations, as well as cultural and gastronomic traditions. Therefore, they rate the quality of the countryside and the conservation of the environment as very important. Equally important is the opportunity to see an abundance of fauna and flora. 40 % of the French people, who would be prepared to buy a trip on the basis of discovering fauna, require a guarantee that they will see animals during their stay. The French are very fond of camping and so are the ecotourists who are most likely to prefer basic accommodation such as guest houses or gîtes (cabins) over more expensive and luxurious hotels.[173]

The Germans are interested in visiting nature/national parks (64 %) and in animal observation (44 %). Most of them want to hike by themselves (without a guide) on well marked trails (46 %) and only 15 % want to go on excursions with a local guide. 41 % expect local cuisine with local ingredients and expect

---

169 World Tourism Organisation 2002c, p. 75.
170 World Tourism Organisation 2002e., p. 49-50.
171 The motivation to meet indigenous people does not correlate with the photographs in the brochures of the tour operators, who put much more emphasis on landscapes and wilderness and do not include many pictures of local people in their promotion material.
172 World Tourism Organisation 2001a, p.58-60.
173 World Tourism Organisation 2002d, p. 76-81.

pronounced hospitality (they want to feel welcome) in small accommodation businesses run by locals.[174]

Italian ecotourists want to be involved as much as possible in the local culture of the destination through direct contacts with locals, by discovering landscapes and local traditions as well as through local cuisine and ingredients. Of secondary importance is a good selection of excursions with well informed local guides or self guided trails. When choosing their holiday destination, nature is the most important factor.[175]

Spanish ecotourists seek mixed packages when they contact a tour operator, with a visit to nature reserves featuring prominently. Encounters with indigenous people are also considered important, as well as contemplation of outstanding landscapes. The report does not give information about the accommodation preferred by the Spanish.[176]

5.1.8 Ecotourism and authenticity

Except for Ceballos-Lascuráin's initial definition of ecotourism, the other definitions mentioned above (see figure 9 on page 53) emphasise the low impact that tourism should have or the responsibility tourists should show towards the context they enter. All above mentioned definitions also evoke images of undisturbed landscapes that can be enjoyed (or gazed at) by the cautious and responsible traveller. Authenticity – although not mentioned specifically – lies under these concepts. Thus, ecotourism attempts to bridge the gap between culture or society and nature, and according to Wöhler[177] this encompasses a certain purification and standardisation. What is perceived as sustainable (or authentic) is fenced in, whereas unsustainable (or in-authentic) things or processes are eliminated or excluded. The process that leads to this regionalisation is an ecological purification including a certain 'sacralisation' of the place.[178] If the term 'ecotourism' is attributed to a specific destination, which also carries the (sacred) label 'national park', this combination serves as a guarantee for authenticity. However, because of the various definitions of ecotourism it cannot formally serve as an internationally recognized label with specific guidelines. It serves as an informal label which nonetheless evokes certain ideas and notions about how such an informally labelled area should look. The lack of precise and concise definitions of ecotourism can lead to diffuse and "romantic" images and expectations with which tourists enter an area they visit as ecotourists. For the man-

---

174 World Tourism Organisation 2001b, p. 34-36.
175 World Tourism Organisation 2002a, p. 55.
176 World Tourism Organisation 2002b, p. 55-63.
177 Wöhler, K. 2001, p. 42.
178 Wöhler, K. 2001, p. 43.

agement of such an area (i.e. a national park) it can be difficult to cope with these notions. Therefore, it can be useful to "stage" authenticity (and structures that are associated with ecotourism) in a transparent and comprehensible way. That does not mean that Potemkin villages have to be built just to meet the expectations of the visitors. On the contrary, often the things that are expected or those that define a conservation area or an ecotourism destination are hidden from the visitor's eye and should be exposed, if not literally then figuratively. Endau Rompin on Peninsula Malaysia is, for example, renowned for its Sumatran rhinoceroses and they have been an important reason for gazetting the area. However, the chances for visitors to ever see a rhino are close to zero. The park management cannot bring the tourist to the elusive animals, and to bring the animals to the tourists would be regarded an intolerable threat to their wellbeing. Therefore, the management has to find ways to cope with the expectation of tourists who want to see a rhinoceros. A ranger could, for example, explain the reasons for its elusiveness or show the visitors traces of where an animal has passed through.

5.2 Impact of (eco)tourism in conservation areas

As in any sensitive environment, it is not easy to introduce tourism into protected areas. Many traps and pitfalls have to be avoided when setting up or maintaining ecotourism in conservation areas. The World Commission on Protected Areas (WCPA) has issued guidelines and caveats for sustainable tourism in protected areas[179] that should help to avoid negative repercussions. They cover aspects of the economy, the environment, infrastructure and information among others.

5.2.1 Economic impact of (eco)tourism[180]

Like any kind of tourism, ecotourism has economic consequences, too. The question is, whether ecotourism can have a more positive than negative impact on sustainable development. For conservation areas it is important that the maintenance of infrastructure and protection can be financed by tourism and that local people can benefit from it.[181] Since many national parks do not charge high entrance fees (or none at all) they do not generate enough revenue to pay for the costs of management. However, there are examples of self-sufficient parks – at least financially.[182] A consequence of this high-price policy could be the exclusion of poorer tourists and the limitation of the number of

---

179 Eagles, P.F.J., McCool, S.F. & Haynes, C.D. 2002.
180 If not stated otherwise the information of this chapter are from Lindberg, K. 2001.
181 See for example Hitchcock, M. & Jay, S. 1998 or Müller-Böker, U. 1996.

visitors. Another economic aspect of ecotourism is that it can reduce access to natural resources by the local population. Conservation areas – that cause this effect – are usually not gazetted for tourist purposes only. Nevertheless, depending on the rules and regulations, tourists can have more access to the resources of a park than the local population, which can have negative consequences, if the lack of access is not compensated adequately. Due to the presence of relatively affluent tourists in an area, prices for consumer goods can rise for the local population, which can cause problems for the poorer of them. Moreover, due to new possibilities of income generation, a new financial elite may emerge and thus cause a disturbance of pre-existing structures. Generally, tourism creates new opportunities that open up new sources of income and access to resources for some people but close other options for others. The degree of revenue sharing and distribution within the host society varies greatly according to the type of ecotourism and the institutions that apply. Therefore, it is not clear if certain economic changes have a positive or a negative impact. A general problem with tourism is the so called leakage of money, that is, money that does not stay in the host country but flows back to the countries of origin of the visitors. Ecotourism with its focus on sustainability – including an optimization of local revenue generation – has the potential to minimise these leakages.

Therefore the WCPA[183] proposes the following guidelines for capturing economic benefits:

- Increasing the number of visitors is only an option if the financial benefits exceed their costs (including environmental damage).
- If the length of stay of visitors is increased, more local goods and services can be sold and costs per visitor can be lowered.
- Attracting richer market niches has to go along with a sophisticated infrastructure that must be cost effective. However, it can exclude less affluent people.
- The purchases per visitor can be increased if more locally-made goods are for sale and readily available for the visitors.
- The park management can provide lodging, where relatively large sums are paid and can be distributed locally.
- Guides provide good sources of information and can enhance the tourists' experiences. Moreover, local people can find an occupation with great potential.

---

182 Monteverde Cloud Forest Reserve in Costa Rica is a self-sufficient private reserve. The entrance fee for foreigners is US$ 23, for residents US$ 2 and for students US$ 1. Thus, by 1994 revenues of US$ 850,000 could be gathered, which covered more than the costs of the parks management (Eagles, P.F.J., McCool, S.F. & Haynes, C.D. 2002, p. 36).
183 Eagles, P.F.J., McCool, S.F. & Haynes, C.D. 2002, p. 26.

- Events such as art exhibitions, crafts and festivals based on local culture can serve as attractions and can increase local economic impact.
- The purchase of local food and drinks instead of imports, can provide income for local farmers.

Interestingly some of these guidelines also apply to positive impacts of backpacking (see "Figure 8: Backpackers and local development" on page 38), which should be all the more a reason not to neglect this form of tourism.

5.2.2 Environmental impact of (eco)tourism[184]

The assessment of the environmental impact of ecotourism depends on the definition of ecotourism and on the affected ecosystem. For example, loud shouting has little or no impact on a bare mountain top[185], whereas in forests it could be a major disturbance to the fauna. The impact can be divided into 'travel' to and from the site, 'accommodation', and specific 'recreational activities'. Along with studies regarding the natural sciences, it is interesting to study how tourists themselves perceive the environmental impact of tourism at their destination. Visual consequences such as trampling or littering have been researched[186], but for other kinds of impact there is little data available. The impact of travel can be rather diverse, including the following consequences:

- The use of airplanes – and with that (global) air pollution – to reach a site is often inevitable for foreign tourists.
- Cars that are used for transport can crush and cut the soil, roads can interrupt surface drainage; the noises of the vehicles disturb animals and their tyres can transport weeds seeds and fungal spores into areas where the do not belong.
- Motorized boats can disturb water fauna and flora by noise, propellers and toxic antifouling paints.

Impact of various types of accommodation, ranging from tents to big lodges may include:

- Permanent or temporary crushing of vegetation
- Soil modifications
- Introduction of foreign weeds and pathogens
- Water pollution from human waste, washing, engine fuel and cleaning products

---

184 If not stated otherwise the information of this chapter are from Buckley, R. 2001.
185 This may hold true according to a Western conception of nature and religion. However, in societies with different religious concepts shouting on a mountain could be regarded as antagonising heavenly or uranic forces.
186 See Chin, C.L.M., Moore, S.A., Wallington, T.J. & Dowling, R.K. 2000 or Baysan, S.K. 2001.

- Air and noise pollution from generators and other machinery
- Visual and audible disturbances
- Wildlife disturbance through all of the above and the presence of food scraps and litter

Regarding activities, the line between acceptable and disturbing practices is very narrow. It depends more on how they are done, than on the type of activity. Almost all activities have a certain impact. Even the footprint of a hiking boot can cause soil compression, thus reducing porosity and increasing surface runoff and erosion.[187] Whether activities are disturbing or not depends on the vulnerability and resilience of the ecosystem. In order to assess carrying capacities, extensive research needs to be done in the respective areas. However, for most conservation area managements it is not possible to organise and pay for this kind of research. Therefore, careful monitoring – including the visitors' perspectives on environmental impact[188] – can help to prevent major damage to a conservation area's ecosystem.

The WCPA[189] proposes a long list of guidelines for environmentally (and culturally) sensitive facilities. They encompass landscaping and site design, buildings, resource conservation and consumption, materials, the use of adequate technology, services as well as impact and quality controls. These may include the reshaping of the visitors' site (e.g. planting trees in order to attract animals) or the use of "vernacular design features" in buildings. In other words, indirectly, a staging of certain aspects of the site is proposed.

The WCPA proposes several strategies to cope with these issues[190]:
- reduce the use of the entire protected area by limiting the number of visitors, the length of their stay, requiring specific skills of visitors, charging higher fees or making access more difficult
- reduce the use of problem areas by informing visitors about problems, discouraging or prohibiting their use, making access harder (and easier to other areas), eliminating facilities or attractions or charging varying visitor fees
- modify the location of use within problem areas by locating facilities on durable sites, concentrating and guiding use through facility design or information, segregating different types of visitors

---

187 For more detailed information on environmental impacts on soil, vegetation, invertebrates, reptiles and amphibia, birds, fish, and mammals, c.f. Buckley, R. 2001; Ceballos-Lascuráin, H. 1996 or Eagles, P.F.J., McCool, S.F. & Haynes, C.D. 2002.
188 See Chin, C.L.M., Moore, S.A., Wallington, T.J. & Dowling, R.K. 2000 and see "2.2.1 Bako" on page 99.
189 Eagles, P.F.J., McCool, S.F. & Haynes, C.D. 2002, p. 26.
190 Eagles, P.F.J., McCool, S.F. & Haynes, C.D. 2002, p. 88-89.

- modify the timing of use by encouraging use outside the peak use periods, discouraging or banning use when impact potential is high, raising fees in periods of high use
- modify type of use and visitor behaviour by discouraging or banning practices that are detrimental to the environment, encouraging or requiring specific behaviour, skills or equipment, teaching wilderness ethics, discouraging or prohibiting overnight use
- modify visitor expectations by informing visitors about appropriate behaviour and uses and informing them about potential conditions in the area
- increase the resistance of the resource by shielding it from impact and strengthening it
- maintain and rehabilitate resources by removing problems and maintaining or rehabilitating effected locations

5.2.3 Conflicts

Conservation areas can be understood as arenas where different people with different needs and desires and the consequences of different actions meet, which can lead to conflicts. More often than not, conflicts are a result of unintended consequences of actions, which makes it generally more difficult to mediate between different stakeholders. The most important field in which conflicts occur is the triangle between the expectations of tourists, the needs of local people and the goals of nature conservation (see figure 15 on page 72). Between tourists conflicts can also occur, which are important in the context of this study. The nature of their conflicts however, is rather short term, because of their limited stay in the parks. Nevertheless, they can be demanding for the park management if they occur frequently. Conflicts between (and among) the local people can have a much longer duration and be more severe on the individual level than conflicts perceived by tourists, who can leave the area and thus leave the conflicts behind.

With human interaction, power relations are never absent. Therefore, potential conflict areas have to be seen in this context too. In conservation areas we have the unique situation that great (formal) power (authoritative resources) is with the agency that has to enforce the protection, which is mostly the state or regional government. Usually, the rules for the use of a conservation area's (allocative) resources are clearly defined – and globally sanctioned through the IUCN. However, in order to be able to enforce rules, actors need to be equipped with resources. Often the park management is understaffed for effectively protecting the area from encroachments and the negative consequences of detrimental tourist behaviour. In cases of emergency, the park management can resort to the resources under the control of the government, which ultimately has to insure the integrity of the protected area. Depending on the laws of the state on whose territory a conservation area is located, the local people can bring forward their claims. Depending on the willingness of the government to allow the use of certain resources within the park, the local people can satisfy their needs. However, apart from the law and the resources of its enforcement apparatus there are other resources that certain people are equipped with. For example, local people can know (an authoritative resource) how to secretly enter a park and use some of its resources without being detected by the park rangers. Tourists and the tourist industry do not have many formal entitlements for the use of park resources. However, with their economic resources they can be an important power factor. This is not only important for individual parks but also for the regional or national economy. If tourists are prohibited from entering a park or from making use of desired resources, they can decide to avoid the whole region or country. Therefore, tourists can also exert power with the threat of possible boycott.

Figure 15: The conflict triangle in a conservation area

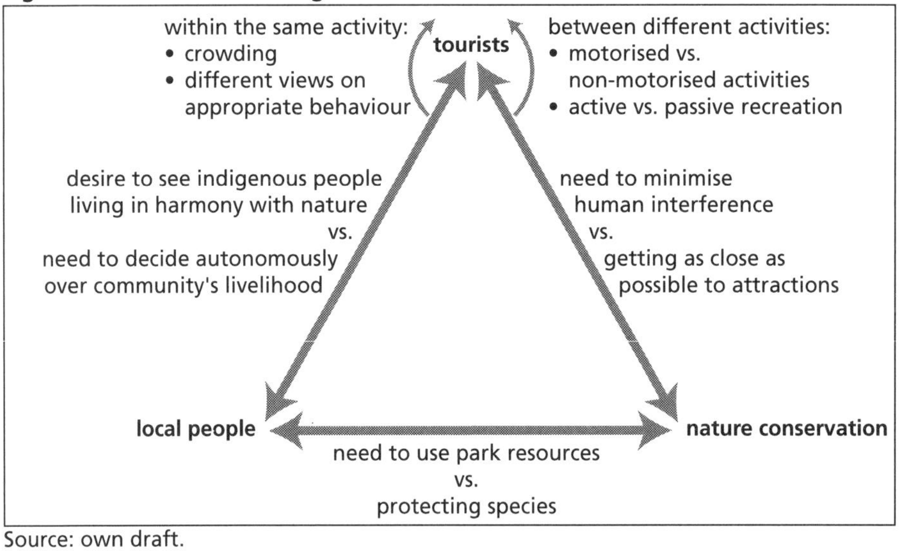

```
                        tourists
    within the same activity:           between different activities:
    • crowding                          • motorised vs.
    • different views on                  non-motorised activities
      appropriate behaviour             • active vs. passive recreation

    desire to see indigenous people     need to minimise
    living in harmony with nature       human interference
            vs.                                 vs.
    need to decide autonomously         getting as close as
    over community's livelihood         possible to attractions

    local people                        nature conservation
                need to use park resources
                            vs.
                      protecting species
```

Source: own draft.

5.2.4 Risk control

Many forms of visitor activities in parks have risks associated with them, and for many tourists they are an integral part of an adventurous journey. However, the park management's task is to minimise the severity of the consequences of risks. It is not possible, and also not necessary, to totally eliminate risk from the visitors' stays. The management needs to identify and assess the level of potential risks, decide which are not too risky, and use appropriate control measures (e.g.

eliminating risk, transferring risk, reducing probability, reducing impact, accepting risk). Activities can be divided into levels of risk and the higher the level the more the management has to invest to reduce probability and impact. Therefore, only a small number of tourists should be allowed to engage in activities of high risk.[191]

There are not only the risks to the visitors' well-being, but also risks to the environment and to the local people that need to be managed. With an increasing number of visitors some activities cannot be accessible to all visitors, because their aggregated impact would be detrimental to the environment.

5.2.5 Ecotourism in rainforests[192]

For many tourists who live in urban areas, rainforests are special attractions. They are probably the most attractive biome on Earth and they are associated with images of a lush, vibrant, complex and mysterious environment. Moreover, a visit to a rainforest is for many tourists an affirmation of their support for the environment, especially since there is a common understanding of their vulnerability and about the threat of their extinction. Therefore, many urban people attribute special values to the environment of rainforests.[193] Most people have a general definition in mind, when they talk about rainforests, which is simply the combination of high rainfall and (dense) vegetation.[194] The increasing public interest in rainforests coincided with its increased global depletion during the 1980's and 90's. Hence, the argument of heritage writers that many things only

---

191 Eagles, P.F.J., McCool, S.F. & Haynes, C.D. 2002, p. 76-78.
192 If not stated otherwise the information in this chapter are from Frost, W. 2001, p. 193-204.
193 On values and entitlements see Kollmair, M. & Backhaus, N. forthcoming.
194 For the purposes of this study this common notion of rainforests should be sufficient. For a more elaborate definition of rainforest types c.f. Frost, W. 2001, p. 194-197, who describes four types of rainforests:
The *tropical rainforest* was first described as rainforest at the end of the 19th century and it is probably the stereotype that is "firmly lodged in the mind of most tourists". Its characteristics are a very wide diversity of plant species (especially trees), a very dense canopy with often fairly open under storey at ground level, trees with large leaves and massive roots and large numbers of thick, woody vines, palms and epiphytes. It requires warm temperatures (above 18°C) and high rainfall (above 100 mm each month) or in other words an Af climate (according to Köppen). *Subtropical rainforest* occurs adjacent to tropical rainforests in areas that are slightly cooler (Cf(a) climates) due to differences in altitude or latitude. They are less luxuriant and diverse than the tropical rainforests. *Dry or monsoonal rainforest* is marked and affected by a dry season which leads to more open vegetation, smaller leaves and smaller trees and a dominance of drought-tolerant species (Am, As, Aw climates). The *cool temperate rainforest* do not really match the stereotypes of rainforests, because they lack the diversity of tropical rainforests and because they are cold and wet. They are not located adjacent to the other types of rainforests and mostly occur on the southern hemisphere (and on the north American west coast). As a rule the have one dominant tree variety, very small leave size, many ferns, mosses and lichens and no palms, figs or epiphytes (Cf(b) climates).

come to be seen as heritage when they are under threat can be applied to rainforests. In the last two decades rainforest tourism has mostly consisted of western, well-to-do tourists who were generally well educated and keen to incorporate learning experiences into their holidays and who were concerned about conservation. The fairly high average costs of US$ 100-200 per day tended to limit the market to older, high income, experienced and highly motivated travellers and to exclude domestic tourists. The limitation to wealthier and older tourists is changing rapidly, because air fares became cheaper during the last decade and access to many conservation areas was improved, so that an increasing number of backpackers and also domestic tourists now can visit these areas. Subsequently, the parks have had to deal with a greater variety and number of visitors as well as with new demands and challenges. A problem related to this increasing variety is adequate information and interpretation, because most visitors want to increase their knowledge which, however, has many different levels. Frost proposes ten messages that should be included into interpretation at all rainforests:

1. What makes a rainforest and the debate over what is and what is not a rainforest
2. The different types of rainforest and, in particular, the type that this rainforest belongs to
3. How indigenous people interact with this rainforest
4. How European colonization or settlement affected this rainforest
5. The major threats today
6. Plant (and especially tree) varieties
7. Animals (especially birds and insects)
8. Special growing conditions associated with this rainforest (e.g. nutrient cycle or the presence of buttressed roots)
9. The fragility and resilience of rainforests in general and of this particular rainforest
10. Any re-vegetation or scientific research projects in progress

It is not easy to adequately put immediate these messages into practice, especially when they comprise conflicting interests (e.g. when a government agency manages the park and at the same time the government is responsible for deforesting rainforests). Therefore, it is important to research the kind of interpretation that is provided in conservation areas (see "3.10 Information centre" on page 237). For experiencing and understanding rainforests there is a wide range of modes, such as guided walks, trails with signage, night-walks, plank walks etc. However, one particular mode has been adapted almost exclusively in rainforests, namely the elevated viewing structure. Since the canopy is one of the most interesting features of rainforests, many tourists wish to be able to see it at eye level. Moreover, elevated viewing structures are thrilling attractions. Frost discerns three different types of structures: the first are publicly owned structures, built to cater for mass tourism (i.e. canopy walkways, see "2.1.1 Taman Negara" on page 93); the second are privately owned structures that are part of an accommodation, that only cater to paying guests; and third, mostly privately owned and operated structures for mass tourism (e.g. cable cars[195]). Structures such as canopy walkways or cable cars are a subject of debate because of their intrusion into the rainforests ecosystem. On the one hand, they are regarded by critics as a sign of the "hardening" of ecotourism and as an inroad of mass tourism into the realm of rainforests. On the other hand their promoters say that the structures keep visitors from straying into the forest and are a means of transportation and education of higher numbers of – and less mobile – visitors.

5.2.6 Images about rainforests[196]

Since tourism has become a mass phenomenon, the images people in the west have had about rainforests has changed over time. A media discourse in Swiss newspapers, conducted by Simone Bossart[197] was instrumental in this change. She analysed 276 articles which can be regarded as representing the discourse in German speaking countries. Although from the sample we cannot deduce the form of the discourse in another context, we can assume that it does not differ greatly from the German discourse. In order to analyse the newspaper articles, different rationales for the protection of nature (including rainforests) are described. Lude[198] makes a distinction between anthropocentric, biocentric, holistic and theistic rationales. Anthropocentric rationales are further divided into aesthetic reasons for protection, those that emphasise the beauty of nature that it has a value of its own, as well as recreational, economic and scientific reasons. The biocentric rationale emphasises that any life-form is relevant and that its value does not depend on its function. The holistic rationale encompasses non-living parts of nature that have an intrinsic value. Finally, according to the theistic rationale, God's creation must be protected by humans. According to a study by Lude, the biocentric and the holistic have the greatest effect on the behaviour of people. However, the anthropocentric rationales are more useful in the public discussion about nature conservation. Others[199] state that nature protection cannot be but anthropocentric, because as humans we cannot leave

---

195 See Moscardo, G. & Woods, B. 1998.
196 Information provided in this chapter are from Bossart, S. (2003) if not stated otherwise.
197 Bossart, S. 2003.
198 Lude, A. 2001 in Bossart, S. 2003, p. 40-41.
199 For example Dünckmann, F. 1999 in Bossart, S. 2003, p. 41.

the anthropocentric point of view. If we stay with this rationale, we can discern the following reasons[200] that are given for the protection of nature:
- The conservation of biodiversity has become one of the most important reasons for the protection of rainforests. Since the 1970's the rainforest has come to be regarded as a reservoir of genetic diversity, as the pharmacy of the future. 50 % of the world's plant species and around 90 % of its animal species are estimated to be found in rainforests. An extensive number of them are still unknown to science and therefore the apparent and hidden genetic resources should be protected.[201]
- Living space of indigenous people is regarded as an important issue; however it is not usually the primary reason for the protection of a certain area.[202]
- The rainforest as source of resources for people in developing countries is a reason that can be debated, because a certain amount of the destruction of rainforests is attributed to people living at their fringes.[203]
- Ecological values such as the protection of water catchments or the prevention of erosion were reasons for the protection of distinct vulnerable areas. In the light of climatic change the destruction of the rainforests can be regarded as a further accelerator of global warming.[204]
- Research: rainforests can be regarded as the biggest outside laboratory of the world and harbours information about evolution. Therefore, the destruction of rainforests can be regarded as a loss of options and opportunities for the future, which is why it has to be protected.[205]
- Socio-cultural values comprise the psychological and cultural well-being of people who live in or near rainforests but also for others who have an affinity toward them. Moreover, recreation and education belong in this category.[206]

The images of the rainforest rendered in Swiss newspapers have changed since the 1970's when they were mostly regarded as hideaways for war veterans and

---

200 For the values that can be found behind these reasons see also Backhaus, N. & Kollmair, M. 2001.
201 Budowsky, G. 1970, Richards, P.W. 1973, WRI et al. 1985, Whitmore, T.C. 1993, 1998, Hupke, K.-D. 2000 in Bossart S. 2003, p. 42-43.
202 Whitmore, T.C. 1993, 1998, Hupke, K.-D. 2000 in Bossart S. 2003, p. 42-43.
203 UNESCO 1978, Golley, F. 1983, Lamprecht, H. 1984, Hupke, K.-D. 2000 in Bossart S. 2003, p. 42-43.
204 UNESCO 1978, Golley, F. 1983, Lamprecht, H. 1984, Hupke, K.-D. 2000, Richards, P.W. 1973, Myers, N. 1983, in Bossart S. 2003, p. 42-43.
205 Richards, P.W. 1973, UNESCO 1978, Golley, F. 1983, Myers, N. 1983 in Bossart, S. 2003, p.43.
206 Budowsky, G. 1970, IUCN, 1974, UNESCO 1978, Golley, F. 1983, Myers, N. 1983 in Bossart, S. 2003, p.43.

as a frontier, where people had to fight for their survival against nature (especially against diseases and wild animals). The power that was at that time perceived as threatening or overwhelming was later seen as awe inspiring and a source of energy and strength. The rainforest's bulk, variety and fecundity sometimes also had erotic associations. During the 1980's tourists started to get interested in rainforests, which were subsequently attributed with romantic features and depicted as the antithesis to cities. Generally the jungle[207] – mostly taken as synonym for rainforest – was regarded as devoid of human beings, in these articles. When indigenous people were mentioned in the 1970's, they were depicted as savage, primitive and in need of pacification and development. Only later, were indigenous people living in rainforests regarded as guardians of an abundant knowledge about properties of plant species that must to be protected, along with their habitat. This image has only recently been modified by reports about some unsustainable practices of indigenous people.

Articles about the protection of rainforests have focused mostly on the Amazon region and Africa, less on Asia. Rainforests should be protected for the preservation of biodiversity and the gene pool, and other resources (e.g. wood, water). Since the 1980's, and increasingly since the Earth Summit on environment and development in Rio in 1992, the rainforest's role in the prevention of global warming has become publicized. At the same time, the issue of the dwindling habitats of indigenous people was made a central focus in the newspapers (within the coverage about rainforests). Tourism or education, however, were not mentioned as reasons for the protection of rainforests. But tourism has emerged as a means for a successful protection, especially since the 1990's.

According to Bossart the discourse about rainforests can be divided into two interlacing threads: the first thread concerns the protection of rainforests, which developed during the 1980's and has been present ever since; the second consists of symbolisations, demonisations or idyllisations which dominated the articles before 1980. The number of articles in the media is highly dependent on other events. Therefore, they are often published when there are no other more pressing topics to be taken into account. The reasons for the protection of rainforests that are given in the newspapers are mainly anthropocentric with an economic-material background. Moreover, the newspapers follow scientific arguments and mostly refrain from using holistic or biocentric arguments that cannot be reconciled with "usefulness".

---

207 According to Merriam-Webster 'Collegiate Dictionary' (2003) the word jungle comes from the Hindi *jangal* forest, from Sanskrit *jangala* desert region, meaning "an impenetrable thicket or tangled mass of tropical vegetation" or "a tract overgrown with thickets or masses of vegetation". It is therefore not a synonym for tropical rainforests only, but also for other types of rainforest (more or less excluding cold rainforests).

The discourse analysis on the images of rainforests mirrors the range of opinions that is present in the (Swiss German) media. Although we cannot draw a direct line from these images to the ones in people's heads, the media give us a rough idea about what potential western tourists who visit rainforests think about rainforests. Most of them have heard about the problems of global warming which are said to increase when rainforests are cut or burned down. Moreover, they have been confronted with different reasons for the protection of the forests. The most prominent reasons are "climate protection" and the conservation of biodiversity. The great diversity of species in rainforests corresponds with the image that is associated with the jungle, a humid forest teeming with life. The situation of indigenous people living in rainforests contributes to the image of a threatened ecosystem that has to be protected for its own sake but also as a living space for indigenous peoples. The latter aspect is probably particularly prominent in the heads of Swiss tourists because of the activities of Bruno Manser in Sarawak (see "4.2.1 Excursus: images of Borneo" on page 46). To sum up, when western tourists visit a protected rainforest, they most likely expect a pristine area with a high biodiversity, impressing trees and indigenous people living their traditional lives.

III Nature conservation and national parks in Malaysia

1 (Eco)tourism in Malaysian conservation areas and national parks

The increasing numbers of visitors who come to Malaysia are, at least partly, attracted by its natural beauties especially its national parks. Many can be regarded as the epitome of tourists' images of tropical rainforests. The Malaysian Tourism authorities assume that ecotourism is a growing segment of tourism, although its economic share is, with RM 655 million (US$ 170 million), still small compared with the estimated RM 24 billion (US$ 6.5 billion) generated by all kinds of tourism in Malaysia in 2001.[208] The definition of ecotourism that is applied here is the one coined by Ceballos-Lascuráin, which is also proposed by the IUCN. It is closely connected to the visiting of conservation areas. Ecotourism is however, not necessarily regarded as a synonym for nature tourism, because the regulations of Malaysian conservation areas mostly prohibit tourist activities that are detrimental to the environment. It is also acknowledged that ecotourism has become a buzzword which is widely used by tour operators for their own promotion. According to a study by Lim[209], travel agencies that offer ecotourism in Malaysia mostly do not understand the principles and concepts of ecotourism. Moreover, most of the activities offered by the agencies tend to be fun-oriented without reference to nature protection or sustainable development. The concept of ecotourism, while used by the authorities, is not well known to the public, or is simply used as a synonym for nature tourism (see "5.1.3 Ecotourism and other types of tourism" on page 56).

In the following section I will provide a brief synopsis of the condition of ecotourism and then an overview of the most important national parks and conservation areas in Malaysia, based on expert interviews, my own observations and secondary data. In the chapter 1.2: "The 'National Ecotourism Plan Malaysia' (NEP)" on page 86 the most important issues of the plan will be addressed.

1.1 Impact of (eco)tourism

1.1.1 Economic situation

There is virtually no national park in Malaysia that generates enough income to cover all its costs. However, there are some parks that have the potential of generating much more revenue than they do today. The Malaysian government wants to provide equal access for a greater part of its society to national parks. Moreover, the government is against a differentiated fee system, where foreigners have to pay more than domestic visitors. Indeed, Sarawak just recently want-

---

208 Badaruddin, M. 2002.
209 Lim, G.L. 1999 in Badaruddin, M. 2002.

ed to introduce such a tiered system but stopped its implementation. Since the entrance fees are comparatively low[210], and because will not charge foreigners more, the parks will not generate much more revenue with increasing the numbers of visitors.

Even if a conservation area does not generate enough money for its own maintenance with its entrance fees, it can generate many jobs in its vicinity[211]. With an increase in the average length of stay the potential of visitors spending more money in the area increases. The increase of visitors' lengths of stay can be a welcome contribution to the regions economy. Whether visitors extend their stays depends on the possibilities a park has to offer. For most parks there is something like an average itinerary of what visitors do which determines their length of stay. A park does not necessarily have to create new attractions or open up new parts of the park for visitors in order to keep them longer in the area. Often, different kinds of attractions could be combined in a way that visitors would not have to choose to do either one or the other. One problem is the rigidity of transport schedules, which inhibit (individual) travellers from extending their stays if they decide to do so. Moreover, many parks do not offer the possibility of just hanging around for one or two days, lets say in between treks or to just relax in a beautiful environment. In many Malaysian parks there could be potential for extending the visitors' length of stay.

Malaysian tourism is aimed toward the more affluent market, which it can certainly appeal to, as the standard of infrastructure and accommodation is quite good. However, to concentrate too much on richer tourists can be a double edged sword. For one thing they tend to stay in hotels with international standards that are mostly owned by foreign corporations or by those from urban centres and not by people from the area. This means that the benefit of more jobs per guest can be eaten up by the leakage of a substantial part of the revenue. Moreover, such a concentration ignores the fact that tourists with a thinner wallet leave a substantial amount of money in the country, because they usually stay longer and a smaller amount of their spending is leaked to other countries.

In most national parks only few local products are for sale. Some hotels try to use locally grown vegetables or rice, but an increase in the production and use of locally made goods would generate more income for locals. Since ecotourism also promotes the use of local products it would also be useful to advertise the

---

210 It has to be noted that most national parks in Europe or in the USA do not charge any entrance fees at all, except for the access to certain attractions. In other areas, for example in Latin America, visitors often have to pay hefty entrance fees. The global tendency of privatisation does not stop at conservation areas. Therefore we can expect that entrance fees will rise considerably where (private) conservation areas have to be cost-efficient.
211 The Swiss National Park generates approximately 200 jobs in its region (Küpfer, I. 2000).

fact that local products are used, if they are used. Most lodging on the premises of national parks used to be managed by the respective park administrations. However, more and more parks are out-sourcing the management of their lodgings to private enterprises. The main reasons for this are the need of the park administration to concentrate on their task of ensuring the protection and maintenance of the area, and on interpretation. Moreover, private companies are regarded as more efficient in providing a relatively high standard of accommodation. Since these companies are mostly not local enterprises, a substantial amount of revenue is removed from the area. Potential conflicts between the needs of a thriving tourist industry and nature conservation have to be carefully mitigated, otherwise, tourism can be detrimental to the park in many ways, including damaging the environment, reducing biodiversity near the lodgings, damaging the image of a park as a pristine and untouched environment).

Guides are regarded as good providers of information and generally as the best means for interpretation. For many local people, guiding tourists through the national parks is a welcome opportunity to earn money. However, since most parks have a tight budget they cannot employ too many guides. Usually, the rangers fulfil this task besides filling their other obligations. Therefore, the local people who want to work as park rangers and guides have to be especially skilled, especially in languages. In the bigger parks, guides are employed by tour operators, who are not always local people. (Tour) guiding is also often short term employment, which is why many good and qualified guides look for other (better) jobs after several years of guiding. Therefore, the park management, as well as tour operators, are constantly training new guides and losing seasoned ones. Although this has to be regarded as a problem the great turnover of (local) employees can also be seen as a good means to involve local people in conservation and tourism and to provide good skills that are useful in other areas.

The bigger parks have started to host events to attract tourists or to make their parks better known. The events themselves do not make a big economic contribution because the costs are generally quite high, and the return questionable. Nevertheless, (cultural or sporting) events have become a means to make a park known to a wide range of potential visitors and thus serve as a valuable promotion tool.

1.1.2 Environmental impact

If we look at the resources of Malaysian park managements and the rules and regulations of park administration, some of the WCPA strategies seem to be more feasible than others. Limiting access to an entire park is an instrument that is not often used. In contrast, access to remote parks such as Gunung Mulu or Taman Negara is constantly being improved. For tourists, East Malaysia on

Borneo is almost inaccessible by sea[212], therefore a great number of domestic tourists have to fly in, for a visit of national parks in Sabah and Sarawak. Smaller aircraft that are used to reach parks in remote areas (i.e. Gunung Mulu National Park; see "VI Tourists in Gunung Mulu National Park" on page 203) are noisy and can disturb animals, especially when the planes pass low over the canopy in order to let the passengers see spectacular sites. In most parks the impact of cars is not an issue, as they cannot be entered by cars. However, roads and tracks at the fringes of conservation areas can have an impact because most parks do not have buffer zones[213]. Boats are more often used than cars, because the extensive river system serves as a good means of transport. . Although residues of fuel and paints can have an impact on water resources, Malaysian rivers suffer more from sediments washed down from areas where forests have been removed for development.[214] Therefore, in many parks the only means available so far to control the numbers of visitors is by the limitation of adequate accommodation.

Reducing of use of problem areas within a park is not always easy, especially if the resource that should be used less is a major attraction of a park Other, less prominent features can be (temporarily) protected by moving access routes and paths to other sites. This is done with well trodden paths where the soil is compacted or roots become uncovered in one place and where they can be closed and left to grow over again. Relocating facilities and infrastructure is not always possible. The easiest way is to remove shelters and huts in order to avoid that visitors stay too long at a place. In caves, the illumination can be turned off – which is done in Mulu during half the day – in order to keep visitors from entering them.

There is great potential regarding the infrastructure and the set up of a park. Sensitive areas can be protected by constructions such as elevated plank walks (i.e. in Mulu) that protect the soil and keeps visitors from going astray. Certain areas can be constructed in such a way as to concentrate certain activities such as picnicking to areas that are not as vulnerable as others. Moreover, walks with well-marked information (e.g. on plates or numbers that are explained in leaflets etc.) could be introduced in order to attract the majority of visitors while only a smaller part look at more sensitive areas.

Until recently, most Malaysian parks did not have problems with seasonal overcrowding. With few exceptions (i.e. Pulau Penyu and parts of Taman Negara and Gunung Kinabalu) most Malaysian national parks are not over crowded,

---

212 A ferry from Peninsula Malaysia to Sarawak was put out of service due to the increasing activity of pirates in the South China Sea.
213 This is problematic insofar as that roads can be built close to protected areas which make it much easier for poachers to enter them (Chin, C.L.M. & Bennett, E.L. 2000).
214 Douglas, I. 1999.

yet. However, since the number of ecotourists has started to increase, more conservation areas with visitor contact will be threatened by too many visitors. The more nature tourism is advertised and sought after, the more people will visit national parks. The peak seasons are mostly during the European, American and Malaysian summer holidays in July and August and around New Year at the end of December. During this time it has become difficult to book accommodations in Taman Negara and Kinabalu Park (especially on the mountain). Travel guide books[215] have already begun to inform their readers that these peak seasons should be avoided and that animals are better viewed just after the rainy season during which fewer visitors are in the park. Most parks are now open during the whole year although during the rainy season (in most areas from November to February/March) some paths may be closed. However, the El Niño phenomenon and weather changes attributed to global warming have changed rainfall patterns in recent years, blurring the differences between the seasons.

Information about the dos and don'ts in national parks is quite clear and widespread. Nevertheless, with an increase of visitor numbers it can be expected that behaviour that is detrimental to nature protection may be on the increase as well. Therefore, even more explicit and clear information is needed and visitors have to be informed what they can expect and what not. The latter is not an easy task especially when the parks are promoted with three hundred different species of birds while visitors can only see a handful of them if they are lucky, because the birds can easily hide in the dense forests.

It is very difficult to improve the resilience of natural attractions in a rainforest. Normally this is only possible if the attraction in question is shielded from detrimental influences, at least temporarily. Therefore, in some parks it is discussed to open up other areas for visitors in order to reduce the impact in one area. A problem with this tactic could be that once new areas are opened and the number of visitors is still growing, damage to the environment could increase. However, on a smaller scale parts of a park (e.g. paths and picnic areas) that have been under stress can recover if they are temporarily closed.

1.1.3 Risk control

The authorities in Malaysia are very conscious about the risks some visitors take in their national parks. Security measures for example on the Canopy Walkway in Taman Negara, in the Mulu caves or on Gunung Kinabalu are very thorough. For seasoned travellers these measurements may take away from the fun and adventure they want to experience. However, many European, American and Australian visitors to national parks are fitter and more used to hiking in rugged ter-

---

215 See LonelyPlanet guide book by Rowthorn, C., Benson, S., Kerr, R. & Niven, C. 2001.

rain than many Malaysian visitors. The reason for this could be that the decision of a foreigner to visit a national park takes more consideration and involves better preparation because it is more expensive and time consuming than a visit over the weekend. Moreover, rainforests are generally perceived in western countries as potentially dangerous places. Domestic tourists know less about risks they might encounter during a visit to one of their national parks[216] and moreover, they are less able to cope with them. However, they may have better skills in dealing with local animals.

1.1.4 Conflicts

Many conflicts can occur when an area is first proposed as a conservation area and there are different interests and notions about the use of its resources. Areas with big trees are a potential income source for logging companies who therefore have an interest in not bringing the area under protection[217]. Local people – especially indigenous people[218] – often use a wide range of forest resources, mostly, but not always, in a sustainable way. In a protected area there are strict rules for the use of its resources, which can cause local people to change their lifestyles considerably. If they are not given any alternatives, they will have problems maintaining their livelihoods. The recent development of participative nature conservation in the discussion about nature protection[219] is being applied in Malaysia. There is a wide range of ways local people can participate in nature conservation, from 'actively consulting' to 'transferring authority and responsibility'[220]. In Malaysia the former is most often practised; so far there are no conservation areas entirely managed by local people. Another new development in nature conservation is the creation of buffer zones around a protected area. Within these buffer zones some limited activities are possible and they serve mainly as a means to better protect the core areas. Local people play an impor-

---

216 A good example is the ascent to Gunung Kinabalu. Many Westerners know what it means to climb more than 2.000 altitude meters. Although, only a minority of them has experience with such altitudes, most have hiked up to mountains and thus can more or less extrapolate their experience to Gunung Kinabalu. Many Malaysians start far too quickly and have difficulties to get into a steady pace and in higher altitudes they suffer from the cold (which can drop to 0°C). Because of this all climbers have to be accompanied by a guide, although it is very difficult to lose one's way (see "2.3.1 Kinabalu" on page 106).
217 Many conservation areas contain forests that were already protected as water catchment areas. Thus, the new conservation areas have only partly economic potential for logging firms.
218 It is not always easy to differentiate between local and indigenous people. The former are people who live in an area regardless of how long (thus including indigenous people). The latter have – as a group – been in the same area for generations. In this study explicitly mentioned indigenous people are the Penan of Sarawak and the Orang Asli in central Peninsula Malaysia.
219 See Soliva, R. 2002, p. 73-74
220 Borrini-Feyerabend, G. 1997.

tant role in maintaining buffer zones, the use of which they actively contributes to the parks protection. However, in Malaysia the authorities are very reluctant to create buffer zones. This is not because they don't appreciate the effectiveness of buffer zones, but because with their implementation there would not be clear park boundaries. In order to effectively enforce park regulations a visible boundary is necessary. Poachers have frequently claimed that they have gotten lost and thought they were outside the park when hunting. Therefore, some parks have even painted the trees forming the boundary red in order to clearly show where park law begins. They feel that if the boundaries are clear, it is easier for the park management to enforce park law with their limited staff. In some areas, such as around Kinabalu Park, a kind of informal buffer zones develop, when local people, tourists, use areas adjacent to the park in a sustainable way.

1.2 The 'National Ecotourism Plan Malaysia' (NEP)

1996 the Malaysian Government has published the 'National Ecotourism Plan Malaysia' (NEP) in order to assist government agencies on the federal and state level in the development of Malaysia's ecotourism potential. It is also to serve as an appropriate instrument for the conservation of the natural and cultural heritage of the country within the overall sustainable development of Malaysia and the economy as a whole. The plan is the result of a study commissioned by the Federal Ministry of Culture, Arts and Tourism to the WWF, Malaysia.[221]

The NEP uses Ceballos-Lascuráin's definition of ecotourism (see "Figure 9: Selected definitions of ecotourism" on page 53) and illustrates its meaning with positive and negative examples, such as the following[222]:

- "Bird watchers who disturb nests in order to get good pictures, or go on tour with a foreign leader and no local counterpart, not paying entrance fees, and bringing all their food in packages from outside the area do not perform ecotourism.
  Bird watchers who are respectful of the environment, make little noise, engage a local guide/counterpart, spend money in the region especially amongst the local people, including buying their simple meal on the spot do perform ecotourism. (...).
- Drivers of four-wheel drive vehicles for purposes of sport, who deviate from approved routes, entering protected areas, driving too fast creating dust and racing, cutting corners and making detours, playing out loud radios, cutting vegetation to make bridges and new access routes do not perform ecotourism. Users[223] of four-wheel drive vehicles where no other access is possible (no

---

221 WWF Malaysia 1996, p. iii.
222 WWF Malaysia 1996, p. 3-8.

landing strip, river access, paved roads), who stay on an approved route, who minimise soil erosion by not making detours and cutting corners, who do not cut trees to make bridges do perform ecotourism. (…).
- Theme parks (such as Disneyworld) in which the main attractions are not natural or traditional, but artificial, using plastic palm trees and rubber rhinos, concrete constructions, bright lights and loud noise, air conditioning, noisy vehicles and huge crowds are not ecotourism.

  Interpretive centres in national parks with modest low-key architecture harmonising with the environment, and the exhibits all orientated towards an understanding of the natural and cultural environment, as a complement to other activities the visitor has performed/will perform in a natural area, never the main attraction are ecotourism. (…).
- Hoteliers who run hotels which do not treat refuse or waste water, keep a caged animal behind the hotel, have inappropriate architecture, do not recycle products, but who advertise themselves as eco-hoteliers do not deserve that label.

  Hoteliers who run hotels with appropriate low-key architecture blending into the natural surroundings that have been disturbed as little as possible, treating refuse and wastes appropriately, recycling products when possible and minimising energy consumption, and do not keep caged animals can call themselves eco-hoteliers. (…).
- Local people who sell unsustainable souvenirs such as 'golden chickens' (fern fronds) in the highlands of Malaysia, conveying incorrect information or none about the souvenir and its significance are not performing ecotourism. Local people who sell fruits from a forest tree, or who have appropriate techniques and permits for making souvenirs from sustainably produced local products, giving correct and sufficient information about them do perform ecotourism."

At the time when the NEP was published, the authors noted that 2,000 tour and travel agencies were registered in Malaysia, and estimated that 800 of them made bookings for nature-based tourism, and that 30 companies specialised in nature or ecotourism. Moreover, there were 3,500 licensed guides in the country. The participation of NGOs in ecotourism was regarded as limited but increasing. The majority of foreign overseas ecotourists visited one or more of approximately 20 sites. 7 to 10 % of all overseas tourists were estimated to engage in ecotourism activities (whereas 14 % were interested in walking, trekking or hiking). Like the participation of NGOs, the participation of the local people is

---

223 The choice of words is interesting. Whereas the non-ecotourist is a *driver* of a four-wheel drive car, the ecotourist is called a mere *user* of such cars, though he/she *drives* all the same.

regarded as inconsistent. In certain area such as Gunung Kinabalu National Park, they are closely involved as guides, staff or in spin-off companies. In other areas they are a 'passive' component of ecotourism and in some areas they are even excluded from the benefits of ecotourism.[224]

The legal aspects of tourism and ecotourism were developed, changed or adapted mostly during the 1990's. The Tourism Industry Act of 1992 regulates the licensing of guides, restaurants and accommodation. The Malaysian Tourism Promotion Act of 1992 was passed in order to stimulate and promote the tourism market. The Sabah Tourism Promotion Corporation Enactment of 1981 (which later established the Sabah Tourism Council), and the Sarawak Tourism Board Ordinance of 1994 did the same at the level of their respective states. The Promotion of Investment Act of 1986 allows the government to give tax incentives to hotels and tourist projects, and the Environmental Quality Order of 1987 regulates Environmental Impact Assessments (EIA)[225]. Regarding natural resources, the Federal Constitution regulates in whose jurisdiction a matter falls. The following matters are within *federal* responsibility[226]:

- Treaties, agreements and conventions with other countries and all matters which bring the Federation into relations with any other country (for example the Convention on Biological Diversity)
- Implementation of treaties, agreements and conventions with other countries
- Maritime and estuarine fishing and fisheries, excluding turtles
- Water supplies, rivers and canals, except those wholly within one state or regulated by an agreement between all the states concerned

The following matters are within *state* responsibility[227]:

- Land matters, including land improvement, soil conservation and licensing of mining
- Agriculture
- Forestry
- Water (including supplies, rivers and canals), control of silt, riparian rights
- Turtles and river fishing
- fore shores

Concurrently managed by the *federal and state* governments are[228]:

- Protection of wild animals and wild birds, national parks
- Town and country planning

---

224 WWF Malaysia 1996, p. 12-13.
225 Hotels with more than 80 rooms, resorts covering more than 50 ha and tourist facilities in national parks or on islands surrounded by marine parks have to be assessed with an EIA.
226 WWF Malaysia 1996, p. 20.
227 WWF Malaysia 1996, p. 20.
228 WWF Malaysia 1996, p. 20.

- Maritime and estuarine fishing and fisheries (only in Sabah and Sarawak).

Ecotourism should also generate socio-economic benefits. Although still a minor contributor to the total tourism revenue, it nevertheless has strong potential for contributing to the development of the rural poor, to village economies. Often local communities living near ecotourism sites have incomes below the national average and a rather limited range of economic options. Therefore, ecotourism can be a very important source of income. According to the NEP the following socio-economic benefits from ecotourism are noteworthy[229]:

- "Ecotourism generates local employment, both direct in the tourist sector and in various support and resource management sectors (…);
- It stimulates domestic industries including hotels, restaurant, transport systems, souvenir and handicraft sales, and guide services:
- Ecotourism generates foreign exchange;
- Ecotourism diversifies the local economy, particularly in rural areas where agricultural, fisheries, and other forms of employment may be sporadic or insufficient;
- Ecotourism stimulates rural economies by creating a demand for agricultural produce, and by injecting capital;
- Ecotourism stimulates improvements to local transport and communications infrastructure, which benefit local people;
- Ecotourism promotes the maintenance of parks and reserves, which can become showcases for the country and which can therefore enhance investment;
- Ecotourism encourages the economically productive use of land which may be marginal for agriculture, enabling larger tracts of land to remain covered in natural vegetation, and safeguarding water supplies and other environmental services."

Besides benefits, there are also costs of ecotourism, especially the maintenance of parks and reserves which cost more than parks normally generate. In 1994 the government agencies' expenditures for the upkeep of parks and reserves amounted to RM 48 million (including both recurrent and capital development spending). Even if we account for a considerable increase of this amount during recent years, the expenditures are still small in comparison with the annual revenue from tourism (then around RM 9 billion), of which an estimated 7 % (or RM 560 million[230]) can be attributed to nature-based and ecotourism.[231] The main strategies of the NEP are:

- to emphasise participation of existing institutions and the local people

---

229 WWF Malaysia 1996, p. 33.
230 This is consistent with estimates made by Badaruddin (2002) for 2000 (RM 655 million).
231 WWF Malaysia 1996, p. 36.

- the encouragement for the establishment of additional areas for ecotourism
- the introduction of innovative funding mechanisms in order to encourage self-financing of parks
- the monitoring of the progress of ecotourism
- to emphasise the importance of manpower training (ecotourism should be a tool for environmental education and ecological awareness)
- to move towards a future where all tourism is sustainable and environmentally responsible.[232]

The NEP operates with three scenarios for the development of ecotourism; each is based on an estimated 12.5 million foreign tourists a year by the year 2000, which, as we know now, was not reached. Only slightly more than 10 million foreigners came to Malaysia during that time (see figure 4 on page 6). The scenarios operate assuming 5 %, 10 % and 15 % ecotourists (including nature tourists) in 2000, and estimate the manpower requirements for guides for 2010 in the ecotourism sector to rise from 675 people in 1994 to 1,700, 3,500 or 5,200 respectively. Moreover, the NEP (in all scenarios) expects a decrease of the average stay of foreign tourists from 19 days in 1994 to 12 days in 2010.[233]

The NEP identifies 37 main issues that should be addressed in the near future in order to implement the plan. Several of these issues will be addressed, in chapters V: "The experts' discourse about nature conservation in Malaysia" on page 171 and VI: "Tourists in Gunung Mulu National Park" on page 203, but mainly in the last chapter 6: "Important issues of the National Ecotourism Plan" on page 260.

Figure 16: Main issues of the National Ecotourism Plan

No	Issue	Explanation/example
1	Conditions for tenure of ecotourism sites not formulated	Many ecotourism sites are free to use, therefore, businesses benefiting from such sites should pay for access
2	Need for carrying capacity limits not appreciated	A methodology for the assessment has to be developed and assessments have to be carried out
3	Ecotourists' expectations poorly understood	There is a lot of knowledge about the expectations but little comprehensive and accessible data
4	Inadequate tourist and nature-based tourist statistics	Different types of surveys should be conducted in order to know the numbers and desires of ecotourists
5	Inter-agency integration inadequate	There are many agencies dealing with (eco)tourism; they should be coordinated and a generalized guidebook for existing or prospective tour operators or developers should be available

---

232 WWF Malaysia 1996, p. 44.
233 WWF Malaysia 1996, p. 61-64.

No	Issue	Explanation/example
6	National objectives of ecotourism unclear	There is a general lack of development and management plans for areas with ecotourism and few enforcement mechanisms to implement them
7	Criteria for assessing proposals and proposers inadequate or non-existent	Tourism developments often get under way without establishment of the legal and administrative framework
8	Land use decisions made on inadequate foundation	Land applications may not take into account traditional use by local communities, or may not consider social impacts of the influx of tourists
9	Shortage of controls for ecotourism activities	There are not sufficient controls about environmental impacts of tourism activities
10	General perception of ecotourism as a poor kind of tourism	Ecotourism is often equated only with low-budget backpacking, even though they stay longer in the area and inject their money with less leakages
11	Shortage of good information of ecotourists	It is often difficult for travellers to acquire information about access, permits, transport to parks as well as maps
12	Few or no benefits to conservation from ecotourism	Fiscal measures may encourage infrastructural development in the more sensitive areas
13	Carrying capacity limits of acceptable change exceeded at identified sites	In some areas eroded tracks, stressed wildlife due to an exponential increase of visitors is detrimental to the environment and the tourist satisfaction
14	Suitable sites remain unidentified	An area suitable for ecotourism may be used for other, environmentally degrading and possibly less economically productive purposes
15	Technical data on sites inadequate	Shortage of information about visitor interests may lead to interference of different tourist types' activities
16	Reserved sites unmanaged for ecotourism	Missed opportunities for fee collection, protection and interpretation may lead to damaging activities and revenue losses
17	State land sites alienated for other purposes	Applications for State land for agricultural purposes, submitted years ago, may continue to be processed, even though recent information indicates that the land has good ecotourism potential
18	Alienated lands lost to ecotourism	A land owner of alienated land may see tourists, who come to see a rare plant, as interference in his agricultural work
19	Sites degrade and lose ecotourism value	Sensitive sites may be degraded through litter or overcrowding if there are not clear measurements and controls
20	Ecotourism contributing little to environmental education and awareness	Insufficient interpretative materials may detract from visitors' enjoyment and un-trained guides may convey messages that are detrimental to the environment
21	Absence of process for assessing and deciding on proposals	There are no comprehensive regulations that assess applications for developments in national parks and other sensitive areas
22	Unsuitable developers entering ecotourism industry	Insufficient knowledge of developers, lax controls or even fraud can lead to damage of the environment

No	Issue	Explanation/example
23	Shortage of innovative entrepreneurs entering ecotourism businesses and developing new products	A small group of tour operators have created many good ecotourism products, they should get more incentives and support from the government
24	Mass tourism occurring at ecotourism sites	Mass tourism can lead to littering or the clearing of large areas for weekend picnicking
25	Unsuitable products under way	Tour operators may encourage the feeding of monkeys or tourist behaviour at a beach that offends the local people
26	Weaknesses in on-site management	Managements (e.g. bookings, accommodation) may be conducted by agencies insufficiently qualified
27	Inadequate on-site staff capacity and capability	Organisations charged with area management may not have (enough) staff qualified in tourism matters
28	Widening gap between manpower needs and supply	Rapid creation of job opportunities may exceed the supply of local manpower, forcing an influx of people from outside the area
29	Inadequate guidance and rules for private sector	Exotic plants may be introduced into natural areas or litter and waste water disposal methods may be inadequate
30	Lack of image leading to inappropriate marketing	Promotion of a site may lead to excessive visitor numbers, without a contingency plan for diversion of tourists to alternative sites
31	Insufficiently developed human resources leading to constraints on further developing ecotourism products	Low levels of expertise may exist among tour guides, business owners, federal and state government agencies
32	Insufficient benefits returned to local people	Local people may not be given access to training opportunities or may be insufficiently consulted when a tourism operation is set up
33	Tourist safety	Boats may be loaded with passengers beyond capacity, tour drivers speed or some reef sites off Sabah are at risk from armed pirates
34	Inadequate taxation and fee collection mechanisms and inappropriate tax incentives persist	Tax relief on capital equipment for development on islands may lead to excessive destruction of the beaches or entrance fees may be too small
35	Due to unsustainable "ecotourism" operations, lack of confidence in ecotourism and reduced inputs to protect and manage significant sites	Obviously unsustainable constructions or operations may be detrimental to the environment
36	Government loses opportunities for sustainable development and forgoes potential revenue	Basically uneconomic businesses may be subsidised by free use of land, leading to opportunity costs
37	Large mass tourism operators retain economic advantage	Small ecotourism operators may not qualify for tax exemptions based upon a minimum number of customers or of economies of scale

Source: WWF Malaysia 1996, p. 71-121.

2 Most important parks and reserves in Malaysia

Between 4.5 to 5 %[234] of the Malaysian surface is protected as conservation areas. Most of the bigger areas are counted among IUCN-category II parks that are open to visitors and have adequate infrastructure. However, there are also a number of smaller parks – many of them within easy reach of cities or towns – which are often used for day trips by Malaysians or passing tourists (see figure 17 on page 94). On the following pages I will introduce the most important parks, describe their features and, if available, their visitor statistics. They represent the range of different features and problems of Malaysian parks.

2.1 Peninsular Malaysia

2.1.1 Taman Negara

Taman Negara is probably the best known park in Malaysia. Taman Negara literally means "national park", which is why many Malaysians[235] refer to it as "Taman Negara Pahang", because its head quarters and main access point are located in Pahang. Taman Negara was the most important conservation area of colonial Malaya, founded in 1938[236] by the Sultan of Pahang in cooperation with the Sultans of Kelantan and Terengganu, and until independence was named "King George V National Park". It covers an area of 4,343 km^2 and is still the largest park in Malaysia[237]. It is located in the centre of Peninsular Malaysia covering territory of Pahang, Kelantan and Terengganu. It harbours the oldest rainforest in the world, said to be more than 130 million years old. With its altitude ranging between 61 m and 2,187 m (Gunung Tahan) it has a great biodiversity i.e. 250 to 300 species of birds and several large mammals such as elephants, tigers, rhinoceroses, gaurs etc.[238]

The number of park visitors to Taman Negara has steadily increased in the last decade. Both the numbers of Malaysian and foreign visitors rose until 1997, after which fewer Malaysians visited the park, but more foreigners did. 1990 and 1994 were "Visit Malaysia Years", when the Malaysian government tried to attract foreign tourists. However, the visitor statistics of Taman Negara do not show a dramatic increase of foreigners.

---

234 The numbers can differ, because in some sources marine parks are included whereas in others they are excluded without mentioning it.
235 Most foreigners who do not understand Malay call it "Taman Negara National Park" which in fact is a pleonasm.
236 According to the World Conservation Monitoring Centre (WCMC) it was founded 1939 (UNEP, W.C.M.C. 1992).
237 WWF Malaysia and Cubitt, G. 1998. p. 65.
238 UNEP, W.C.M.C. 1992.

Figure 17: Location of Malaysian national parks

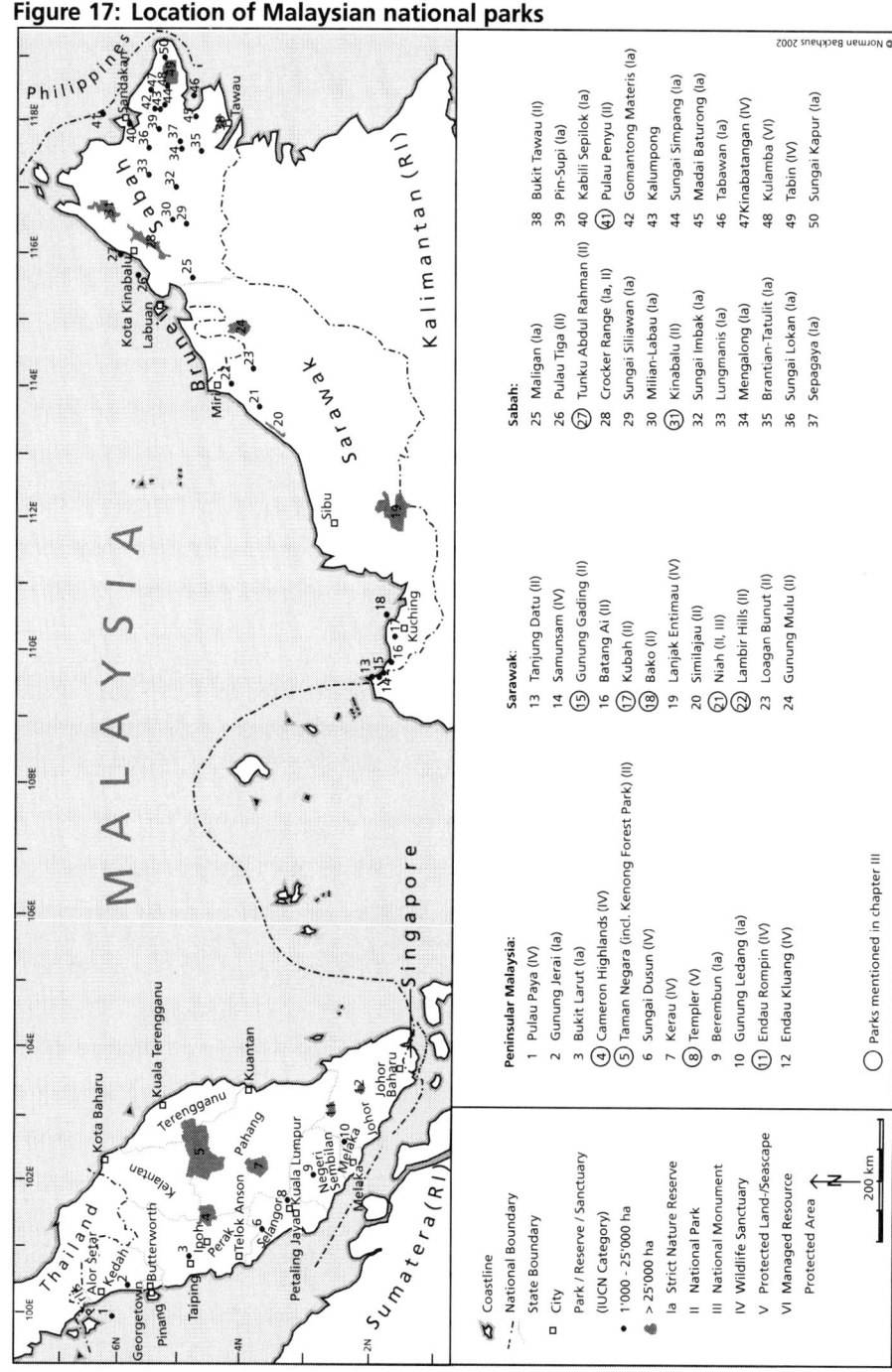

Source: own draft; data: IUCN 1994; UNEP, W.C.M.C. 1992.

1997 and 1998 was the time when a considerable part of southeast Asia was suffering from the haze, when the whole region was covered in smoke from great fires in Kalimantan and Sumatra. Interestingly, the number of Malaysians decreased, but not the number of foreigners. This could be explained with the Asian financial crisis that hit the Malaysian economy 1997 and 1998. For many people the financial situation was problematic, which could be the reason why they decided against a visit to Taman Negara.

The nearly 60,000 visitors per year is not distributed evenly throughout the year. Most of them travel in the months from March to September, with a peak in July and August, when there are school vacations in Europe, the USA and in Malaysia. Sometimes more than 500 visitors visit the park in one day, which exceeds – according to NGOs – the carrying capacity of the park.

Although almost never visible to the visitor, large mammals are a major attraction. The antiquity of the rainforests' ecosystem[239] is an attraction that is often advertised[240], though it is even less visible. The age of the rainforest indicates an unspoilt authentic environment, which is an attraction in itself. Visitors can hike along many treks around the head quarters at Kuala Tahan. The exhausting trek to Gunung Tahan takes the better part of a week, but people can also take the short stroll to the nearest observation platform in order to wait for animals to show themselves. Besides the treks, and the fauna and flora there are other attractions. Taman Negara features the (so far) longest canopy walkway (400 m) in the world. The system of connected suspension bridges allows visitors to see the jungle at the canopy level, where many birds and monkeys can be seen. Furthermore, fishing is allowed in the park and river trips are advertised. One can explore the jungle on his or her own on the sign posted trails around the head quarter, but it is also possible to hire a guide who can show one the secrets of the jungle. In the survey, one respondent mentioned the Orang Asli as an attraction too. These indigenous people have lived their nomadic lives in the area of Taman Negara for a long time before the park was gazetted. Today they are allowed to use its resources in a limited way. They can hunt animals with traditional weapons (no firearms) and remove wood (but they are not allowed to log). However, the Orang Asli of the Taman Negara area have settled down in villages outside the park and are not (fully) dependent on its resources any more. In the past some of them worked as guides for visitors[241], but nowadays most of the guides are not Orang Asli and come from all parts of the Pe-

---

239 Mainly lowland and hill dipterocarp forest (biogeographical province: 4.07.01 Malayan Rainforest; UNEP, W.C.M.C. 1992).
240 Taman Negara Resort n.a.
241 With their extensive knowledge about the jungle they also proved to be invaluable guides for researchers, leading them to the right spots and ensuring their safety.

ninsula. When hunting animals or gathering plants Orang Asli sometimes pass through the area of the park headquarters where they encounter tourists. For many tourists the presence of an Orang Asli is a sign of the authenticity of the environment. The Orang Asli are thus regarded as a part of it, only, however, if they are dressed in attire that tourists perceive as more or less traditional.

Accessibility here does not only comprise how quickly you can reach a park, but also how easy or difficult it is to organise travel and accommodation. Taman Negara is not a destination for a day trip for people living in or near Kuala Lumpur. However, the access is a combination of comfortable travel and adventure. From Kuala Lumpur good roads lead over the mountains into Pahang and to Tembeling, which can be reached by bus or private car. There, visitors pay their entrance fee of less than ten RM (including the camera fee) and get registered. The park entrance at Kuala Tahan is located 50 km upstream from Tembeling. In roofed long boats visitors embark on a journey into the jungle. For many the "adventure" of visiting the jungle already starts with the trip up river. It is also possible to hire a speed boat that brings people in one hour instead of two to three hours to Kuala Tahan. Access via road on the east side of the Tembeling River is new, and makes day trips possible from nearby towns.

Figure 18: Visitors of Taman Negara National Park

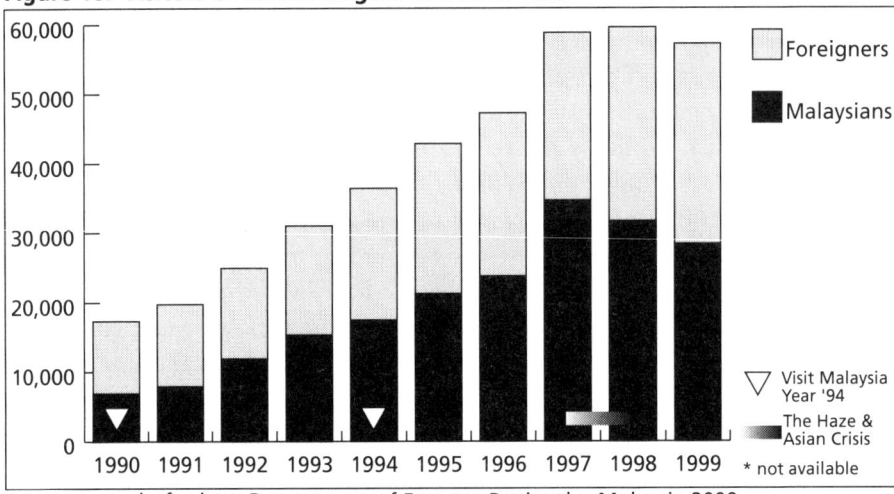

Source: own draft; data: Department of Forestry Peninsular Malaysia 2000.

A few years ago people could show up at the park office in Tembeling and try to book accommodation there. This is not longer possible since more and more visitors want to visit Taman Negara. Now accommodation inside the park has to be booked in Kuala Lumpur with a private company that runs the "Taman Negara Resort" which has close to 300 beds. They also provide transportation to and from the park. The resort is usually fully booked in the high season from March to September, especially on weekends. Opposite the resort – across the river and thus outside the park boundary – is a small village called Kampung Tahan where the newly built road ends. It provides accommodation too, for about as many people as the resort. Mostly they provide cheaper accommodation, which is why travellers with flexible schedules often book one or two nights in the resort in order to be sure to have accommodation, and then move over to the "cheaper" side of the river.

To sum up, we can say that the accessibility of Taman Negara is quite good, even though the resort is often fully booked. The possibility of staying in a hostel outside the park makes it possible to visit the park on rather short notice. For the park management the number of visitors poses a problem. Nevertheless, each year the Department of Wildlife and National Parks organises the Taman Negara Fest in November, in order to attract more visitors to the park.[242]

2.1.2 Cameron Highlands

Next to Taman Negara, the Cameron Highlands is the most favoured conservation area of the respondents. Besides having been a hill resort since colonial times, the Cameron Highlands are a wildlife sanctuary (IUCN category IV). The 64 km^2 area was gazetted 1962 as an outstanding example of mountain environment.[243] It was developed in the 1930's as a hill station for the British but also as an area for tea plantations. The fact that a large part of the area is situated on a plateau of 1,200 to 1,800 m, made the highlands an ideal spot for the British (and nowadays Malaysian and foreign tourists) to escape the hot and humid lowlands. Within the park there are still several tea estates and three villages. The protection of the sanctuary is less strict than that of a national park of category II, and the area surrounding the park is more densely populated than other conservation areas (i.e. Taman Negara, Gunung Mulu or Endau Rompin). Hence, the pressure on the park for wood is also greater than in other parks and therefore the few park rangers often report illegal logging in the protected area[244].

The wildlife sanctuary is not the main attraction of the Cameron Highlands. It is more the combination of freshness, the possibility of hiking and the unique landscape of the tea plantations, which attract people. There is also a great biodiversity, but much less spectacular – in numbers – than in the Taman Negara, for instance. It reveals itself not only in the forest, but also in vegetable and flower gardens. Some tea producers also offer tourists the possibility of observing the

---

242 Department of Wildlife and National Parks Malaysia 2002.
243 WWF Malaysia and Cubitt, G. 1998. p. 37.
244 UNEP, W.C.M.C. 1992.

tea processed from the leaf to the teabag. A newer development is the golf course that has attracted some more expensive hotels.

The Highlands can be reached easily from Kuala Lumpur, by road from the west (Perak). However, for a day trip it is quite far and many people from the lowlands and the cities want to spend enough time at altitude to enjoy the cool nights. A road connecting several hill resorts is planned for the near future. It will make the area much more easiliy accessible from Kuala Lumpur and it is believed that the development of many more buildings and hotels will follow.

2.1.3 Templer Park

Templer Park is gazetted as a Multiple-use Management Area[245] and a state park of Selangor state . Originally it was established as a botanical reserve and recreation area, but was declared a park in 1955. It is situated only 22 km North of Kuala Lumpur and can be easily reached by bus or private car. It has become an important recreation area for day trippers, featuring a waterfall, walks, ponds and a scenic limestone formation jutting out like a thumb. Moreover, a world renowned golf course has been established that attracts affluent Malaysians and Japanese. Out of 1,011ha, 400ha have been set aside as jungle reserve that has to remain untouched. Unfortunately there are no visitor statistics available, but the fact that many respondents have visited it, shows that it is an important recreation area for the urban population around the capital.

2.1.4 Endau Rompin

Endau Rompin was founded in 1989 and is located in the south of Peninsular Malaysia at the border of Johor and Pahang and comprises 800 square kilometres. Visitor statistics are not obtainable, but up to now only few visitors have found their way to Endau Rompin[246]. Before it was gazetted as a conservation area,Endau Rompin's resources – mostly rattan – were used by the Orang Hulu, a Proto-Malay ethnic group living in the area. Visitor facilities have only been built recently and are basic.

Endau Rompin features a great variety of forest types, due to different soils, and besides tigers, sambar deer and tapirs, there are still a few Sumatran rhinoceroses. Although these 'charismatic' mammals are rarely seen (the chance of seeing a Sumatran rhinoceros is virtually nil), their presence in Endau Rompin distinguishes it as a unique and unspoiled eco-system. As in most other Malaysian parks, there is also a great diversity of bird species (more than 200[247]), which makes it attractive for bird watchers. Although Endau Rompin is situated not

---

245 World Conservation Monitoring Centre & IUCN 1998.
246 Oral information by Malaysian Nature Society, Kuala Lumpur.
247 WWF Malaysia and Cubitt, G. 1998. p. 49.

far from Johor Bahru, it is not easily accessible. It cannot be reached by bus or ordinary car; at the least, a four wheel drive is necessary to contend with the dirt road to the head quarters at Kampung Peta. An alternative is to reach the park via boat. Both forms of transportation have to be arranged in advance, for there is no regular service. This, and the fact that entry permits have to be obtained in Johor Bahru, make it advisable to visit the park with a tour operator. However, during the coming years an improvement of infrastructure and access possibilities will probably lead to a more steady flow of visitors.

2.2 Sarawak

2.2.1 Bako

Bako is situated on the coast of Sarawak in its 'first division', 30 km from the capital Kuching. The 2,728ha area on a peninsula comprises a plateau of sandstone with cliffs rising up to 50 m. The soil is mostly sandy and therefore the environment is very poor in nutrients[248]. Nevertheless 25 vegetation types have been identified, ranging from mangrove forest at the coast to open scrubland on the sandstone plateau[249]. Founded in 1957 it is the first national park of Sarawak and still one of the most visited. In 1999 it was visited by more than 18,000 people, a quarter of them Malaysians (see figure 19 on page 100). 1995 was the peak year with more than 20,000 visitors. Most of them were Malaysians. Their number has decreased continuously from 1993, whereas the number of foreign visitors has slowly increased, with the exception of the years of the Asian currency crisis 1997/98, which overlapped with the haze. One can only speculate about the reason for the decline of Malaysian visitors to Bako. It could be that other parks became more attractive and/or that Malaysians tended to visit a variety of other parks. Many foreigners visiting Kuching include Bako in their itinerary, since it is not far from Kuching, the main entry point to Sarawak.

Although Bako is a small park, it features many attractions. In a small area the visitor can find many different vegetation types that can be easily seen within a few hours. However, the best known attractions are the sandstone sculptures on the coast. Marine erosion has formed bizarre columns and pillars that are unique to Bako. They can be observed from beaches that invite hikers to a swim. Besides the geomorphological forms and the vegetation some interesting species of mammals can be seen in Bako. The long-tailed macaque is ubiquitous and can be a nuisance when it is looking for food in visitors back packs, safe in the knowledge that they are protected here. Wild boar and sambar deer are not as easily spotted as macaques. However, the most charismatic animal of Bako is the

---

248 WWF Malaysia and Cubitt, G. 1998. p. 91; Laman, T. 2002.
249 UNEP, W.C.M.C. 1992.

proboscis monkey that can be seen not far from the headquarters, although the population consists of only a few dozen animals. With its long nose, the monkey has become something of an emblem of Borneo.[250] Bako is the most easily accessible place in Sarawak to see a proboscis monkey in the wild, a reason more for foreign travellers to visit the park.

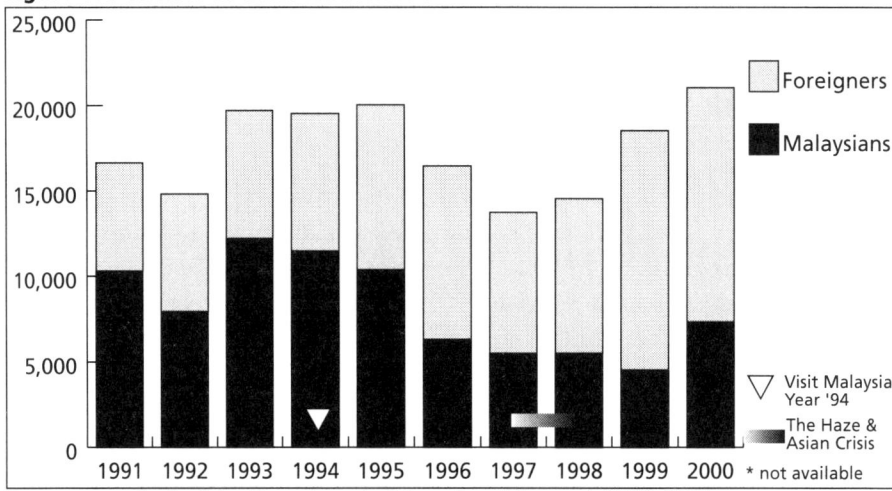

Figure 19: Visitors to Bako National Park

Source: own draft, data: Department of Forestry of Sarawak 2000, 2001.

As mentioned above, Bako is situated not far from Kuching, 35 km north of the city. Since 1984 there has been a road to the border of the park and a regular bus service connecting Kuching with Kampung Bako. The 45 minute ride is inexpensive, costing a mere RM 1.5 and leads through suburbs and newly cleared areas along the road. Although the elevation of the sandstone plateau virtually looms above Kampung Bako, and the park border is near, it cannot be accessed from there. The visitor has to enter it by sea. The villagers provide transport with small outboard vessels that can carry up to seven passengers. To hire the boat visitors have to pay RM 30 for a round trip, which is not much if the fee can be shared. However, many foreign travellers come alone or in pairs and often complain about the price which they consider stiff compared with the bus fare or even the cost of a taxi from Kuching. The income thus generated is vital for the community of fishermen and their families. As in Taman Negara, the access is a combination of a comfortable (and rather quick) transport via road and the adventure with the boat. Especially at low tide the boat tends to run aground in the shallow mound of Bako river, where it has to be freed by the pushes and

---

250 The official emblem of Sarawak is the hornbill that adorns the states seal.

pulls of the boatman (and sometimes by the passengers). Moreover, the trip leads along or through (depending on the tide) mangrove swamps – where occasionally flying foxes can be seen – and sandstone cliffs.

2.2.2 Gunung Gading

Gunung Gading is situated near the western tip of Borneo, close to the border with Indonesia. This park of only 41 square kilometres comprises an isolated mountain, and was gazetted in 1983. Foreign tourists have only recently started to visit Gunung Gading, and even today the majority of visitors are Malaysians. 1995 was a peak year (see figure 20 on page 101), when the visitor facilities were completed and many curious Malaysians came to the park. However, the number of visitors declined considerably after 1995 and has increased since mainly because of foreign arrivals.

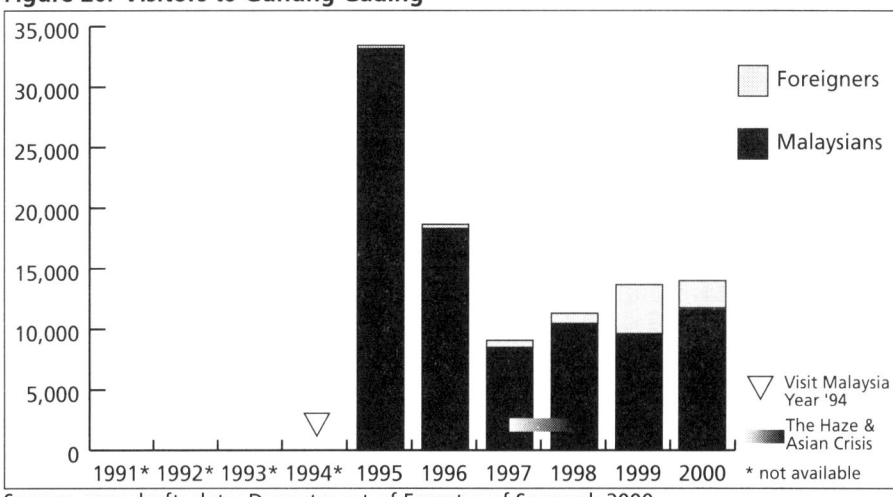

Figure 20: Visitors to Gunung Gading

Source: own draft; data: Department of Forestry of Sarawak 2000.

Most people go to Gunung Gading in order to see Rafflesia[251] bloom, although the blossoms of this gigantic flower are only in bloom for a few days before they decay, and they rarely bloom. Nevertheless, besides Crocker Range (and Kinabalu), Gunung Gading is one of the best places to see the rare flowers at all. The Amorphophallus, a giant lily which blooms even less often, is also found in Gunung Gading. When one of these plants is about to bloom, the rangers inform

---

251 Rafflesia are rootless, leafless and stemless parasitic flowers that grow on lianae and have huge fleshy flowers. The red flowers can have a diameter of up to 100 centimetre and thus are the biggest flowers in the world. They emanate a rotting smell that attracts carrion-scavenging insects, which pollinate the plant. After a week of bloom the flower decays. In Malaysia 8 species (of 15-18) are found (Wong, M. 2002. p. 20-27; Mohamed, I.A. 2001).

the tourist office or travel agents who then make this fact known to their customers. Besides these spectacular plant species, Gunung Gading offers streams and ponds to bathe in, as well as hiking. In addition to that, beaches are not far from the park. The park is mostly visited on week ends when people from Kuching go there for recreation. The visitor centre is built in the shape of a traditional Bidayu head-house (the house in which the heads of slain enemies were kept) and shows an exhibition about *Rafflesia*.

From Kuching, Gunung Gading can be reached within two hours by car and three by bus, via the small town of Lundu. The drive itself is quite scenic, first moving through the outskirts of Kuching through agricultural land, crossing a river on a ferry and finally arriving at the sleepy border town of Lundu, an entry point for Indonesian traders and workers, from where a smaller bus brings visitors close to the park entrance.

2.2.3 Kubah

Kubah National Park was gazetted 1989 for its wealth of palm species. On its 22 km^2, 98 species of palm trees have been recorded, which makes it one of the richest – if not the richest – palm habitat anywhere in the world.[252] The Visit Malaysia Year in 1994 was the one year with by far the most visitors (more than 45,000 in one year), who were all domestic visitors. Afterwards their number decreased to fewer than 10,000 annually. Kubah has only in recent years become a destination for foreigners, although their number is still quite small.

Although the abundance of palm trees was the reason for the park to be gazetted, people come to Kubah more often to hike or just to spend their week end. Groups of younger people from the Kuching area especially, come to the park in order to spend a night or two with their friends just relaxing and enjoying themselves, without having to walk far from the headquarters to where the accommodation is located.

The Matang Family Park is situated just next to Kubah National Park. Here, there are facilities to picnic and barbecue along an inviting river. A small restaurant provides meals and drink. The family park is fenced in and people have to pay a small entrance fee. It is frequented much more often than the nearby national park and almost exclusively visited by Malaysians. On the other side of the national park (and a part of it) is the Matang Wildlife Centre where orangutans, as well as other species, who were raised in captivity, are being rehabilitated and returned to the wild. The wildlife centre also attracts quite a number of people who watch the semi-wild primates being fed.[253]

---

252 WWF Malaysia and Cubitt, G. 1998. p. 95.

Kubah is situated 25 kilometres west of Kuching and can be reached by local busses within forty minutes, an ideal destination for Kuching city dwellers looking for a spot in unspoiled natural surroundings. Foreigners with limited time may prefer Bako to Kubah, if they want to make a day trip from Kuching. Bako offers proboscis monkeys and the sea and even the possibility of visiting the Sarawak Cultural Village near Damai Beach on the same day.

Figure 21: Visitors to Kubah National Park

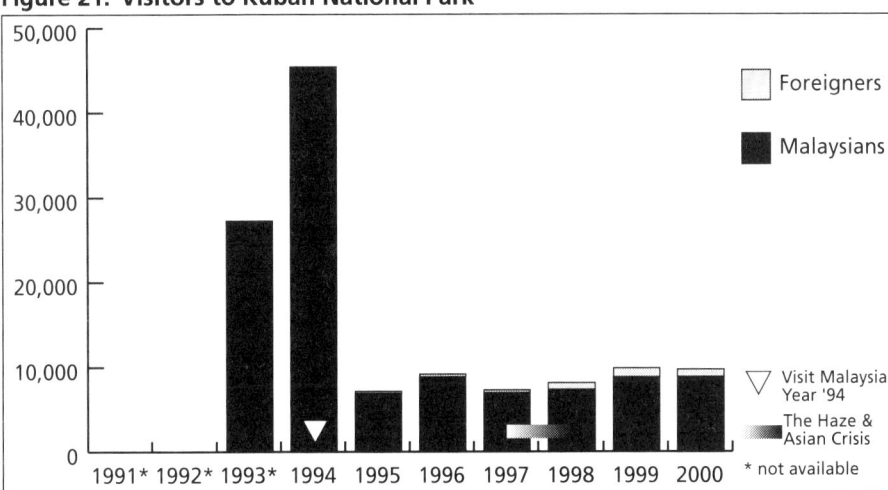

Source: own draft; data: Department of Forestry of Sarawak 2000.

2.2.4 Niah Caves

During the 1950's, various archaeological expeditions discovered the remains of human dwellings and their inhabitants, dating back as far as 40,000 years ago in a giant cave between Miri and Bintulu. It seemed to have been inhabited until recently.[254] The cave is also the main reason why people come to Niah and why the park has been put under protection in the first place, 1971 as a natural monument and then in 1974 as a national park. The park covers an area of 3,140 ha (the monument of 71 ha is a part of it).[255] Before its protection, the cave was used to gather swiftlets' nests and bat guano which is nowadays restricted. This is now a problem for the park management, because people still want to use the cave as a resource for income.[256] Before 1990 fewer than 2,000 visitors[257] came

---

253 The Wildlife centre was opened in 1996 and has more than 50,000 visitors per year (totally 253,725 from 1996 to June 2001), of which are 97 % Malaysians and 68 % return visitors. Foreigners come to see animals that are to be rehabilitated to the forest, most Malaysians go there to have picnic and enjoy themselves near the waterfall (Saifuddin, B.S. 2001).
254 Cranbrook, G.G.-H., Earl of 2000.
255 UNEP, W.C.M.C. 1992.
256 Lim Chan Koon 2000.

to Niah, after 1990 more than 10,000 (see figure 22 on page 104). The majority of visitors are Malaysians which make up fifty percent to two thirds of the visitors. In the peak year of 1995 the number of foreigners was particularly high. An explanation could be the "Visit Malaysia Year" in 1994, where the authorities advertised Malaysia – and with it Niah – abroad. Like with most destinations, the number of visitors to the park declined due to the combination of haze and the Asian financial crisis of 1997/98. Afterwards numbers increased again.

In the cave, remnants of human habitation, human skulls and bones and the only haematite cave paintings[258] on Borneo were found. Moreover, fossils of extinct giant pangolins have been excavated. At least five entrances lead into the cave at Subis Mountain. Plank walks make it conveniently accessible.

Figure 22: Visitors to Niah National Park

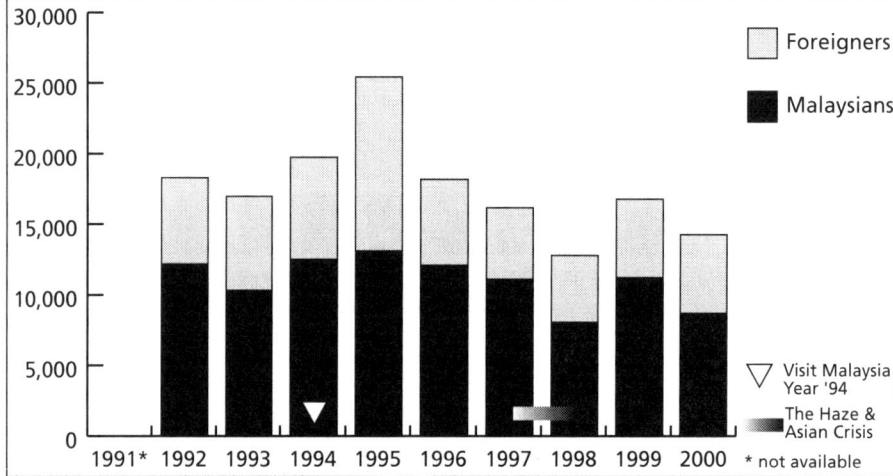

Source: own draft; data: Department of Forestry of Sarawak 2000.

Since the park is situated between Miri and Bintulu it can be reached by bus in two or three hours, which makes it attractive for day trippers. From the park head quarters the caves can be reached via plank walks. The walk takes less than an hour. Compared to Mulu which has a greater variety of attractions, Niah is better accessible, which could be one reason why more people come to Niah than to Mulu. Furthermore, the trip is cheaper, because it does not include an air fare. Last but not least, Niah can be visited in one day and therefore does not require any bookings, which probably contributes to its comparatively high number of visitors.

---

257 Kassim and Ngui 1989 in: World Conservation Monitoring Centre 2002.
258 Walsh 1981 in: World Conservation Monitoring Centre 2002.

2.2.5 Lambir Hills

Lambir Hills – a 70 square kilometer sandstone outcrop – was established in 1973 as national park. On just 0.5 square kilometer, more than 900 different species of trees have been found, which makes it the most diverse site for trees in the world. Due to its geomorphology it features many waterfalls plunging down steep cliffs. Currently it is mainly visited by Malaysians. As with Kubah, the figures in 1993 and 1994 show a very high number of visitors (over 60,000 in 1993) compared to later years (see figure 23 on page 105), which has to be explained by differences in the counting methods, rather than with the actual number of people coming to the parks. Although in 1997 and 1998 the number of visitors declined in Lambir Hills too, the decrease was not as grave as in other destinations. The number of foreigners is rather small compared to domestic visitors; it has even decreased during the last years.

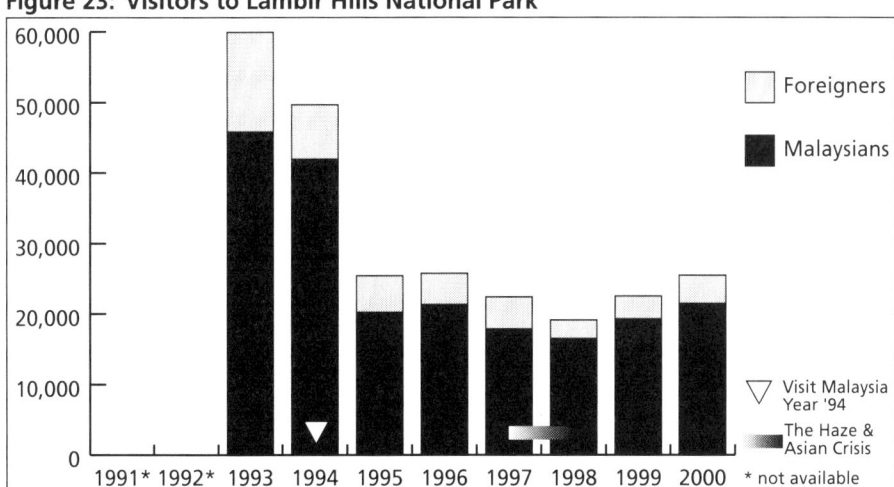

Figure 23: Visitors to Lambir Hills National Park
Source: own draft; data: Department of Forestry of Sarawak 2000.

Although the great diversity of tree species was the main reason for gazetting Lambir Hills, it is the waterfalls, pools and trails that attract most people to the park. Most of them are people from Bintulu or Miri who come there on weekends. Just outside the park, some Iban long houses can be visited by tourists. They also offer their handicrafts and wild fruits for sale. The combination of nature and traditional lifestyle is a great attraction.

The park headquarters are located on the Miri-Bintulu, road 32 kilometres from Miri. It is therefore accessible from Miri within 30 minutes, and it is even possible to make a short stop at Lambir Hills Park. The good accessibility and location can be seen as the main reason for many domestic visitors to come to

Lambir. Foreigners would rather go to the much better known Gunung Mulu and Niah Parks when they are in Miri.

2.2.6 Gunung Mulu

Gunung Mulu National Park is one of the best known attractions of Sarawak, although up to now comparatively few visitors visit this remote park (see figure 24 on page 106). In this study I did a survey asking visitors about their experiences in Mulu (see "VI Tourists in Gunung Mulu National Park" on page 203). The explanations about the context of Mulu are given in the afore mentioned chapter.

Figure 24: Visitors to Gunung Mulu National Park

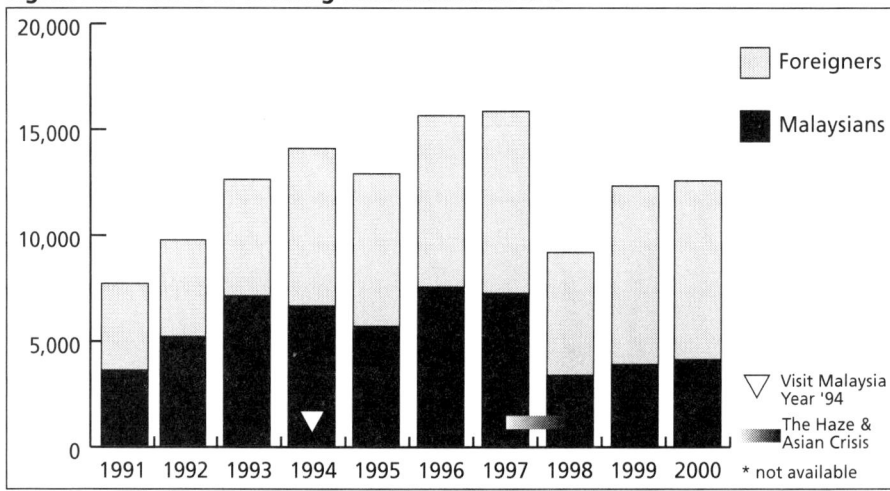

Source: own draft; data: Department of Forestry of Sarawak 2000.

2.3 Sabah

2.3.1 Kinabalu

Gazetted in 1964, Kinabalu park harbours the most prominent landmark of Sabah, and Gunung (or Mount) Kinabalu, which, at 4,096 m[259] is the highest peak of south-east Asia. Due to an altitude range of 152 to over 4,000 m, the park features one of the world's greatest biodiversities, which is the main reason for it to become gazetted as a World Heritage Site by UNESCO in 2000[260]. The mountain is a clearly visible and free standing phenomenon, towering over Sabah. It is the remnant of a magma intrusion that lifted the overlying marine

---

259 Older sources mention a height of 4,101 m (Wong, K.M. & Phillipps, A. 1996), however satellite measurements in 1999 corrected it to 4,096 m.
260 UNESCO 2000.

sediments, due to complex crustal movements, forty millions years ago. The mound consists of mainly granitic rock including older metamorphic rocks that have been brought up with the intrusion[261]. Subsequently, erosion (hydraulic and glacial) formed the current distinct shape of the mountain with a plateau around 3,800 m, many peaks, and sheer cliffs of which Low's Gully[262] is the steepest and deepest.

Mount Kinabalu has played an important role to many ethnic groups living in its vicinity. The Lotud, a Dusun/Kadazan tribe, describe how the mountain was created by their supreme deities Kinohoringan and Umunsumundu: "Umunsumundu created the earth while Kinohoringan created the sky, cloud and all above the earth. The eagle, Kondiu, was sent to inspect all that they had created. Alas, the report was that the cloud was too small in relation to the earth. Kinohoringan (…) was ashamed. (…). This was a blow to his pride. Umunsumundu understood his feelings and decided to reshape the earth instead, to make it equal in breadth to the cloud. She decided to create a mountain which she called Kinabalu[263] or Kinorungoi. This mountain was to be the heart of the world."[264] Rituals involving the sacrifice of cocks and eggs are performed on the mountain in order to honour the spirits of the dead.[265]

The symbolic importance of Gunung Kinabalu reveals itself in the flag of Sabah where its outline is depicted. But it can also be seen in the fact that many Malaysians visit Kinabalu Park in order to see the mountain's majesty. During the last decade a steady flow of visitors came to the park (see figure 25 on page 108).[266] Kinabalu Park has an average of more than forty percent of the visitors of all Sabah parks, and more than fifty percent of the Malaysian visitors of all Sabah parks[267].

The greatest attraction of Kinabalu Park is obviously Gunung Kinabalu. It is a hot spot of biodiversity, which[268] draws it to the attention of bird watchers (306 species of bird, according to Jenkins et al.[269]; 289 according to the

---

261 Lee Tain Choi, D. 1996. p. 19.
262 1994 a british military unit descended into the gully and went missing. An SAS team had to be dispatched to the soldiers' rescue.
263 The name Kinabalu probably comes from the word *nabalu* (any big boulder associated with spirits) and *Ki* (occurrence of boulders) (Regis, P. 1996. p. 35).
264 Regis, P. 1996. p. 31.
265 Regis, P. 1996. p. 37.
266 According to Liew (Liew, F.S.P. 1996. p. 468) the numbers of visitors varies from 163,337 in 1984 (before only people were counted that inscribed themselves in the visitors book) to 210,988 in 1986 to 173,459 in 1989.
267 Sabah Parks 2000.
268 World Conservation Monitoring Centre 2002.
269 Jenkins, D.V., de Silva, G.S., Wells, D.R. and Phillipps, A. 1996. p. 397.

WWF[270]) and plant enthusiasts (9 species of pitcher plants alone, of the nepenthes family, according to Corner & Beaman[271]). Besides climbing the mountain, visitors can hike on many posted paths, at its foot, and around the park head quarters. There are many inviting picnic sites. Furthermore, there is an orchid garden and the park provides guided tours. Last but not least there is a small information centre with an exhibition.

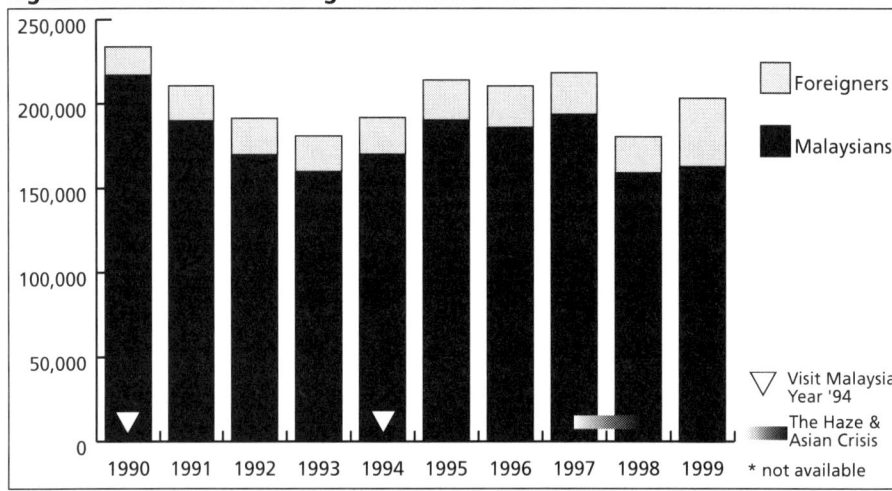

Figure 25: Visitors to Gunung Kinabalu National Park

Source: own draft; data: Sabah Parks 2000. 'Visitor Statistics'. Kota Kinabalu.

For many people the climb of the highest mountain in the area is a challenge not to be missed. However, if we look at visitors' statistics the climbers only make about 15 % of all visitors, but close to 50 % of all foreign visitors (see figure 26 on page 109). The climb takes two days with an overnight stop at Laban Rata at 3,600 m. Although the path is marked very well, climbers must hire a guide for the trip (at 35RM), which cost can be shared by a group. Many travellers – mostly foreigners – doubt the usefulness of these guides, because it is almost impossible to go wrong on the trail. However, the guide serves as insurance for the park administration in case something happens, and as a "watchdog" to prohibit visitors from going astray and disturbing the delicate environment. The income generated by the guides helps them to sustain their livelihood[272] Usually the climbers meet their guide in the morning, take a bus (provided by the park) to the end of the road, 1,800 m from where they start their ascent. This leads them over thousands of steps through changing vegetation up to the

---

270 WWF Malaysia and Cubitt, G. 1998. p. 145.
271 Corner, E.J.H. and Beaman, J.H. 1996. p. 117.
272 The park administration does not collect a share from the guides' fee.

mountain camp near the tree line. In the early hours of the second day the climbers ascend above the tree line where they walk on the rough granite of Low's Peak, the highest elevation, which they try to reach before sunrise. The whole trip from the end of the road to the summit is only 10 km; however, the climbers have to contend with an altitude change of 2,300 m. The descent to the head quarters takes only a few more hours, and most climbers check out and leave the park for Poring (also a part of Kinabalu park on the opposite side of the mountain) where they soak their weary bodies in hot springs. Most foreigners who climb the mountain have little or no problems doing so. They have mostly planned their trip months in advance and are used to hiking and – probably more importantly – to temperatures not much above zero degrees celsius. In contrast, many Malaysian climbers are not well trained for the climb. They mostly travel in groups to Kinabalu, and especially Sabahans want to have climbed their great mountain at least once in a lifetime. For them, the group experience is more important than exercise or contemplation. High altitudes and very cold temperatures are a strain on many Malaysians.

Figure 26: Climbers of Gunung Kinabalu

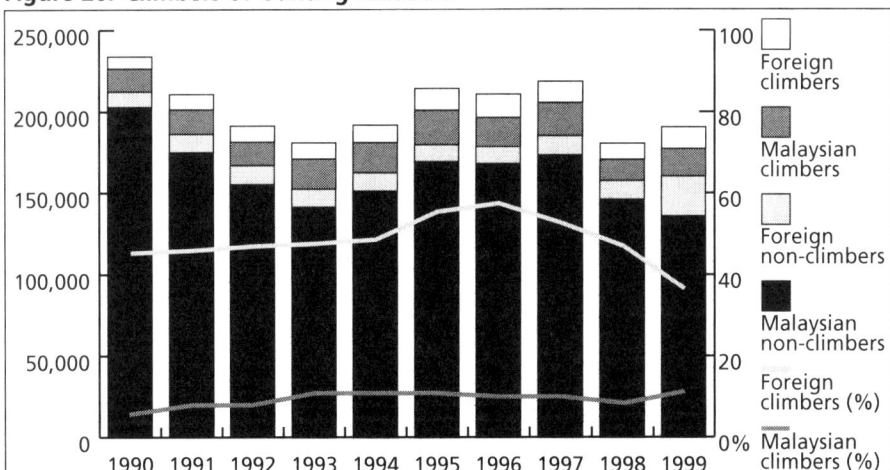

Source: own draft; data: Sabah Parks 2000.

From Kota Kinabalu, the head quarters of Kinabalu Park can be reached within two or three hours by bus or car. The trip is rather scenic, especially where the roads lead up into the mountains. However, due to the steep slopes, the streets are often covered with debris from minor landslides or have even been partially destroyed after heavy rains. Of course for many visitors this can be a nuisance, but it also adds to the adventure. The road to Kinabalu Park is the same road that leads further east to Poring (also part of the park) and to Sandakan and other conservation areas (i.e. Kinabatangan or Sepilok). Therefore, Kinabalu Park is not only a highlight on the itinerary of visitors to Sabah, but also a convenient stop along the way to the east. Good accessibility enables people from Kota Kinabalu to even visit the park without an overnight stay. Many picnic places invite them to just relax and enjoy their stay in the coolness of the mountain area with a splendid view of Mount Kinabalu.

For visitors who want to stay overnight it is not feasible to just show up at the head quarters hoping for a place to stay, for most beds are booked far in advance. The privately owned "Kinabalu Gold Resorts Sdn Bhd", which manages accommodation and restaurants in the park, has offices in Kota Kinabalu, where stays and trips to the mountain can be booked. Even more than accommodation around the head quarters, the beds in the Laban Rata area on the mountain are frequently booked. People willing to climb Mount Kinabalu often have problems booking their stay, because there are few beds (around 130) on the mountain. However, for people who do not want to climb, there are many guesthouses around the park that offer reasonably priced accomodation.

Although the majority of the visitors does not (want to) climb the mountain (see figure 26 on page 109), the good accessibility of the peak is an attraction in itself. There are not many mountains higher than 4,000 m that are as accessible and easy to climb as Mount Kinabalu.

Buses frequently enter the park and unload their passengers right in front of the registration office, which gives it the impression of being a bus stop rather than the entrance of a national park with a great biodiversity. In the Tourism Masterpla[273] of the Government of Sabah moving the car and bus park outside the park has been suggested, in order to uphold the image of an intact and unpolluted environment. However, even if it is moved a minimum of traffic remains, because the buildings in the head quarters area are quite scattered.

2.3.2 Tunku Abdul Rahman

Tunku Abdul Rahman (or TAR for short) National Park consists of five islands (Gaya[274], Manukan, Mamutik, Sapi and Suluk) that are situated just off the coast of the Sabahan capital Kota Kinabalu. It was gazetted 1974[275] aand named after the second prime minister of Malaysia. Although the park is comprised of 50 square kilometres, the islands are rather small. Before 1995, slightly

---

273 Institute for Development Studies 1996.
274 The easternmost part of Pulau Gaya is not included into the national park, for there is a fishing village and its inhabitants would have been forced to abolish fishing with nets, while living in the park. Moreover, it is a policy of the Sabah park administration to either remove local people from parks or to not include their villages into parks.
275 WWF Malaysia and Cubitt, G. 1998. p. 141.

more Malaysians visited the park than after 1995. The number of Malaysians declined at the same time that the number of foreigners increased (see figure 27 on page 111). As early as 1992, more than 100,000 visitors came to the park, mainly to Pulau[276] Manukan and Pulau Mamutik. Although after 1995 the number of visitors decreased a little bit, TAR Park did not suffer as much from the haze and the Asian financial crisis as did other parks. Kota Kinabalu is planning to build a new waterfront in the harbour, which will allow visitors to stroll along the coast; the islands of TAR will then be more easily seen from the city and possibly attract more people.

Figure 27: Visitors to Tunku Abdul Rahman National Park

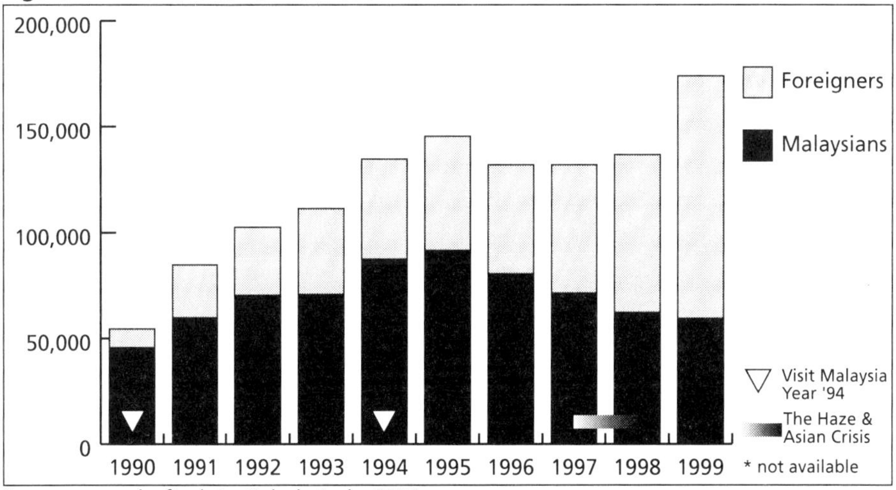

Source: own draft; data: Sabah Parks 2000.

TAR's main attractions are coral reefs around the islands. In most cases they can be reached easily from the beaches and simple snorkelling gear is enough to allow one to watch fish and the reef life. However, the condition of the reefs is not the best. Due to their proximity to the shore they are frequently trampled on by tourists and some of them suffer from coral reef bleaching. The near vicinity of Kota Kinabalu and its mainly untreated waste water is detrimental to the coral, too. Nevertheless, the beaches attract more and more people, who mainly visit the islands for recreational purposes and less because they are part of a conservation area. In recent years, travel agents from hotels around Kota Kinabalu and Tanjung Aru bring groups of up to a hundred tourists (mainly from Taiwan and Japan) to the islands, where they entertain them with games and barbecues. Since TAR is very near to Kota Kinabalu, on week ends many local people spend

---

276 "Pulau" means "island" in Malay.

afternoons swimming or snorkelling on one of the islands, from which Mount Kinabalu is clearly visible (which it is not from Kota Kinabalu). Its vicinity to the capital, Sabah, makes TAR attractive and unappealing at the same time. People who are looking for a nice day at the beach, where they can snorkel and have a picnic will like it. Those who are looking for natural attractions such as unspoiled coral reefs and birds are more likely to avoid its busy beaches.

Due to its proximity to Kota Kinabalu, TAR can be reached within twenty minutes by boat. For the individual traveller, the rather aggressive offers of boatmen to bring them to the park can be perceived as a hindrance. However, the official boat service to the park is fairly cheap and reliable, which makes it possible to visit the islands without prior reservations.

2.3.3 Pulau Penyu

Pulau Penyu Park ("turtle island park" in English), comprises three small islands of 15 ha (Pulau Selingan, Pulau Bakungan Kecil and Pulau Gulisan) and their surrounding waters (1,725 ha). Established as a game and bird sanctuary in 1972, the enactment was revoked in 1977 and the status of the park changed to national park, which again was repealed in 1984 when the park became a state park.[277] Situated 40 kilometres north-east of Sandakan near the Philippine border it is an important tourist attraction of Sabah. More than 90 % of the visitors are foreigners, who come here to watch turtles breeding or hatching. Since the islands cannot be visited as a day trip, the number of visitors is restricted to the available accommodations, which are managed by a private company.[278]

As the name of the park already suggests, the main attractions of Pulau Penyu are the sea turtles that lay their eggs in the sand of the beaches, at night. The green turtle lays them between July and October and the smaller hawksbill turtle lays them from February to April. The eggs are collected by park rangers who bring them into protected hatcheries on the islands where they are safe from predators and illegal collection. There are also several species of dolphins and even dugong living in the waters of the park.[279] However, the visitors mainly come to see the adult turtles lay their eggs or the young hatching and scuttling into the sea. The islands – and especially the turtles – cannot bear masses of tourists, which is why officially only twenty[280] people are allowed to the park at the same time.[281]

---

277 UNEP, W.C.M.C. 1992.
278 Rowthorn, C., Andrew, D., Hellander, P. & Lindenmayer, C. 1999. p. 504.
279 UNEP, W.C.M.C. 1992.
280 Lutterjohann, M., Homann, E., Homann, K. & Kuster, R. 1998. p. 536.
281 Until 1998 it is comprehensible to have only twenty visitors per day. Since 1999 the number was increased to 53 people (information by Crystal Quest Sdn Bhd, 2002) (more than 9,000 people visited the park, which makes an average of 25 people per day).

From Sandakan, a short boat ride brings the visitors to Pulau Selingan where the chalets are situated. Since the whole trip has to be booked in advance in Sandakan, the transport is organised too. The restricted number of visitors allowed, especially during the peak season, and the comparatively high price for the compulsory overnight stay (RM 245-270 per person) are the main factors in keeping potential Malaysian visitors from making the trip.

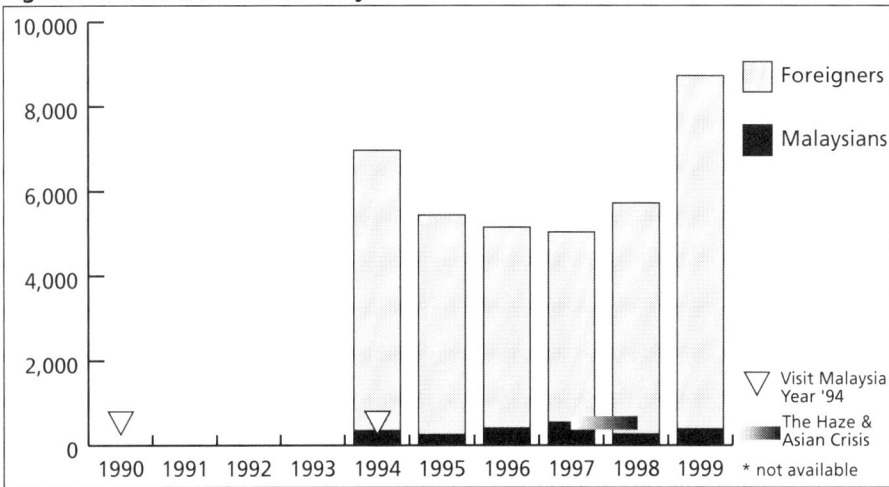

Figure 28: Visitors to Pulau Penyu National Park

Source: own draft; data: Sabah Parks 2000.

2.4 Conclusion: different developments and problems

If we take a closer look at the relative visitor development of the most important parks, we can see considerable differences (see figure 29 on page 114). Roughly we can discern three groups:
- Parks with a considerable growth of visitors: Taman Negara, Tunku Abdul Rahman (TAR) and Mulu. The latter experienced a decrease in 1997/98 due to the detrimental effects of the haze. Although Taman Negara and Mulu are bigger, better known conservation areas, we cannot say that the big parks have growing numbers of visitors and the small ones not, because Tunku Abdul Rahman is a rather small park. Accessibility is also not a decisive factor, because Mulu and Taman Negara are not very close to major centres, whereas TAR can be reached from Kota Kinabalu within half an hour.
- Parks with a more or less stable development: Pulau Penyu, where the number of visitors is strictly limited; Bako which is increasingly popular because of its beaches and vicinity to Kuching; Niah which is similar to Mulu; and Kinabalu which has had a constant high number of visitors for years.

There are also different reasons for the stability of the visitor numbers in Pulau Penyu, Bako, Niah and Kinabalu. Since the turtle island limits its visitors to very few, the numbers cannot vary much. However, its newly acquired status as a World Heritage Site will probably increase the number of foreign visitors in the near future. Bako and Niah are small, but well known parks near towns, which makes them well accessible and attractive for day trippers.
- Parks with a decreased number of visitors: Gunung Gading, that was very popular just after it opened to the public, but that is not near bigger centres; Lambir that is very close to Miri but lost its popularity probably due to the better accessibility of Mulu; and Kubah which is near Kuching but borders on a popular recreational park, which attracts a great number of local visitors, who go can there to have barbeque and a bath in the river. Foreign tourists tend to visit Bako, when they make a day trip from Kuching. Gunung Gading, Lambir and Kubah are newer parks, which had sudden peaks in visitor numbers when they opened to the public, but are – with the exception of Kubah – not as close to towns as are other small parks.

These different developments show that not all park administrations will have the same conditions in the near future regarding their visitors. This could be used to possibly shift visitors from parks that suffer from a high demand to parks with low visitor numbers. In order to achieve this, adaptations would have to be made regarding the demands of tourists and what the parks have to offer them.

Figure 29: Indexed development of selected parks

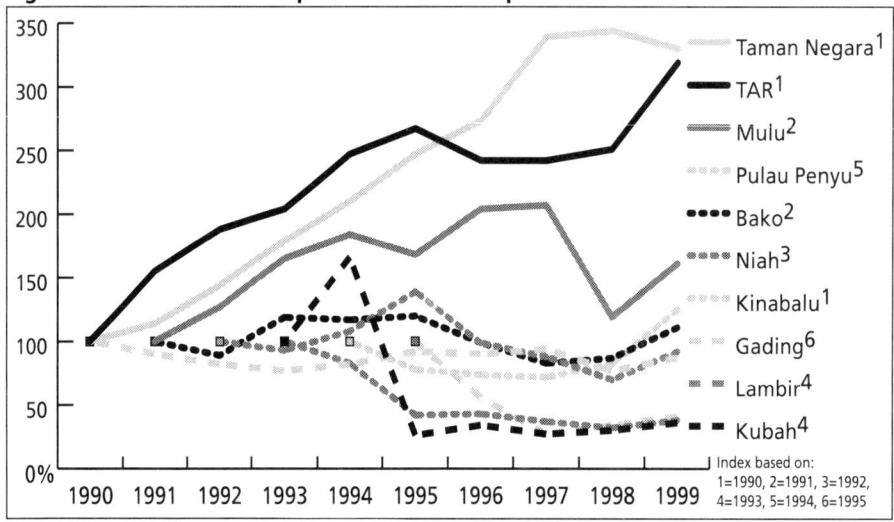

Source: own draft and calculation; data: Department of Forestry of Sarawak 2000; Sabah Parks 2000; Department of Forestry Peninsular Malaysia 2000

Analysis

IV Malaysian urbanites and their national parks

1 Introduction

Nature protection strongly depends on revenue from tourism, and most conservation areas (IUCN categories II-VI[282]) also have an educational function. Therefore, for the upkeep of a conservation area and its acceptance by the public it is important to know the opinion of the people who might visit such an area. If the inhabitants of a country do not support the idea of protecting specific areas – and thus precluding it from most other uses –, effective conservation is difficult to achieve. People visiting national parks generally come from urban or suburban areas, or have an urban lifestyle. People living in rural areas, tend to visit conservation areas less often. This is even more so in areas where nature poses a threat (wild animals or encroaching vegetation) or where people recently have had to reclaim land from the wilderness or the jungle. In order to learn more about what Malaysians think about nature and its conservation, their expectations for future visits, and their experiences with past visits, we have to survey people living in urban areas of the more densely populated regions of the country.

Almost two thirds (62 %[283] in 2001) of the Malaysian population live in urban areas. There is great potential for an increasing number of visitors to national parks, because, since 2000, government employees have at least one Saturday off per month[284]. This allows them to make weekend trips with an overnight stay at times other than their regular holidays. Their potential as visitors of national parks makes people living in urban or suburban surroundings ideal targets for a survey. Because visiting a conservation area is a leisure activity like sightseeing or visiting a theme park, a few questions were asked about the interviewees' visits of and experiences with theme parks.

In recent years, a considerable number of theme parks have sprung up in the surroundings of Kuala Lumpur and other urban areas (Ipoh, Taiping, Melaka). With this survey, we attempted to see whether comparisons can be made between people's impressions of conservation areas and theme parks (see "VII: Regionalising conservation areas" on page 245).

---

282 IUCN 1994.
283 Department of Statistics Malaysia 2001.
284 In Malaysia people generally work six days a week, from Monday to Saturday. In more and more private companies Saturday is not a work day any more. The government is following this practice to a certain extent.

2 Methods

In public or semi-public locations of the greater Kuala Lumpur area, 500 standardized interviews were carried out (see figure 30 on page 118). The interviews were conducted by five Malaysian geographers, who could read and understand the questionnaire, which was written in English, and to translate the questions into Malay or Chinese[285]. The pre-tests showed that some questions had to be clarified or reformulated, because they could not easily be translated into Malay or Chinese. Answers of the open questions were recorded in English or in Malay by the interviewers. Each interview took fifteen to twenty minutes to complete. The interviewers reported no problems with acceptance by the people they interviewed, which can be attributed to their familiarity with the context (they had grown up in or near Kuala Lumpur), to their language skills[286], to their comportment and probably also to their youth.

The sample was not taken randomly in the statistical sense: rather – as in most social studies – it was taken arbitrarily. For a true random sample, one out of every 3,000 inhabitants from the 1,379 million population of the greater Kuala Lumpur area (Wilayah Persekutuan Kuala Lumpur) would have to have been selected for an interview, i.e. using an alphabetical list or house numbers. After establishing this random sample it would have been important to actually interview the selected person.[287] Only then can the sample be termed representative in the statistical sense. However, it was not feasible within this study to attempt to get such a random sample. The costs would have been too high, and the interviewers would have had to visit or phone the designated interviewees several times. Using phone numbers would have had the added difficulty that phone numbers change often and their entries into directories are rarely up to date. Thus, the sample was chosen arbitrarily in the statistical sense. Respondents were approached in public or semi-public places in the greater Kuala Lumpur area such as shopping malls or train stations (see figure 30 on page 118). The survey gives us a good idea about what people in this urban area think, and we found several major trends. In order to reinforce results from the analysis,

---

285 Besides Mandarin, several other languages from South China are spoken in Malaysia, namely Hakka, Teochiew, Hokkien, Cantonese and Hailam (Watson Andaya, B. & Andaya, L.Y. 2001. p. 5). The interviews with ethnic Chinese respondents were mostly conducted in Mandarin or Hokkien or a mixture between Malay and a Chinese dialect.
286 Even though many Malaysians speak English well, the resistance to give an interview in English to a foreigner would probably have been greater.
287 This is the reason why telephone interviewers rather ask to be allowed to phone again at a later time to conduct an interview instead of just move to the next person in the alphabet or the next house in the street, if the selected respondent is not willing to participate in the survey at the moment.

chi-square tests were made where necessary. They help to strengthen an argument, but they are also not representative in the statistical sense.

The interviewers were instructed to ask people whether they were interested in answering some questions. If they were not, the interviewers were not to try to convince them to participate in the survey. Thus, the sample consists of questionnaires answered by people who are interested in the topic. This of course means there is a slight bias, but one that serves the aim of the study, because answers by interested people – whether they are in favour or against nature conservation – are in this case more valuable than the ones given by indifferent people. This is because the results shall serve as information for orientation and planning for organisations that are concerned with nature conservation. The sample used in this study comprises answers of people interviewed in public places (streets, squares) or semi-public places (shopping malls, train or bus stations). By selecting these places we have two advantages: In public spaces people are better able to say no, if they are not inclined to answer the questions and therefore they do not feel put under pressure when asked to participate.[288] People who use public places such as shopping malls are likely to have an urban lifestyle.

Figure 30: Places, where the interviews were conducted

Place	Kind	Percentage of interviews
Amcorp Mall	shopping mall	0.2
Bandar Utama	shopping mall	2.0
Central Market	market	4.8
Damansara	shopping mall	1.6
Jaya Jusco	shopping mall	7.0
Jaya Park	shopping mall	1.8
Klang bus station	station	2.0
KLCC	shopping mall	4.6
Kota Raya	shopping mall	5.4
Lot 10	shopping mall	3.6
Metrojaya	shopping mall	0.8
Mid Valley Mega Mall	shopping mall	6.2
National Library	public library	1.4
One Utama	shopping mall	11.6
Petaling Street	street	1.4

---

288 Since other studies (Saifuddin, B.S. 2001) show that local people are generally quite reluctant to participate in interviews, it is quite important to have respondents who gladly participate in the study.

Place	Kind	Percentage of interviews
Puduraya	station	7.4
Railway station	station	1.4
Salak South	station	1.0
Six College	university campus	5.2
Sogo	shopping mall	16.4
Sungai Wang	shopping mall	1.4
Tasik Jaya	shopping mall	5.0
UH, KL	university campus	2.0
Petaling Jaya	street	5.2
Pantai Dalam	shopping mall	0.4

Source: own survey.

2.1 The sample and statistics of Malaysia and Kuala Lumpur

In an arbitrarily chosen sample it is more difficult to select people according to specific categories such as ethnicity, religion, or occupation. Therefore, we compare the sample with the statistics of the Federal Territory (Wilayah Persekutuan) of Kuala Lumpur. The comparison with Malaysia shows that urban areas – and especially Kuala Lumpur, the capital – have a different compositions of population. The sample is quite near to the actual composition of Kuala Lumpur, however, it differs in some aspects. Since it was not the aim to interview foreign tourists, the interviewers did not approach people whom they thought were foreigners. Hence, they also did not interview foreign residents, and therefore the sample consists of 100 % Malaysian nationals.

While in the whole of Malaysia the *Bumiputera*[289] make up almost two thirds of the population, in Kuala Lumpur, their number equals, with more than forty percent, the number of ethnic Chinese. The reason for the higher number of Chinese in Kuala Lumpur (and other cities and towns) can be found in colonial history. The British encouraged Chinese immigration (mostly from southern China), because they thought their industriousness to be superior to that of Malays. As a consequence, the Chinese mostly settled in the area of tin mining (i.e. around Kuala Lumpur) or in commercial centres, and less in rural areas.[290] The sample shows a bias towards ethnic Chinese. This can be explained either by their lifestyle, which is probably more urban than that of the minority Bu-

---

[289] Bumiputera means literally "sons of the soil" and stands for "native" or "indigenous" people, comprising the Malays, the Orang Asli and other ethnic groups (i.e. the Dayak, Bidayu, Penan etc. of Borneo).
[290] See: Watson Andaya, B. and Andaya, L.Y. 2001. pp. 177-184.

miputera, making the Chinese feel more comfortable with shopping malls etc. It might also be because the interviewers were ethnic Chinese and were more likely to approach people of their own ethnic background.

There is also a considerable Indian community in Malaysia, especially in the cities. They immigrated in the wake of British colonial rule from (South) India and the former Ceylon. Because they were more accustomed to British rule, Indians filled the lower ranks of the colonial bureaucracy. The number of ethnic Indian respondents in the sample comes close to their actual percentage in Kuala Lumpur.

Figure 31: The sample compared with Kuala Lumpur and Malaysia[291]

Category (%)	Malaysia[a]	Kuala Lumpur[a]	Sample[b]
Citizenship			
- Malaysian	94.1	93.3	100.0
- Foreigner	5.9	6.7	0.0
Ethnic group			
- Bumiputera	65.1	43.6	37.5
- Chinese	26.0	43.5	50.1
- Indian	7.7	11.4	10.8
- Other Malaysian	1.2	1.5	1.6
Religion			
- Islam	60.4	46.2	37.2
- Christianity	9.1	5.6	13.7
- Hinduism	6.3	8.4	7.8
- Buddhism	19.2	34.2	33.4
- Taoism	2.6	2.7	4.4
- other religion	1.2	0.7	0.6
- no religion	0.8	0.9	2.8
- unknown	0.3		0.6
Median Age	23.6	26.6	20-29
Sex ratio			
- male	52.0	51.3	49.8
- female	48.0	48.7	50.2

a. Source: Department of Statistics Malaysia 2001.
b. Source: own survey.

In Malaysia religion is closely related to ethnicity, especially with the Malays who are Muslims by definition. Hence, the sample mirrors religion and ethnicity well (see figure 32 on page 121). Christians seem to be over-represented in the sample, because a large number of Chinese were interviewed, and many of them are Christians. In the sample all Malays are Muslims, whereas Chinese, Indians, other Bumiputera and other Malaysians have different religions.

---

291 Department of Statistics Malaysia 2001.

Figure 32: Ethnicity and religion of the sample

Category (%)	Muslim	Christian	Hindu	Taoist	Buddhist	other	none
Malay	100.0						
Chinese	0.8	20.0		9.0	65.3	0.8	4.1
Indian	1.9	22.6	71.7				3.8
Other Bumiputera	50.0	50.0					
Other Malaysians	25.0				37.5	12.5	25.0

Source: own survey

The median age in Kuala Lumpur is higher than in the rest of Malaysia, probably due to a higher number of unmarried people and a higher average age of first marriage. In the sample, people were – out of courtesy – asked their age group, rather than their actual age. However, the median age, "20-29" corresponds with the median of Kuala Lumpur (and Malaysia). Malaysia is one of the few countries with a higher proportion of males in the population, and Kuala Lumpur is no exception. However, the sample differs from these numbers. Relative to their actual percentage, slightly more women were interviewed.[292] Either there were actually more women present in the places were the interviews were conducted, or more probably, the fact that all the interviewers were women is responsible for this slight bias. However, in a partly Muslim society male interviewers would have had much more difficulty interviewing (Muslim) women and therefore I am convinced that the bias would have been much greater (however in the opposite direction) if the interviewers would have been male.

2.2 Other characteristics of the sample

2.2.1 Age and marital status

The largest segment (56.2 %) of the interviewees is between 20 and 29 years old. Together with those below twenty (16 %) they make close to three fourths of the sample. The group of people between 30 and 39 comprises 17 %, the ones between 40 and 49, 7.8 % and those above 50, 3 %. This reflects the high percentage of young people in Malaysia. Consequently, most people (71 %) of the sample are not married yet, while 27 % are married and only 2 % are divorced, and 77 % have no children. Of those people who have children, 18 % have one, 35 % two, 20 % three, 16 % four and 11 % five and more children (the highest number of children was ten).

---

[292] However, the difference is not statistically significant ($\chi^2 = 0.045 \leq 3.841$ at 5 %; df of 1).

Figure 33: Place of residence of the respondents[293]

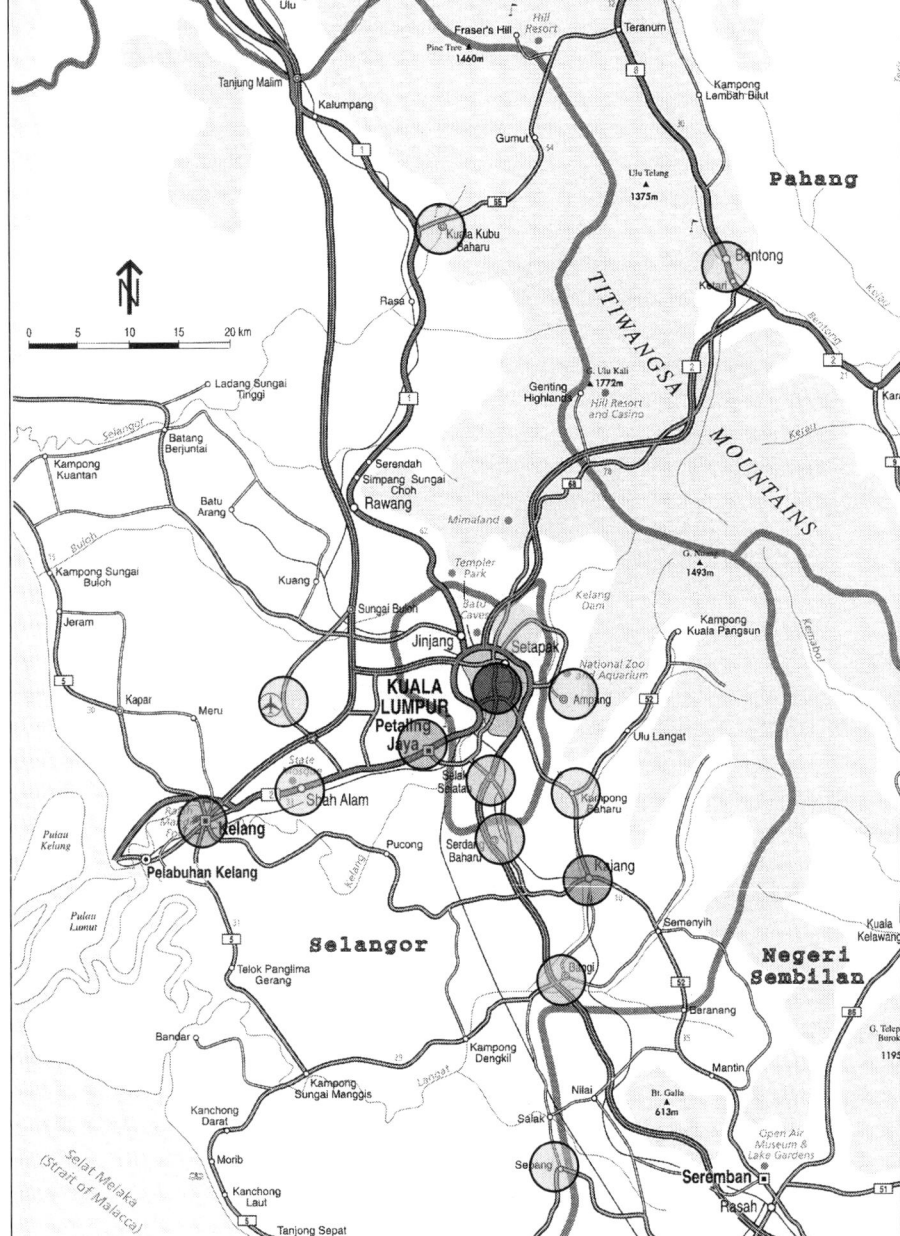

Source: base map of Road Atlas of Malaysia 1996; data: own survey.

---

293 Most respondents live in Kuala Lumpur, Petaling Jaya, Kalang and Kelang. Six live in Ipoh, Kota Kinabalu, Kuala Kangsar, Miri and not specified places in Terengganu and Pahang.

2.2.2 Occupation

The number of students is – according to age structure – at 47 %, rather high. However, Kuala Lumpur has grown to be a university city with many institutes (public and private) springing up in the last decade. The other respondents work mainly in the third economic sector (services) (see figure 34 on page 123), only a small proportion work in manufacturing, and none work in the first sector (agriculture, forestry, mining), which is not surprising in an urban setting. In Kuala Lumpur, there are 5,676 people per square kilometre.[294] Moreover, in its suburbs there is virtually no land to till and the great tin mines were exhausted years ago and now serve as residential area or as site for theme parks (see "6: Recreation and theme parks" on page 164).

Figure 34: Occupation of the sample

Occupation	Percentage
Student	47.1
Teacher, nurse	3.9
Sales(wo)man, business(wo)man, manager	14.6
Bank teller, office clerk, government employee	11.6
Engineer, inspector, operator	6.9
Worker, mechanic	4.9
Hawker, taxi driver	2.6
Housewife	5.1
Other	3.4

Source: own survey

2.2.3 School

Of the 500 people interviewed, only 11 (2.2 %) finished their formal school education after primary school, 34.5 % attended middle school, 26 %, high school and 37 %, university. The ones who had only attended primary school are distributed among all age groups. Since people under twenty were also interviewed, the probability that a significant number of them will go to university is high. Summarising, we can say that the sample consists of rather well educated people, since 63 % have at least gone to high school.

2.2.4 Place of residence

In one section of the interview people are asked which national parks or recreation areas they have visited (see "4: Visited parks and recreation areas" on page 128). In order to estimate the distance of these places from their home-

---

[294] Department of Statistics Malaysia 2001.

towns, they were asked their place of residence. The overview map (see figure 33 on page 122) shows the areas where those interviewed reside. They are also asked whether they like it where they live or not. Three quarters say they like it; close to one quarter say they do not. There are various reasons for approval and disapproval of the place of residence (see figure 35 on page 124). Most like their place of residence because of good facilities and convenience. The ones who dislike where they live do so mostly because of noise and pollution. Whether approval or disapproval of one's place of residence has something to do with the interviewee's opinion about nature or not will be discussed below (see "3.2.7: Place of residence and the respondents' opinion about nature" on page 128).

Figure 35: Reasons for approval and disapproval of the place of residence

Reasons	Percentage[a]
Approval[b]	75.4
- good facilities, convenience[c]	30.7
- nice surroundings[c]	12.2
- near work place, school, university[c]	11.6
- quiet, peaceful, safe[c]	10.0
- entertainment[c]	7.8
- not much pollution[c]	5.5
- hometown[c]	5.0
- good work opportunities[c]	3.6
- other[c]	13.6
Disapproval[b]	23.4
- too noisy, busy, polluted[c]	61.7
- too crowded[c]	19.1
- anonymity[c]	3.5
- too far from work, school, university[c]	3.5
- no place for children[c]	1.7
- high rent[c]	0.9
- other[c]	9.6

a. 0.8 % are missing values: 75.4 % + 23.4 % = 99.2 %.
b. Percentage of all interviewed respondents.
c. Percentage of their respective groups (approval, disapproval).
Source: own survey.

In the following chapters the results of the survey are presented according to the major topics of the questionnaire: "Connotations of nature" on page 125, "Visited parks and recreation areas" on page 128, "Opinions about nature protection and tourism" on page 144, and "Recreation and theme parks" on page 164.

3 Connotations of nature

3.1 Associations about nature and its opposite

3.1.1 What comes to mind with the word 'nature'?

The respondents are asked what comes to their mind if they hear the word nature. The aggregated answers do not differ from what people with a (middle) European cultural background[295] would say.[296] Half of the respondents mention elements such as flora, fauna, trees, forest etc. (see figure 36 on page 125). Those whose answers are included under 'Other', mention environment, beauty and harmony[297].

Figure 36: 'Nature' and the 'opposite of nature' according to the respondents

Topics	Percentage
What is 'nature'?	
- Flora, fauna, trees, green	31.0
- Environment in general and elements of physical environment	21.3
- Jungle, forest, park	19.0
- Original, unspoiled, clean	18.1
- Harmony, peaceful, to be protected	4.1
- Beauty	4.0
- Made by God	2.6
What is the 'opposite of nature'?	
- City, buildings, concrete	27.8
- Man made	23.8
- Pollution, waste	18.8
- Artificial	10.4
- Changed by humans	8.8
- Other	5.4

Source: own survey

---

295 See: Schiemann, G. 1996.
296 That does neither mean that there is a clear and outspoken definition of what nature means in Europe nor that all people share the same opinion about it.
297 5 % did not answer the question.

3.1.2 What is the 'opposite of nature'?

The question about the 'opposite of nature' shows similarities to the separation of nature and culture. More than 60 %, of things mentioned are man made or artificial. For many, the city itself is the 'opposite of nature'. The category "changed by humans" or "pollution, waste" shows what people perceive as the interference of humans with what is seen as (unspoiled) nature. From these we can conclude that life in the city, or an urban lifestyle, is not regarded as a part of nature. The respondents associate nature with things or elements they do not have (much) daily experience with. We can also conclude that there is no significant Malaysian cultural influence on the respondents' notions about nature.

3.2 Differentiation according to specific groups

3.2.1 No differences between the sexes regarding nature

If we compare the answers of men and women, we do not find big differences, except in the category "nature is made by God", which is mentioned by many more men (70 %) than women (30 %). However, statistically the difference seems coincidental[298], and since only 2.6 % of the respondents mention this category at all the difference can in fact be attributed to coincidence. The question about the 'opposite of nature' is not answered differently by men and women.

3.2.2 Age groups: differences only with aggregated categories

As with the sexes, age groups do not differ much in their answers about nature. Looking at the 'opposite of nature', there is only a significant difference when the age groups are aggregated. If we compare the respondents below forty with those above, there is a significant difference in the category "city, buildings, concrete", which is more often regarded as the 'opposite of nature' by older people[299]. We could assume that this is because most of the people above forty have spent their childhood, or a part of it, in a rural area or in a quarter of a city with a more or less rural lifestyle, i.e. a *kampung*[300]. Often these memories are "glorified" to the extent that people only see the positive things that they experienced in their youth[301]. Thus, the kampung-life seems to be more natural compared to the city with its multi-storey buildings.

---

298 Chi-square (χ^2) of 2.896 at 1 % probability of error and a degree of freedom (df) of 1 does not exceed the value of 3.841, which would be necessary to reject the null hypotheses that there is no significant difference between the values.
299 $\chi^2 = 5.05 \geq 3.841$ at 5 % (df of 1).
300 The Malay expression kampung literally means village. When people migrated from the countryside to the growing towns they often kept up a village-like lifestyle in the suburbs where they settled down.
301 See: Huber, A. 1999.

3.2.3 No differences between those with children and those without

One might assume that once people have children they change their opinion about what is nature because they either reflect more about the state in which they will leave their environment to the next generation, or because they want to let their children grow up in a "healthy environment". However, the respondents with children do not answer differently from those with no children, to the first questions about nature. Therefore, people do not tend to judge an environment that many termed as not suitable for children (see "3.2.7: Place of residence and the respondents' opinion about nature" on page 128) as opposite to nature.

3.2.4 Little differences between ethnic groups

Regarding nature, different ethnic groups might have different opinions according to their cultural background. However, statistically the differences tend to be coincidences rather than based on actual differences within the sample.

If we look at what people from different ethnic groups say about the 'opposite of nature' there are (statistically) significant differences. Disproportionately many Malays see it as "changed by humans"[302], many Chinese see it as "man made"[303] or "artificial". Of course we can argue that these categories are quite similar in their meaning, but even if we aggregate these three categories[304], we still have more Chinese and many fewer Indians who share this opinion.

3.2.5 Religion shows more significant differences

Regarding the category "flora, fauna, trees, green" there is a difference between Muslims and Christians. The former mention it much less often than expected, the latter much more[305]. However, the "book religions", Islam and Christianity combined, mention the expression "made by God" more than statistically expected[306]. This is probably because for Hindus, Buddhists and Taoists it is neither customary nor easy to credit a divine being with making or shaping nature. Moreover the Muslims emphasise "beauty" and "unspoiled" much more[307] than people with another religious background.

Regarding the 'opposite of nature' there are no significant differences between people of different religions, although slightly more Muslims to see "pollution" as the 'opposite of nature'.

---

302 $\chi^2 = 17 \geq 6.653$ at 1 % (df of 1).
303 $\chi^2 = 8 \geq 6.653$ at 1 % (df of 1).
304 $\chi^2 = 5.3 \geq 3.841$ at 5 % (df of 1).
305 $\chi^2 = 7.7 \geq 6.653$ at 1 %. and $5.1 \geq 3.841$ 5 % (df of 1).
306 $\chi^2 = 7.1 \geq 6.653$ at 1 %(df of 1).
307 $\chi^2 = 4.2 \geq 3.841$ at 5 % and $\chi^2 = 7.1 \geq 6.653$ at 1 %(df of 1).

3.2.6 Occupation and formal education have little influence

Since the occupations of the respondents are rather diverse (resulting in a high number of categories) and since there is a greater proportion of students in the sample, we examine the differences between students and people with other occupations. However, the occupation of a person does not seem to have any influence on his or her 'attitude' toward nature. The only significant difference occurs in the category "artificial". There, the number of answers by students is disproportionately high[308].

3.2.7 Place of residence and the respondents' opinion about nature

At the end of the interview the respondents are asked whether they like their place of residence. People who were not happy with their place of residence mention the physical aspects[309] of nature such as flora, fauna, or the jungle less often than harmony, an unspoiled clean place etc. of nature. It is not easy to explain that result. Perhaps people, who perceive their immediate environment as unfavourable, project their longing for harmony and cleanliness (most complained about pollution and noise) on what they perceive as nature. Nature consequently serves as a place where the squalor of everyday life is absent.

4 Visited parks and recreation areas

4.1 Expectations of a visit to a national park

In most so-called industrialized countries, nature conservation is well accepted. A long tradition of nature conservation is one reason, but also the mostly negative aspects of modern life, which lead people to cherish unaltered areas. In industrializing countries such as Malaysia, we cannot expect the same attitude toward nature conservation of the ideas of nature conservation. Therefore, it was an aim of this survey to know more about this issue.[310]

The respondents were asked, whether they would like to visit a national park or a conservation area in the future. The overwhelming majority (93.8 %) answered yes. This is a clear sign of the acceptance of nature conservation by the Malaysian urban population. Even if a part of those who answered yes were sceptics and would only like to visit a conservation area in order to confirm their reservations (which we think is not the case), the high number proves that most people are not indifferent about conservation issues. However, there are still a

---

308 $\chi^2 = 4.1 \geq 3.841$ at 5 % (df of 1).
309 $\chi^2 = 7.1 \geq 6.653$ at 1 % (df of 1).
310 Figure 37 on page 129 shows conservation areas that were visited by the respondents.

small number of respondents (5 %) who would not like to visit a conservation area. The most important reason is a dislike or fear of trees and the jungle.

Figure 37: Location of Malaysian national parks and visits by the respondents

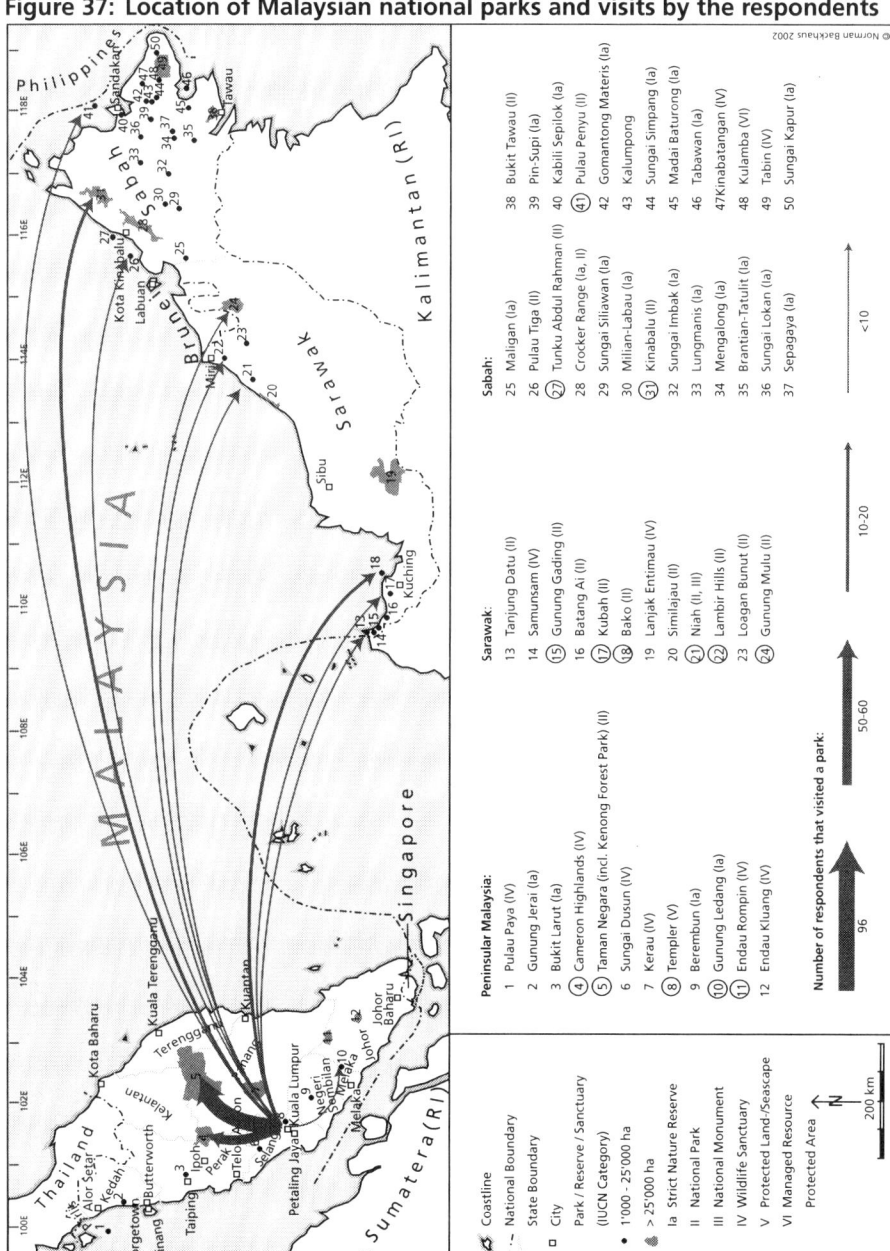

Source: own draft; data: IUCN 1994; UNEP, W.C.M.C. 1992.

Fear of animals is only mentioned once[311], (specifically, a dislike of mosquitoes), which is surprising as Malaysian conservation areas harbour many species that could be dangerous for people. Standing beneath the canopy of an ancient dipterocarpacean forest can indeed intimidate the visitor, which makes the answer more comprehensible to the western European observer, who probably would not expect such an answer in his/her own society. However, jungles have also long been regarded as an obstacle for – rural or industrial – development, and only a small part of the population – e.g. the Orang Asli of the Peninsula – actually used its resources extensively. Other reasons why people do not wish to visit a national park are that they do not have the time or the money, that they prefer the city, that the parks are too far away, or that one should not disturb the unique ecosystem. Three quarters of those who would not like to visit a park have not ever been to a park.[312] Therefore, their reluctance cannot come from bad experiences. However, the result could also be a consequence of the bad image of national parks. If that is the case, it is important to change that image in the near future.

The respondents who would like to visit a park are asked what they would expect of such a visit (see figure 38 on page 130). Since more than half of all the respondents have already been to a park, the expectations stated are probably close to what people actually can expect when visiting a conservation area.

Figure 38: Expectations about a future visit to a conservation area

Category	Percentage[a]
Activities, camping, hiking	42.2
Relax, holiday, getaway, enjoy	22.3
Beauty, contemplation	20.3
See plants, animals, Orang Asli[b]	12.3
Barbecue, be together with friends	2.9

a. Many respondents give more than one answer. The percentage refers to all the given answers, which therefore with 528 answers exceeds the number of respondents of 500.
b. Orang Asli (Malay: "original people", that can be translated with indigenous people) were mentioned only once, together with plants and animals (!), which is why they are in the same category.
Source: own survey and draft

The table shows that plants or animals are not the main things people expect to see and/or do. They are more interested in enjoying themselves and being active, which is not what most western tourists come to Malaysian national parks for. They are more interested in seeing the flora and fauna[313]. Since Malaysian vis-

---

311 The answers do not show a bias towards a certain age group or sex.
312 $\chi^2 = 14 \geq 6.653$ at 1 % (df of 1).

itors emphasise enjoyment and activity when they visit a conservation area, this could be a problem for park management, because although they encourage recreation, the parks are not designed to function as picnic areas, etc.

4.2 Most visited parks and recreation areas

Of all respondents, 60 % have visited a national park (or what they thought to be a national park). When they are asked which national parks they have visited, they mention up to five different parks each, with a range of over sixty parks. Although Malaysia has more than fifty national parks (of the IUCN categories I to VI) and many more state parks, only 46 % of the mentioned parks are actually conservation areas (see figure 40 on page 132). Many respondents mention destinations of recreation which they think that they were national or state parks (54 %; see figure 39 on page 131[314]).

Figure 39: Most favoured recreation areas (excl. national parks)

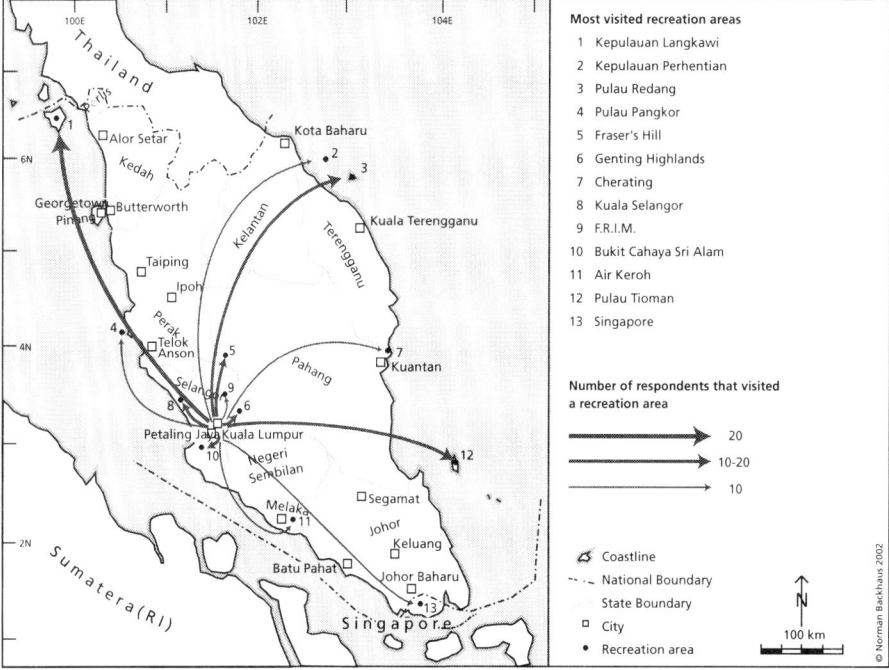

Source: own draft

---

313 An analysis of travel-books (Lutterjohann, M., Homann, E., Homann, K. & Kuster, R. 1998; Rowthorn, C., Andrew, D., Hellander, P. & Lindenmayer, C. 1999) shows that national parks are advertised with their abundance of species and great biodiversity which is a sign that western tourists actually are attracted to areas with these attributes.
314 The respondents only mention recreation areas on the peninsula.

Figure 40: Favoured parks (conservation and recreation; ranked by number of visits)

Area/park	Kind	State	No. of visits[a]	Percentage
Taman Negara	National park	Pahang, Terengganu, Kelantan	96	19.75
Cameron Highlands	National park	Pahang	54	11.11
Kepulauan Langkawi	Recreation area	Kedah	25	5.14
Pulau Tioman	Wildlife reserve	Pahang	18	3.70
Pulau Redang	Recreation area	Terengganu	17	3.50
Bako	National park	Sarawak	16	3.29
Kinabalu	National park	Sabah	15	3.09
Bukit Cahaya Sri Alam	Recreation area	Selangor	13	2.67
Genting Highlands	Recreation area	Pahang	12	2.47
Fraser's Hill	Wildlife Sanctuary	Pahang	12	2.47
Templer	National park	Selangor	12	2.47
Kuala Selangor	Nature park	Selangor	12	2.47
Niah	National park	Sarawak	12	2.47
Gunung Ledang	National park	Johor	10	2.06
Pulau Pangkor	Recreation area	Perak	9	1.85
FRIM	Research station	Selangor	9	1.85
Gunung Mulu	National park	Sarawak	8	1.65
Air Keroh	Recreation area	Melaka	6	1.23
Kepulauan Perhentian	Marine park	Terengganu	5	1.03
Cherating	Recreation area	Pahang	5	1.03
Tunku Abdul Rahman	National park	Sabah	5	1.03
Singapore	Recreation area	Singapore	5	1.03

a. Only areas with 5 or more visits were included (= 77 % of all mentioned areas).
Source: own survey and draft.

4.3 Most favoured Malaysian national parks

Fewer than half of the mentioned "nature destinations" are in fact national parks. Figure 41 on page 133 shows the national parks which were visited by the respondents. The figure shows that only the two most visited conservation areas are on Peninsular Malaysia, followed by parks from Sarawak and Sabah which are much further away from Kuala Lumpur.

In order to reach the parks in Sarawak and Sabah, people have to fly; there is no regular ship service between the Peninsula and Borneo[315]. This is rather remarkable, because the air fares are not cheap. However, accessibility is not the only determinant of a respondent's decision to visit a park. Accessibility can also not simply be measured by distance. In the following sections we will take a closer look on the visited parks.

Figure 41: Visited Malaysian national parks (by number of visiting respondents)

Name of the park	State(s)	No. of respondents	No. of visitors 1999[a]	Malaysian visitors (%)[a]
Taman Negara	Pahang, Terengganu, Kelantan	96	57,255	49.6
Cameron Highlands	Pahang	54	n.a.	n.a.
Bako	Sarawak	16	18,520	24.5
Gunung Kinabalu	Sabah	15	190,806	80.1
Niah	Sarawak	12	16,770	33.1
Templer	Selangor	12	n.a.	n.a.
Gunung Ledang	Johor	10	n.a.	n.a.
Gunung Mulu	Sarawak	8	12,230	31.2
Tunku Abdul Rahman	Sabah	5	174,027	34.1
Endau Rompin	Johor	2	n.a.	n.a.
Gunung Gading	Sarawak	1	13,675	70.4
Kubah	Sarawak	1	9,892	88.8
Lambir Hills	Sarawak	1	22,487	85.6
Pulau Penyu	Sabah	1	8,732	4.4

a. Sources: Department of Forestry of Sarawak 2000; Department of Forestry Peninsular Malaysia 2000; Sabah Parks 2000.
Source: own survey and draft.

The most attractive parks, as well as those most visited by the respondents, can be grouped according to their visitor structure (see figure 42 on page 134). Some parks are visited by more Malaysians than foreigners and others more by foreigners. This shows that the parks are not equally attractive to both groups. Parks that are easily accessible and where the visitors can relax with friends or family, where they can have a picnic or have fun in ponds under waterfalls, are more often visited by Malaysians. Matang Wildlife Centre is an interesting ex-

---

315 There used to be a ferry between the east coast and Sarawak, but due to piracy in the South China Sea the service was stopped and the ferry was converted into a floating restaurant.

ample. Here, animals raised in captivity are rehabilitated to the forest. Although, the main attraction (and the main purpose) of the centre seems to be the animals, most domestic visitors come there because it is near to Kuching and because it is a nice area to have a picnic and relax, whereas the few foreigners come exclusively to see the animals.[316] 90 % of all visitors to Kubah – situated adjacent to Matang – are domestic tourists. This site offers facilities for groups of visitors and on most week ends the chalets are fully booked. Near the entrance to Kubah is the Matang Family Park, an enclosure where people can picnic, barbecue and bathe in the river that flows from the national park. There is an entrance fee (RM 3), which makes it a mixture of conservation area and theme park. The family park is almost never visited by foreigners.[317]

Figure 42: Visited national parks and percentage of domestic visitors

Park	Region	1999	1990-99	Major attractions	Leisure[a]	Access
Matang	Sarawak	97	98	Animals, waterfalls	++	++
Kubah	Sarawak	89	98	Landscape	+(+[b])	++
Lambir Hills	Sarawak	86	81	Ponds, Waterfalls	++	+
Gunung Kinabalu	Sabah	80	89	Mount Kinabalu	++	+
Gunung Gading	Sarawak	70	93	Rafflesia	+	+
Niah	Sarawak	67	63	Cave, archeological site	+	+
Cameron Highlands[c]	Peninsula	≥50	≥50	Freshness, flowers, tea plantations	++	++
Templer[b]	Peninsula	≥50	≥50	Limestone formations, waterfall	++	++
Taman Negara	Peninsula	50	50	Animals, canopy walkway	+	–
Tunku Abdul Rahman	Sabah	34	59	Reefs	+	+
Gunung Mulu	Sarawak	31	45	Caves, Bats	–	– –
Bako	Sarawak	25	48	Proboscis monkey, limestone	+	+
Pulau Penyu	Sabah	4	12	Turtles	+	– –

a. Such as the possibility to have a picnic, play games, go fishing, river rafting etc.
b. Including the Matang Family Park.
c. For the Cameron Highlands and Templer Park were no visitor numbers available. Nevertheless, we can assume that these destinations are visited by more domestic tourists because of their vicinity to cities and specific attractions.

Source: own draft; data: Department of Forestry Peninsular Malaysia 2000; Sabah Parks 2000; Department of Forestry of Sarawak 2000.

---

316 See Saifuddin, B.S. 2001.
317 When I wanted to visit Matang Familiy Park, I was first asked to the "real" park's entrance.

If we compare the average number of domestic visitors of the last decade with the numbers of 1999, we can see that the percentage of domestic visitors has, in general, decreased. Not shown in the table is that there was a steady increase of visitors to Malaysian national parks. The National Ecotourism Plan[318] predicts as many foreign as domestic ecotourists (or nature lovers); in the future, and generally an increase in the number of tourists. The fact that there is a difference within the visitor structure needs to be recognized by the respective park managements, if they want to avoid discrimination and/or conflicts.

4.4 Evaluation of visited parks

The respondents are asked to evaluate their visits to the park they liked best. Of the 273 respondents who have visited a park, 96 (35 %) have only visited that specific park, 111 (41 %) have also visited a second park, 47 (17 %) a third, 16 (6 %) a fourth and 3 (1 %) a fifth. In order to establish how the respondents evaluate the conservation areas, they are asked a number of questions. These include the length of their stay, whether they visited the area on a weekend or not, whether it was their first visit (and if not, how many times they have been there), by how many people they were accompanied, whether it was an organised trip or if they used a private vehicle. They are also asked what they remember most vividly, what they like most, what was not so good, why they went there in the first place, whether they would like to go there again, and whether they think that the area was overcrowded or not.

4.4.1 Length of stay

Taken all respondents who have been to a park together, a quarter (23.2 %) went on day trips, another quarter (25.8 %) spent two days and over half of them (51 %) spent three or more days. For many Malaysians it is not easy to stay overnight in a park, because until recently they worked six days a week. Therefore, they either had to take a day off or to drive to a park in the evening after work. However the numbers show that most of the respondents could afford to stay two or more days, which is also necessary for some parks.

We can group the most often visited parks according to the number of times each is mentioned in each category. The result is that most parks were visited for three or more days, but parks were mainly visited for only two days or for a day trip (see figure 43 on page 136).

In the category "mostly day trips" we find parks and recreation areas that are easily accessible either from the Kuala Lumpur area (i.e. Bukit Cahaya Sri Alam, F.R.I.M., Genting Highlands, and Templer) *or* from a city (i.e. Tunku Abdul

---

318 WWF Malaysia 1996. p. 62.

Rahman from Kota Kinabalu, Niah from Miri and Gunung Ledang from Johor Baharu). They are relatively small and can easily be seen in one day. The relative smallness of some of these areas can be interpreted as a sign that smaller areas have importance in the opinions of the respondents. Even if such an area offers a wide range of attractions that could "last" for more than one day, people do not regard it as worthwhile spending more time. For example, the *F.R.I.M.* (Forestry Research Institute of Malaysia) is basically a research station with a botanical garden (mostly dipterocarpaceae), and an area of primary and secondary rainforest where people can hike on well marked paths. Bukit Cahaya Sri Alam is a small park south of Shah Alam near Kuala Lumpur, that was specifically designed for day trippers and which is accessible by private car in less than an hour from the capital. The Genting Highlands is most often visited by people who want to play in the casinos that are located in the hill station. Besides that, it is also possible to hike there.

Figure 43: Categorisation of parks and recreation areas: length of stay[319]

Mostly day trips	Mostly two days	Mostly more than two days
Bukit Cahaya Sri Alam	Cameron Highlands	Air Keroh
F.R.I.M.	Cherating	Bako
Genting Highlands	Kuala Selangor	Gunung Mulu
Gunung Ledang	Pulau Redang[a]	Kepulauan Langkawi
Niah[a]	Singapore	Kepulauan Perhentian
Templer		Kinabalu
Tunku Abdul Rahman[a]		Niah[a]
		Pulau Pangkor
		Pulau Redang[a]
		Pulau Tioman
		Taman Negara
		Tunku Abdul Rahman[a]

a. Parks or recreation areas with just 50 % in two categories are listed in both categories.
Source: own survey

In the category "mostly two days", we find destinations that are a bit further away from Kuala Lumpur or other centres. The drive up to Cameron Highlands takes a while and many people like to stay one night in the coolness of the

---

319 Only parks that were visited 5 or more times were considered, and 'mostly' means that 50 % or more respondents visited the respective park in a day trip, for two days or three days or more respectively.

mountains. The area is quite extensive with the possibility of hiking and seeing attractions like tea plantations or orchid gardens. In the future when the Cameron Highlands are linked to the Genting Highlands with a highway, there will be probably more people who stay for shorter periods.

Cherating is basically a tourist area near Kuantan on the east coast of the Peninsula, which used to be famous for the turtles which came ashore to lay their eggs. However, due to poaching, fewer and fewer turtles come to its beaches. Cherating's beaches are themselves a reason to come there and spend a day or two in a guest house.

Kuala Selangor is a nature reserve at the mouth of the Selangor River, around 60 kilometres from Kuala Lumpur. Its major attraction are the fireflies (Malay: *kelip-kelip*) that inhabit the *Berembang* trees at the river. At night billions of fireflies glow and illuminate the trees – a sight rare in the world and unique to Malaysia in this concentration. Many tourists watch them in electrically powered boats after dusk. Besides the fireflies, Kuala Selangor[320] contains a mangrove swamp and is good for bird watching. The old town of Kuala Selangor is also a tourist attraction where people often stay overnight, which explains why the majority of the respondents spent two days in Kuala Selangor in spite of its vicinity to Kuala Lumpur.

Pulau Redang is a small island off the coast of Terengganu that can be reached by boat from Merang near Kuala Terengganu. The island is part of a marine park and offers beautiful coral reefs for snorkelling. People stay there at least one night, but many stay there longer. Some respondents visited a recrea-

---

[320] The nature reserve is threatened by the construction of a dam according to Malaysian NGOs concerned with the environment such as the Malaysian Nature Society (MNS) (Malaysian Nature Society 2000a; Malaysian Nature Society 2000b; Magick River, A. 2002). Selangor State and the Wilayah Persekutan Kuala Lumpur fear a fresh water shortage during the next years which can be prevented with the construction of a dam in the Selangor river. According to the Consumer Association of Penang (CAP) the dam leaves not enough water in order to sustain the ecosystem of the nature reserve and floats extensive land including two Orang Asli settlements (Consumers' Association of Penang 1999). The proposed completion of the dam was scheduled for the end of 2002. However, geological surveys showed that the dam is situated near a fault line which makes it necessary to strengthen it. The high costs of its construction is also a source of critique, which is sometimes expressed in an ironical way (see the "Billionaire ad").

tion park in Singapore, which was probably during a short trip to the city state on the southern tip of the peninsula.

Most people stayed for three or more days in parks or recreation areas; the majority of visited areas are in the category "mostly three or more days". In *Taman Negara*, the park visited by most people, the overwhelming majority (83.6 %) spent three or more days. Although the accessibility from Kuala Lumpur is quite good, it takes some hours to reach the headquarters, especially if one goes by boat. Nowadays it is possible to go there by road too, which makes it easier for people with limited time. An increasing number of day trippers, however, could lead to an exceeding of the carrying capacity which already happened at peak times before the road was completed. The fact that Taman Negara is the biggest park in the country and its first, enhances its significance in the perception of the visitors. It seems to be that if people want to visit a national park, they have Taman Negara in mind. In fact, its very name (taman negara means national park) suggests that it is *the* national park in Malaysia.[321]

The *Langkawi islands* are too far away from Kuala Lumpur and the mainland for people to take day trips there. Three quarters of the respondents (77 %) spent three or more days there. Since there is an airport, it would even be possible to fly there in the morning and return in the evening.[322] But not many people who travel to a recreation area spend the money for a flight in order to just stay for a day.

With *Tioman Island* it is more or less the same, nobody goes there for a day trip, although many people spend only two days there. However, most respondents went there for three or more days. Although Tioman has a wildlife reserve, people are mostly attracted to its beaches.

Pulau Redang (mentioned above), figures in this category too, because with its beaches and coral reefs it invites people to stay more than a couple of days.

The *Perhentian islands*, just north of Redang, are also part of a marine park. The two islands, (Perhentian Kecil, Malay for "small", and Perhentian Besar, Malay for "big") were "discovered" by foreign individual travellers who were looking for beaches off the beaten track. Since then, the islands have developed into a growing tourist area[323] with a variety of accommodation. The coral reefs

---

321 It has its similarities in Switzerland where until now there is only one national park, which is also called *the* "Nationalpark".
322 Domestic flights also depart from Subang airport, the former international airport near the centre of Kuala Lumpur. The new Kuala Lumpur International Airport (KLIA) in Sepang that was opened 1998, is located 70 kilometres to the south of the city and only recently the railway line was opened which makes it now possible to reach the airport within half an hour, where before at least 90 minutes had to be budgeted for the transport.
323 For more information on tourism on the Perhentian islands see: Kamphues, M. 1998.

are now protected from extensive fishing, and access is limited. Since the islands can only be reached by ferry (from Kampung Kuala Besut) and their frequency is not as high as to Redang, people stay for a longer period on Perhentian.

Pangkor Island is situated off the west coast of Perak state and features similar infrastructure to Redang. It can be accessed quite conveniently by a short ferry ride from Lumut, which can be reached within approximately two hours from Kuala Lumpur, but there are also flights with small aircraft from Subang. It is mostly visited for its beaches and clear waters.

Air Keroh is a green belt around Melaka with a variety of attractions such as a zoo, fishing pond, golf course and crocodile farm. There are also resorts to stay overnight. Air Keroh is a place for extended family outings with many ways to spend some leisure time. The other destinations in this category are national parks in Sabah and Sarawak: *Kinabalu, Tunku Abdul Rahman, Mulu, Niah* and *Bako*.

Tunku Abdul Rahman and *Bako* are rarely visited for more than two days. However, even though they are rather small and easily accessible, people rarely spend more than one night there. The reason for the fairly high average stay could be found in the way the question is perceived by the respondents. They probably flew to Sabah or Sarawak in order to visit these parks, and transferred the duration of their stay in the respective states to the park they visited even though they only spent a day there. This could be an explanation for the surprising results for these smaller parks. For the bigger parks it is quite probable that visitors spent more than two days there.

4.4.2 Most recent visit

More than half of the park visits date back two years or more prior to the survey, a third took place the previous year, and an eighth took place the year of the survey.[324] 1998 was the year when Malaysia suffered most from the Asian currency crisis, when most people were careful not to spend too much money on holidays. Therefore, most visits probably occurred before the crisis. However, the Asian crisis could actually have been a reason for people to visit destinations within their own country rather than to travel abroad. Although neighbouring Thailand became cheaper for Malaysian tourists by 25 %, and Indonesia by 75 %, Malaysians are reluctant to visit these countries.[325] This could be because the Malaysian government encourages their citizens in times of crisis, to spend their holidays in Malaysia and contribute to the improvement of the economy.

---

324 The survey was conducted in spring 2000.
325 From 1997 to 1998 Malaysian tourism to Thailand decreased by over 12 % and it picked up only 1999 with an increase of almost 8 % (Tourism Authority of Thailand 2002).

4.4.3 Visit on weekends or on week days

Most parks (59.1 %), were visited on weekends, especially those easily accessible from the Kuala Lumpur area. These are also the areas that cater for weekenders and that feature attractions that can be seen within a day or two. The parks that were mainly (over 60 % of the respondents) not visited on weekends are the bigger parks – Taman Negara, Kinabalu and Mulu – which could also be accessed within a few hours, but that feature a great variety of attractions. It is not only this variety but also the size of the areas, the fact that they are each called a national park – and therefore have many visitors –, that can be the reason for people to take more time to visit them.

4.4.4 First visit or not?

Most respondents (56.6 %) have visited the respective park or recreation area for the first time, but almost half of them (43.4 %) have already been there at least once. This relatively high number indicates that these are the areas which they like most. With the exception of Bako, all the areas that have been visited more than once are (also) recreation areas – Cameron Highlands, Langkawi, Genting, Fraser's Hill, Templer[326] and Air Keroh – which people also visit for vacations.

The majority of those respondents who have already visited a park or recreation area have been there more than twice (57 %). More than a quarter (28.2 %) have visited the area twice before and only 14.8 % have been there only once. We cannot make a distinction between different characteristics of the areas which might explain these numbers. It seems that the respondents visit their favourite parks frequently and that they become attached to them.

4.4.5 Organisation of the trip

82.1 % were accompanied by three persons, when they visited the park or recreation area. A group of four seems to be the customary entity of participation when Malaysians travel to parks and recreation areas. Since the sample consists of mainly unmarried people it is not merely families that account for the high percentage, although the majority of couples have two children. Groups of five persons and more were formed only in 4 % of the cases, groups of three in 8.6 %, couples in 4 % and only two respondents went alone (to Taman Negara). This result corresponds with the fact that Malaysians visit their parks and recreation areas not primarily in order to see flora and fauna, but for activities such as hiking, camping or barbecuing (see figure 38 on page 130), which they

---

326 Templer is a national park in the IUCN category V/VIII that does not envisage a strict protection. Templer is known mainly as a recreation area. The Cameron Highlands comprise a wildlife reserve (category IV), but villages and tea plantations etc. are also a great attraction.

mostly enjoy in groups. It is also a sign of a less individualised society that not many people travel alone, which occurs much more in western countries.

Most respondents (71.9 %) went on their own to the respective areas; less than a third booked a package tour. Only the holiday resorts Tioman and Redang were often visited as part of package tours. Most parks can be easily accessed without help of a tour operator. Accommodation at Taman Negara has to be booked with the office of the "Taman Negara Resort" in Kuala Lumpur; so many people who want to stay in the park also book their transport to the park at the same time. This accounts for the comparatively high percentage of group travellers (41.8 %) to Taman Negara. Parks that are more difficult to reach by private means, such as Endau Rompin – which was not included in this evaluation, because it was visited by too few respondents – are therefore less frequented. Especially in times when people have to carefully look at how much they spend, they tend to organise things themselves instead of making use of the services of a tour operator.

Slightly more than half of the respondents (54 %) used a private car in order to get to the recreation or conservation area. The rest used public transportation or the vehicles of a tour operator. Cameron Highlands, Fraser's Hill, Templer, Kuala Selangor, Gunung Ledang and Cherating are mainly accessed by private car, because the roads to these destinations are good and it does not take long to get there from Kuala Lumpur. Langkawi and Pangkor were also mainly visited in private cars. Either the vehicles were left in the harbour area from where the ferry leaves, or they were taken on the ferry in order to be used on the islands. People also visited Bako and Niah with private cars, for all of the respondents who had visited these parks are from the Kuala Lumpur area. They either had access to a private car or perceived a hired taxi as a private vehicle.

4.4.6 Reasons for the visit

As reasons for the visit of a park, the respondents say that they went there to relax and enjoy themselves (34.7 %), to spend their holidays (17.5 %), be active (10.4 %) and see the nature (7.7 %). Some just went there to be with their families (7.7 %) or friends (5.4 %) or because the park or recreation area was near where family or friends lived (2.7 %). 5.1 % went there with their school or company.[327] To observe nature is therefore not the foremost reason for people to visit a park[328]. Only for Taman Negara, Bako and the visited recreation area in Singapore, did more than the average number of the respondents express this reason. Only Taman Negara, Bako and the recreation area in Singapore were

---

327 8.8 % had various other reasons.
328 This is consistent with other studies (e.g. Saifuddin, B.S. 2001).

visited by at least half of the respondents to observe nature. Most people visit parks and recreation areas because they want to enjoy themselves, spend leisure time or be active.

Figure 44: Parks and reasons for visiting them

See nature	Relax	Leisure	Be with family	Be with friends	Near family/ friends	Activity	With school/ company
≥ 10 %[a]	≥ 40 %	≥ 20 %	≥ 10 %	≥ 7 %	≥ 5 %	≥ 15 %	≥ 7 %
Taman Negara	Langkawi	Cameron Highlands	Taman Negara	Taman Negara	Langkawi	Kinabalu	Cameron Highlands
Bako	Tioman	Langkawi	Bako	Langkawi	Bako	Kuala Selangor	Bako
Singapore	Redang	Tioman	Fraser's	Bukit Cahaya	Singapore	Ledang	Bukit Cahaya
	Fraser's Hill	Redang	Templer	Pangkor		Air Keroh	F.R.I.M.
	Templer	Genting	Niah				Air Keroh
	Kuala Selangor	Kuala Selangor	Ledang				
	Ledang	Niah	Perhentian				
	Pangkor	Mulu					
	F.R.I.M.	Singapore					
	Mulu						
	Perhentian						

a. The percentages in this table rank above the actual average of the respondents' answers. Accordingly, the parks listed in each category of reasons for the visit are those standing out.
Source: own draft.

If we look at the parks that were visited for specific reasons (see figure 44 on page 142), we cannot say that the kind of park or recreation area solely determines the reason for its popularity. Parks which are not easily accessible, such as Mulu, are all visited for relaxation. Recreation areas in urban Singapore are visited in order to see nature. Social reasons (that people went with their families, friends, schools or companies) were mentioned as reasons for respondents' visits. This is another indication of the importance of sharing a group experience when visiting a park or recreation area.

4.4.7 Evaluation of the visit

The respondents are asked what comes to their mind first, when they think about their last visit to the park or recreation area, and what they like most.

Most (34.1 %) remember the flora and fauna, although that has not been the primary reason for their visit. More than a quarter (28.4 %) remember that it was beautiful and enjoyable, 6.8 % remember the peacefulness and 7.1 %, the clean environment. There are also negative memories: some found it annoying (4.7 %), tiresome (1.4 %) or hectic (1 %). Although not many have negative memories, it still surprises that negative answers occur at all, because the respondents were talking about their favourite parks. The memories are for the most part positive. Again there is no discernable pattern according to which some kind of parks or recreation areas invoke specific memories. It is therefore not the case that national parks are associated more with flora and fauna or clean environment than are recreation areas near agglomerations.

When people are asked what they like most about their most recent visit, natural attractions rank highest (35.7 %), before "fresh air and coolness" (21.2 %). 15.5 % like most that they saw special plants or animals, 7.4 % enjoyed the activities (e.g. rafting, swimming, hiking) most, and 5.7 % liked non-natural attractions (e.g. canopy walkways, picnic areas, casinos etc.) most. Natural attractions are not necessarily named first by people who have visited parks with an exceptional biodiversity. People who have visited Cherating, Perhentian and Redang mention attributes fitting this category, however this means that, while parks with an (advertised) high biodiversity may attract people with that fact, but that other destinations may feature similar characteristics in the eye of the visitor. From this we can conclude that people may enjoy a park more for attractions which are not necessarily advertised, or that they were not expecting at that specific park.

Clean and fresh air is important for people living in urban areas, especially when they are living in congested places where they suffer from pollution. However, people who do not like the place where they live do not necessarily mention cool and fresh air more than the others. Destinations that are located at higher altitudes (i.e. Genting Highlands, Fraser's Hill) have higher percentages of respondents who mention cool air as the characteristics they like most.

When asked what they do not like about their last visit, most (29.8 %) criticize the insufficient infrastructure. For established recreation areas – especially for the islands – it looks a little bit better. They have fewer restrictions, because in a conservation area, accommodations and other infrastructure are usually located outside the protected area. Moreover, on islands the protected areas are not the only attractions people come for. This means that income is not merely generated by the conservation area but by other features too, which allows a higher amount of investment into infrastructure.

Apart from insufficient infrastructure, people complain about rubbish, waste and vermin, or that the place was generally dirty (17.7 %). This applies for the more crowded areas such as Taman Negara, Langkawi, Redang, Templer, Ledang, Pangkor and Mulu. This could be a problem, especially for extensively visited national parks. Combined with the notion that the infrastructure is insufficient, it can damage the reputation of an area considerably.

Although the respondents list some negative aspects of their visits, the majority of them (57.8 %) do not think that the parks and recreation areas are overcrowded. However, a sizeable minority (42.2 %) think that there were still too many people there. The areas that are regarded as the most crowded are not the national parks – with the exception of Mulu (66,7 %), Ledang (60 %) and Templer[329] (100 %) –, but the holiday destinations of Cameron Highlands (64.7 %), Langkawi (53.8 %), Tioman (71.4 %), Genting (83.3 %) and Pangkor (66.7 %). Therefore, in the national parks, carrying capacities do not seem to be exceeded in the perception of the majority of the visitors. This either means that the park management is doing a good job in restricting people or that the limit of tolerance for overcrowding is rather high.

Nearly all respondents (95.6 %) would like to revisit the park they like best. Only single persons declare that they do not want to visit these areas again (Taman Negara, Cameron Highlands, Kinabalu and Pangkor). This shows that all of these parks and recreation areas tempt people to come more than once. Of course, this result does not mean that people really *will* go there again, because the wishes people have and what they actually do, can differ quite significantly from each other.

5 Opinions about nature protection and tourism

After the respondents are asked about specific parks, they were confronted with questions about tourism and nature protection in general. They are asked whether Malaysia should establish more national parks and why, and they are requested to comment on statements that are read to them, using an adapted Likert method (see "5.2.1: Methodology" on page 146).

5.1 Establishment of new conservation areas

The overwhelming majority of the respondents (91.8 %) favour the idea of Malaysia establishing more conservation areas in the future, a small minority (7 %) is against it and a few persons (1.2 %) do not answer. This result shows that na-

---

329 Templer Park has to be regarded as a (suburban) recreation area rather than a conservation area in the perception of the visitors.

ture conservation is regarded as something good that the government should support it. When people are asked why Malaysia should establish more parks, the answers could be grouped as follows (see figure 45 on page 145). Most of the respondents perceive beauty and natural balance as something worth protecting. Some people find that Malaysia does not have a sufficient number of parks and that there should be more. An important reason for adding more parks, would be to attract more tourists. By tourists people mainly mean foreign tourists. The respondents agree that tourism is an important economic (and maybe political) factor for the development of the country. This may be because they have been influenced by the promotion of "Visit Malaysia Year" in 1990 and 1994. Moreover, the Malaysian government urged Malaysians to spend their holidays in their own country during the Asian currency crisis, so they are aware that the country needs tourist dollars.

Figure 45: Reasons for the establishment of new conservation areas

Category	Percentage
Preservation of beauty and natural balance	26.5
Insufficient number of parks	18.8
Attraction of more tourists	18.2
Protection of the environment	11.4
Relaxation and ease of tension	11.2
Education and heritage for the next generations	9.0
Other reasons	4.9

Source: own survey and draft.

Most Malaysians are not as aware of environmental protection, as they are of the idea that nature is beautiful and that a natural balance should be protected. "Beauty" and "balance" are concepts which people can relate to emotionally, whereas "environment" is rather used in scientific and political sense. Therefore, people who have visited a conservation area – the majority of the respondents – and who liked the experience, tend to express their thoughts about conservation areas in a more emotional way. The category "Relaxation and ease of tension" refers to experiences the respondents had or think they will have. The importance of parks for education, and the preservation of parks for the next generations is a less important issue.

The few that were against the creation of more parks mostly argue with economic reasons (see figure 46 on page 146) or with the argument that Malaysia is already doing enough. They seem to be aware that the conservation of large areas costs the government a lot of money, even though entrance fees are collected. However, the fees are rather small and the visitors realise quickly that they are not enough to sustain a whole park[330]. The fact that economic reasons are brought forward shows also that conservation is regarded as a luxury.

Figure 46: Reasons against the establishment of new conservation areas

Category	Percentage
There are already enough parks	42.2
Slowing down of economic development	18.2
Costs: money and space	15.2
No resources for the maintenance	9.1
Other reasons	15.2

Source: own survey and draft.

5.2 Attitudes towards nature conservation

5.2.1 Methodology

In order to establish an aggregated opinion of the respondents regarding nature conservation and tourism, they are confronted with fifteen statements. To each statement they have to agree or disagree or neither agree nor disagree. This part of the questionnaire was designed according the principles of the Likert-method[331] and have two aims: first, to learn the urban Malaysian population's opinion about specific issues and second to establish groups of respondents according to their aggregated answers (taking the average value of all answers of each respondent). Applying the Likert-method, researchers use five, six or even seven categories in order to find out whether the interviewees "strongly agree" or only "slightly agree" etc. However, for the purpose of this study, we have simplified the mode of collecting opinions. Although the respondents live in an urban context in an industrializing country, they are probably not used to being interviewed and to making very detailed statements. Often, the interviewers have to translate the statements into a different language for which it is easier to only have three possible categories to answer instead of five or six. In addition, with only three categories we can achieve a better polarization of the opinions. The statements with which the respondents are confronted are listed in figure 47 on page 147.

---

330 The fees are in general around 1 to RM 5per person and day. In many parks there is an additional camera fee of RM 5 and where fishing is allowed the hobby angler has to pay up to RM 10 for a license. However, Sarawak plans to raise the entrance fees from RM 3 to RM 10. According to a study by Azahari, B.O. (2001) such a raise is not accepted by all visitors. Most foreigners do not mind it, but many Malaysian visitors find the raise to high.
331 Schumann, S. 2000. pp. 42-47.

When using the Likert-method we try to grasp the general attitude of individual persons about a specific topic which we cannot have access to by simply asking them directly. This latent variable should be expressed in the statements the respondents are confronted with. However, in the actual survey we have to use statements that can be answered easily by the respondents and that do not annoy them.

The latent variable behind the statements is the respondents' attitude towards nature conservation. The hypothesis is that people who are environmentally conscious "achieve" a low score of aggregated points in the various categories, whereas people who are less environmentally conscious or think that economic development is more important than nature protection, score higher.

When we first look at what the average of the respondents say to each statement, we get a heterogeneous result (see figure 48 on page 148). It shows that the respondents differentiate their opinions when reflecting on each statement. We can discern the following clusters of statements according to the scores they received:

I   low scores (1.0-1.6): 2, 7, 12, 13, 15
II lower medium scores (>1.6-2.0): 6, 8, 14
III higher medium scores (>2.0-2.4): 1, 5, 11
IV high scores (>2.4-3.0): 3, 4, 9, 10

Figure 47: Statements the respondents are confronted with

No.	Statement	Codification[a]
1	"Tourism is bad for nature"	1,2,3
2	"Economic development is more important than the protection of nature"	3,2,1
3	"Establishing and improving public tourist facilities is a waste of tax money"	1,2,3
4	"There should be more attractions like the Canopy Walkway in the trees or river rafting in national parks"	3,2,1
5	"Attractions like the Canopy Walkway in the trees or river rafting attract the wrong people to the parks"	1,2,3
6	"If people want to have fun, they should go to theme parks instead of to the jungle"	1,2,3
7	"Tourists come to Malaysia mainly because of its natural beauty"	1,2,3
8	"Ecotourism is a major economic factor for Malaysia"	1,2,3
9	"Places of nature tourism have mostly positive effects on local people living in or near the place"	3,2,1
10	"Tourism has negative effects on Malaysian Culture"	1,2,3
11	"The national parks are already too crowded with tourists"	1,2,3
12	"Malaysia should have much more conservation areas"	1,2,3

No.	Statement	Codification[a]
13	"Malaysians should rather visit their own national parks instead of travelling to other countries"	1,2,3
14	"Other governments do nothing but blame Malaysia for cutting down its rainforests"	1,2,3
15	"Five percent of the country's area is protected, this is enough"	3,2,1

a. Most questions are coded in the following order: "I agree"=1, "I neither agree nor disagree"=2, "I disagree"=3 (1,2,3). However, some have to be put in a reverse order because there meaning is opposing the latent meaning behind the statements, that have to be formulated positively in order to avoid misunderstandings (3,2,1).

Source: own survey and draft.

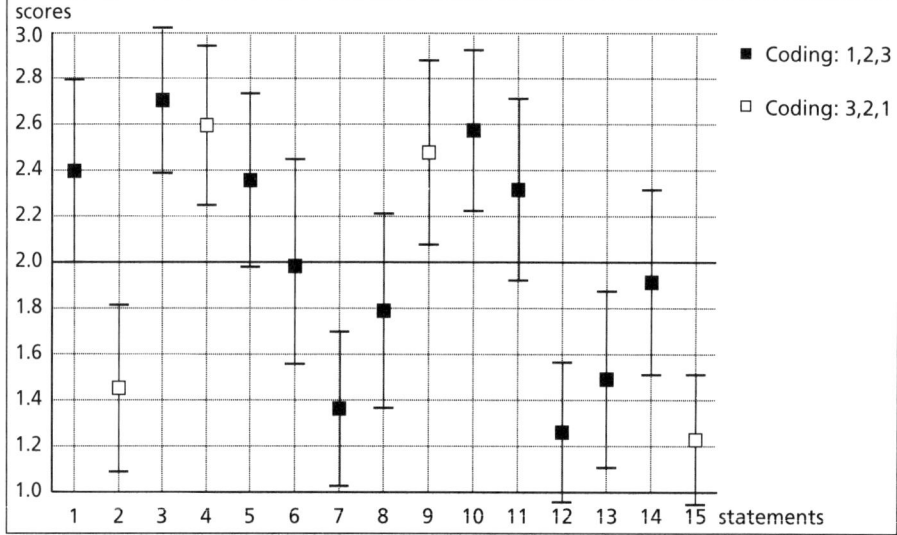

Figure 48: Average score to each statement (including standard deviation)[332]

Source: own survey and draft.

5.2.2 I: Low score appraisals

The statements with the lowest scores (group I) receive the strongest environmental support. Statement 2 *"Economic development is more important than the protection of nature"* is strongly denied (agreement with the statement received 3 points, disagreement, 1). The respondents either do not think that nature protection should be sacrificed for economic development, or they do not think that nature protection and economic development oppose or even exclude each other. However, economic development ranks very high on the agenda of the Malaysian government. In his "Vision 2020" (Malay: Wawasan 2020) former Prime Minister Mahathir wants Malaysia to achieve the status of a fully indus-

---

332 Statements with a reverse order of coding are highlighted with white diamonds (2, 4, 9, 15).

trialized country.[333] Therefore, respondents who favour "nature protection" over "economy" make a strong statement against national policy.

The high valuation of nature – or the natural environment of Malaysia – shows itself in the appraisal of statement 7 *"Tourists come to Malaysia mainly because of its natural beauty"*. Although some regions are advertised for their shopping facilities (i.e. Kuala Lumpur or Selangor), all destinations (or states) promote their natural beauty and even ecotourism or agritourism. The current slogan of Malaysia tourism, however, is "Malaysia – Truly Asia"[334] which does not directly advertise its natural beauty. Nevertheless, Malaysians regard their natural environment as an important attraction for foreign tourists. If we look at figure 4 on page 8, tourist arrivals grew to over 12 million in the year 2001, which is more than Thailand, that only had 10 million figure 4 on page 6, in that year, although Thailand generated more revenues with less tourists.

Statement 12 *"Malaysia should have many more conservation areas"*, is in line with statement 7. Most respondents think that Malaysia does not have enough conservation areas and that it is still possible to gazette new national parks. Since the respondents do not think that tourism is a threat to the environment (see "5.2.4: III: Higher medium score appraisals" on page 151) and that tourists mainly come to their country because of its natural resources, it makes sense to "provide" them with more reasons to visit Malaysia. However, we should not explain the respondents' approval solely with their economic awareness. It also has to be regarded as statement for the conservation of nature in general.

Statement 13 *"Malaysians should visit their own national parks rather than travelling to other countries"*, was less strongly accepted but is still in the group of low scores. It certainly mirrors the current policy of the government of keeping travel expenses of Malaysians within the country. Therefore, this statement refers more to economic and development issues than the former. It also reflects the notion that Malaysians should see and enjoy their own country's beauty before travelling to other countries.

The last statement in the group of low scores is number 15 *"Five percent of the country's area is protected, this is enough"*. In order to formulate it positively, the coding was reversed (3,2,1). The figure of 5 % is rounded up from the actual value of 4.5 %[335] or 4.75 %[336], according to different sources. In fact, the number has not yet been reached. However, it is a realistic figure and may reached within the next decade. The respondents do not think that five percent

---

[333] see: Crouch, H. 1996; Gomez, E.T. and Jomo, K.S. 1997; Watson Andaya, B. and Andaya, L.Y. 2001.
[334] Tourism Malaysia 2002.
[335] Badaruddin, M. 2002.
[336] UNEP, W.C.M.C. 1992.

of Malaysia[337] under protection is enough. Malaysia is not very densely populated[338] and still has comparatively vast areas covered by rainforests. Therefore, there is no great population pressure on these areas. However, rainforests are cut down for the export of wood and in order to convert areas to plantations, mostly of oil palms. We can assume that the majority of the respondents knows about these developments and is aware that at present only the conservation of and the "label" of national or state park or forest reserve can save these areas permanently – or at least for a long time.

5.2.3 II: Lower medium score appraisals

The statements that are grouped together in the category of "lower medium score" can be seen as environmentally "friendly" although not as strongly as the former group.

Statement 6 *"If people want to have fun, they should go to theme parks instead of to the jungle"* is the most ambivalent statement, with the highest standard deviation of means. The formulation of the statement probably does not invite the respondents to strongly disagree. This is because nature conservation is generally seen as rather serious business and because the association of "fun" with "theme parks" produces a certain image of people enjoying themselves in a theme park. This image does not fit very well with a conservation area. Nevertheless, if we recall the main reasons why the respondents visit national parks (see figure 44 on page 142) – relaxing, activity and leisure – we can see an affinity for "having fun". Therefore, many respondents probably neither agreed nor disagree with the statement, because they also like to have fun when visiting a park.

Statement 8 *"Ecotourism is a major economic factor for Malaysia"* more clearly belongs in this category. The reason that the affirmation is not stronger could be that the respondents think that ecotourism is good for the Malaysian economy (and ecology) but that it has not yet become an important factor for the Malaysian economy. The term ecotourism has become a buzzword[339] that is used for almost any activity that is conducted in nature. Therefore, the contribution of ecotourism – in a stricter sense – (see "5.1.3: Ecotourism and other types of tourism" on page 59) to the Malaysian economy is probably overestimated by the respondents.

Statement 14 *"Other governments do nothing but blame Malaysia for cutting down its rainforests"* was formulated in a rather straightforward manner. There-

---

337 5 % of 330.355 square kilometres are 16.517 square kilometres, which is about 40 % of the area of Switzerland, 45 % of Pahang, little less than the area of Johor or 13 % of Sarawak.
338 Malaysia has 69 inhabitants per square kilometer, Thailand 117, Indonesia 108, the Philippines 248, China 614, Singapore 6101, and Switzerland 173 (Fischer Weltalmanach 2001).
339 Hitchcock, M. & Jay, S. 1998.

fore, its score of below 2.0 can be interpreted as a slight assent. The fact that Malaysia has often been criticised from abroad for destroying its rainforests, is something that has not remain hidden from the public in Malaysia[340]. Moreover, former Prime Minister Mahathir has often stated that Malaysia is going its own way and that governments of industrialised countries that have already cut down their own forests should not meddle with development issues of Malaysia. Although, the respondents acknowledge the presence of foreign tourists and perceive them as an important contribution to the economic development of the country, they resent the criticism of other governments. Most of them probably oppose the excessive cutting down of rainforests for the exportation of wood – which is why they plead for more conservation areas – but they do not want to be told that by foreigners or foreign governments.

5.2.4 III: Higher medium score appraisals

The statements in the category of "higher medium scores" have (in a strict sense) a slight anti-environmental tendency. That does not mean that the appraisals can be termed anti-environmentalist, but that the respondents do not have a basic understanding of the relationship of nature conservation and tourism.

Statement 1, *"Tourism is bad for nature"* receives a score of 2.4 which means that the respondents disagree, but not vehemently. Most of them have visited conservation areas as tourists, and it would be a strong self-criticism if they would strongly agree with the statement. Moreover, many of them think that if their tax money is used for nature conservation, they have the right to visit national parks as tourists. IUCN-categories II, IV, and VI provide for recreation, which is why the parks are accessible in the first place. However, the statement is not entirely disapproved of, which shows that the respondents are aware of the delicate balance between tourism and nature conservation.

Statement 5, *"Attractions like the canopy walkway in the trees or river rafting attract the wrong people to the park"* is aimed at eliciting similar information as statement 1. The canopy walkways may be seen as a means of getting closer to the wonders of the rainforests. On the other hand when visited by many people it can be seen as an attraction that rather disturbs the environment which people want to experience at close range. Since most respondents who have visited a national park visited Taman Negara, which has the longest canopy walkway in the world, most of them have experienced and probably enjoyed it. Therefore, we cannot expect vehement criticism by the respondents regarding this feature. As previously discussed, important reasons for visits to national parks are the activ-

---

340 See for example INSAN, Institute for Social Analysis 1994.

ities and the group experiences which might very well include the canopy walkway or rafting down a vivid river.

Statement 11, *"The national parks are already too crowded with tourists"* sheds more light on the respondents' relationship with nature-tourism. The respondents do not strongly feel that the carrying capacity is exceeded in the national parks. They see it as their right to visit their parks and a restriction on visitors would infringe upon this right. In addition, ecotourism is seen as an important economic factor for Malaysia, and this should not be compromised by too many restrictions.

5.2.5 IV: High score appraisals

The appraisals of the statements in the "high score" category can be interpreted as disagreement with a fundamentalist view of nature conservation or as in favour of a tourist oriented conservation management. The statements in the "high score" category can be interpreted as being at variance with a concern with nature conservation, or as being in favour of conservation management aimed at the tourist trade. Two of the four statements (4 and 9) in this category have a reversed codification (3,2,1). The respondents do not share the opinion that "establishing and improving public tourist facilities is a waste of tax money".

Statement 3 – which receives the highest score of all 15 statements – refers to future developments, too. This statement also implies the question, are the respondents prepared to see their tax money invested in infrastructure projects in national parks? If we keep in mind that among the negative aspects the respondents criticise in parks and recreation areas, insufficient infrastructure figure highly, the appraisal of this statement is to be expected. It is also a sign that the improvement of infrastructure in parks should be taken seriously by the park management. Satisfied visitors of a park make a positive contribution to nature conservation and the improvement of infrastructure is an important tool to achieve that.

In line with statement 3 is statement 4 – albeit with reversed codification (3,2,1) – is that *"There should be more attractions like the canopy walkway in the trees or white water rafting in national parks"*. Most respondents strongly agreed with that opinion, because they perceive these features as an asset to a park and not as a liability. This result matches the results of a study done by Gianna Moscardo and Barbara Wood[341] in the Wet Tropics World Heritage Area in Queensland. The park management had installed a 'skyrail rainforest cableway', with which visitors are transported in gondolas above the canopy. They can stop at two stations along the route, take a walk and get some information. The ap-

---

341 Moscardo, G. & Woods, B. 1998.

proval of the skyrail was great, especially because it was combined with good information along the route. Therefore, the combination of attraction and interpretation can be beneficial for the visitors, the park management, and conservation. The visitors have a good and interesting experience, the park management can better focus and channel the flow of visitors, and if it is well done it allows a greater number of visitors to be led through a park without having a bad influence on the environment.

A different topic is touched on by statement 9 (codification: 3,2,1), *"Places of nature tourism have mostly positive effects on local people living in or near the place"*. Most respondents agree with the statement. They regard the existence of a park as an opportunity for local people, rather than a constraint, because it offers a range of new income possibilities. Moreover, the general attitude of urban Malaysians towards indigenous people or Orang Asli is a feeling of superiority, at least in terms of development. They regard them as in need of development, in terms of education, housing and work. Therefore, it is no surprise that they are not very critical about an issue that is controversial, especially when looking at cultural issues[342].

The respondents are not concerned that *"tourism has negative effects on Malaysian culture"*, statement 10. The reason could be that they find it difficult to define Malaysian culture because of its ethnic mix.

People living in urban areas have often changed their lifestyles considerably in recent years, due either to development or to a move from the countryside. Therefore, they either do not have a great problem with cultural change or they do not think that tourism can cause any serious cultural change.

5.2.6 Correlation of statements with the profile of the sample

After having analysed how all respondents react to the statements, we want to know how specific segments of respondents react. Is there a correlation between ethnic or religious background, age, gender and education? The interpretation of the data refers to "extreme" values and has to be seen in relation to the averages of the statements.

If we compare different *age groups* and their notions about the statements, we may assume that the youngest and the oldest are furthest apart from each other in their opinions. Regarding the graph (see figure 49 on page 154), that is true for statements 2, 4, 7 and 12. The younger respondents agree less that economic development is more important than the protection of nature, but they want more non-natural attractions in national parks as well as conservation ar-

---

342 See for example: Brosius, P.J. 2000; Eaton, P. 2000; Khaidir, A. 1994; Lee, B.T. & Bahrin, T.S. 1998; Sanggin, S.E., Noweg, G.T., Abdul, R.A. & Mersat, N.I. 2000.

eas, and they think that tourists come to Malaysia mainly because of its natural beauty[343]. If we look at statistically significant differences, statement 8[344] emerges. Younger people believe more strongly that ecotourism is a major economic factor for Malaysia, and older respondents think that tourism could have negative effects on Malaysian culture, whereas middle aged people do not agree with that statement. We conclude that young urban Malaysians see the potential of a combination of tourism and nature conservation, while the older generation are a bit less enthusiastic about that issue, and also more fearful of its negative effects.

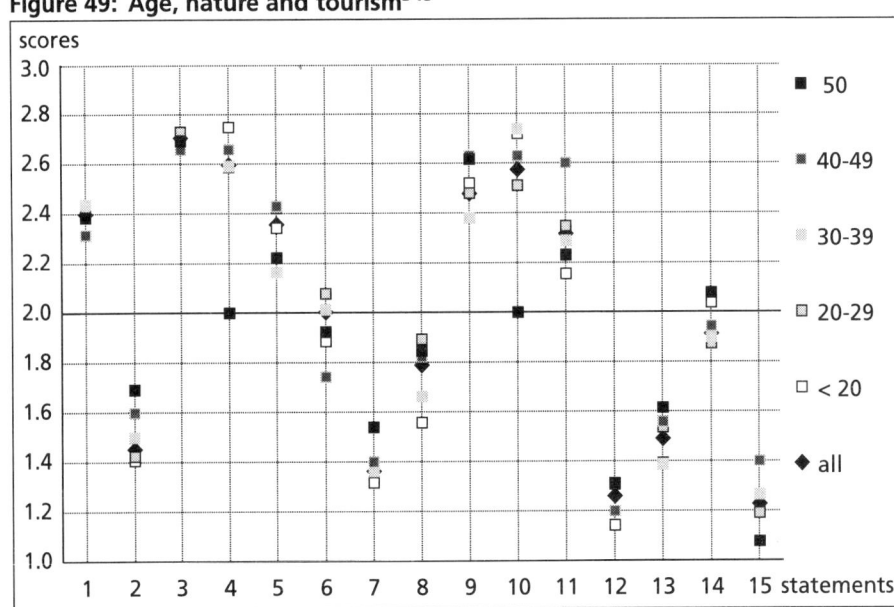

Figure 49: Age, nature and tourism[345]

Source: own survey and draft.

If we look at the *educational level* of the respondents, the hypothesis that people with lower education tend to have more extreme notions, holds true (see figure 50 on page 155). Their answers show a rather positive attitude toward environmentally fundamentalist statements. They believe less in establishing and improving the infrastructure of conservation areas, for they regard it as a waste

---

343 However, considering all categories the difference is not statistically significant.
344 $\chi^2 = 18.250 \geq 16.8$ at 1 % (df of 6).
345 In order to be able to apply a chi-square test the categories "≥ 50" and "40-49" had to be combined. Otherwise there would have been cells with values below 5, which is against the rules of the test. For illustrative purposes the graph was kept in the more differentiated version.

of tax money[346]. They rather think that non-natural attractions attract the wrong people to a park and that those people should go to theme parks[347]. For them, tourists come to Malaysia for its natural beauty, and ecotourism is a major economic factor for Malaysia[348]. They think tourism has negative effects on Malaysian culture[349] and that the national parks are already too crowded[350]. Furthermore, they think that Malaysians should visit their own parks, rather than go abroad. Respondents with university education show a less clear picture than others, although they often oppose the opinions of the ones with lower educations. They especially do not think that non-natural attractions attract the wrong people, and that those people should visit theme parks (see footnote 347 on page 155). They have more doubts about the statement that ecotourism is a major factor for the Malaysian economy (see footnote 348 on page 155). Regarding the other statements, they score very close to the average of all respondents.

Figure 50: Education, nature and tourism

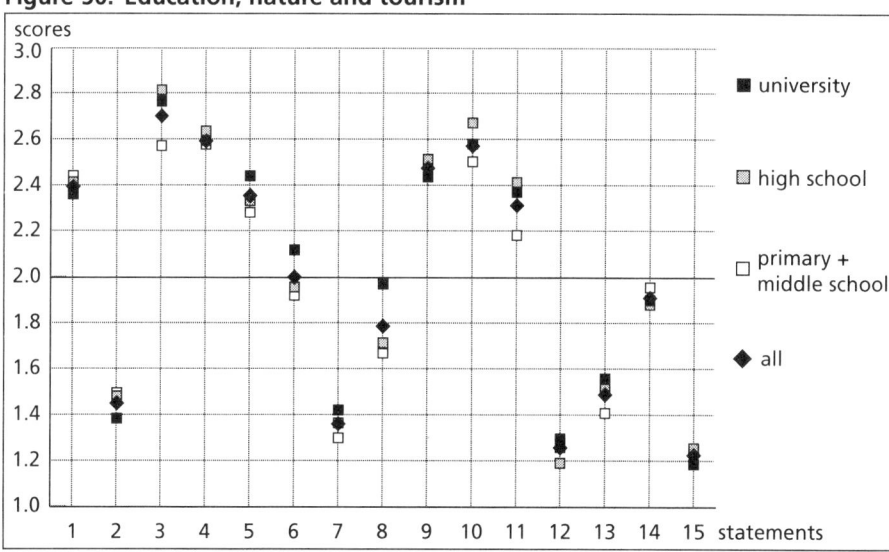

Source: own survey and draft.

Ethnic background – like religion – does not give a clear picture (see figure 52 on page 158) of mental attitude toward nature and tourism[351]. The Malays disagree most with the statement that tourism is bad for nature, and with the notion

---

346 $\chi^2 = 25.283 \geq 18.5$ at 0.1 % (df of 4).
347 $\chi^2 = 8.988 \geq 7.78$ at 10 % (df of 4).
348 $\chi^2 = 12.465 \geq 9.49$ at 5 % (df of 4).
349 $\chi^2 = 8.118 \geq 7.78$ at 10 % (df of 4).
350 $\chi^2 = 15.746 \geq 13.3$ at 1 % (df of 4).

that economic development is more important than the protection of nature. They favour the idea of having more non-natural attractions in the parks and they find it too crowded in the parks. They want to have more conservation areas and think that their fellow countrymen should visit their own parks instead of going abroad. Indians agree slightly more with the statement that non-natural attractions attract the wrong people, but disagree more with the statement that fun seeking people should go elsewhere. They are the least likely to think that foreigners come to Malaysia mainly for its natural attractions. They think that 5 % of the country's area under protection is enough.

Figure 51: Ethnicity, nature and tourism

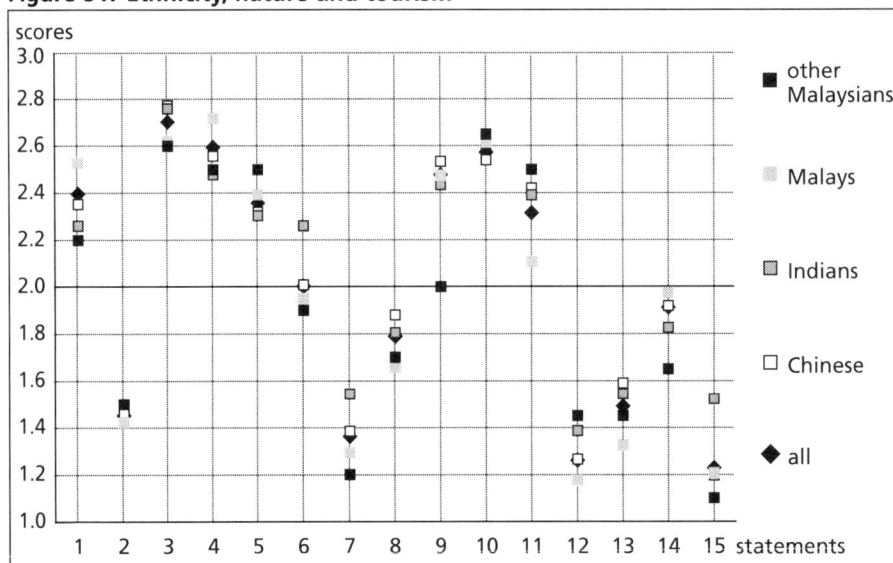

Source: own survey and draft.

The Chinese – as the majority of the respondents – scored nearest to the average of the sample. They only disagreed most with the statements that ecotourism is a major economic factor for Malaysia and that Malaysians should visit their own national parks. They think that local people can benefit from nature conservation and do not think that tourism has negative effects on Malaysian culture. Other Malaysians think that tourism is bad for nature, but disagree with that non-natural attractions attract the wrong people to conservation areas. Consequently, they would prefer that these people visit theme parks. They agree most with the statement that tourists mainly come to see the nature of Malaysia and

---

351 As with religion it was not possible to conduct a proper chi-square test (see footnote 352 on page 157).

disagree that local people benefit from nature conservation. The reason for this could be that among this category are Bumiputera from Sarawak who are familiar with the problem of land rights of indigenous peoples, who are often threatened not only by conservation projects but by logging activities. In terms of cultural change, they do not think that tourism is a relevant factor. In contrast to the Malays, they do not think that national parks are already too crowded, and are less likely to think that Malaysia should have more national parks. However, they strongly disagree with the statement that 5 % of the country's area under protection is enough. They agree that Malaysia is often blamed by other countries for cutting down its rainforests.

Regarding the category *religion* (see figure 52 on page 158) we cannot see a clear pattern[352], but we can discern some distinctions. Muslims, more than those of other faiths agreed that establishing and improving tourist facilities is a waste of tax money. They agree more that people who want to have fun should not go to national parks, as well as that national parks are already too crowded. They think that Malaysians should visit their own parks instead of going to other countries. The Christians disagree more with statement 1 "Tourism is bad for nature" than others, they agree strongly that ecotourism is a major economic factor for Malaysia, and do not think that Malaysian national parks are already too crowded. Hindus would like to have more attractions in the parks. Although they also tend to think that these things may attract the wrong people, they do not think that these people should go instead to theme parks. They think least that foreigners mainly come to Malaysia because of its natural beauty, but have slightly more concerns about their influence on Malaysian culture. They are also least in favour of the establishment of new national parks and think that 5 % of protected area is enough.

    Buddhists and Taoists strongly disagree that the establishment and improving of public tourist facilities is a waste of tax money, and they would not like to have more non-natural attractions in the parks. They disagree most that ecotourism is a major economic factor for Malaysia, but they think that local people can benefit from nature tourism. Like the Christians, they do not fear that tourism has a negative effect on Malaysian culture, and they do not share the impression that other governments accuse Malaysia of cutting down its rainforests. Among the category of "other", are mostly people who are self-declared atheists or "free thinkers" and a very few who follow "local" religions. The "others"

---

352 With that many categories it was not possible to follow through a proper chi-square test, because there were frequently cells with values below 5. And it was not possible to combine any more two categories (Buddhists and Taoists have already been merged into one category). However, the numbers of the "faulty" chi-square test still show tendencies which also can be seen in the graph.

think that tourism is bad for nature, but they do not feel that non-natural attractions attract the wrong people, and they do not think that national parks are too crowded. Finally, they are more likely than others to think that Malaysia should have more national parks.

Figure 52: Religion, nature and tourism

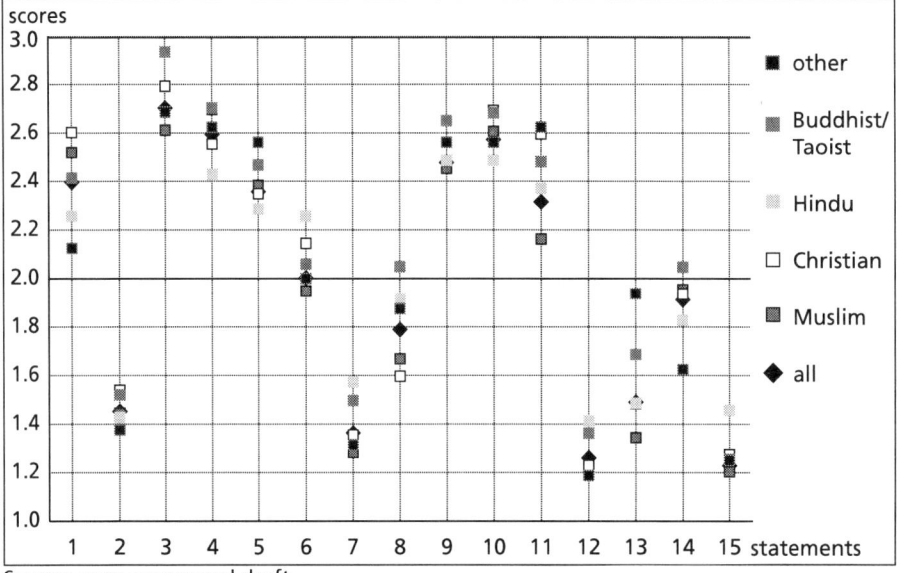

Source: own survey and draft.

If we compare how *women* and *men* answer to the statements (see figure 53 on page 159) we can see that the scores do not differ much from each other (and from the mean of all respondents). The chi-square test shows a functional correlation in statement 5[353] and 11[354]; the values for the other statements are lower[355]. Women disagree more with the statement that attractions like the canopy walkway attract the wrong people and they think less that national parks are already too crowded. Both statements show that women are more tolerant than men in general, are even more tolerant toward people who come to a park mostly because of its non-natural attractions. An explanation of this could be that Malaysian women – who mostly live in a traditional family model – are more

---

353 χ^2 = 5.489 ≥ 4.61 at 10 % (df of 2).
354 χ^2 = 6.050 ≥ 5.99 at 5 % (df of 2).
355 Looking at the graph (see figure 53 on page 159), statement 6 seems to depict a more significant correlation than statements 5 and 11. However, we have to bear in mind that the scores are an aggregation of the answers "I agree", "I disagree" and "I neither agree nor disagree". Statement 6 consists of more neutral answers and therefore the chi-square test yields only a value of 3.094 which is just short of significant.

occupied with children than men are, and that for children non-natural attractions are more important than for adults. This explanation is more plausible than the assumption that women are less environmentally concerned than men.

Figure 53: Gender, nature and tourism

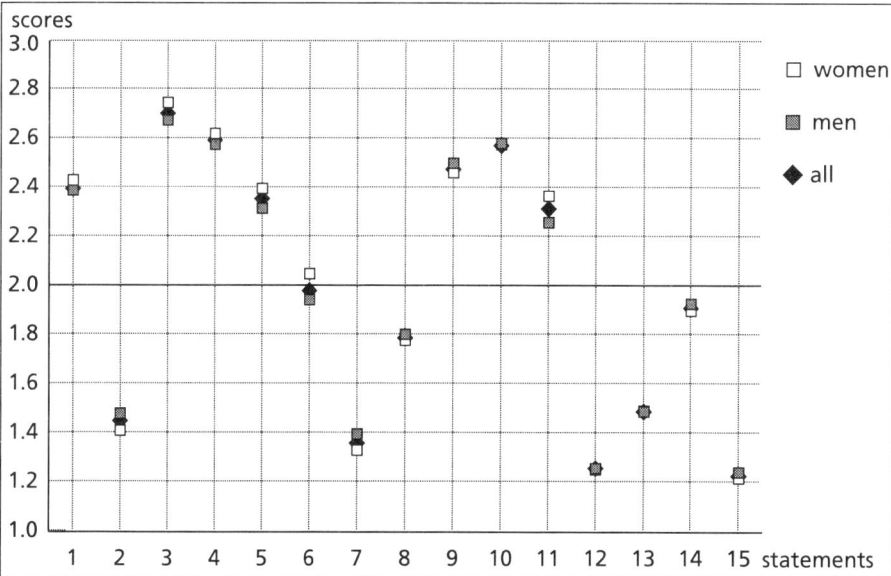

Source: own survey and draft

5.2.7 Aggregated individual scores

We have already looked at the aggregated opinion of the respondents to our fifteen statements. In the following we want to aggregate the opinions of each respondent and make a longitudinal section where before we made a cross section through the sample. The aim of this procedure is to see whether we can identify specific groups of respondents. In order to achieve this, the statements have to be coded in a way that allows an inference to the latent meaning behind the statements – the respondents' mental attitudes towards nature conservation and tourism. Therefore, some statements are coded in reverse order (3,2,1), as we have seen above (see figure 47 on page 147). The average mean score of all respondents is 1.997, which is very close to the neutral value of 2. This result suggests that there is no bias toward a more "environmentalist" or a more "liberal" attitude towards nature conservation and tourism in general.

If we look at figure 54 on page 161 we can see the aggregated values of each respondent sorted in ascending order. The dots describe a nearly logistic curve, with the proportion of values around the middle value of 2 suggesting a normal distribution[356]. If we examine the outlines, we can see that there are more in the

lower range of scores. Obviously there are a few rather vehement environmentalists among the respondents, whereas the majority is more moderate in their opinions. If we count the values according to the categories of scores, we get the following result:
- Low scores (1.0-1.6): 24 respondents
- Lower medium scores (>1.6-2.0): 178 respondents
- Medium high scores (>2.0-2.4): 256 respondents
- High scores (>2.4-3.0): 11 respondents

Although the mean score is below 2, there are only 202 respondents in the two categories with lower scores, whereas there are 267 in the categories of higher scores. This shows that the opinions of the former are more distinct compared with the latter. The median of the sample is between 2.0 and 2.1 and therefore slightly above the mean of 1.997 (see figure 54 on page 161).

In the following, we shall analyse whether the individual aggregated scores show differences between different groups of respondents. Figure 55 on page 163 gives an overview of the scores according to age, education, occupation, ethnicity, religion, family and marital status and gender. The scale is spread out in order to make the (small) differences more easily legible. According to an ANOVA comparison of means[357] only the categories "education" and "occupation" show significant differences between specific groups. There are also trends to be seen in other categories, even though they are not statistically significant.

Regarding *age groups*, the oldest and the youngest are furthest apart. The respondents above fifty have the lowest scores and therefore have a more eco-friendly attitude, whereas those below twenty tend to have a more liberal attitude. The other age segments have scores nearer to the average.

It is not easy to explain the results in the category *education*, although they show significant differences. The more liberal ideas of persons with university degrees contrast with those with high school diplomas, whereas those with the shortest duration of school attendance are in the middle range. It could be that university students (a substantial part of the sample) are financially more challenged and therefore tend to have more economically concerned attitudes toward nature conservation. Or it could be that high school graduates had a more ecologically concerned education, whereas those who only went to middle school or less did not. If we support this interpretation we have to conclude that in university students learn to be more economically minded. There is probably not just one factor responsible for the result, but a mixture of several factors.

---

356 According to the Kolmogorov-Smirnov-Test the sample significantly (1.662 ≥ 1.645 at 10 %) follows a normal distribution.
357 Wittenberg, R. and Cramer, H. 2000. pp. 209-213.

Figure 54: Scores of aggregated answers about nature conservation

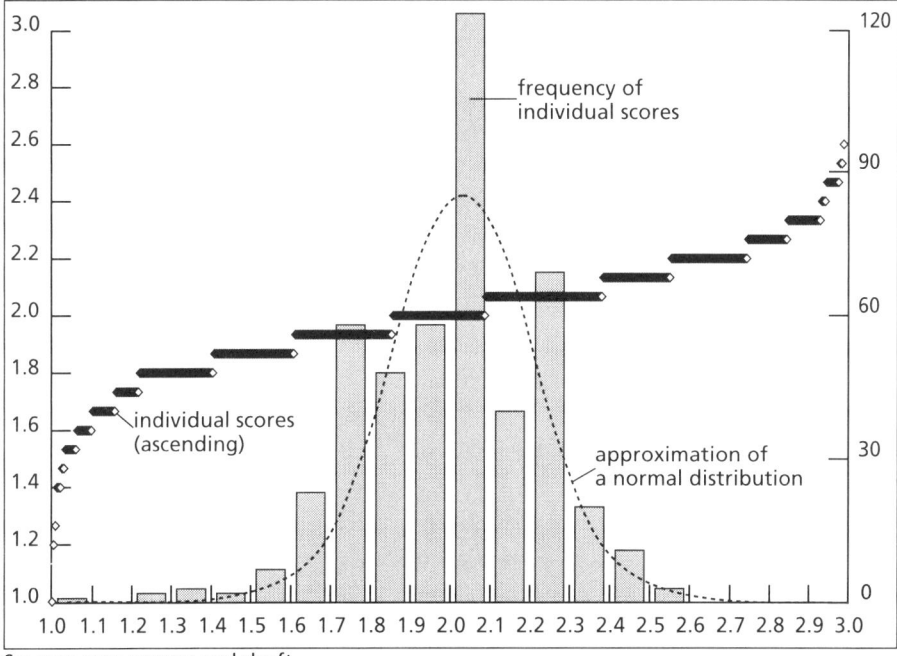

Source: own survey and draft.

The results in the category *occupation* are statistically significant and likewise difficult to explain. The students – the majority of the sample – score close to the average of the whole sample, together with the workers. Business people and housewives have a more economic attitude, a bit less so teachers, nurses and engineers. Office clerks are more environmentally minded but not as much as street vendors and taxi drivers. The latter is a surprising result because commonly, people with these types of jobs are not known to be especially ecofriendly. However, both street vendors (or hawkers) and taxi drivers are in contact with many people[358] and therefore a variety of views, and while working in the streets are exposed to pollutants. Teachers and nurses talk to many people as well, but they do it more in their professional capacity, where they cannot make much small talk with other people. Nevertheless, this is probably not a very strong reason for the result. We have to bear in mind that the survey was done in the af-

---

358 A study on hawkers in Telok Bahang on the island of Penang shows that many of them favour the job of hawking over work in a factory or an office, because they can be their own masters and can work according to their own pace. In addition, they mention that being able to talk to people is a great advantage of hawking. They also have more critical attitude towards economic growth, because along with emphasizing economic development the government tries to get the informal hawkers off the streets and into special hawker compounds which the hawkers mostly resent (see: Backhaus, N. & Keller, S.A. 2001).

termath of the Asian currency crises, when the country was still struggling to achieve pre-crisis economic growth rates. Business people and housewives are among those who felt the impact of the crisis strongly and immediately and therefore tend to emphasise economic development more that others.

If we look at the category *ethnicity* we can see that the Malay are the most economically minded. This position, which contrasts with that of the Chinese population, could be interpreted as the result of former Prime Minister Mahatir's[359] successful appeal to the Malay population to become more conscious of individual economic development. On the other hand, there could be a contradictory interpretation. Economic vulnerability, not economic awareness, may have made the Malays rate the statements in a more economically minded manner. The category of "other Malaysians" consists of indigenous people from Borneo, who live and work in or near Kuala Lumpur. They are probably more aware of forest degradation in the vicinity of their hometowns and are therefore more ecologically minded.

Since ethnicity and religion are closely related in Malaysia, we are not surprised that the Muslims score as high as the Malays. Very close to their score, is the one of the "others" – atheists, agnostics or "free thinkers" as they call themselves – who seem to be less ecologically conscious than the average respondent. Buddhists and Taoists score like the Chinese, whereas the Christians (consisting of mostly Chinese, other Malaysians and some Indians) score lowest. It is difficult to relate the scores directly to the different religions. It is probably a combination of ethnic background and religious affiliation that leads to the distribution of scores.

It is often said that when people have *children* they think more about the future and what their generation leaves for the next generations. However, there is almost no difference between the scores of respondents with children and those without. Therefore, people with children are not more environmentally or economically minded.

There is also almost no difference between married and single respondents. However, divorced respondents score lower than any other category. Since the scores do not differ in a statistically significant way from one another, we can assume that the score of the divorced is an outlier.

There are differences according to *gender* although they are not statistically significant. Men tend to be more economically minded, whereas women tend to be a little bit more environmentally conscious.

---

359 see: Watson Andaya, B. and Andaya, L.Y. 2001. pp. 333-336.

Figure 55: Differences between specific groups of respondents

Source: own survey and draft.

6 Recreation and theme parks

6.1 Theme parks: the epitome of artificiality

At first glance it seems strange to include a chapter about theme parks in a study about conservation areas. For theme parks are often seen as the epitome of artificiality, which strongly contrasts with national parks that have the connotation of authenticity. However, both theme parks and conservation areas are used for recreational purposes. It is not easy to clearly define what a theme park is. Generally theme parks can be described as non-places, according to the French anthropologist Marc Augé[360]. Non-places are not rooted or embedded into the context of their surroundings; they could be anywhere, since they have no history and serve only commercial purposes. Theme parks are non-places designed for recreation and pleasure. This is their sole purpose apart from generating income for their owners, whereas a conservation area is primarily gazetted for the purpose of protecting a specific environment. In recent years many theme parks were erected around Kuala Lumpur, mostly in abandoned tin mines. Since the definition of theme park cannot be regarded as common knowledge, the respondents are presented with a list of several known theme parks, and given the possibility of adding others. Nevertheless, some of them also mentioned conservation areas when they were asked what other theme parks they have visited.[361] This shows that many respondents do not draw a clear line between a theme park and a conservation area, which in itself is an interesting result.

As we have seen (see "4.1: Expectations of a visit to a national park" on page 128), recreational activities – also offered by theme parks – are quite important to the respondents. Hence, they are asked whether they have visited a theme park, which one they like most, and why. The majority (408) of the respondents has visited at least one theme park (or what they think to be a theme park). Compared with the total sample, the respondents who have visited a theme park do not differ regarding general categories (i.e. age, gender, marital status, religion, ethnicity, occupation, education). Almost half (247) of the respondents have visited at least both one conservation area and one theme park. A third (161) has visited at least one theme park but no conservation area, a bit more than a tenth (56) has only visited a conservation area but no theme park, and 6 % (33) have neither been to a conservation area nor to a theme park.

---

360 Augé, M. 1995.
361 Since multiple answers were possible all respondents who mention a conservation area as a theme park which they have visited, also mention at least one "real" theme park.

6.2 Most visited theme parks

Figure 57 on page 167 shows the most visited theme parks. Genting Theme Park[362] (30.3 % of all visits) and Sunway Lagoon[363] (29.5 %) attract the most visitors, followed by The Mines Wonderland[364] (19 %), A'Famosa Waterworld[365] (6.7 %), Bukit Merah[366] (6.4 %) and Waterworld[367] (5.1 %).[368] Other "theme" parks attracted less than 1 % each and only 3.1 % combined. This is most certainly a result of the design of the questionnaire, where a list of the first six theme parks – comprising the most important theme parks around Kuala Lumpur – was given.

Figure 58 on page 167 shows how much the respondents like the theme parks they have visited. The result suggests that they like what they visit and visit what they like. Accordingly, Genting Theme Park (41.7 %), Sunway Lagoon (34.5 %) and The Mines Wonderland (11.5 %) are the most favoured theme parks.[369] Bukit Merah (4.8 %), A'Famosa Waterworld (3.5 %), and Wetworld (1.1 %) are less popular.

Since theme parks do not depend on a specific environment – apart from (affordable) space – they are erected as closely as possible to potential customers (see figure 56 on page 166). Therefore, we find a concentration of theme parks around Kuala Lumpur, Petaling Jaya, and Shah Alam, near Ipoh and Taiping as well as in the vicinity of Melaka. Genting Theme Park is not as close to urban areas as other parks, however it is located at a hill resort favoured by many day and weekend tourists. Genting combines the cool environment of a hill resort, with the possibility of hiking in natural surroundings, and gambling in one of the casinos, making it one of the most visited destinations in Malaysia.

---

362 http://www.genting.com.my/en/themepark/index.htm (accessed 5th August 2002).
363 http://www.sunway.com.my/lagoon/index.asp (accessed 5th August 2002).
364 http://www.countryheights.com.my/wonderland/index.html (accessed 5th August 2002).
365 http://www.afamosa.com/water/index.html (accessed 5th August 2002).
366 http://www.bukitmerahresort.com.my/waterpark/index.html (accessed 5th August 2002).
367 http://www.wetworld.com.my (accessed 5th August 2002).
368 The average of all respondents visited a bit more than two (2.2) theme parks (including conservation areas mentioned in this category; excluding conservation areas 2.1). The average of the respondents who have been visiting at least one theme park is 2.65 (respectively 2.56).
369 The percentages can be misleading, because only a visited park can be favoured over others. Important is the ranking and the difference between percentage of visits and percentage of favoured parks.

Figure 56: Map of most visited theme parks

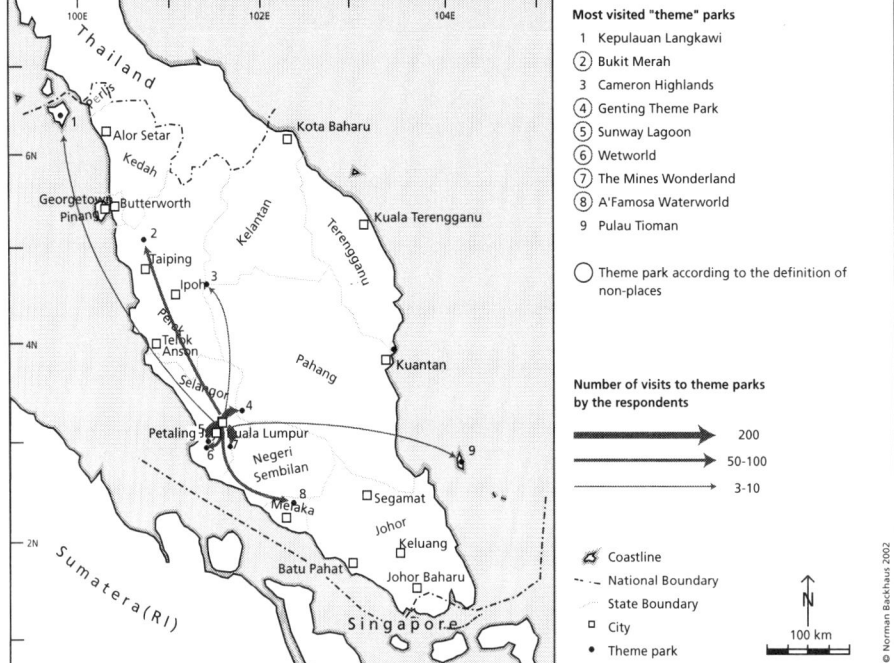

Source: own survey and draft.

6.3 Evaluation of the theme park visits

The great number of visits (over 1,000 visits for the whole sample) shows that theme parks have become an important factor leisure activity in Malaysian society. They are conveniently located and offer a variety of possible activities for the whole family. Often theme parks are attached to shopping malls where the need for the 'tourist activity' shopping can be satisfied. This is a reason why existing theme parks are constantly being overhauled and if possible extended. Almost a must for any theme park seems to be a section with water activities (rafting, swimming, sliding), which for climatic reasons can be used year round without the need to heat the water.

When the respondents are asked what they like best about their visit to theme parks, most mention "fun and entertainment" (36.1 %), followed by "fresh air and cleanliness" (29.3 %)[370]. Much less mention "natural attractions" (8.1 %), "good facilities" (5.5 %), "beauty" (4,2 %), "closeness" (3.9 %), "suitability for families" (3.4 %) or "feeling comfortable" (2.4 %).

---

370 This category was mostly mentioned by those who have visited Genting Theme Park which is located around 1,500 m over sea level, where people can indeed experience fresh air.

Figure 57: Most visited theme parks

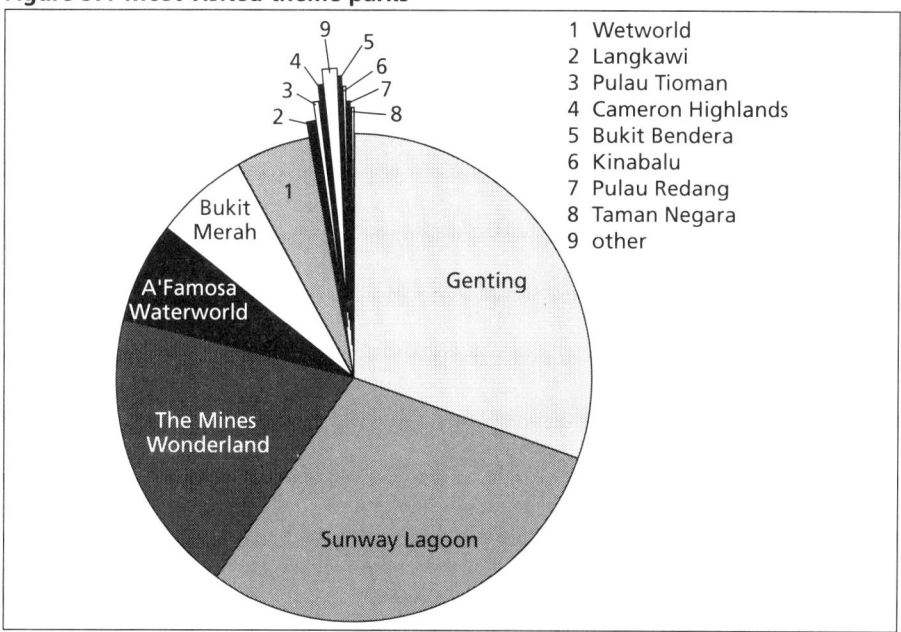

1 Wetworld
2 Langkawi
3 Pulau Tioman
4 Cameron Highlands
5 Bukit Bendera
6 Kinabalu
7 Pulau Redang
8 Taman Negara
9 other

Source: own survey and draft.

Figure 58: Most favoured theme parks

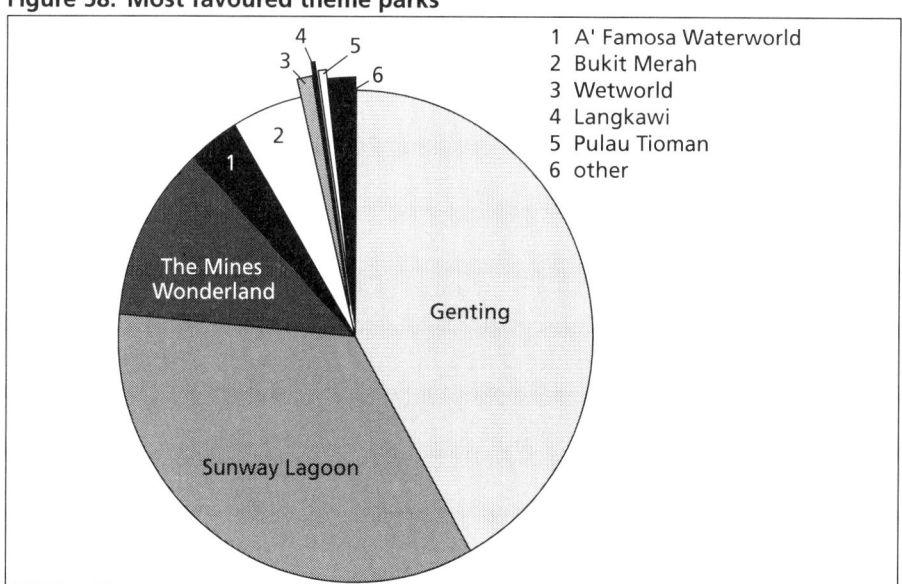

1 A' Famosa Waterworld
2 Bukit Merah
3 Wetworld
4 Langkawi
5 Pulau Tioman
6 other

Source: own survey and data.

Their greatest dislike is that theme parks are "too expensive" (29.3 %). Sunway Lagoon (41.5 %; prices for adults RM 39, for children RM 26), Genting Theme Park (32.2 %; RM 20-34 and RM 12-18), and The Mines Wonderland (26.9 %; RM 25 and RM 17) are considered especially expensive. In fact, compared with A'Famosa Waterworld (RM 18 and RM 13), Bukit Merah (RM 19 and RM 14), and Wetworld (RM 7 and RM 4) they are among the most expensive recreation areas, especially if we bear in mind that the entrance fee for national parks is 3 to RM 10. Moreover, the parks are often considered to be "too crowded" (21.4 %), especially Sunway Lagoon, Wetworld and Genting. On week ends – the only time when families usually can spend a whole day together – the parks are very crowded. For some, the attractions are "not satisfying" (10.9 %) or too "artificial" (10.2 %). But there are also respondents who have "nothing" (9 %) to criticise about the theme parks they have visited.

7 Summary

The aim of this part of the study was to ascertain what (potential) domestic visitors of Malaysian national parks think about (their) conservation areas, why they visit them and what needs and wishes they have for future visits. The results help us to understand what claims the increasing numbers of domestic visitors of national parks make, and whether they are in line with the goals of nature conservation. The results help the park management to see where the biggest problems are today and in the future and to adapt their policies if necessary.

The respondents seem to have a 'nature vs. culture' concept in mind when they try to define nature and it's opposite. Nature is therefore seen as 'unspoiled', 'clean' and 'made by God'; whereas it's opposite is 'artificial', 'polluted' and 'made by humans'. Thus, the respondents' notion of 'nature' corresponds with most concepts of authenticity. The Malaysian discourse about nature and environmental problems is, therefore, more or less in line with the discourse in western countries. The notion that the environment needs to be protected against pollution and degradation meets the guidelines of all conservation areas. Consequently, park managements should not have problems with the environmental awareness of domestic tourists.

Regarding the expectations the respondents have when they think about a visit to a conservation area, many mention fun or leisure related activities. However, what they remember most after a visit are natural attractions. Therefore, a combination of leisure and educational activities is called for, if the park managements want to meet their domestic visitors' expectations and the often stated need for environmental education of the Malaysian population.

60 % of the respondents have already been to a conservation area and most of these have visited Taman Negara, the flagship of Malaysian national parks. Some parks are almost exclusively visited by domestic visitors (i.e. Kubah, Matang) and some mostly by foreign guests (i.e. Bako, Pulau Penyu). The former are easily accessible and allow for leisure activities. This result suggests that parks don't necessarily have to cater for the same mix of visitors; there is room for specialisation, which should be coordinated between the different parks.

Visitors stay longer in the bigger parks, however, parks that do not offer many leisure activities are rarely visited more than once. 80 % of the respondents visited parks in groups with friends or families. The group experience is an important aspect of a park visit, but often the infrastructure does not cater to it. Either there are no or too few places for having a picnic, or the accommodation is not suited for bigger groups. The fact that more than 80 % of the respondents have visited a theme park further emphasises the importance of leisure and being together with friends. If the needs of domestic visitors for leisure activities and group experiences could be better integrated into the setup of parks, the educational aspects of nature conservation could be better passed on.

Since, in most parks, the majority of the visitors are from Malaysia, domestic visitors form a powerful group of actors whose needs should not be neglected. An integration of more leisure activities that do not compromise conservation (much), would be more ecologically sound, than attempting to keep people who are mainly seeking fun out of conservation areas. This does not mean that parks should be opened to as many people as possible. It is feasible to have limits of visitor numbers, but for those who can visit a park, the visit should be worthwhile, fulfilling and in the best case heighten their environmental consciousness.

V The experts' discourse about nature conservation in Malaysia

1 Introduction

The protected areas of Malaysia have become important tourist attractions. They are renowned for their biodiversity as well as for their unique geological and geomorphologic features. As previously mentioned, two of the larger Malaysian parks – Gunung Mulu and Gunung Kinabalu Park – have received the status of World Heritage sites, proving that the management of the parks is regarded as of a high standard. Malaysia has a large community of people who are professionally involved with nature conservation. It is the aim of this chapter to establish the Malaysian discourse on nature conservation in connection with (eco)tourism. Naturally we cannot expect that all participants or contributors to the discourse share the same opinion. I have tried to clarify the range of positions involved in this discussion. The following pages serve as a synopsis of different positions (opinions) regarding nature conservation and tourism in Malaysia. The respondents were chosen as representatives of the organisations they work with and not as private individuals. When doing research from an action oriented perspective, the distinction of an individual as a member or representative of an organisation and as a private person can pose difficulties. From the perspective of systems theory[371] the 'opinion' of an organisation can probably be more easily understood, than that of an individual. Using the theory of structuration that tries to combine individual action with structure (see "Theory of 'structuration'" on page 15), it is possible to view a respondent as a representative of an organisation, where an aggregation of individual actions within the context of the organisation forms a more or less distinct 'corporate identity'. This 'corporate identity' can be regarded as a structure or framework for the people working within the organisation. These structures become important guidelines when members of an organisation communicate with outsiders such as an interviewer. Hence, while interviewing individuals, I can recognize opinions and notions that are embedded in or derived from the above mentioned 'corporate identity'.

First, I will describe the method of the content analysis, before I outline the discourse with respect to the topics of park management, participation of local communities, privatisation, and tourism.

---

371 See for example Treibel, A. 2000, p. 21-48, or Korte, H. 2001, p. 81-96.

2 Method

2.1 Content analysis of interviews

A qualitative approach proves more useful for describing the discourse of nature conservation and tourism in Malaysia, than a quantitative one. It is not my aim to show how many times a specific argument has been proposed, and whether there is a statistically significant difference between different groups of respondents. It is more important to show the range of opinions and make them accessible for the reader[372]. Although I am writing about discourses, I am not conducting a thorough or deep discourse analysis in the strictest sense[373]. While all qualitative approaches share a concern with the meaning of social life, discourse analysis tries to explore how socially produced ideas and objects are created and maintained over time[374]. Although, I will try to refer to the context of topics and statements, I cannot provide a full analysis of the meanings behind specific topics. The reasons for this can be found primarily in the 'language'. Discourse analysis is very sensitive to language, because it is language that is responsible for constructing the phenomena we are analysing. Since I conducted my interviews in English, a language that is neither my mother tongue nor in most cases my respondents', it is difficult to adequately attribute the deeper meaning of certain expressions. However, it is possible to show, with the data, how social phenomena – such as different aspects of nature conservation – are pondered and revealed in spoken language. In doing so I hope to be both fair to my respondents and to the aim of the study.

2.2 Profile of the sample

In order to delineate the range of positions, I selected respondents from NGOs, the scientific community, the administration as well as from the private sector and tourist operators. All of them have to be professionally engaged in either nature conservation and/or tourism connected to nature conservation. Thus, they form a group of experts on various aspects of nature conservation. The potential respondents and/or organisations were contacted by phone in Malaysia. Some of the contacted experts could not be interviewed, mostly because of time restrictions. All in all I conducted twenty four interviews in all parts of the country. Most interviews were recorded on tape, a few respondents preferred me to take notes. The interviews were conducted with one person, except one once

---

372 Lamnek, S. 1995.
373 For a concise introduction into discourse analysis see Phillips, N. & Hardy, C. 2002.
374 Phillips, N. & Hardy, C. 2002, p. 6.

when two people were interviewed together. Subsequently, the interviews were transcribed, digitised and later categorised (see "Categorisation" on page 174). Names and affiliations of the respondents were kept out of the analysis sheet for reasons of privacy protection. Since the interviewees were interviewed explicitly as representatives of their organisations and not as private persons, they indicated when they uttered a personal opinion or view of a certain issue.

2.3 Categorisation

To analyse the data, I used 'atlas.ti', a software application designed for the analysis of qualitative data. The data consisted of 24 text files each containing the transcript of one interview. The texts were first categorised according to the respective affiliation of the respondents:

- Seven texts that corresponded with interviews of experts in the administration or management of national parks on different levels and in different states, were labelled with the code word *'administration'*. All respondents within this category were in positions that involved them in various issues connected with nature conservation. Since it was their task to maintain or implement the protection of specific natural areas, they were confronted with problems similar to those of management of conservation areas.
- The four representatives of Malaysian NGOs[375] were grouped together under the label *'NGO'*. The NGOs chosen are exclusively or partly concerned with the conservation of nature. Their goal is to strengthen nature conservation in general and in the long run to gazette more conservation areas.
- The category *'scientist'* comprises representatives of the natural and social sciences, who are affiliated with university institutes. Each respondent from the scientific community has their own research projects and/or are teaching classes and programmes in the field of nature conservation and tourism.
- The last category *'tour operators'* comprises respondents working in (national) organisations either in the private sector (as tour operators or as managers of resorts in national parks) or in government institutions concerned with the promotion of tourism.

These four categories of respondents serve as the cornerstone of the following analysis of the discourse (see figure 59 on page 175). The categorisation was done in two consecutive steps. Since the interviews focus nature conservation and tourism, the categories formed from the transcribed texts do not differ from this given framework. In the following chapter the results of the text analysis will be presented.

---

375 The NGOs operate on the national level and are national organisation, although they have close ties to international NGOs.

Figure 59: The analysed discourse threads and the respondent categories

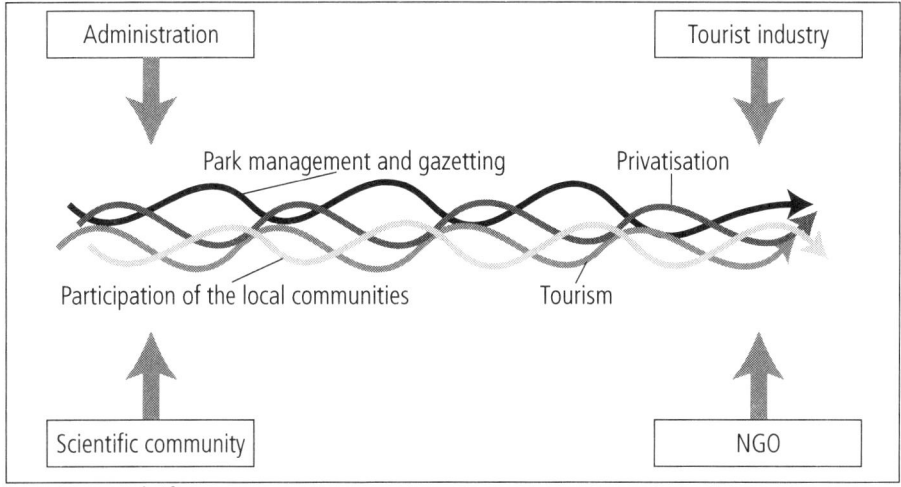

Source: own draft.

3 Important topics of nature conservation

3.1 Park management and gazetting

3.1.1 Gazetting of new parks

Institutions involved in the *management* of parks (category 'administration') generally favour the gazetting of new conservation areas and nobody questioned the need for additional protected areas in Malaysia. The majority of them are looking forward to having more areas under protection. In several states the procedures for the establishment of a new park have been streamlined so that in the future it will take less than the average ten years that it now takes.[376] In the future these respondents want to have more marine parks and want to advance a proposition of the IUCN to increase the size of the protected land area in Sarawak from the present 3 % to 10 % in the near future. However, a minority is more sceptical about the feasibility of the gazetting of new areas. According to the majority it is increasingly difficult to propose new conservation areas because there are more and more stakeholders who oppose the idea. This often is because they want to use the area for a future theme park for agricultural pur-

---

376 We have to discern between state parks and national parks. Sarawak and Sabah have a special status within the Malaysian confederation and can decide independently from Kuala Lumpur whether an area becomes a national park or a state park. The Sultanates of the Malayan Peninsula can gazette state parks independently – if they are not covering terrain of a neighbouring state – but have to get the consent of the national government when trying to gazette an area as a national park.

poses[377]. Therefore, they say it is important to combine nature conservation with tourism to cover potential economical losses of the local communities when a park and its resources become protected.

Taking the initiative to propose areas for conservation is an essential function of the *NGOs* (category 'NGO') we contacted. They have distinct notions about the process of gazetting a park. Although they are all happy that the acreage under protection is increasing in Malaysia, they propose not so much the increase of the size of the conservation areas but the protection of specific and unique habitats, which makes the gazetting of new areas more difficult. This is because there are few unique habitats that are at the same time pristine and untouched enough to fulfil the requirements to be gazetted as a park. They share the opinion of those respondents of the administration, that their work is increasingly more controversial, because many areas that are suitable for conservation are contested by other stakeholders for their own purposes. For instance, one respondent tells the – in his view successful – story of the prevention of a proposed theme park with replicas of the inner cities of Chicago, London, Paris and an original Malayan village (that should have attracted many tourists). The project had to be cancelled and instead the NGO's proposition to gazette a part of the area as state park has now good chances to be implemented. The respondent stated that the local inhabitants who would have formed the Malayan village would have been like animals in a zoo. This shows that the NGOs are increasingly concerned with the local people. Another example is the protection of the habitat of billions of fireflies, by preventing that it be converted into a golf course. Moreover, such successful recent examples, where business interests (that were regarded as detrimental to the nature and the local people) were not put before the conservation of nature, are most welcomed by the NGOs. This is because in Malaysia many projects work according to the principle "what is working here, is also working somewhere else". Increasingly, the members of the NGOs serve as informants of publicists of critical situations or threatened species and habitats. The respondents stated that although their work is not always easy and that they sometimes don't prevail, the situation of nature conservation in Malaysia has considerably improved. Therefore, they try to implement more 'showcases' of special habitats or protection concepts with the aim of promoting them and promulgating them. One respondent said that it is high time to improve nature conservation as a whole, because there are fewer and fewer areas left that can be protected. He complained that there is no overall management

---

377 With oil palm plantations investors can get a reasonably quick return. An informant said that with the currently high prices a return on investment can be achieved after three to five years. Therefore, oil palm plantations are regarded as a good business opportunity.

plan and that most conservation areas are isolated from each other, which prohibits the exchange of animal populations between various parks. Thus, the number of Sumatra rhinoceros is bound to decrease because the small populations of Endau Rompin Park in Johore cannot mix with those of the Taman Negara.

The *scientific community* (category 'scientist') is generally in favour of, and see the need for more and larger conservation areas. The respondents emphasised involving many stakeholders in the process of protecting new areas for conservation. They see their own contribution as providing scientific background for the authorities and often work together with NGOs. One respondent pointed out that it proved very useful to provide this knowledge to the authorities through field trips to the respective areas. That way, problems can be shown much more directly and visibly.

Tour operators and the respondents from the private sector did not explicitly discuss the issue of gazetting new parks, probably because they mostly entered the field when parks are already gazetted. However, they regard conservation areas as an asset and an important source of income.

3.1.2 Financing parks

Once parks are gazetted and implemented, their maintenance and management cost money which has to be provided on a long term basis. All conservation areas in Malaysia are under the jurisdiction of either the respective state or the central government, there are no privately owned parks, so yet. Respondents working within the *administration* explain that all income generated within the parks – mostly through tourism – flows back into the state coffers, from which the parks are funded. Most parks produce a deficit, only very few such as Kinabalu would manage to cover their expenses. The respondents did not comment on the system of distribution of funds via the state, and that the state has therefore disproportionate control over the parks. However, there is a great discussion about raising the entrance fees in order to cover park deficits. According to one respondent, studies have shown that most visitors would be prepared to pay more for park entry[378]. On the Peninsula, one respondent argued that visitors should pay more but that they should also be better able to see what they get for their money, meaning the money should be put toward visible improvements of the park. Thus, new tickets were designed, with colourful images of the park and the name of the visitor printed on them. In Sarawak there are two positions regarding raising entrance fees. One faction within the administration wants to

---

378 Indeed my own study does not contradict this but the interviewees were not enthusiastic about the prospect of a substantial raise (see "Tourism and its potential in Gunung Mulu" on page 211).

introduce a system that would distinguish between foreigners and Malaysians. The former should pay more than the latter, because Malaysians already pay for nature conservation through taxes. The other faction is against this, arguing that Indonesians and Filipinos would have difficulty paying the higher fee, because their purchasing power is even lower than that of Malaysians. In general the interviews gave the impression that the administration is having trouble with the question of raising prices, although the need for more income is evident. They do not think that parks have to be profitable businesses with the task of protecting species and habitats and of providing education and recreation to a wide range of people.

Besides generating revenues for nature conservation by raising entrance fees, the administration could tax pharmaceutical firms using substances found and gathered in Malaysian forests. In Sarawak where the Sarawak Biodiversity Council was recently established, the hopes for such income sharing are especially great.

Most *NGOs* are very conscious of the financing of nature conservation, because it is their daily business to gather funds for their own projects. While they point out the problems that can arise with tourism in protected areas, they see tourism as a good means to generate income for nature conservation, if it is done in an ecofriendly way. According to one respondent, the connection of tourism to nature conservation has recently become much more important. Areas can only reasonably be proposed for conservation if tourism is included as a means to raise money, for the park management as well as for the local people who want to profit from tourism. In general the NGOs state that in Malaysia there is a gap between the need for economic development and nature conservation, which is not easily bridged. Although people in Malaysia were more sensitive to economic development during and after the Asian currency crises, the NGOs think that people also feel that nature conservation is important.[379] Therefore, NGOs favour a price system with higher entrance fees for tourists while maintaining cheaper fees for Malaysians. One respondent emphasised that the local people around a new park do not understand that people have to pay to enter an area which they were free to enter before it was gazetted. Therefore, he states, it is also important to inform the local people about the reasons for and benefits of raising entrance fees. NGOs did not have as much trouble with funding during the Asian currency crisis as they had feared, mostly because foreign donations were not affected by the crisis. However, donations are increasingly tied to

---

379 The NGOs do not do polls about this issue, however, my own study (see "Malaysian urbanites and their national parks" on page 115) shows that many people think it is important to have more areas under protection.

specific projects. People tend to give money for the protection of charismatic species such as the tiger or the proboscis monkey but much less for habitat protection or less spectacular animals. Therefore, the NGOs sometimes have to deal with constraints on the use of their money.

The *scientists* are probably most critical of combining tourism and nature conservation in order to gather income. They say that sometimes the park management forgets that the tourist industry's primary focus is to earn money which can contradict conservation issues. However, they agree that for the conservation of nature, money is a critical issue and that some projects were slowed down or downsized during the Asian currency crisis.

Although the tourist attraction of conservation areas may be diminished by charging higher entrance fees, the respondents from the *tourist industry* did not openly oppose the idea, nor did they encourage an augmentation of the existing fees. They think that most western tourists would accept such a raise but that the Asian tourists might not. They sometimes do not understand that it costs a lot of money to protect an area covered by vegetation that existed long before people thought about nature protection.

3.1.3 Enforcement of park regulations

The enforcement of park regulations, especially the prohibitions against hunting and plant gathering, is regarded as a problem. The respondents from the *administration* all stated that parks do not have enough rangers to enforce the ban on hunting, or to catch poachers. Some think that they will never be able to stop poaching in their parks, although they try to prevent/reduce it. They distinguish between different kinds of "poachers":

- There are people such as the Penans who have always hunted animals and gathered plants in today's parks, for subsistence purposes. They are usually allowed to proceed with hunting in the parks because their livelihood would be severely threatened if they could not use the natural resources they used for centuries. However, in certain parks (i.e. Mulu) the management has observed that the populations of certain mammals have diminished because of this practise.
- Another category is poachers who sell wild meat at local markets. For some wild meat is a necessary source of income, which they claim would be a financial hardship to lose. Two respondents agreed that it is not enough to simply forbid hunting without presenting alternatives. In Sarawak, where it is generally forbidden to sell wild meat at markets, the rules have been altered slightly. Now hunters may legally hunt ten animals per month in forests, but not in protected areas and sell them in the market. A consequence of this

change is that the stocks of animals have recovered and therefore hunters can find their prey outside of conservation areas.
- The third category is plant collectors who cut down precious trees such as sandal wood, or who steal rafflesia in order to sell them on the international market. The park managements try to sensitise the population living around conservation areas to the importance of nature protection and thus hope to get their help catching illegal plant collectors. However, this only works if local people have incentives (i.e. income from tourism) that help them to appreciate the conservation areas.
- The last category is 'biopirates' who collect plants for pharmaceutical firms that seek extracts usable for the production of new medicines. Since 'biopirates' come as tourists, it is difficult to apprehend them (for more about the topic of the genetic resources of parks, see "Research and biodiversity" on page 181).

Because hunting or poaching are regarded as problematic, the park administrations favour the model of a 'hard' boundary without buffer zones. They argue that park boundaries are often not visible in the terrain, which is why hunters can claim to have lost their way when caught poaching inside a park. Some parks (i.e. Kinabalu) have even painted the trees at the boundary red, in order to make it visible. They maintain that official buffer zones would make it less obvious when poachers enter the forbidden hunting grounds.

The *NGOs* also recognize the problems of poaching and 'biopiracy', and they emphasise the difficulties arising from different jurisdictions within and outside the parks, and differing interests within the arena of nature conservation. They would appreciate the creation of buffer zones, which would bring greater areas under the control of the park management. However, one respondent pointed out that, in that case, large wooded areas would be taken from the control of the Forestry Department, whose power is directly related to the acreage of forests it controls. Therefore, NGOs think that the Forestry Department should be allowed to use buffer zones. This poses another problem, because the roads that have been built into forests in order to be able to cut and move trees, allow easy access for poachers. Because of these various problems, NGOs propose some kind of decentralisation within the park administration which would give individual parks more room for negotiation and adaptation of rules for specific situations.

Since some *scientists* have research projects in marine parks, they mostly talked about the protection of reefs and fish. In some areas they think would be advantageous to have a 'hard' boundary, too, in order to prohibit fishermen from catching fish in marine parks. However, the costs for marker buoys are too high. In Sabah many reefs were threatened or destroyed by dynamite or poison fishing before they could be protected[380]. On the Peninsula vast areas of mangrove swamps are being converted into shrimp farms, which is very problematic for the coastal environment and can threaten nearby reefs. In Sarawak, shrimp farms can only be set up when they meet the highest environmental standards. However in Sarawak, the biggest problem seems to be over-fishing by trawlers. The law regulates how much they are allowed to fish, but it is not well enforced.

One scientist disagreed with the idea that conservation areas need more staff in order to more efficiently enforce park regulations. He claims that the existing staff in the parks is not well managed, so that a lot of time is wasted, that could be used for other tasks (i.e. enforcement of park regulations). Contrasting to the last opinion, are those of the respondents from the *private sector*. They feel that there are not enough rangers in the parks to stop poaching or illegal logging, and that more financial backing is needed for this great task. However, they did not mention from where this money should come from.

3.1.4 Research and biodiversity

The administrations of Sarawak, Sabah and the Peninsula have recognised the potential of the biodiversity within their forests, and they want to have a share of the income thus generated. Sarawak was first to introduce its 'Biodiversity Council' (SBC) in 1998 (Sabah followed soon), which monitors research concerning the biology of plants and animals in Sarawak. Every research project connected to biodiversity has to be approved by the council. It tries to assert property rights regarding flora and fauna. All respondents from the administration have great hopes of benefiting from medicines that are developed from the flora or fauna of their forests. When a company or an institution discovers something of commercial value, it has to (according to the contract with the SBC) contact the council and start to negotiate with the state attorney about remittances. Some respondents who were not directly involved in the activities of the Council, stated that at the beginning some mistakes were made which kept researchers away from Sarawak. The procedure to obtain a research permit took too long, and the additional requirements were regarded as unreasonable. Another task of the SBC is to get an overview of all biodiversity-related research in Sarawak in order to avoid the duplication of research projects. It also attempts to provide information about Sarawak's biodiversity for tourists.

The *scientists* are quite critical about the SBC, because they think it inhibits research. The rule that scientists have to submit all the papers they publish about biodiversity related research in Sarawak to the Council *before* they can submit

---

380 It has to be noted that dynamite and poison fishing is prohibited throughout Malaysia.

them to journals is regarded as constraining free research[381]. Scientists are sceptical about revenue generation from biodiversity related research, because they think that pharmaceutical companies are powerful enough to avoid sharing their profits. They also say that it is very difficult to verify whether a chemical substance used in a medicament comes from a specific plant that only occurs in Sarawak[382].

Park managements do not have enough funds for general research. Kinabalu has probably the biggest research unit of a Malaysian park, but they also depend on researchers from the outside who share their knowledge and findings with them. In the case of a planned or proposed conservation area, *NGOs* conduct a lot of scientific research with the help of their members who often donate a great amount of their free time and of their knowledge to the cause.

3.1.5 Political collaboration

In national parks, different actor groups' interests converge, and it is necessary to have institutions regulating them, and there are different opinions about how this should be done. The representatives of the *administration* did not dwell long on this topic, probably because they are in charge of making the rules and because they feel more or less comfortable with the way things are. However, they admitted that the political situation around Taman Negara is less than satisfactory. This is because there are four policies – the state policies of Pahang, Terengganu and Kelantan (policy Sultan) and the federal policy (policy Agung) – which need to be coordinated. Fast changes or adaptations are virtually impossible because all four parties concerned have to agree on an issue.

The *NGOs* have much more to say about collaboration with the authorities, because they often oppose government policies deemed to cause environmental or social damage. They complain that the politicians who have to decide about issues related to nature conservation often do not have adequate knowledge about the issue and that they subsequently sign bills or contracts that are detrimental to the environment. Some NGO respondents say that the situation has recently improved because a younger generation with better education are now in political offices and a greater awareness concerning environmental issues has developed in Malaysia. The former Prime Minister's proposal for the renaturation of Paya Indah wet lands near the new international airport in Sepang, is only one example of this development. The interviewees emphasise that for

---

381 The council argues that it wants to keep control on what is published but it also wants to be able to edit any critical remarks about the SBC or Sarawak.
382 Moreover, it is sometimes very difficult to attribute a certain chemical to a plant when it is not constantly produced by the plant due to seasonal or other changes and differences (see for example Swerdlow, J.L. 2000).

them it is very important to back up their arguments scientifically. Otherwise, their cause might be regarded as political opposition. In addition to scientific reports, some NGOs have started to organise site visits for politicians to contested regions, which proved to have more impact than a report alone would have had. Moreover, they try to involve all relevant stakeholders of an issue, and they are more focused on the result of their undertakings than on getting the credit for the protection of a certain area. They say that this distinguishes them from politicians. They are aware that the power and prestige of forestry departments rise with the amount of area under their control. This area becomes smaller if forests become gazetted as conservation areas and the jurisdiction over them moves to other branches of government. Therefore, the NGOs propose that forestry departments should also play an important role in conservation areas, and they should receive credit for their commitment. They see a great problem with the loosening of regulations concerning the involvement of foreign companies. Where previously it was not possible for a foreign enterprise to own the majority of a company, in Malaysia it is possible now. The consequence is that local companies (especially small scale enterprises) cannot compete with big international corporations. Another field where NGOs oppose decisions of the government – or the lack of enforcement of laws – is logging, which has led to an increased fragmentation of forest land. The lack of a forest and conservation management plan makes the protection of habitats and species difficult.

Scientists basically see themselves in a role similar to NGOs. Most of them want to increase the number and acreage of protected areas in Malaysia. They also concede that nowadays it is easier to propose an area for protection and to have it gazetted, than it was ten years ago. This is because of the greater acceptance of nature conservation by the younger generation of government officials, who studied environmental issues at high school or university. In addition to and probably as a consequence of that, government officials are more willing to learn more about their environment and ecology. So far, only the top levels of the government and private companies are difficult to reach and to motivate for such environmental training and information. Getting the consent of the local population to protect an area is generally fairly easy, because obedience has a long tradition in Malaysia as pointed out by one respondent. Therefore, decisions from 'above' are mostly well accepted, on the Peninsula, especially when they come as Malay projects. If projects have a 'non-Malay smell' more opposition can be expected, but with conservation areas this is rarely the case.

The *tourist industry* is divided about the role of the government in regulating tourism in conservation areas. Those who manage resorts in or near national parks emphasise that they fully support the regulations of the parks and that they acknowledge the priority of conservation over tourism. The tour operators who do not own or lease accommodation in or near parks are a little bit more critical. Although they admit that governmental control is necessary and that regulations have to be made, they are critical of specific regulations. However, they do not favour less strict regulations; they stated that some government regulations are too targeted at fostering mass tourism instead of an environmentally and socially friendly tourism. As an example, one respondent mentioned the discussion about extending the runway on the Mulu airstrip, in order to bring in more tourists to the national park. The consequence of the construction (and eventually the extension) of the airstrip and at the same time of the failure to further the transport by boat, was that tourists spend less time in Mulu. They spend less money, cause more costs per individual and decrease the air fare to a sum which is much lower than the cost of a boat trip. An extension or upgrade of the system of river transportation would have generated more jobs at the local level and would not have made the extension of the runway necessary. Apart from such criticisms, tour operators concede that working together with the government generally functions quite well.

3.2 Participation of the local communities

3.2.1 Participation and income

The participation of the local population in conservation issues is generally regarded as very important. Without their acceptance, it is difficult to effectively protect a national park. This opinion is also shared by the respondents of the *administration*. Since the concept of participatory or community based conservation[383], which mostly encompasses a zoning of the protected area (with core and buffer zones), is relatively new, most parks in Malaysia were not gazetted according to its principles. Therefore, according to the respondents, the local population was not involved much when a conservation area was gazetted. They say that most such areas were not densely inhabited, or they would not have been gazetted. Today the administration tries to involve the people living just outside the parks. Except for a few nomadic people such as the Orang Asli on the Peninsula or the Penan in Sarawak, people are not allowed to live in protected areas[384], in order to effectively protect the area. In Kinabalu the administration tries to recruit park rangers and other employees from the nearby villages. The rangers thus serve as intermediaries between the park and the villagers in its vicinity. This also shows that the park provides sources of income without ex-

---

383 See Soliva, R. 2002, p. 73-74.
384 When I conducted the interviews in Sabah, one family was still living on the premises of Kinabalu Park. The administration is trying to find an alternative for them outside the park.

ploiting its natural resources. In order to maintain a high number of local staff, people from further away are discouraged from seeking employment in the park. However, the respondents claim that it is not always easy to integrate the locals because most do not speak English well enough to be used as guides for foreign tourists. Since more and more domestic visitors come to conservation areas, locals could in future be used primarily for that group of tourists.

The system of employing local people and of providing them with information to set up their own tourist related businesses has developed to the extent that today proposed conservation areas have a chance for implementation only if opportunities for local people to gather income can be demonstrated. In order to maintain the protection of a park, the income of the local people has to be more or less stable otherwise they may resort to poaching. Since the transport to and from a park can provide possibilities for income generation, the way tourists access a park has to be planned carefully. In Bako for example, the park management refrained from building a road to the park. Instead the fishermen of Bako village provide transport via boat to the park entrance. Thus they have a more or less steady income without needing to resort to old hunting practices.

NGOs also point out the importance of the integration of local people into the park management. But some of them criticise how, in some cases, people are baited with income opportunities in order to get them to consent to a tourist project near a park (and their villages). According to NGOs, local people often do not have the right education to be able to benefit from tourism, or they are not willing to change their livelihood in favour of tourism. This is happening in the Kinabatangan floodplain, which is one of the newest conservation projects in Malaysia. Tourists go there in order to view the famous proboscis monkeys from boats in the river. These tourists find it difficult to understand why some villagers throw their garbage into the river, or even why they continue to hunt monkeys[385]. However, the tourists do not see that their presence can be not only an opportunity but also a constraint for the villagers, who mostly do not have the know-how to fully appreciate the benefits of tourism. They are not surprisingly sometimes unwilling to change their lifestyles just to 'please' the tourists and the tour operators, who skim off most of the money spent by the visitors. Because of these problems, the NGOs stress that it is very important to provide the villagers with adequate education, and to give them a chance to continue with their traditional lifestyle. In Endau Rompin, for instance, the local

---

385 See also Schulze, H. & Suratman, S. (1999, p. 5) with a drastic statement by a villager in the Lower Kinabatangan Area: "Why should the tour operators make money at our expense? If we cannot benefit from tourism we will shoot the last proboscis monkey so that the tour operators will have nothing to show their tourists!"

people who used the resources of the park before it was gazetted, are still allowed to gather rattan in the park for their subsistence production. "They must have a stake in the park, to give them a reason to protect the park as their heritage", one respondent summed it up.

The *scientists* regard the participation of the local people as a precondition for the efficient protection of a park. They also emphasise the need for adequate education of the locals, if they cannot continue to use park resources as they could before. This ranges from participating in (eco)tourism, to new cultivation techniques replacing shifting cultivation, to growing new products such as seaweed, (eco)shrimp or giant clams in order to prohibit them from reef destroying dynamite or poison fishing. One respondent concedes that he does not know whether the local population are happy with these changes or not. The participation in tourism has proved difficult, not only because of the lack of language skills of many locals, but also if their expectations are too great and cannot be fulfilled. This happened for example in Mulu, for example, where the local Berawan opened lodges for tourists with a capacity that exceeded the number of tourists by far. Most of the lodges had to close down and their investments had to be written off.

The *tour operators* that have accommodation in parks say that they want to employ local people, because live nearby and tend to remain longer in the jobs, but these are mostly menial positions. Since most of these private companies are relatively new in the parks they hope to improve the skills of their local staff in the coming years. Especially in remote areas (i.e. Mulu or Taman Negara), resorts depend on the local people either as workers, guides or to provide local products to the restaurants. The tour operators say that it is not easy to employ some local groups that are less employable than others, and that they cannot employ everybody. For instance, in Mulu it proved impossible to employ Penans for longer periods, because they find it difficult to adapt to routines. Therefore, they are now employed on a contract basis, where they might, for example, build a boat for two or three weeks and then do something else. Some tour operators complain about that local people do not acknowledge the benefits they get from tourism in national parks, and about the reluctance with which they have accepted tourism. The tour operators criticise that some – especially older – local people think that villagers who work with tourists are tempted to having an affair with the foreigners. One respondent said that local people should not have any reason to be against the protection of nature and tourism in conservation areas, because these areas belong to the heritage of the Malaysian people, to which they belong, too.

The tour operators who do not own accommodation have a slightly different view. They also emphasise the importance of the participation of local people, but they go further and think that locals need to be given the ownership of the resources they use and provide for tourism (i.e. longhouses, natural resources, culture). These tour operators work in a multi-tiered way. When they see or hear about a village with the potential to become a tourist attraction, they approach the villagers and explain to them what might be of interest to tourists. Subsequently, the villagers decide themselves whether and how they want to participate in the tourist activities provided by the tour operators. If they want to co-operate, the tour operators provide information about how things could be set up. They have had the experience that villagers wanted to do too much, and they have had to caution them not to compromise their natural environment or their culture. After a while, however, 'it clicks' and the people understand the importance of protecting their resources, because they will only be valuable in the context of tourism when they can be sustained.

3.2.2 Resource use and education

The use of natural resources in a national park is generally regarded as a problem by the *park administration*. Although, they concede that for local communities it can be difficult to stop using conservation areas as hunting grounds or for collecting wood and plants. Therefore, the use of natural resources is allowed for the local people to a certain extent. Nevertheless, the administration launches information campaigns and provides business incentives in order to reduce this impact which is detrimental to the parks' ecological integrity. Some respondents suggested lectures and posters in order to inform the local people (as well as the wider range of domestic tourists), others say that this is not enough, and that such information campaigns need a lot of time. Moreover, some respondents emphasise that during the time it takes to educate people, the local people should be protected from business competition from the outside. Otherwise, it is almost impossible to close the knowledge gap between outsiders and the local people.

According to the experiences of *NGOs*, capacity building is a difficult task, because the local people cannot be regarded as a homogenous group. Some of them are eager to embrace new opportunities whereas others want to keep things the way they are. According to the NGOs, the greatest problems occur if tourism is involved. Although tourism is also seen as one of the greatest opportunities for local people to generate income to compensate the loss of natural resource use, the confrontation with different groups of tourists can cause friction. The NGOs also state that the urban population in Malaysia – especially the middle class – has developed an environmental awareness that is lacking the rural population. Since the biggest threat to the environment (of conservation areas) comes from the latter, it is regarded as important to invest in their education, which is not as easy as it is with urbanites. Urban people do not directly use many natural resources, so the notion of protecting certain species or habitats does not pose a problem for them. People who lose access to a vital resource find this less acceptable. It is not easy to explain to fishermen not to cut down mangrove swamps which they do to have better boat access to the sea, when they have done this for generations. The mangroves are now threatened, however, and with them fish hatcheries. Another example is that people have learned not to litter in parks but do it just outside the park entrance.

The *scientists* discern between a short and a long term focus, and between different groups of people. They say that it is most important to sensitise the children to environmental issues, for they expect it to take two or three generations for a country to become ecologically aware. However, some habitats – especially the reefs – are threatened today and cannot wait until another generation protects them. Immediate action is called for, which is very difficult, because the ones who destroy the reefs with dynamite and poison fishing[386] are among the poorest in Malaysia. If they have no other source of income, they cannot survive.

The scientists say that one must distinguish between middle class and lower class, with regard to environmental awareness. The former has only developed since the independence of Malaysia and have grown up during the economic boom of the 1980's; its members are well educated and environmentally aware. People in the lower class are poorly educated and often do not understand the importance of nature protection. The scientists also criticise that the unequal enforcement of laws. For example in most national parks it is prohibited to kill any animal or to pick any plant. However, even rangers often go fishing, which they feel is acceptable, whereas they would never think of hunting in a park. Thus, it is also allowed for tourists to go fishing in protected rivers or the sea.

Some of the *tour operators* seem to be have little patience with local people. Some of them would prefer if locals would more readily accept tourism and its benefits. At the same time, they castigate the media which paint an exaggerated picture of the problems of the local people. Others claim that there is no problem of integrating locals – especially nomads – into the rest of the society, because development is what these groups want. This statement was emphasised by the comment that "people in Malaysia are different from those in Africa and that the Penans should not live in the trees and hunt wild boar, that instead they should be capable of domesticating them".

---

386 One respondent said that in Sabah in the average each reef is hit more than forty times per day by an explosion in its vicinity.

3.2.3 Excursus on the activities of Bruno Manser

Towards the end of each interview I asked some questions about the Swiss environmental activist Bruno Manser, who lived for six years with the Penan in Sarawak during the 1980's. During his stay in Sarawak he helped to organise several roadblocks by the Penan who protested logging activities that threatened their habitat. In 1991 he decided to return to Europe after having been almost captured twice by the authorities, who had declared him persona non grata, and wanted to deport him. Back in Europe, he founded a charitable trust under his name and campaigned to inform the public of the situation of the Penan in Sarawak. In 1999 he flew into Kuching with a motorised hang glider, in order to meet the Chief Minister and to plead with him to withdraw any logging concessions from the lands of the Penan[387]. He was apprehended by the authorities and sent back to Switzerland. In 2000 he tried to enter Sarawak from Indonesian Kalimantan and has been missing ever since and is now declared dead. There were many speculations about his disappearance. First it was thought that it was a 'PR gag' and that he would suddenly emerge somewhere in Sarawak in order to create media attention. But most people are convinced that he was killed either in an accident crossing the border or by his enemies, who were mostly among logging companies. Since I am Swiss myself, I expected that some interviewees would try to avoid the topic. However, that was not the case. I raised the issue of Manser towards the end of the interviews, so that the interviewees had enough time to judge whether I was trustworthy or not, and subsequently nobody avoided the topic although their words were sometimes carefully chosen.

As expected, the respondents of *government agencies* were the most cautious about Manser. At first one interviewee said 'I don't even know what he was doing' but then went on and said that Manser was only living with the Penans for the adventure and that he wrote articles and made films and probably earned a lot of money with them. Manser's activities are seen as problematic and damaging and causing problems for the government. One respondent thought that Manser wanted to preserve the Penan's culture the way it was hundred years ago, which the interviewee regarded as neither feasible nor desirable. The last of the respondents had a different slant on the question. He conceded that there are problems for the Penans, but he thinks it is unfair to come from abroad and denounce the government as Manser did. For the government it is difficult to go into the issue, if it is attacked so fiercely. This procedure may be adequate with obstinate governments, it was argued, but not with Sarawak which is not a "dif-

---

387 Manser, B. 1999, p. 2-8.

ficult" government. Manser simply did it the wrong way and thus did not help the Penans much.

The *NGO* respondents see it the same way, and emphasise that the meddlesome 'greenpeace approach' is generally not successful in Malaysia. If this is the case, the NGOs say, the doors of the government close quickly and cannot be opened as easily again. It is regarded as a matter of saving face, which is why most NGOs in Malaysia try to work together with the government. Nevertheless the name of Bruno Manser apparently often springs up in meetings with the government and one respondent remembers the following statement regarding the development of the Penans, which he heard in such a meeting: "I wonder how the Swiss would feel, if the Romans would have left them in their caves."

The *scientists* concede that Manser has raised the issue of the Penans and their problems, which has meant the government has had to deal with it. Even after his disappearance, tourists visiting Sarawak often ask about the Penans and after their welfare. The respondents say that it was not the right way to do things in Sarawak and that Manser's activities did not help them with their work.

The *tour operators* also say that Manser's activities were counter productive, because although he publicized the Penans plight, their situation has not improved. Another respondent added that their land rights have not changed at all. There was more money dedicated to their development, but that was not really what they (and Manser) wanted. Yet, with all this criticism they admit that what he did was astonishing.

3.3 Privatisation

There is a discussion in Malaysia today about privatising services that are provided by the park administration such as restaurants, canteens, accommodation or guiding. The government wants to withdraw from activities that are not primarily connected to the protection of a park and to concentrate on these aspects only. In Taman Negara the accommodation and guide system was privatised in 1989, in Kinabalu in 1998, and in Mulu in 2002. The authority to privatise does not lie with the park administration but with the government. Therefore, it is possible that the park management not favour the decision to privatise, which can lead to problems with the collaboration of resort and park, as has happened in Kinabalu.

The *administration* generally favours such privatisation because that way they can put more resources into conservation issues. Moreover, they hope that the visitors get better services from companies whose sole business it is to cater for tourists. The employees of the parks are not regarded as being well enough equipped to run guesthouses and restaurants, and the government is not seen as having the funds to invest in the skills necessary for that task. Although the general opinion about privatisation is positive, there are also negative aspects. The biggest problem is that private companies need to make a profit and that the pursuit of profit can detrimentally effect a conservation area. The orientation toward profit may cause prices to rise which makes it impossible for less affluent people to visit a park. Moreover, the managers and staff of privatised resorts are not necessarily aware of conservation and therefore can cause (mostly unintended) problems. In order to avoid conflicts caused by different interests, the park administration maintains jurisdiction over the resorts located on the premises of parks. In Taman Negara there are monthly meetings where problems are sorted out and solutions tried. The park administration always has the last word. They must be careful not to stifle the resort businesses with tough restrictions. In Kinabalu there were even greater problems, because the resort was given the mandate of managing the restaurants and accommodation of several parks in Sabah. This proved to be too big a task for them, and the park administration subsequently heard many complaints from tourists who were not satisfied with the infrastructure and service. Since visitors do not know the difference between the management of the park and of the resort, they complain to anybody who looks like they work in the park. This leads to a situation where a visitor might complain about the bad food in the restaurant to a park ranger, and seek information about specific animal species from a resort receptionist. According to one respondent, this leads to visitors not being able to get answers to their questions, which is a frequent criticism of tourists.

The park administration does not like independent changes to buildings or roads, because that could pose environmental problems. Therefore, the management of the resort must ask the park administration when they want to change anything to do with buildings or roads, even if it is the colour of the buildings.

The *NGOs* did not have much to say about the issue of privatisation. They see a problem with the resorts' focusing on profit, but they also see that resorts benefit tourists. In Taman Negara they would like to see a decrease of visitors in Kuala Tahan, the park headquarters. The resort's tendency to expand is seen as a problem there, but in contrast to the lodges just outside the park, the resort's development is under control of the park administration, and can therefore be constrained.

Some *scientists* were preoccupied with the immanent privatisation of their universities and did not say much about privatisation in national parks, except that dependence on market forces can be an advantage if the economy is booming.

Tour operators generally favour the privatisation of park facilities, because they say that they could better look after the tourists with a steady source of revenue. The respondents from the resorts that have accommodation in parks, said that in the beginning they found it difficult to work together with other stakeholders such as NGOs who they thought were against privatisation because of a "narrow understanding of ecotourism". They included park administrations and NGO's in this group. However, during the first years of operation most problems were solved and now the parks and the resorts have developed a good system to deal with problems. In Kinabalu, the restriction that nothing may be changed without the consent of the park administration posed some difficulties. Accommodations was designed for individual low budget travellers or for families; there were almost no ordinary double rooms. A conversion of the buildings was proposed, but not well received by the park management. The tour operators also think it is necessary to educate their own staff better regarding conservation issues.

3.4 Tourism

3.4.1 Demands of tourists

The increasing numbers of tourists visiting conservation areas have different needs and demands regarding attractions, infrastructure and information. The park management now has the difficult task to try to satisfy these various needs and to protect the area from detrimental influences. Moreover, they have to provide for the safety of the visitors. This is not always easy, especially when physical exertion is involved, such as on the assent to Gunung Kinabalu, where ten people have died in the last twenty years, mostly due to heart problems. Since more than 300,000 persons have climbed the mountain in that time, ten fatalities do not seem much.

Respondents from the *administration* are concerned about the increasing heterogeneity of the tourists who visit national parks. A few years ago mostly nature enthusiasts (e.g. bird watchers or hobby botanists) came to these areas, whereas nowadays the national parks have become a destination for (international and domestic) mass tourists too. On the one hand the respondents approve of this development, because more people have the opportunity to learn about and enjoy nature. On the other hand they fear that some groups of visitors – namely those from ASEAN countries – do not understand when they have to pay an entrance fee or when they cannot roam freely. The increasing interest of domestic tourists and those from neighbouring countries is seen as a result of rapid urbanisation during the last twenty years, because rural people rarely come to visit conservation areas. Slight adaptations of the visitor infrastructure and the park management are possible but according to one respondent the visitors should adapt rather than the parks.

Respondents from the *NGOs* have the same opinion as those from the administration about these problems. They fear that many domestic visitors seek something in the parks which they do not find. Moreover, the NGOs believe that because the parks are on Malaysian soil, they belong to all Malaysians and can be used by them, at will. Many Asian tourists visit Malaysia for two weeks and most go shopping during the first week. Since Malaysia is also advertised as a nature destination they think "let's go and see some nature". The NGOs fear that the Asian tourists often enter the parks with a consumer's attitude and just want to see certain animals, like in a zoo. Thus the probability of a disappointing experience is great. For other respondents of the NGO-group, the advertisement of destinations and especially nature destinations is generally seen as detrimental to the areas and the people who are visited.

Because some decisions regarding tourism and the promotion of destinations are made from the top, the 'visited' tend to become victimized in one way or another, because they are expected to conform to the tastes of other people. Moreover, the NGOs say that foreigners are perceived by the local population in a way that can cause additional problems. The interviewees see the root of these problems in colonialism, and perceive tourism as something like a "return" of the imperialists.

The *scientists* see the problem of cultural change and the resulting friction between local people and foreigners in a slightly different light. Although they acknowledge that tourism can be problematic for the culture of the visited, they do not perceive the problem as dramatically as the NGO-respondents do. According to the scientists, the contact between tourists and the local people goes much less deep than it is often thought and that the latter also have the means to protect themselves. They also see an increasing difference in the various needs of tourists. The origin for the increasing popularity of conservation areas with the urban population can be seen on the one hand in colonial times, when the British started to walk in the forests of the hill resorts, and on the other hand in the increasing number of people living in (often congested) urban areas, and in the growing middle class that can afford to travel.

The *tour operators* are not less critical than the other experts about the problems between different needs of tourists. This is probably because they are confronted directly with the opinions of tourists. They think that the biggest problems occur with (mostly domestic) tourists who have African safaris in mind when they come to a Malaysian national park. However, the tour operators have often had the experience that these tourists quickly see the importance of a habitat even if they do not see the animals they came to see. Moreover, they are happy when they can discover "small" things and still have a good experience. The respondents within this group have different opinions about the role of the government's tourism promotion. Some say that certain destinations and attractions should have their price and should therefore not be accessible to everybody. Others want to propagate cheap air fares in order to bring as many people as possible to Malaysia and to its national parks.

3.4.2 Ecology and tourism

Malaysia has had a National Ecotourism Plan[388], since 1998, which was worked out together with the WWF Malaysia. The *administration* is happy with the plan, although the respondents regard it as difficult to implement. This is because – the parks need make decisions independently from their respective governments. The plan requires that carrying capacities be defined for every park, and according to the respondents, most parks have not set such limits in their management plans. This group is not in agreement about whether carrying capacities are exceeded or not. Some say that the parks are still far from being overcrowded; others state that there are already problems in certain areas (i.e. on Gunung Kinabalu, in Taman Negara and in the Mulu Caves). The number of visitors is – with very few exceptions (i.e. Pulau Penyu, see "Pulau Penyu" on page 112) – only limited by the accommodation. The carrying capacity is linked to the infrastructure of the parks, which in many cases is regarded as in need of improvement. Sanitary facilities and sewage are often in unsatisfactory condition, which is problematic for the environment, and for the well-being of the tourists.

Although the *NGOs* are very much in favour of the ecotourism plan, they are also critical of it. They admit that it probably will take a few years for the plan to be implemented. However, since it presents only guidelines but no specific numbers of visitors, this could exceed the respective carrying capacities of the parks; it is regarded as unlikely that the plan will have a great impact on the issue. The NGOs propose extensive studies about carrying capacities in the parks, which could be carried out by the NGOs themselves. Although somebody stated that "a federal plan is a federal plan" (meaning that it has not the highest priority in the states), the plan is regarded as very useful in order to start a discussion about issues of ecotourism and ecology in conservation areas. The NGO respondents emphasised that they were surprised how little the tour operators knew about ecotourism (according to the definition of Ceballos-Lascuráin, which is used in the plan; see figure 9 on page 53) and therefore were glad for

---

388 WWF Malaysia 1996.

the plan's input in order to launch the discussion. They say that a discussion is very important, because "people do not understand how the environment works". For example (mostly domestic tourists) obey the rule not to litter on the park's premises, but do so as soon as they are outside its boundaries. Another example is the Kuala Selangor Nature Reserve with its glowing fireflies: politicians wanted to build a road to the site, in order to provide better access to the attraction. This would have most certainly driven the insects away. In general the NGOs representatives fear that many parks will soon be overcrowded at certain times and at specific places (i.e. near major attractions and especially over reefs) and therefore they propose a management that will deal with overcrowding.

The *scientists* basically share the opinion of the NGOs; some formulate their opinions more bluntly. They welcome the discussion about ecotourism that was launched with the National Ecotourism Plan. Some scientists think that the economically minded tourist industry has such different interests nature conservationists, that they only offer ecofriendly attractions when they are forced to. They want the park managements to enforce the guidelines of ecotourism. The greatest problems are seen in the management of water and waste, and the reefs. In some areas – especially islands – water is scarce and has to be brought from far away, often for nearby golf courses. Waste disposal, especially sewage, is a problem in the parks, because it is rarely treated.[389] Many reefs are in danger, even though they are supposedly protected, mostly because of sewage, over-fishing and trampling by tourists. Scientists are not very happy with the label 'ecotourism', because there is no common definition of it. Some say that this buzzword will disappear within a few years. The problem is to convey the meaning of ecotourism – as sustainable and not harmful to the environment – to the tourists and the tourist industry without an adequate label. Now, the discussion is about ecotourism, but everyone has a different opinion about it.

The *tour operators* who I interviewed did not seem to resent the National Ecotourism Plan, but seemed to welcome it. They say that with ecotourism the tourist industry is protected too. However, the understanding of what ecotourism is varies greatly within this group. Some see it as a synonym for 'nature tourism', whereas others try to avoid the label but monitor their 'package trips' regarding ecological aspects. One tour operator always asks his customers to evaluate their trips, and since many of them are ecologically minded, they provide feedback about issues regarding ecotourism.

---

389 On the slopes of Gunung Kinabalu the park management had the same problem. The toilets stank considerably. However, today there is a sewage system in place which cleanses the water to such an extent that it can be released into the soil with no harm to the environment.

3.4.3 Guides

The respondents of the group, *administration*, regard guides as an important tool for both informing tourists about the park and its ecology, and preventing damage by visitors. However, the respondents state that most parks have neither enough guides nor are they sufficiently qualified. Since it is a policy of most parks to engage local people as guides, the respondents often find that guides do not speak English well enough to convey their knowledge about nature adequately to tourists. Once they are trained and have experience, "they are pinched by the tourist industry", because the tourist industry offers better salaries than the park administration can. Because there is too little money for employing enough guides and because guiding is not a well-paid job, there are almost no students who work as guides during the peak season, as is the case in western countries. The park administration is reluctant to use rangers as guides although they currently have the best training for the job. The rangers are needed for the enforcement of park regulations and for the monitoring of fauna and flora, more than for guiding. Therefore, the respondents think that guides should be employed by tour operators or be able to work independently, although their skills should be controlled by government agencies.

The *NGO* respondents did not say much about guides. They regard it as the business of tour operators to train and educate guides, and only state that there is a need for better training and for more guides in most parks.

Some of the *scientists* offer courses for members of the park administration, including units on guiding and information. One respondent draws a distinction between guiding and interpretation. The latter should contribute to the visitors' appreciation of a park. Moreover, the politicians and the park administration should realize the value of a park and consequently be prepared to spend more money or political energy for conservation issues. Guides have the goal of seeing that their clients have a good time. Therefore, interpretation and guiding do not necessarily have the same goals. The park managers can be sympathised with, because they have a difficult time, because circumstances change rapidly and funding for additional rangers or guides is difficult to get. Moreover, until some years ago national parks were considered a "dumping ground" for people who could not find an employment elsewhere. Therefore, according to this respondent, many parks are stuck with "under performers", which is why parks should invest in upgrading their staff. Although guides are regarded as important interpreters, they should not be compulsory for all tourists, as they are when tourist want to climb Gunung Kinabalu.

When I talked to the *tour operators* about guides, it was quickly apparent that there is a big difference between those who use guides in order to travel with a tourist group to different destinations in Malaysia (often including a visit of a longhouse), and those who only provide guides for a trip in the park. The former are considered an important asset of the tour operator's organisation and therefore are selected, trained and monitored very carefully and paid comparably well. Guides who only operate within parks (i.e. the ones who accompany climbers to the summit of Gunung Kinabalu or those leading trekkers up Gunung Mulu), are not well trained nor well paid. Sometimes it is not clear whose responsibility it is to train them and to test their performance, especially when the resorts do not earn any money from the guides (like in Kinabalu and Taman Negara). Therefore, the tour operators in resorts often hear complaints about the guides.

3.4.4 Information

The *administration* is well aware of the need of adequate information about the parks and their regulations. Therefore, all parks have an interpretation (or information) centre where this information should be provided. However, the information is not always regarded as adequate by members of the park administration; because it often happens that tourists do things they should not do or ask questions about important things that they should know. Maybe this is because tour operators and guides are still regarded as the best sources of information by the respondents.

The *NGOs* emphasise the importance of information about environmental issues and about specific parks. They say that there is still much to be done, and provide courses where adequate information is taught. Moreover, they say that education and information has to be provided on both ends: to the visitors and to the visited. Many local people have special knowledge about plants and animals, but not about sharing this knowledge with foreigners. Therefore, some NGOs have programmes where the locals are taught to teach courses about the environment to their neighbours and to tourists. The information that is given to the tourists is – according to some respondents – often insufficient and it is mostly given too late, when they are already in the park. The tourist information offices and booking offices in the cities should hand out information about the dos and don'ts in parks when people are considering a visit to a park.

The *scientists* stress the need for information even further. They claim that certain segments of tourists (especially backpackers) are not provided with adequate information, because they travel independently. Therefore, the important and relevant information should be found in travel guide books, as well. The Lonely Planet guide book is regarded as a good example, but it should involve the park administration more, so that they can assure that the information printed is adequate. Since the number of guides in the parks is limited and since not all people want to engage a guide, one respondent proposes more 'track side interpretation', but that this must entail more than putting up signs with the botanical and the native names of trees. In general the park managers need to be more creative, because in the future the parks will have to compete with each other for visitors and for revenue.

The opinions of the *tour operators* are again divided. Some say that all necessary information is available for the tourists if they only would ask for it, which they often do not. Furthermore, they trust their guides to provide the necessary information during the journey. Therefore, they do not see a need for much more information. Others think that there is still a demand and need for information at various places and on various levels.[390]

3.4.5 Image and promotion

The image of a destination is very important in tourism. Therefore, incidents such as the Asian currency crisis or the haze can taint the good image of a region. However, the *administration* does not think that these specific incidents have had a great impact, because tourist arrivals did not decrease much, and because there were no lasting effects from them. Regarding logging activities – the respondents admit – Sarawak does not have such a good image in western countries, although they claim that the situation has improved considerably and that the image was exaggerated in the first place. Sabah is said to have the problem of not having much of an image, which is why it is not well known abroad. Promotion is regarded as very important for the creation of the image of a tourist destination, which was proved by the peak of visitor numbers during the 'Visit Malaysia Year 1994', when the country was promoted heavily in Europe and the USA. On a smaller scale, the respondents favour events (e.g. the sporting events, 'climbathon' in Kinabalu or the 'Battle of Borneo' in Sarawak) that primarily serve as promotional tools, because the events themselves do not bring in much revenue.

The *NGOs* are also aware of the importance of the image of a country or a destination. Regarding the image of logging activities, my respondents did not all share the same opinion. Some said that the situation has improved now that stricter laws are in place, and that the logging companies do not clear cut whole forests anymore. Others say that although there are stricter laws, the logging goes on pretty much on the same scale as before, because of loopholes in the law. One respondent stated that there is no clear understanding about what image Malaysia should have and develop for tourists, and that the ministries want

---

390 The fact that a tour operator was asked at a travel fair in Singapore "how is the shopping in Mulu?" shows that there is in fact a need to provide information about nature conservation widely.

more tourists but do not ask the tourists what they want. Moreover, the respondents state that the visited are not asked about tourism development.

The *scientists* did not talk about the image of Malaysia as a whole, but about the image of specific destinations. They say that it is difficult to create adequate images for conservation areas because these should remain authentic. It is much easier to promote the Langkawi Islands as the place where 'Anna and the King' was shot or as a destination for golfers. The idea that solitude is an important aspect of a visit to a national park (at least for westerners) is seen as conflicting with increasing the number of visitors. Moreover, a single area has to be promoted for an increasingly diverse clientele without compromising its conservation, which is very difficult.

The *tour operators* are used to creating images, and live from the images they provide for the tourists. Those who promote their products abroad admitted that it is difficult to associate Malaysia with a distinctive image or label.[391] They said that Malaysian multi-culturalism is more difficult to promote than the multi-ethnicity of Indonesia. The fact that the majority of the Malaysian population are Muslims is not regarded as something to be promoted in the west, especially in the USA. Therefore, the promotion "Culture, Nature and Adventure" was changed to "Malaysia, Truly Asia"[392]. Nature is also seen as an increasingly important item on the promotion agenda. Since tour operators are dependent on the number of visitors who come to Malaysia, they suffered more from incidents such as the haze, or the kidnapping at Sidapan. However, the Asian crisis was regarded as a lesser problem and was also balanced by the political crises in Indonesia, which caused many tourists to prefer to travel to Malaysia. Some of the respondents of the tour operator group were not so much concerned about (true) authenticity, as were the scientists, for as one tour operator said "authenticity is in the eye of the beholder". This should not lead to the conclusion that "anything goes" but to a concentration on the product itself. This means that the visited especially should be more involved in the process. Sometimes this can lead to arrangements that may differ from the images tourists have. One respondent was of the opinion that if these arrangements are true to the needs of the local people, they will be perceived as true or authentic by the visitor. Another offered the hypothesis that the density of memories of a trip correlates with the bonding of the visitors with the local people. He discovered that if the

---

391 First Malaysia was promoted with a hibiscus flower, then with an orang-utan, after that with a turtle, subsequently with the Kuala Lumpur train station and eventually again with the hibiscus flower.
392 In recent years the relative peacefulness of Malaysia (apart from the kidnapping on Sidapan and some demonstrations in favour of Anwar Ibrahim) was also considered an asset that could be promoted.

tourists know the name and family of their guide, they take home more intense memories. Therefore, image creation is seen as strongly connected to personal relations and information.

3.4.6 Income
Tourism has become an important source of income for Malaysia. The notions about how this income should be generated differ greatly. The park administration is generally not much involved in these questions, because the income that is generated by the parks goes directly into the coffers of the states, from where their expenses are paid. Nevertheless, the respondents hope that if more people visit the parks and spend money, the expenditures can be better covered. As a means of increasing the number of visitors, the government has decided to introduce Saturday as a free day for government employees. With this they want to enable more Malaysians to stay overnight in parks which was previously almost impossible for them on weekends.

NGOs say that the government often disregards the needs of the local population in their plans for tourism. The construction of big hotels and resorts – mostly owned by big (foreign) corporations – is considered much more important by the government, than are small scale enterprises. The NGOs feel that the government should invest fewer in large projects and more in smaller local ones.

The *scientists* are also aware of these problems, and say that the number of tourists alone does not indicate the amount of revenues that stay in the country.[393] The scientists also criticise the government for concentrating too much on an upmarket clientele such as golfers, who in the end do not bring much revenue to Malaysia. According to studies from New Zealand that were mentioned by a scientist, backpackers spend more or less the same amount of money in the country as people who stay in five-star hotels, because backpackers stay longer, and their money stays in the country more than money spent by those who stay in resorts. One respondent mentioned that compulsory air access to Mulu only costs less than the boat trip to the park, because it is heavily subsidised by the government. This is also a reason why a regular boat service cannot compete with the air traffic.[394]

The *tour operators* feel the ups and downs of the market rather strongly. Depending on their focus, they cater for different clientele. They are not very much interested in backpackers, because these rarely book trips with travel agencies.

---

393 Malaysia has more arrivals than Thailand per year, but much less income through tourism.
394 According to a respondent more than 10,000 visitors came to Mulu at the time when the boats went more or less out of service, and stayed there an average of 3 nights. Today come as many people but they only stay one or two nights.

Generally tour operators are pleased if air fares become cheaper and if the Ringgit is not too strong, because Malaysia does not have the image of being a cheap destination (like Indonesia or Thailand). For smaller tour operators, marketing is difficult, because it is very expensive. Therefore, they very rarely advertise, widely. They concentrate on some trade fairs and tend to invite journalists and photographers to Malaysia. These may publish their impressions of their journeys or special events. Especially among smaller tour operators, the competition is strong and a dramatic slump of visitor arrivals is a great problem for them.

4 Summary

There seems to be little conflict between the different groups of experts. It has to be noted that open conflict is generally avoided in Malaysia, and that there is a general understanding that most issues are better solved in private discussion and compromise. All in all I had the impression that nature conservation works quite well in Malaysia and that most experts who are engaged in different organisations agree.

According to the experts, the biggest problems are financing parks, poaching, participation of local people, and the increasing heterogeneity of visitors. It is debated whether fees should be raised or whether they should only be raised for foreigners. In order to minimise the park managements' expenses, some infrastructure is privatised, which is criticised by the NGOs. While visitors can thus be catered for more professionally, the parks lose a source of income, and since the park administration have to supervise the private companies, their work loads remain high. The hope of generating income from pharmaceutical companies is probably exaggerated, since it is difficult to trace ingredients of medicaments back to a certain plant or area. In many parks, poaching is a problem because there are not enough resources to apprehend poachers. Because of the poaching problem, the park administration is reluctant to introduce buffer zones, which are seen as an easy access for poachers. The fact that in other countries buffer zones are used as a tool to prevent poachers from entering parks is not acknowledged, much. The participation of local people is regarded as important, but only as a means to coerce them to consent to conservation issues. Therefore, a bottom-up approach should be considered more, even if it is not in line with the general policy.

Most stakeholders in conservation work well together, which makes nature conservation in Malaysia less contested than it is in some other countries. Nevertheless, a better coordination between these groups would be helpful to tackle new challenges of nature conservation.

VI Tourists in Gunung Mulu National Park

1 Introducing Gunung Mulu National Park

1.1 The context of the park

Gunung Mulu National park is often called the "pearl" among the national parks in Sarawak. Although it has many outstanding attractions that many want to see, it is not visited by as many tourists as the other two big parks, Kinabalu (see "2.3.1: Kinabalu" on page 106) or Taman Negara (see "2.1.1: Taman Negara" on page 93). However, the newly acquired label of "World Heritage Site"[395] will enhance its attractiveness. It is therefore, a good example of a Malaysian national park that will have to face an influx of visitors and their different needs and demands in the near future. In contrast to the study about the notions of urban Malaysians about nature conservation (see "IV: Malaysian urbanites and their national parks" on page 115), the focus of this chapter is on the differences between individual and group travellers. Each group tends to visit distinct kinds of destinations when travelling. But in national parks and conservation areas, their paths meet, which can be a challenge for the park management.

Figure 60: Visitors to national parks in Sarawak 2000 (monthly)

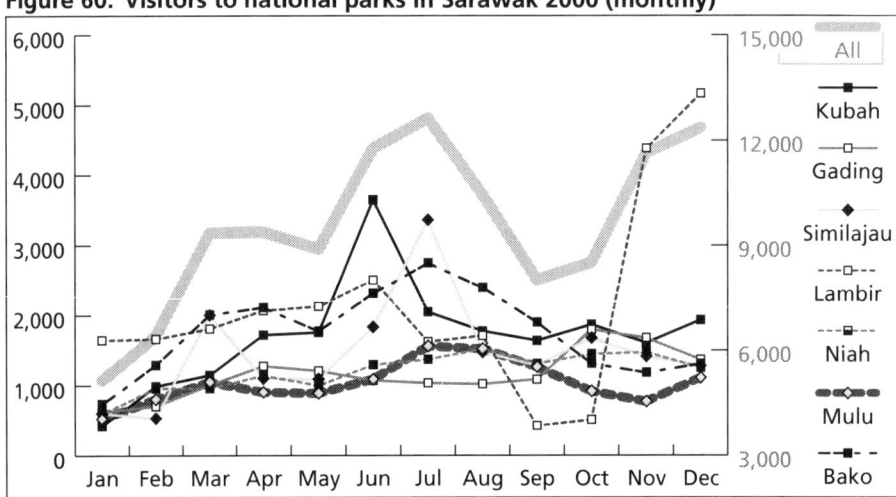

Source: own draft; data Department of Forestry of Sarawak 2001.

Figure 60 on page 204 gives an overview of the visitors of national parks in the year 2000. In that year there were a total of 517,558 arrivals by air (365,373 Malaysians and 152,185 foreigners); 114,599, or more than a fifth (77,682 Malaysians and 36,917 foreigners) of them visited Sarawak's national parks, and

---

395 Gunung Mulu and Kinabalu were both awarded the label of a World Heritage Site at the end of 2000. Taman Negara is next on the list of Malaysian applicants.

12,396 (4,002 Malaysians and 8,394 foreigners) visited Mulu. That means 2.4 % of all visitors (including business travellers) or 10.8 % of those who visited any national park, went to Mulu. There is a clear peak of total visitors in June and July and at the end of the year. Yet, if we take a look at individual parks, those which are visited mostly by Malaysians show very distinct peaks in June and July, during the Malaysian school holidays, whereas the parks with a majority of foreign visitors such as Mulu and Niah show a more balanced gradient. June, July and August are also the driest months in the area, which makes the parks more attractive.

Figure 61: Climate data of three stations near Mulu in East Malaysia

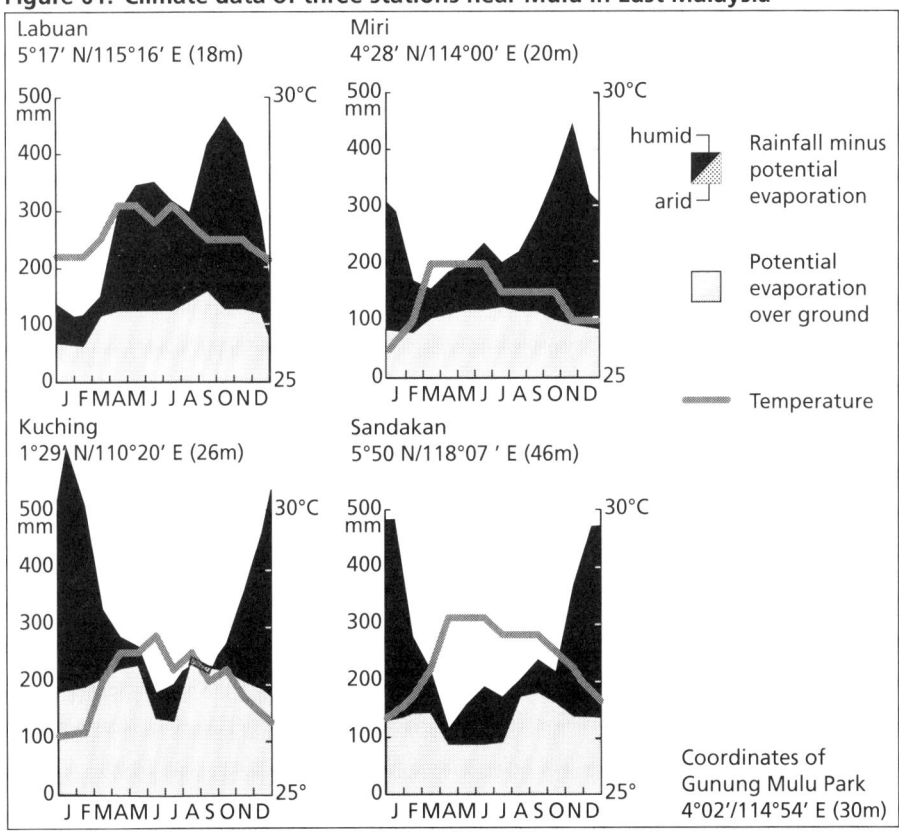

Source: Frankenberg, P., Lauer, W. & Rheker, J.R. 1990.

In February 2002 the park management was turned over to the privately owned company Borsarmulu. The company wants to improve facilities in order to meet the expected number of visitors. The survey was conducted before the change in management. The data gathered show the possibilities and constraints of the site and should be useful to the new management as well.

Figure 62: Sketch of the Gunung Mulu headquarters

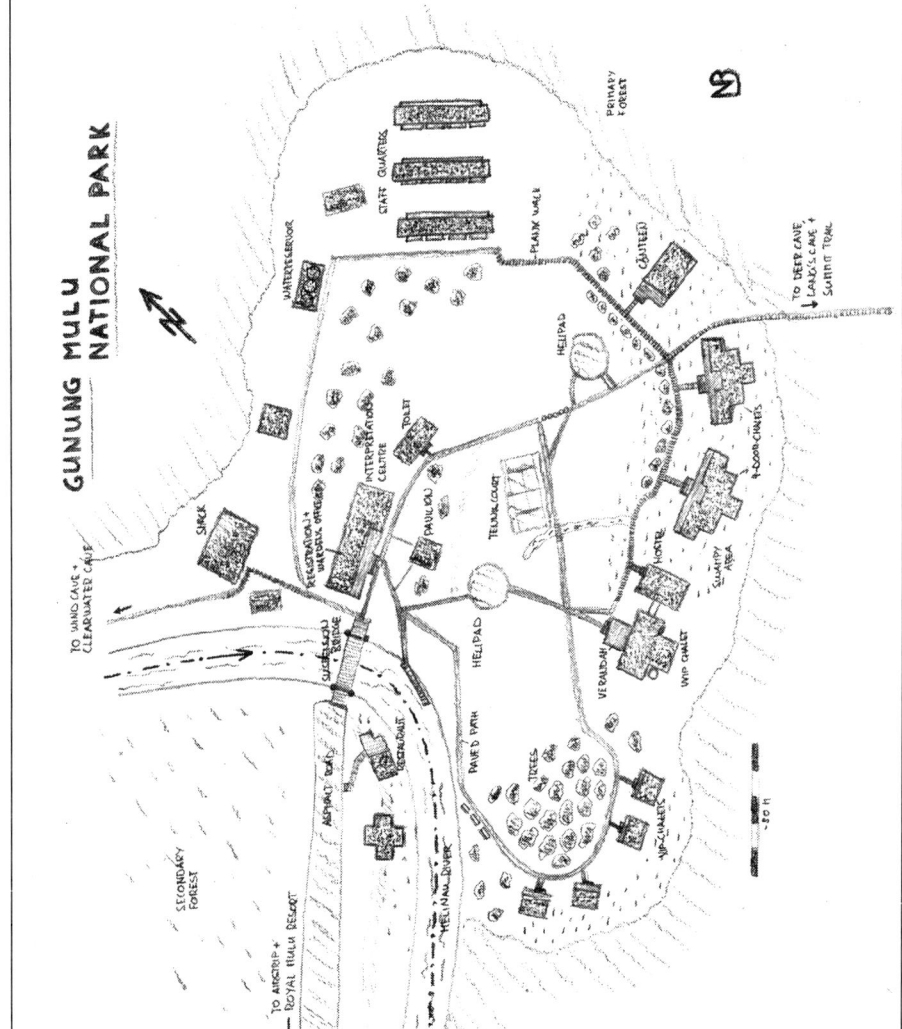

Source: own draft.

1.2 Setting and major attractions

Gunung Mulu is situated adjacent to the border of Brunei Darussalam. Its climate is tropical. Between July and September is the best time to visit the park, because there is little rainfall. Climate charts for the park were not available; therefore, diagrams of locations in its vicinity are displayed in figure 61 on page 205 showing the meterorological conditions of the region. There are no roads leading to the park, it can only be reached by boat, by air or on foot.

Figure 63: Gunung Mulu National Park

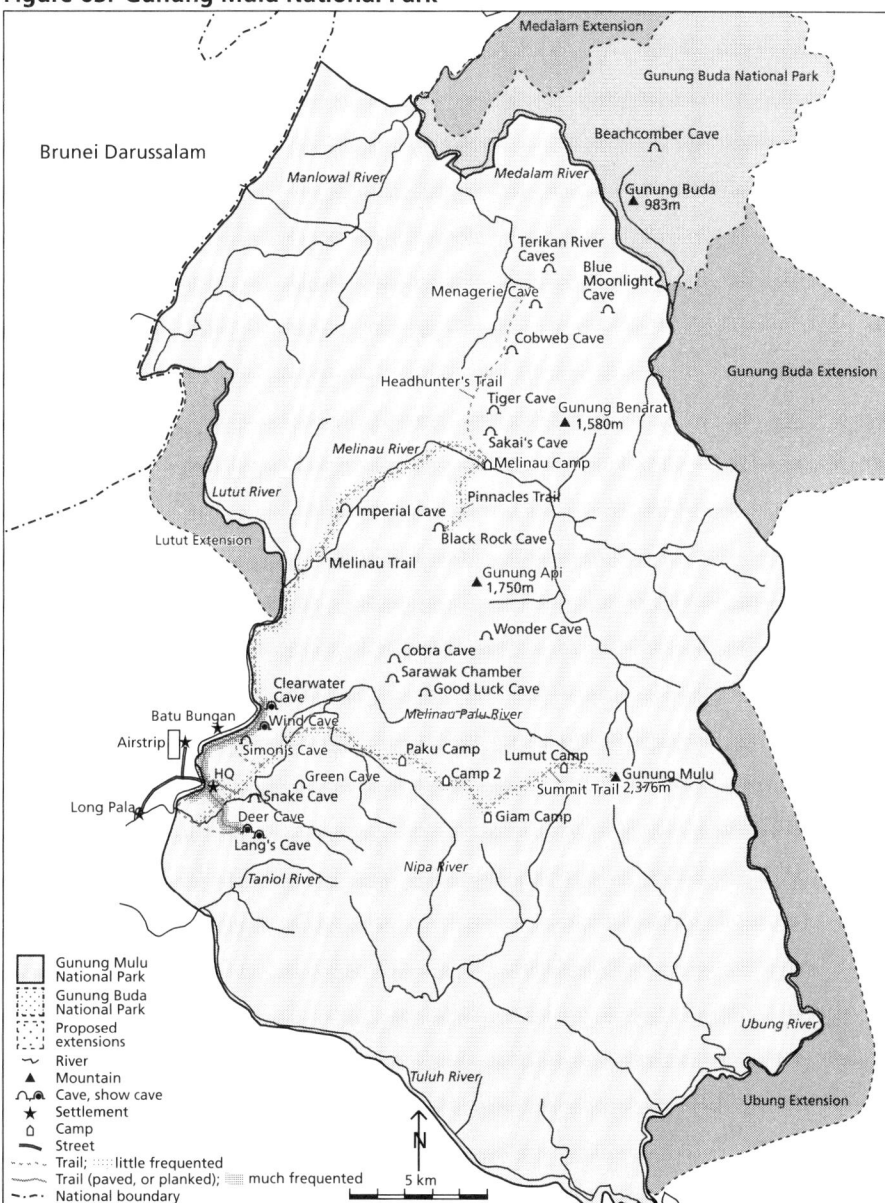

Source: own draft; map basis and data: Periplus Editions n.a.; Thorsell, J. 2000.

The area is sparsely populated, mostly by sedentary Berawans and a few non-sedentary Penans (most of whom have become sedentary in recent years)[396].

---

396 King, V.T. 1993, p. 46, 170.

The 528 square kilometres were gazetted as a national park in 1974, opened to the public in 1985, and at the end of 2000, became a World Heritage Site.[397] The park comprises altitudes between 30 m and 2,376 m, and has a great biodiversity. However, the fauna and flora are not the main attractions of the park. The world's biggest known cave chamber (the Sarawak chamber), the world's largest cave entrance (Deer Cave) and the world's largest and oldest (2 to 3 million years old) cave system are the features that attract most visitors. In fact, Gunung Api is probably the most cavernous mountain in the world.[398]

The highest elevation of the park – Gunung Mulu – is a sandstone outcrop; the caves were hollowed out from limestone formations on its shoulder. The annual rainfall of over 5,000 mm sustains the tropical rainforest in the lowlands. Due to the varying geology and the different altitudes, some 16 vegetation formations have been described, comprising all formations that occur in Sarawak. Moreover, over 60 species of mammal, over 260 bird species and 25 snake species occur.[399] In the southern part of the park, nomadic Penans use the forest's resources. Most of them have now settled permanently outside the park, but around three hundred still live in the nearby forests. They are allowed to hunt in the park, but only for animals that are not endangered, and only with traditional weapons, and are allowed to collect plants to a limited extent. They are not allowed to cut down trees for building material, which makes their traditional livelihood more difficult. These things all make Gunung Mulu park a unique environment and a prime destination for nature based tourism.

2 Methods

The survey conducted in Mulu was set up as a standardised interview with a few open questions. It was designed to be filled in by the respondents themselves. People were approached at different (departure) times in order to avoid biases corresponding with the time when people leave Mulu. Like the survey in Kuala Lumpur, the sample was not taken in the purely random fashion as would be necessary for representative statistics. Nevertheless, I am confident that the sample is representative, at least regarding the visitors who happened to be in Mulu during the time when the survey was done. The questionnaires were subsequently coded and analysed quantitatively using SPSS. The statistics thus compiled show distinctions and similarities between group travellers and individual travellers.

---

397 UNESCO 2000.
398 Meredith, M. & Woolridge, J. 1992; Thorsell, J. 2000.
399 World Conservation Monitoring Centre 2002.

2.1 Profile of the sample

Interviews were conducted with visitors to Mulu, during one week in August 2000. Eighty-two individuals filled in the form, which is roughly a third of all the people who stayed in Mulu during that week. Most of the respondents were approached at the Mulu airstrip before their departure.[400]

Figure 64: Respondents' origin and all visitors of Mulu during interview period

Region	Sample	Sample %	All[a]	All %	5 %[b]	1 %
Europe	60	74.1	159	58.5	yes	no
North America	13	16.0	16	5.9	yes	no
Australia/NZ	3	3.7	17	6.2	no	no
Asia	2	2.5	21	7.7	no	no
Malaysia	2	2.5	47	17.3	yes	yes
Africa	1	1.2	12	4.4	no	no
Total	81[c]	100.0	272	100.0		

a. The park administration registers the visitors when they enter the park's premises for the first time.
b. Percentages of the respondents and of all the visitors were tested for statistically significant differences. 'Yes' in the column of '5 %' means that both groups actually differ significantly at the interval of confidence of 5 %. The same applies for column '1 %' with the interval of confidence of 1 %.
c. One person did not declare his or her country of origin.
Source: own draft and data; data from all visitors by Gunung Mulu Park Administration.

Usually airports are not ideal spots to conduct interviews, because people are pressed for time or anxious to embark. In Mulu, however, it was first obvious that most of the people present half an hour before a departure were waiting for a plane to leave Mulu. Secondly, the passengers did not seem to be anxious about missing their plane because there is only one plane at a time that lands before it leaves with passengers to Miri. Thirdly, due to the schedule, it was easy to know when only the people were on the airstrip, who were departing instead of arriving and who therefore had spent some time in the park. Most people who were approached agreed to fill in the questionnaire.

2.2 Origin of the respondents

The majority of the respondents (more than 80 %; see figure 64 on page 209) are from so called western countries, which is – compared to the westerners registered at the park entrance – a slight bias[401]. This bias, as well as the one against Malaysians – Mulu is visited by 30 % Malaysians (see figure 24 on page 106) –

---

400 Since most people coming to Mulu by boat leave by air plane, it was possible to include them.
401 Only 70.6 % of the visitors at the registration desk were Westerners ($\chi^2 = 4.949 \geq 3.841 =$ significant at 5 %; df of 1; but not significant at 1 %).

in the sample, can be attributed to coincidence because at the time of the survey I did not encounter many Malaysians when I was at the airport distributing questionnaires. If we look at the rest of the sample, some figures only differ significantly at the 5 % interval of confidence (see figure 64 on page 209).

2.3 Gender and age

The gender ratio is 48.1 % male to 51.9 % female[402] visitors, which is fairly well balanced. The age distribution is as follows:
- 10 % of visitors are below 20
- 24 % between 20 and 30
- 24 % between 30 and 40
- 23 % between 40 and 50
- 15 % between 50 and 60 and
- 4 % over 60.

Hence, three quarters of the visitors are between 20 and 50, which is the age group which tend to travel most. There are not many children coming to Mulu with their parents, although the caves and bats are things children would probably like to see. However, the rest of the park does not feature many things that are specifically appealing for children. I consider a fifth of the visitors who are over fifty a rather high number for a tourist destination. It shows that conservation areas are destinations more and more sought after by the elderly.

2.4 Individual and group travellers

The ratio of individual travellers to group travellers of the sample is 31 to 50 (38.3 to 61.7 %)[403]. Hence we see that more people travel to Mulu using a travel agent[404]. Not all of these travel in a group for their whole journey. Often they come to Kuching on their own, where they book a tour including a visit to Mulu with a local travel agent. It is therefore not easy to make a clear distinction between individual travellers and group travellers. Because of this I am not using the terms "backpackers" and "package tourists" because they tend to evoke images which are not accurate anymore (see "3.2.4: Individual travellers vs. group travellers" on page 35). Nevertheless, tourists who take guided tours have different experiences than to people who come to a park on their own. They probably also have different expectations about their stay in a conservation area.

---

402 The gender ratio in Malaysia shows reverse numbers (48 % female and 52 % male), but the numbers do not differ significantly in a statistical sense.
403 The park administration registered the same ratio during the survey period 38.6 to 61.4 %.
404 The respondents used the services of 13 different tour operators, during the period of the survey 25 travel agents (half of them Malaysian) were entering the park with a group.

Women and men do not differ much regarding their status as travellers. Regarding the age groups only the category "20 to 30", with much more individual travellers, differs significantly[405] from the whole sample. This does not surprise, because this is the age when people – at least in western countries – are able to take some time off and travel abroad. The country of origin has no influence on the manner of travel to and in Mulu.

3 Tourism and its potential in Gunung Mulu

Although more and more foreign and domestic tourists are interested in visiting conservation areas, not all the areas have the same potential to attract and satisfy tourists. Not only are natural attractions such as charismatic species or spectacular landscapes important, but also what other recreational activities can be provided for the tourists. The World Tourism Organisation (WTO) and the United Nations Development Programme (UNEP) developed a checklist[406] on tourism potential of protected areas, which I adapted and amended for Mulu. Its questions (see figure 65 on page 211) shall be answered with data from the survey as well as with own observations in the following chapters.

Figure 65: Checklist on tourism potential of Gunung Mulu

	Questions	Rating[a]
1)	Is the protected area close to an international airport or major tourist centre?	+
2)	How comfortable is the journey to the area?	+/–
3)	Does the area offer: charismatic species? other interesting wildlife? distinctive wildlife viewing?	– + +
4)	Is successful wildlife viewing possible?	+/–
5)	Does the area offer more than one feature of interest?	++
6)	What standards of food and accommodation are offered?	++ to – –
7)	Does the area have additional cultural interests?	–
8)	Does the area differ much from other visitor reserves?	+
9)	Does the area have recreation facilities?	–
10)	Are the explanations in the information centre adequate?	+/–
11)	Is the area close enough to other sites of touristic interest?	– –
12)	How attractive is the surrounding area?	–

a. The rating is based on own observations and categorised from ++ (= very much) to – – (= not at all).
Source: adapted and amended from WTO/UNEP 1992, p. 17.

405 χ^2 = 10.828 ≥ 6.653 at 1 %; df of 1.
406 WTO/UNEP 1992, p. 17.

3.1 Proximity to an international airport or a major tourist centre

The closest international airport to Mulu is Miri, although for most international destinations passengers have to change to connecting flights in Kuching, Kota Kinabalu or Kuala Lumpur. With frequent flights from Miri to the Mulu airstrip, visitors can reach the park fairly quickly. The difficulty of getting there is not a problem of the lack of flights but the fact that they are often fully booked.

Although Miri serves as a tourist destination for workers from the nearby offshore oil rigs and for people from Brunei (where it is forbidden to drink alcohol), it is not a great attraction for visitors who are interested in nature tourism. It is known for its entertainment and red light district which may actually repel tourists, rather than attract them. Therefore, Mulu is not only geographically located in a remote area it is also remote from other tourist attractions. However, Mulu in itself is very attractive and has the potential to be a stepping stone to other destinations. Near Miri there are some beaches which are slowly being developed into tourist destinations with hotels. They serve as a base for tourists who want to visit Mulu, Niah and/or Lambir Hills, which can be easily accessed from Miri. Therefore, Miri serves as a centre from where the important conservation areas of the region can be visited. If these draw more tourists to the region, Miri has the potential to grow into a relay station or a minor tourist centre.

3.2 Comfort of access

The main entry point from which to access Mulu is, as explained earlier, coastal Miri; only very few use the so called "Headhunter's Trail", that goes through the park, to enter Mulu. The flight from Miri airport to the Mulu airstrip takes around forty minutes to cover the 100 km distance, and is an adventure itself, because only small planes flying low over the canopy can land on the short airstrip. Since weight is crucial for the small 19-seater aircraft, not only the luggage (10 kg per passenger) is weighed, but also the passengers. By air fewer than one hundred persons can reach Mulu per day, if everything goes smoothly. This was different before 1998, when three different airlines flew into Mulu. The haze and the Asian Currency Crisis, however, caused two of them to collapse leaving only the state owned Malaysia Air System (MAS). In addition, MAS categorised Mulu as Rural Air Service Sector, meaning that MAS is flying there more as a social obligation than for commercial reasons.[407] Therefore, not much is invested in the maintenance or replacement of the old Twin Otter aircraft. In addition, the booking system is not very transparent. Flights are often declared fully

---

407 Tan Chin Siang 1999.

booked, when in reality there are still seats available. Moreover, it is not easy to change the departure date or time from Mulu. Due to the specific availability of activities in the park (see "3.5: Variety of attractions" on page 220) individual travellers often want to change the date of their return flight, which cannot be done in advance. As a consequence they have to take their chances, show up at the desired date and time and hope that there are still seats available. Nonetheless, most people come to Mulu by plane, mostly due to time constraints. There is a boat service too, but it takes roughly a day from Kuala Baram near Miri, and passengers have to frequently change to smaller boats the further they get upstream. The schedule is unreliable because in the upper regions boats only depart once they are full. Moreover, sometimes in the dry season[408] the park is inaccessible by boat, and finally the trip cost as much or more as the flight. Therefore, not many visitors choose this way to get to the park.

3.2.1 Results from the survey

If we look at our sample, 75 % of the respondents came by air plane, whereas 25 % came by boat. The latter number is rather high because four tour operators choose to travel by boat to Mulu. For them it is easier to fill a river boat and to ask for a smoother schedule than for a single individual traveller. Tour operators also have problems with the booking system of the flights, which can make it impossible to bring in a whole group of travellers at the same time. In addition they reported that their customers liked the river cruise that leads them into the jungle of Mulu, as long as the connections functioned smoothly. The tour operators in question combine boat and air travel, because they let the groups that came in by boat fly out by plane.

Figure 66: Evaluation of transport[409]

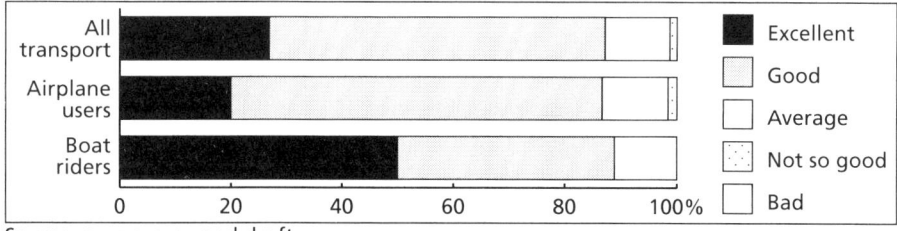

Source: own survey and draft.

Figure 66 on page 213 shows that the majority of the respondents were satisfied with the transport. The ones who took the boat ride were more enthusiastic than those who came in by air plane. This shows that the transport was reliable – at

---

408 There are no distinct seasons in the region, but during August and September considerably less rain is falling which can render the rivers near Mulu un-navigable even for small boats.
409 The evaluation refers to the transportation that was used on the way *into* Mulu.

least during the period of the survey. The rather good rating shows that it is not so important to have a modern mode of transport. Tourists like to view transport as a part of the whole experience, which can have some adventurous aspects or – in other words – aspects of (not undesirable) adventures.

3.2.2 Future prospects: better access, better coordination

If Mulu becomes more attractive because of its status as a World Heritage Site, transportation issues have to be addressed. There are several possibilities, including access by air and by boat. The discussions about the lengthening of the airstrip are not new. Depending on the prospect of many more passengers, MAS will probably have to invest in the extension, as well as in larger air planes. However, they will only do this if tourists can find adequate accommodations. For the four star Royal Mulu Resort (RMR) this could result in a much steadier flow of more affluent visitors and to a higher occupancy of rooms. But it will also have the consequence that people may stay for shorter periods, making the one-night stay the rule, which raises the costs of the hotel business in Mulu. The park administration is privatising their accommodation (as has already been done in Taman Negara and Kinabalu). Generally this causes prices to rise, leaving space for local, lower budget enterprises. The experiences travellers will have when flying into Mulu with a bigger (and air conditioned) aircraft will be different from the one available today. The trip will be shorter, smoother and less adventurous than before. Vision Air Malaysia – a branch of American based Vision Air – is currently setting up air travel from Kota Kinabalu and Miri to Mulu. They want to provide more than just transport, but fly over the landmarks of the park: the Pinnacles and Mount Mulu (and Mount Kinabalu). Upon request, some of the pilots of MAS are doing this too. Whether this practice is disturbing to the wildlife in the park depends on the altitude in which the detours are flown. The fares of Vision Air are considerably higher than those of MAS, where a flight costs around RM 60 for a return ticket from Miri to Mulu. The new airline charges RM 170 for the same trip in an air conditioned 19-seater Dornier air plane, and RM 360 for the longer trip from Kota Kinabalu and back.[410]

There is great potential in the access by boat, although it takes much longer than the flight. If it were possible to have a regular boat service, not only for groups but also for individual travellers, the boat trip could be an attractive alternative to the plane ride. Once there is a steadier stream of boat passengers

---

410 Vision Air (2001) claim on their homepage that visitors have doubled since the introduction of the second air link with four inbound flights in May 2001. However, this holds not true if we compare their data (provided by the registration office of Mulu) with the statistics of the year 2000. In May there was an increase of 44 % compared with May 2001, in June a plus of 34 % and in July even a very slight decrease of 1 %.

who want to visit the park, it will create jobs for local boatmen as well as at kiosks or small restaurants at stopovers. The experience is quite different – especially in the upper reaches of the river – from the flight, and could be advertised as an enjoyable adventure, rather than merely serving as transport. A flexible solution would be to enable the combination of boat trip (one way) and flight (return) for attractive (or even equal) prices. People who travel a whole day in order to reach a destination tend to stay longer than just one night, which would reduce costs and distribute the pressure on specific sights within the park.

3.3 Attractiveness of flora and fauna

3.3.1 Hidden treasures

Travel books, leaflets and films advertise[411] Mulu as a place of high biodiversity with a great variety of birds (over 260 species[412]), among which are all the hornbill species of Borneo. The 16 vegetation formations[413] comprise all the formations known in Sarawak. Moreover, it is one of the richest sites in the world for palm trees, with 109 species. Thus, the visitor expects a rainforest teeming with life and reverberating with the sounds of animals that live under the canopy of giant dipterocarpaceae. Indeed, when entering the park, loud chirping greets the visitors. However, the animals that can be heard can rarely be seen. The birds are even shyer than the mammals that hide away from the park headquarters or the much frequented walks. For many visitors this can be disappointing. There are several reasons why many animals are rarely seen. First, they shy away from the two major trails leading to the four show caves, because of the heavy foot traffic. Second, the indigenous Penans are still allowed to hunt in the park.[414] Hunted animals hide much more and better than those who have learned that there is no harm from humans. A great attraction are the roughly two to three million bats[415] that during the day hang on the roof of Deer Cave and at dusk emerge from its great mouth. They fly in sinuous curves and produce a swishing sound with their wings when they fly over the jungle in order to devour several tons of insects during their nightly forage. In another cave there are also several million swiflets. In the caves there are many species of cave animals that can be seen when caving with a guide.

---

411 See Lutterjohann, M., Homann, E., Homann, K. & Kuster, R. 1998. Rowthorn, C., Andrew, D., Hellander, P. & Lindenmayer, C. 1999. Sarawak Tourism Board 199?.
412 270 according to Thorsell, J. 2000.
413 17 according to Thorsell, J. 2000.
414 Formally they are allowed to hunt with firearms too. However, the government and park administration tries to restrict them to traditional weapons (i.e. blowpipes, bows, traps).
415 Twelve species were counted among which the wrinkle-lipped bat (*chearephon plicata*) is the most numerous (Hall 1992 in Chrismond S.P. 2001).

3.3.2 Results from the survey

Figure 67 on page 216 survey shows the main reasons for a visit to Mulu. Fauna and flora do not rank very high, unless the all-encompassing category "nature" is seen as mainly consisting of fauna and flora. The bats were exclusively mentioned by group travellers. They were probably told by their guides what kind of spectacle to expect and it is a fixed item on the schedule of almost all groups that go to Mulu. Seeing the bats emerge from the cave mouth was one of the best experiences the visitors had (see figure 71 on page 225).

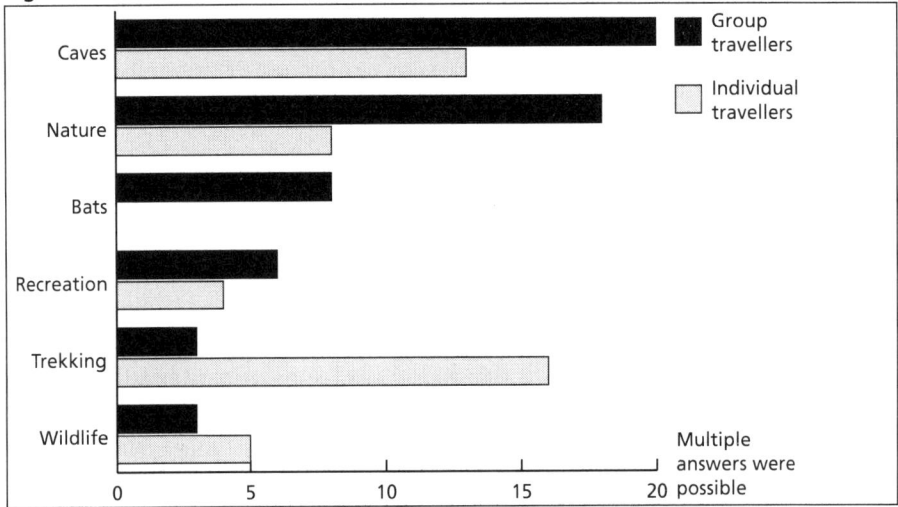

Figure 67: The main reasons for visitors to come to Mulu

Source: own survey and draft.

Again, the group travellers liked watching the bats more than the individual travellers, some of whom also disliked watching the bats. The reason for this could be that the bats do not always come out. If it is raining they tend to stay in the cave, unless they have not been out for two or three days. Waiting for them to come out and to having to go back to the accommodation in the rain and darkness is not fun. Especially when people have not much time at their disposal, not seeing the bats – or other animals for that matter – can become a critical situation, which dampens the whole experience. A study conducted by Chrismond Sem Pasan[416] mentioned that most visitors (91 %) who went to see the bats (and 98 % of the park visitors did so) were either happy or very happy with the experience (all of them actually witnessed the bats to fly out).

---

416 Chrismond (2001) counted 205 Asians and 95 Europeans (probably including Americans) that visited the observation platform during six consecutive days in June 2001.

3.3.3 Future prospects: fewer animals in high impact areas

The more visitors come to a certain area, the shyer some of the animals become, while others get used to visitors. However, if they are also hunted, they hide even more which reduces their visibility considerably. The bats have become a major tourist attraction and the expectations grow especially when "watching the bats" is a fixed item in the itinerary of visitors with limited time at their disposal. Some rangers have already expressed concerns that the bats are disturbed by the visitors to the cave during the day, and by the spectators on the observation platform one hundred meters from the cave entrance (at times there are well over 120 people waiting and chatting there) at dusk. Up to now it cannot be predicted whether the bats will fly on a specific day or not. The fact that the area surrounding Mulu is being logged and converted into oil palm plantations also has an effect on the bats (and the swiftlets). Because their foraging perimeter is around 25 km and they can catch fewer insects over the plantations, the availability of food is diminishing.

If the bottleneck of the air access widens, the pressure on the ecosystems, especially in the caves, rises. Bird watchers already have difficulties seeing the animals they have come to observe, in areas where many tourists walk through. A possibility would be to open specific areas for people who are accompanied by a guide. However, this only works when the guides have specific skills and knowledge and when they can earn a living with this activity. In order to achieve this, the quality of the 'bird watching' or 'night walking' has to be satisfying for the visitors, and the price structure has to be transparent. Often tourists are reluctant to pay a – by all means reasonable – price for a service when they get the feeling of being cheated. Their safeness can be increased with explanations about the costs of certain goods and services provided by the park administration.

3.3.4 Hunting and the participation of indigenous people

Hunting is a very difficult issue. By prohibiting the Penans from hunting wild pig and deer within the park's premises, the protection of species and the desire of the tourists to see them is favoured over the desire of the Penans to continue living their traditional life. However, the Penans' methods of resource use can be seen as a traditional lifestyle that should be protected too. The problem of overpopulation of some species, such as wild pig, which may threaten the ecological balance, is not addressed by the management at all. For some tourists the presence of Penans in Mulu is a sign of its authenticity, which could lead both to the conservation and to the museamisation of their lifestyle (although this contradicts the policy of the government). The protection of environments – especially rainforests – is often closely connected to the protection of indigenous people who live in such environments. In the discussions about this conservation, the aspect of value is very important. It therefore has to be worthwhile to protect the habitat of certain people. Many NGOs stress the immense knowledge of indigenous peoples about medicinal plants which can be used in western medicine. Moreover, the indigenous peoples' lives seems to be shrouded in a mystic aura when their relationship to certain plants or landscape features is described.[417] The extent to which native hunting practices disturb the wildlife or make them shy is debatable. That Penans are present in the park can be viewed in different ways: they can be accused of disturbing the wildlife and even of threatening the biodiversity, they can be ridiculed for their "backwardness"[418] or they can be glorified as keepers of a vast store of knowledge and guarantors of sustainability. However, it should be possible to combine the objectives of the park administration with the needs of the Penans and the tourists in a mutually satisfying manner. The settlement of sedentary Penans at Batu Bungan has already become a tourist attraction, where tourist groups pass by when returning from Clearwater and Wind Caves (especially when the river has little water). The Penans sell some of their handicrafts and thus earn some money. However, being watched and visited like a species in a zoo is not always easy for them. They also complain that they are not allowed to cut down trees in the park for firewood or for building purposes, which they did before the park was gazetted. This problem could be solved with the establishment of buffer zones, where natives would be allowed to use more natural resources than within the park boundaries. However, as we have pointed out in the previous chapter, the government is still reluctant about this because if such zones cannot distinctly be separated from the core areas of the park, it is argued that they open a path for poachers into the park[419]. Although, a clear and visible boundary is helpful for the apprehension of poachers it also has some disadvantages. For example in Taman Negara the development of tourism just across the river from the head quarters cannot be controlled by the park management. This leads to disturbances (e.g. noise, waste disposal) that start to have an influence on certain animals in the park. With a buffer zone in place around the park these effects could be controlled much better.

---

417 J. Peter Brosius (2000) explains the mechanisms and problematic of the mystification of the Penans in the environmental discourse comprehensively.
418 The fact that two Penan families have built huts right in front of the primary school near the Mulu airstrip, to be close to their children caused astonishment but also disdain because the huts were made of used boards drawn from rubbish piles instead of forest material.
419 This is also a reason for the park boundary to mostly follow rivers which serve as a clear and distinct demarcation line. In Kinabalu for instance the park management started to mark the park boundary not only with signs but with red paint on the trees that are near that line.

If the people who are allowed to use resources in such a buffer zone identify themselves with the overall idea of the conservation of the whole area, they themselves help to deter poachers from the park. This only works when they can share in the income that is generated by the park. This is not as easy as it sounds. Of course they already generate some income by selling handicrafts, although not much. A regular job in the park, in a hotel or guesthouse, where indeed people are needed, does not fit well with their lifestyle. On the one hand they should be given the opportunity to decide for themselves how they want to participate in the tourism business. Without experience they do not have adequate information about their opportunities and about the constraints they are facing. Only a slow process of first leaving them with the possibility of keeping their old lifestyle (including using natural resources of the park) and then introducing them to the new opportunities (buffer zone management, participation in the tourist business), can lead to a mutually satisfying combination of their livelihood, tourist activities and conservation.

3.4 Wildlife viewing

Whereas the attraction of the wildlife is great, viewing it, is more difficult in Mulu. Compared with Taman Negara or even Kinabalu with much more visitors in Mulu it is not as easy to spot charismatic species. For another thing the foliage of Mulu is rather dense and there is no canopy walkway where visitors are at eye level to species roaming the upper stories of the jungle. Moreover, the animals in Mulu have not the long experience of being undisturbed by people, because visitors have come to the park in larger numbers only since 1990. The problem of hunting was mentioned above (see "3.3.4: Hunting and the participation of indigenous people" on page 217). Since the main attractions are the caves, most resources have been spent for the building of safe walkways and lighting in the caves. Maintenance is not an easy task and ties up a lot of money. Therefore, there are not many observation platforms from which wildlife can be observed, with the exception of the huge platform for watching the bats. The platform covers a circle of more than twenty meters, has a shelter and toilets. On certain days close to 120 tourists gather there in the late afternoon waiting for the bats to fly out of the cave. Often the rangers ask the spectators to be silent in order not to disturb the bats which have to pass over the platform. However, the admonitions are not heeded for long and a considerably high level of noise rises over the platform. What causes the bats come out and for which reasons they remain in the cave have not been thoroughly studied. If it is raining they come out less often, but there is no rule to their behaviour that allows a prognosis by the rangers. However, rangers who have spent a lot of time there, say that the behaviour of the bats has changed during the last years, due to an increase in visitors. Therefore, the observation platform for watching the bats is at the same time an opportunity for and a threat to the possibility of seeing them. Better information on site is needed. The platform is a good place to post information because people often spend more than an hour there and have ample time to read posters or other information about the bats and about the park in general (see "3.10: Information centre" on page 237).

3.4.1 Future prospects: use of independent guides and better information

The park has only employed a few rangers. Beside their duty to enforce the protection of the area they guide people either through caves (adventure caving) or on trails. They often have little time to spare for smaller tours for watching birds, or to see other animals or plants. For these tasks, local people could be employed if they are ready to acquire the knowledge needed to work as a guide[420]. Once a steady demand for such tours can be established (like in Taman Negara or Kinabalu) these guides can generate their own income. The park administration need only monitor the quality of their work but does not actually have to employ them.

3.5 Variety of attractions

Most people have a fixed itinerary when they come to Mulu. In the morning they either walk or take a boat to the Wind Cave and Clearwater Cave, north of the headquarters. The walk takes 45 minutes to an hour on a good trail through the forest and a small cave. Both caves offer different insights into the limestone formations of the park. Many group travellers do not walk to the caves but go there by boat which takes around 20 minutes. Below the mouth of Clearwater Cave there are a pond where one can swim and shelters to have picnics, which most of the group travellers take advantage of. On the way back, group travellers pay a short visit to the Penan settlement which is located across the Lutut River, while the individual travellers walk back to the headquarters. Around noon the lighting in the caves is turned off and the rangers who were posted at the entrance in order to give information or assistance go back to the headquarters. They or their colleagues proceed to the other two show caves (Deer and Lang's Caves) which are located southeast of the headquarters, while most tourists have lunch either in one of the restaurants (canteens) at the headquarters or in the RMR. After lunch they visit the remaining two show caves to which they have to walk about 45 minutes. Those visitors who arrive in the morning start with the "afternoon programme" and visit Clearwater and Wind Caves the next

---

420 On the importance of guides see Black, R. 1999.

morning. There is ample time to see the caves before people gather on the observation platform in order to see the bats. At dusk, after the animals have emerged, the visitors head back to their accommodation. During the walk back the tropical night falls and flashlights are needed in order not to loose one's footing on the plank walks that lead through peat swamp.

For those who want to stay longer, the trails are another attraction of Mulu. Two trails are well maintained and frequently used: the Pinnacles Trail and the Summit Trail. The Pinnacles are a spectacular limestone formation where rain has washed out the smooth limestone, physically and chemically eroding it and leaving razor sharp needles protruding from the forest. The Pinnacles can be reached within two days with an overnight stay at Melinau Camp, a basic shelter. On the third day most visitors go straight back to the confluence of the Melinau and Lutut river where they are awaited by boatmen who bring them back to their accommodation. The trek is rather exhausting but manageable. More arduous is the trek to the summit of Mount Mulu, where more than 2,000 m of altitude difference have to be covered within two days. The camps along the way are very basic and during the night it can get rather cold. Usually two overnight stays are needed to go up and back down. For both treks the hire of qualified guides is compulsory. The Headhunter's Trail leads north from the Pinnacles Trail to the Limbang River, from where a boat can be taken to Limbang. A few travellers use the trail in order to enter the park, but it is not often used.

"Adventure caving", takes only a few hours. Small groups of four or five visitors follow a guide through a part of the vast labyrinth of caves and passages using carbide lamps for illumination. Visitors who do the trip have to be fit, unafraid of narrow passages and able to squeeze themselves through small holes. Depending on the rainfall the group sometimes has to wade through waist-deep underground rivers.

Treks and adventure caving have to be organised by the visitors themselves, which sometimes can be difficult for individual travellers who have to find other people interested in making a trip and sharing the costs for guides and transport. Sometimes, therefore, the length of stay in Mulu cannot be planned well in advance, because the travellers do not know whether they can make a trek at a certain date or not. Moreover, it is not so easy to find provisions for the treks. There is only one small shop that mostly caters for the employees of the park and which has only a limited variety of goods. Bird watching and the observation of wildlife in general are attractions that are not unique to Mulu, although for the hobby ornithologist there are species to be discovered that are unique to the area. The rangers and guides are mostly used for the treks and in the caves, which is why they have little time left for visitors who want to observe wildlife.

Just outside the park boundary there are several trails suitable for mountain bikes, but they are very rarely used. For most Euro-Americans the tropical heat and humidity is not conducive to making exhausting bicycle rides, although a famous race "The Battle of Borneo" takes place here. In addition, there are not many mountain bikes to be rented and to take one's own bike is difficult. Lastly there are rocks for climbers, which are also rarely used, mostly because the region is not known as a good climbing area and the rocks are reportedly not especially good.

Figure 68: Visited attractions by individual and group travellers

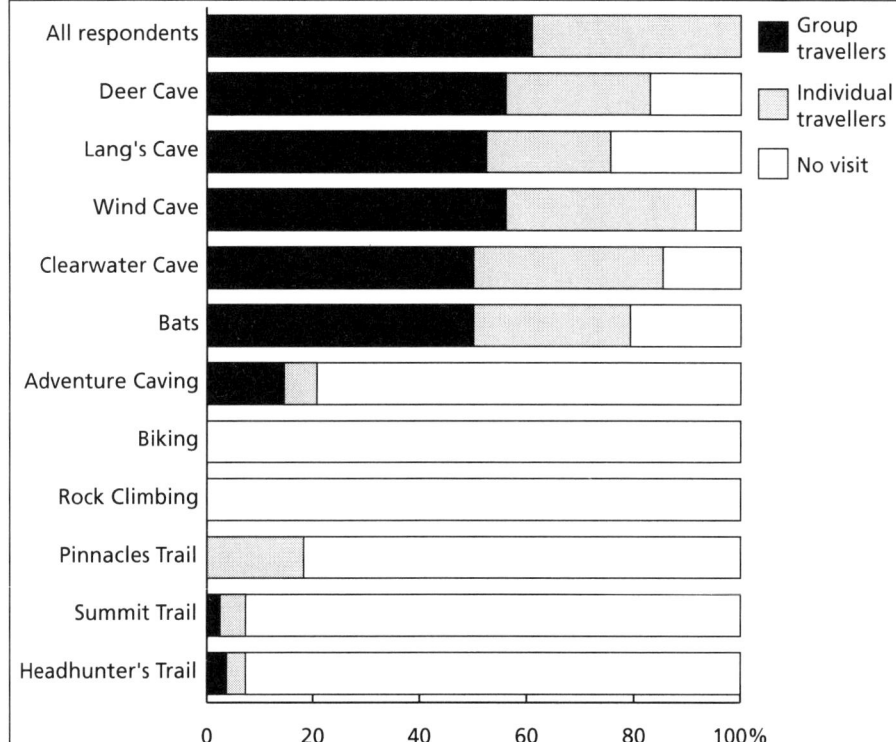

Source: own survey and draft.

3.5.1 Results from the survey: caves and bats are a must

The respondents of the survey considered the four show caves to be the biggest attractions (see figure 68 on page 222) of the park and all visitors have visited at least one cave. Since the bats can be watched conveniently after the visit of Deer Cave where they sleep during the day, most visitors got to watch them at least once. The more time consuming an attraction is, the less often the tourists visit them. But it is not only time constraints that causes tourists to refrain from going on a trek. Many individual travellers would like to make a trek on their third day but often they fail to bring a group of like minded people together for a specific day or there is no guide available.

Figure 69: Length of stay

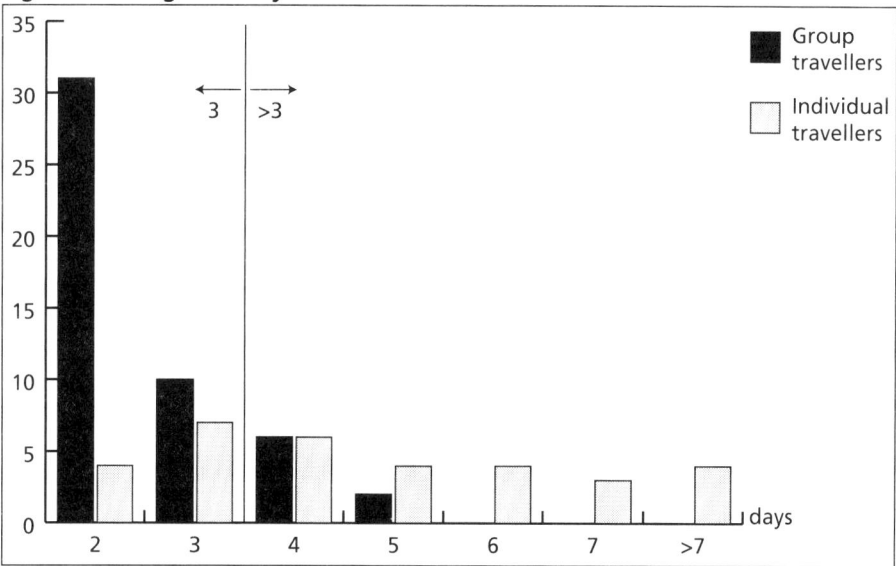

Source: own survey and draft.

Figure 69 on page 223 shows that the majority of the visitors to Mulu stay for only two days which means that they spend only one night there. If they fly in from Miri in the morning on the first day there is enough time to visit Deer and Lang's Caves and to see the bats in the afternoon. The next morning they can visit the other two show caves and take a flight out of Mulu in the late afternoon. Interestingly those who stay longer do not visit all the caves, but do some additional things (see figure 70 on page 224). Some of them – not the majority – often make a trek and therefore visit only a few caves. Wind Cave and Clearwater Cave are the most visited attractions, because they are located along the boat ride to the starting point of Pinnacle Trail and can therefore be visited conveniently by those heading there. Also the bats are more often visited by people who stay a shorter period than by the others, who do not pass by this area when going on a trek (or returning from one).

Around twenty percent of all respondents did some guided adventure caving which is a lot, considering that the availability of guides is not very good. The trails are more frequented by visitors who stay longer. However, there are also people – exclusively group travellers – who upon their arrival embark on a trail and return to Miri without visiting many other attractions.

Figure 70: Length of stay and visited attractions

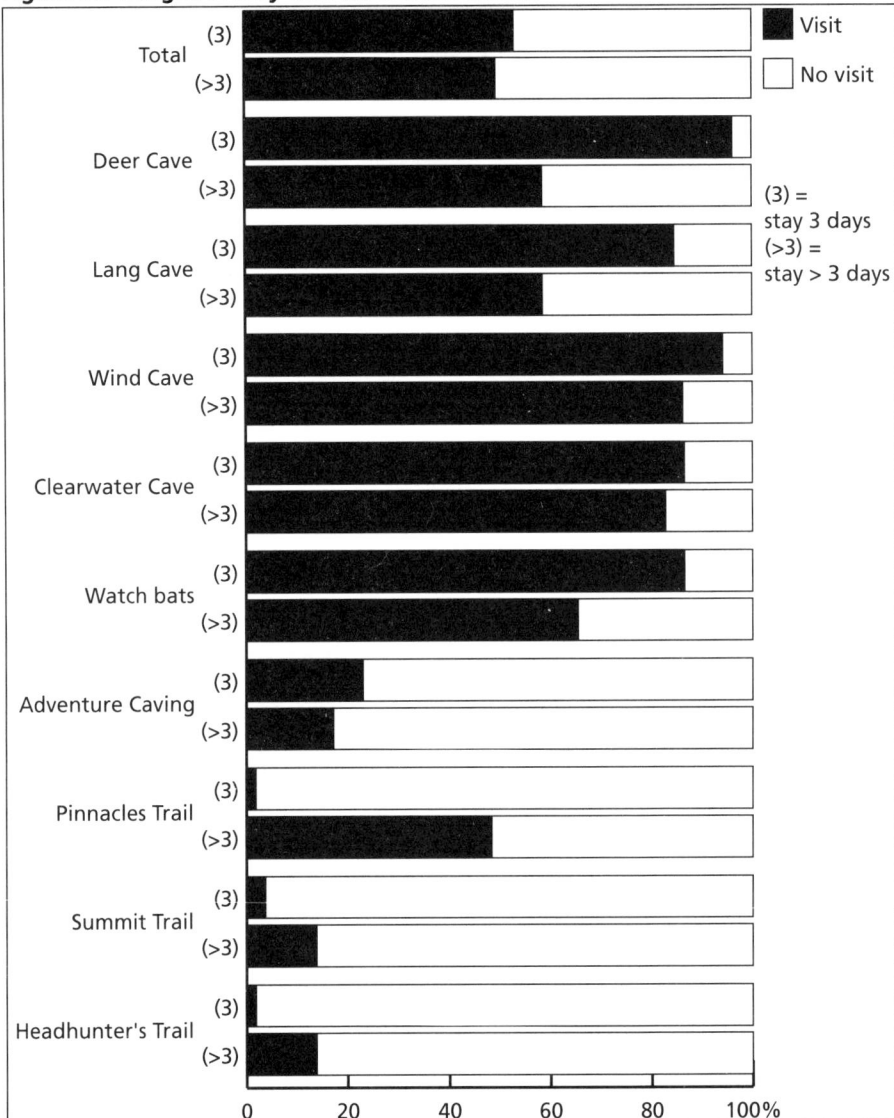

Source: own survey and draft.

Looking at how many attractions the respondents visit we see a surprising result. Those who stayed longer visited fewer attractions than those who stayed for a shorter periods.[421] Statistically the difference is not significant but since the re-

---

421 Figure 70 on page 224 depicts a value of 53 % of all attractions (excluding climbing and biking, because nobody did that) that were visited by the short term visitors and 49 % by long term visitors.

spondents who stay longer had – on the first glance – more chance to visit more attractions, the result is nevertheless interesting.

Figure 71: Evaluation of the attractions by the visitors

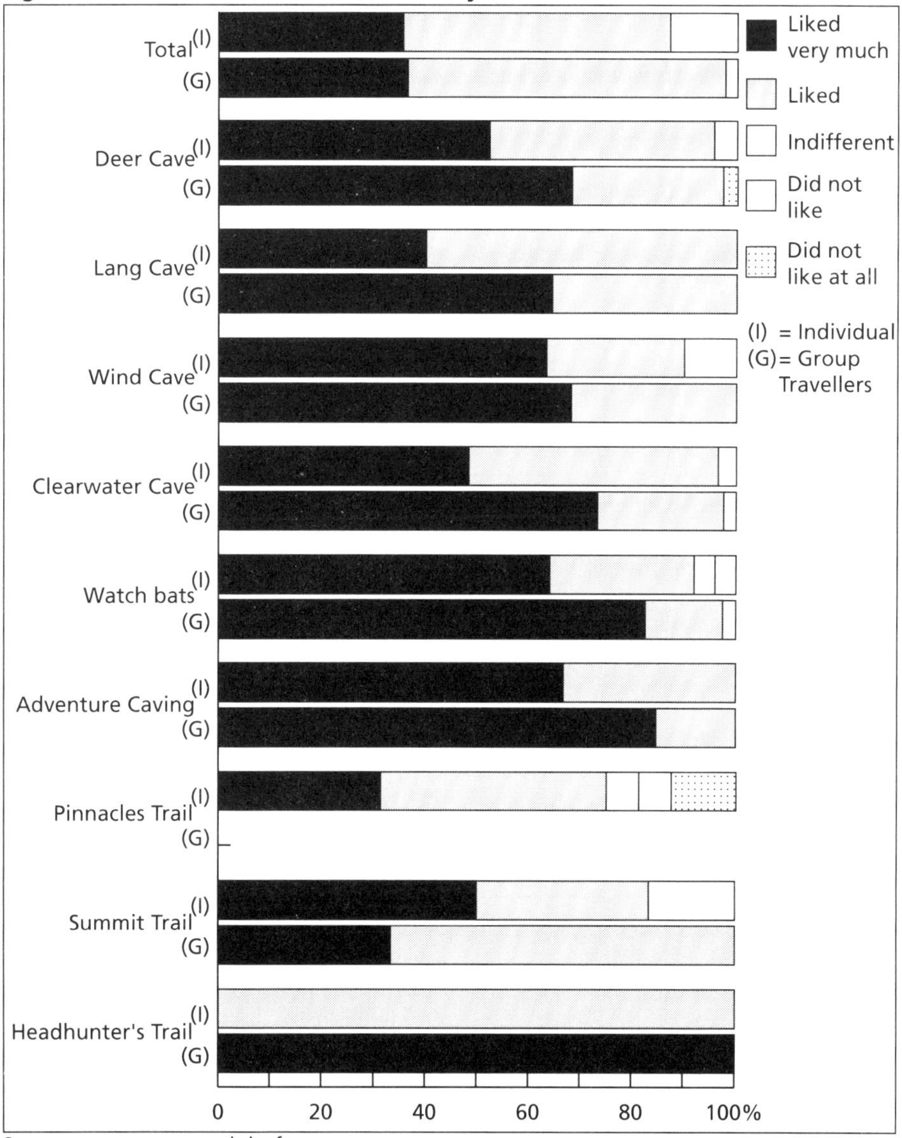

Source: own survey and draft.

Many travellers make the decision between going on a trek and staying near the headquarters in order to visit the attractions there. Between individual travellers and group travellers there is no difference, each visited 52 % of all nine attractions. However, if we split these groups into short and long stay visitors, we get a different picture. Group travellers who stay three days or less, visit most attractions (5.7 or 64 %), followed by the other group travellers who stay longer (5.25 or 58 %). The short staying individual travellers visited 4.9 attractions (or 55 %) and the long staying ones only 4.5 (or 51 %). To sum it up: the more organised and the shorter the stay of a visitor the more attractions she/he visits.

The evaluation of the attractions is positive. Most attractions were "liked" or "liked very much". Even if we imply that tourists tend to evaluate attractions they have visited positively unless they have had specifically negative experiences, the result can be rated as good. Individual travellers are more critical than group travellers. This could be because individual travellers are usually travelling for a longer duration, have visited other parks and therefore compare them. Moreover, group travellers specifically book a tour including Mulu and therefore probably are less critical because they pay an organisation to let them provide the experience they expect. A survey done in 2001 confirms the enthusiastic evaluation (see figure 71 on page 225) of the adventure caving.[422] At that time ten percent of the visitors did adventure caving, 80 % of them were travelling in a group and the caving was organised by their tour operator. Adventure caving is not advertised very well considering the potential of visitors' satisfaction it is able to generate. However, Lawai Anak Kumpang also states that it is crucial that the guides are well trained and should have some basic medical skills.

Figure 72: Costs for various activities and attractions in Mulu

Item	Price (RM)	Remarks
Adventure Caving: guide	88	for a group of 4; 4-5 hours
Adventure Caving: carbide lamp/helmet	40	Rent per person; lunch has to be brought individually
Adventure Caving: boat trip	85	Boat to Wind Cave and from Clearwater Cave
Pinnacles Trail: guide	110	Food has to be brought individually
Pinnacles Trail: accommodation	16	RM 8 per night
Pinnacles Trail: boat trip	350	Boat to and from the river fork of Melinau and Lutut River
Summit Trail: guide	264	Food has to be brought individually
Summit Trail: accommodation	24	at RM 8 per night

Source: own data; Rowthorn, C., Benson, S., Kerr, R. & Niven, C. 2001.

During the survey the park management was charging an extra fee for the entrance to the show caves – to recoup high maintenance costs – which exceeded

---

422 Lawai Anak Kumpang 2001.

the park entrance fee of RM 3. The experiment was stopped after a while because so many visitors complained about it. Visitors have to pay extra fees for the guides and for accommodation for the trails and adventure caving (see figure 72 on page 226). More than half of the respondents (57 %) who went on a trail considered the costs high or very high, whereas the rest found they were reasonable[423] (nobody found it was cheap). The fees for the guides were not objected to, although one person doubted the need for a guide for the Pinnacles Trail. However, the most objectionable factor was the boat ride to the starting point of the Pinnacles Trail, which costs hefty RM 350 per boat, round trip. The trip is so expensive, because the boatmen have to make the trip four times and if the water level of the river is low – which is the case when most tourists come to Mulu – they have to frequently shove the heavy boat over shallows and risk damage of their propellers. Moreover, the petrol costs twice as much as in Miri at the coast, because it has to be transported up the river.[424] The problem for individual travellers is to assemble a group of people willing to share a guide and to share the costs for the boat trip. The boats can transport up to six or seven passengers at one time (including the guide). Therefore, even a group of four people has to pay RM 350. The boatmen have to pass a test in order to be allowed to drive a boat and are organised in a union of twenty Mulu boatmen. They each ask for the same fees and take turns in transporting goods and people. The visitors have little information about the background of the costs which on first glance seem to be rather high.

3.5.2 Future prospects: better coordination for guides and treks

The range and variety of attractions in Mulu is rather good and there are no further attractions needed. However, the coordination of the present attraction could be improved especially if we consider the shortage of guides and resources.

The idea of charging an extra entrance fee for the show caves was abandoned by the park management after an unsuccessful trial, because tourists did not understand why they had to pay twice, because most of them just came to Mulu in order to see the show caves (and the bats). Nevertheless, with the low entrance fees of RM 3[425] the costs for the maintenance of the caves and other facilities cannot be covered[426]. Therefore, the state government of Sarawak decided to raise the fees to all its national parks and wildlife reserves to RM 10 per adult

---

423 The group travellers found it adequate, probably because it was included in their package or because they just booked "the Pinnacles" with their tour operator, paid and the rest was organised for them.
424 This is also the reason why a sack of cement costs double, which is an important factor for the construction and renovation of buildings.
425 To the RM 3 of entrance fee come RM 5 of camera fee, which has to be paid by the majority of the visitors, because almost everybody carries a camera.

and RM 5 per child. Most respondents feel that this is reasonable. More of the group travellers thought it was low or very low (see figure 73 on page 228). When they were asked how much they were prepared to pay, the majority wanted to keep the fees as they are (see figure 74 on page 229[427]). The reluctance to admit that one is prepared to pay more is probably more a methodological problem than the respondents' actual opinion. If such a question is raised within a questionnaire the respondents think that the park management is thinking about a raise and therefore do not want to cut off their noses to spite their faces in admitting that they would be prepared to pay much more.

Figure 73: Evaluation of the entrance fee

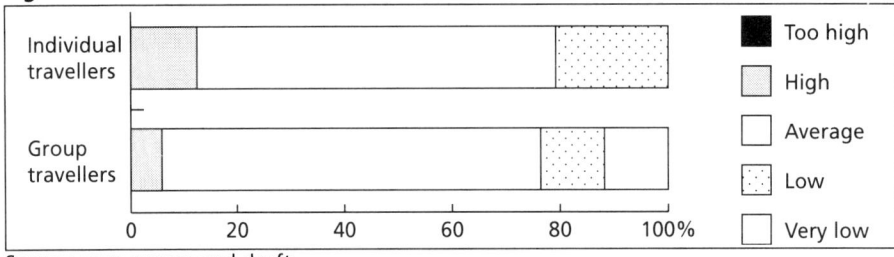

Source: own survey and draft.

For most of the foreigners coming to Mulu the entrance fee is not an issue, because even the RM 10 they have to pay now is not much money compared to the rest of their travel expenses. With the domestic visitors it could be different. Azahari Bin Omar[428] found that many of the domestic visitors to national parks would think twice about visiting a park when the entrance fee is raised again considerably. However, if we compare the fee to what people have to pay for a theme park, the visit of a national park is still much cheaper. The government wants to instil a sense of ownership in the visitors when they have to pay more and thus contribute to its conservation. It is doubtful whether this works with domestic tourists, because most of them think that national parks belong to them anyway. It might be better to point out what the visitors get when they come to Mulu and also how the money they pay is spent. If the latter is not possible due to the system of revenue collection it is still important that the visitors know what expenditures are incurred on their behalf. The same applies for the activities with additional costs (i.e. treks, adventure caving). The visitors need to be told why boat rides are comparatively expensive. It should also be made more transparent what the guides' roles are in order to prevent misunderstandings.

---

426 Most respondents gave good marks for the state of maintenance of the infrastructure. However, one respondent complained about the bat droppings in Deer Cave.
427 Camera fees are included because virtually everybody is carrying a camera and pays RM 5.
428 Azahari, B.O. 2001.

Figure 74: How much the respondents are prepared to pay

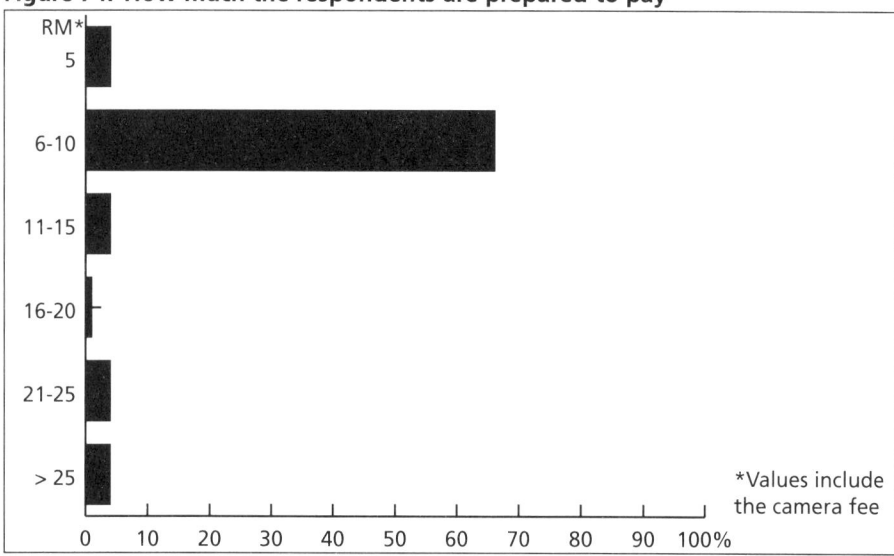

Source: own survey and draft.

Individual travellers often face the problem that they would like to make a trek but that they do not know whether they can join a group and when. Up to now the park administration just waits until they are asked to provide a guide for a certain trek or adventure caving. Planning would be much easier if they would keep a list of people interested to go on a trek or to even set up a schedule of their own. Especially for the adventure caving that would make more sense, because there seem to always be enough people interested in participating. Therefore, there could be an adventure caving tour/expedition organized every day providing that at least three (or four) people are interested. It would not only stabilize the work of the guides but also keep people a day or two longer in the park, which would reduce costs for accommodation and generate more revenue for local people. This is because people who stay longer, tend take a look at things (i.e. markets, kiosks, restaurants) outside the park. Better coordination helps the park management to react better to changing visitor numbers and demands (i.e. upgrading of the guides' numbers or skills, opening new trails or temporarily closing parts of trails that are overused).

3.6 Standard and availability of food and accommodation

The available accommodation exceeds the number of visitors because of the bottleneck of the access. In the park headquarters around 100 beds are available. In the Royal Mulu Resort (RMR), a Japanese owned four star hotel outside the park in Long Pala, there are also 180 beds and in two small privately owned guest houses, around twenty beds. The RMR especially has problems to fill its rooms, whereas the cheaper rooms in the park headquarters are often fully booked. Since the booking of flights and of accommodation cannot be made simultaneously, travel agents as well as individuals sometimes have difficulties to coordinate flights and desired accommodation. Since there is no cancellation fee, those who can book tend to book more seats than they effectively need. Another problem is the lack of accommodation in the lower middle price range which excludes an important segment of visitors. All the available accommodation consists of one storey buildings on stilts or platforms, although their style and infrastructure varies considerably. The RMR was built on a huge platform – in which also a swimming pool was integrated – partly over the river.[429] The rooms are in bungalows of different sizes, which were constructed mostly from local materials in a style found all over Southeast Asia. The appliances in the rooms are western and the same as can be found globally in most better hotels.

The accommodations in the headquarters are wooden bungalows erected on concrete stilts. Their style is a non-descript mixture of traditional Malay houses, local longhouses and colonial barracks. They were constructed to house groups of self catering travellers. Therefore, big kitchens were built in each bungalow which nowadays are rarely used, take up a lot of space and do not work properly anymore. Moreover, many rooms were fitted with the tinted windows that are common in many Asian office buildings, but which make them very dark. Individual travellers as well as some groups stay mostly in a big dormitory with twenty beds, because it is cheap. The showers and toilets were not constructed to withstand the humid climate of the rainforest, and do not appear to be clean although they are cleaned regularly. This is also something people often complain about. The two Berawan owned lodges are very basic and do not have electricity. They do not advertise much and can easily be overlooked upon arrival.

There are four restaurants in and around the park. In the headquarters' compound there is a canteen managed by a tour operator, and just outside the park on the other side of the river is a restaurant, where group travellers can have a cup of tea or a glass of beer after visiting one of the caves. Inside the RMR is a large restaurant and just outside the RMR is also a small restaurant that mostly caters for the local people.

---

429 When the RMR was built on that site there was a strong opposition from the Berawans who lived in the area for centuries and who claimed that the resort was built on their land without paying any compensation. The government refused to negotiate the issue with the indigenous Berawans, who formed a picket line at the airstrip in order to inform the arriving tourists about the issue (Asia Pacific Solidarity 1993). Today the Berawans do not oppose the RMR anymore. For many of them it has become a major income factor (Sanggin, S.E., Noweg, G.T., Abdul, R.A. & Mersat, N.I. 2000).

3.6.1 Results of the survey

There is only a slight tendency for individual travellers to favour cheaper rooms, but most accommodation is used by both individual and group travellers. In the RMR there are more group travellers to be found who have booked a whole package tour through Malaysia but there are also individual travellers. The presumption that individual travellers – mostly denoted as backpackers – travel cheaply and therefore do not bring much revenue into the area cannot be verified.

Figure 75: Accommodation used by the respondents

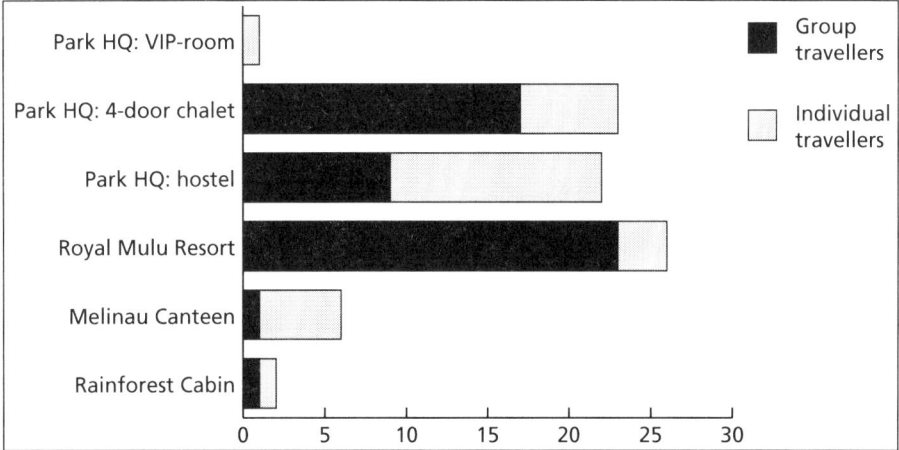

Source: own survey and draft.

Figure 76 on page 232 shows that there are some differences between individual and group travellers in their evaluation of accommodation. Regarding cleanliness, individual travellers tend to be more tolerant than group travellers. They gave better marks to all the accommodation. More than half of the group travellers found that the cleanliness of the rooms of the headquarters was not so good. The four star RMR costs more but also offers cleaner rooms according to the respondents, although not all were that enthusiastic about them. The lodges are very basic; nevertheless the individual travellers found the cleanliness excellent or good.[430] The infrastructure of the rooms in the headquarters was not rated very differently by individual and group travellers, although there are some of the latter who think it was not so good. Interestingly the individual travellers expected a better infrastructure in the RMR than those travelling in a group. The simple infrastructure of the lodges was regarded as good by most of the respondents. The space in the headquarters' rooms is mostly regarded as good or very good with few differences between the groups.

---

430 Only few (5) respondents stayed in the lodges. Therefore their evaluation cannot be regarded as representative for a larger group of tourists.

Figure 76: Evaluation of specific accommodation

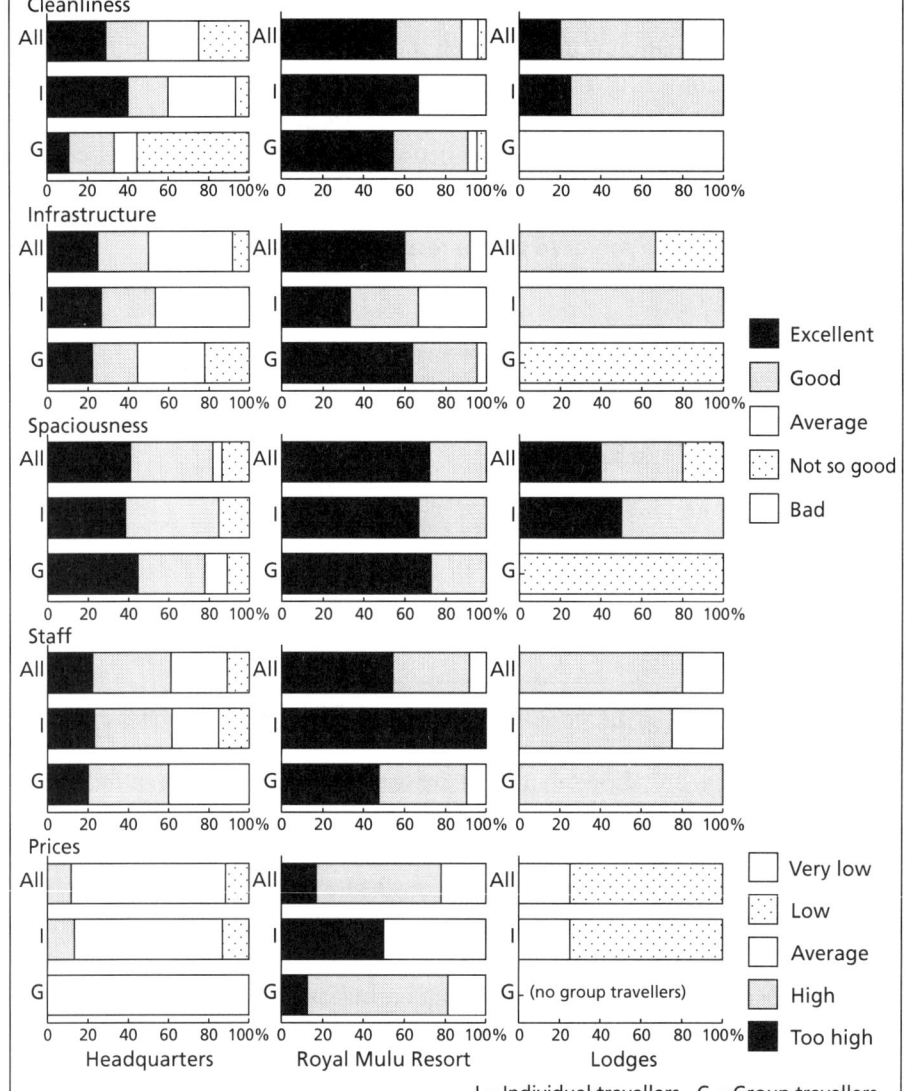

Source: own survey and draft.

Those who were more critical mostly referred to the hostel which can be cramped at times. The RMR offers ample space and the rooms in the lodges are also not regarded as too small. The staff (mostly Berawan from the area) of the headquarters was seen by 60 % as good or excellent. Only a few individual travellers found it less than satisfactory. The staff of the RMR got better marks; the individual travellers unanimously found it excellent. The staff of the private lodges was regarded as good. The prices were mostly acceptable for the rooms of the headquarters, whereas the RMR was considered (too) expensive, especially by the individual travellers.[431] The lodges are regarded as rather cheap.

Mulu is not exactly a destination with a great culinary variety, which may also not be necessary, but there is room for improvement in general. The restaurant in the RMR has the most variety and highest standards, but also the highest prices. Because the canteen in and the restaurant outside the headquarters are more or less run (if not owned) by local people, I wanted to know more about these places. The restaurant outside the headquarters is not visited by many tourists, only a third of the individual travellers and even a smaller part of the group travellers have been there. The staff there received a wide range of evaluations from those who have been there. Half of the individual travellers thought the staff was good or excellent, the other half found them average or not so good. The group travellers were more critical and only a third found the staff good or excellent, most found them average and some not so good or even bad. The prices are not regarded as low or very low[432]. Compared to what you get for your Ringgit, the prices are rather high, which is a consequence of the high transport costs.

3.6.2 Future prospects: more diligence

The evaluation (see figure 76 on page 232) is in general rather good for all the accommodation in the park. Tourists probably do not expect very much coming to the jungle, although some of them are glad to be able to sleep and rest in a four star hotel such as the RMR. However, there is still room for improvement, especially at the headquarters, but also in the RMR and the lodges. The rooms in the headquarters were designed for larger groups (of researchers) who spend more than two or three days in Mulu and who bring their own food. Nowadays this design is not adequate and during the next renovation it should be changed if possible. The sometimes cramped hostel is especially unappealing to people who might want to stay longer than one or two nights. There is almost no space to store one's belongings, let alone to keep valuables. A simple locker system with rentable keys could solve this problem. There should be a simple solution for the rather drab toilets and showers. If shower heads tend to clog and the flushing system of toilets does not work they do not necessarily have to be re-

---

431 Group travellers have mostly paid the costs for accommodation within a package and are not presented with a bill at the end of their stay, whereas the individual travellers have to pay their rooms upon departure, which may result in a different evaluation of the prices.
432 One respondent was upset that the restaurant and the canteen did not sell a specific beer brand which at that time was on sale throughout Sarawak, whereas he had to buy his beer for a higher price, which he found, was not acceptable.

placed with expensive systems. For example the washing area could be placed outside with blinds protecting them from unwanted looks. Thus, they would more resemble a traditional airy "mandi", where (clogged) shower heads are supplanted by buckets pour over oneself during washing, which is more efficient, cleaner, and more refreshing. The use of (semi-)traditional architecture could thus be turned to advantage by providing something exotic for the visitors, which at the same time works better. Modernity is not what tourists want or expect when coming to a national park, but they do seek authenticity and comfort, which both can be achieved with more traditional (and cheaper) means.

To invest in the education of the (local) staff is always worthwhile, as we see by the example of the RMR. If the management of the national park is partly or entirely put into private hands, it will be necessary to set up a system to constantly improve the skills of the staff, who will thus be able to work much more efficiently.

The lodges are almost invisible and only rarely do guests stay there. In terms of capacity, the lodges should be at least considered when the rooms at the headquarters are fully booked, which was rarely the case at the time of the study.

The restaurants in Mulu – maybe with the exception of the one in the RMR – provide only basic nourishment so that people have something to eat and drink. The variety is small and consists of meals that can be called "pan-Asian", because travellers get fried rice, fried noodles, chop suey, banana pancakes etc. at almost every tourist destination of the region. Moreover, often most items on the menu are not available. Of course, there are problems with the transport and Mulu is not a beach resort, where tourists can regale in all the treats that Malaysian cuisine has to offer. However, if it is important that visitors should stay longer in Mulu, that they take home a good image of the place and that the local economy should be able to benefit from the visitors, the restaurants can play an important role and should be upgraded. I do not want to say that the food should be better or that the variety should be greater. I suggest that it could even be narrowed down to just a few different meals. Thus the restaurants might follow the example of Malaysian hawkers[433], who only provide one or two meals, but make them fresh and tasty. It might suffice to have a few local items such as a tea or a soup made of special herbs growing in the area, or a "Berawan" or "Penan" dish. If the restaurants improve their menus and service, they can become a good place to work for local people and thus a good source for income. Now it is rather a spare time job for the youth of the area, and less often a career for adults.

---

433 More on Malaysian hawkers c.f. Backhaus, N. & Keller, S.A. 2001.

Figure 77: Evaluation of the restaurant and the canteen near the headquarters

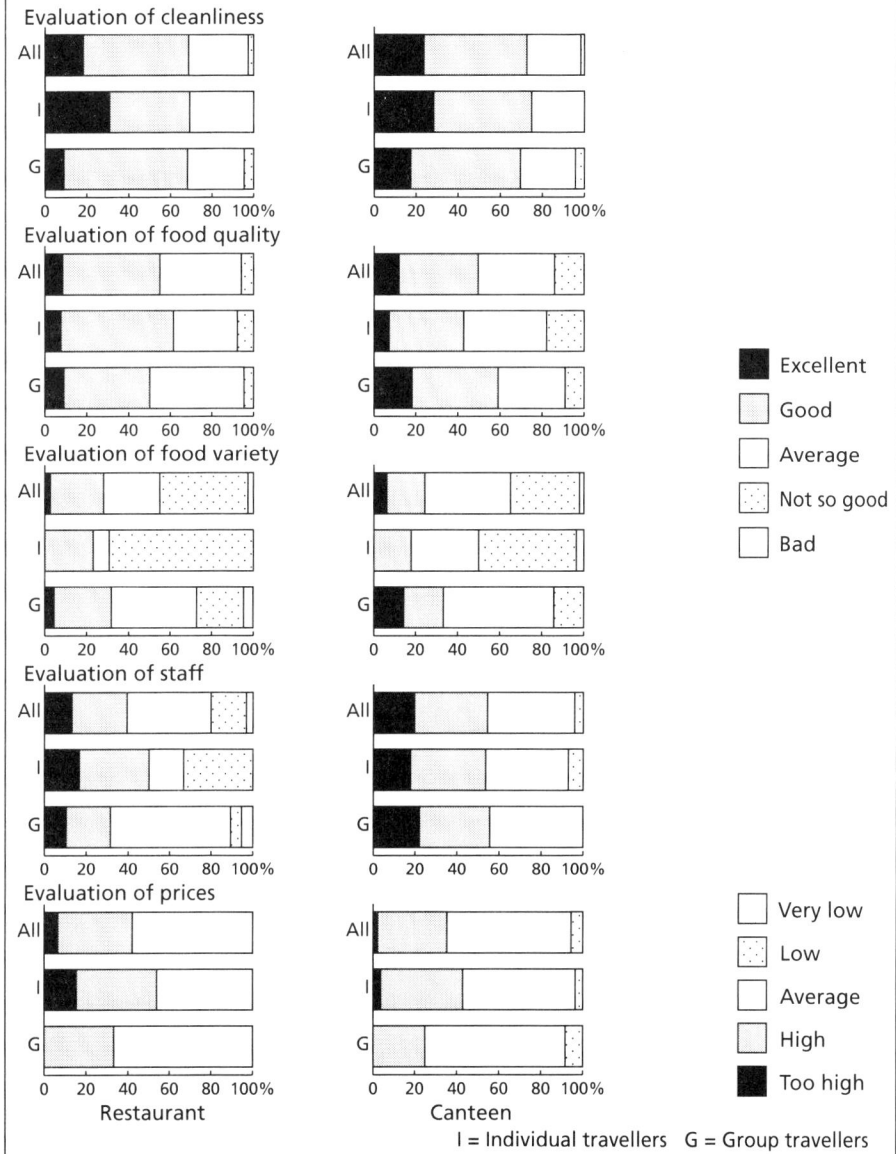

Source: own survey and draft.

3.7 Cultural interests

Visitors do not come to Mulu because of its cultural amenities. Not too many people live in the area and their cultural activities are not included into itineraries of travel groups, nor are they advertised. Nevertheless, since two indigenous groups – the Berawans and the Penans[434] – live in the area, cultural activities could indeed become an attraction. The indigenous people chose (actively or unintentionally) for the most part not to present their lives or a part of them as an attraction for tourists. However, the Penan village opposite Wind Cave has already become a (small) tourist attraction. After some tour groups have visited the caves they make a stop at the village and some buy handicrafts made by the Penans. The whole affair is a mixture between watching poor people made sedentary and visiting the "famous and gentle people from the forest", so many of us have heard of at home.

Unless the Berawans and/or the Penans want to present their mode of living to tourists, it is not feasible to try to set up cultural attractions just because they would be nice to have near a national park. The natural attractions – along with the history of the discovery and the gazetting of Mulu – seem to be sufficient attractions for visitors. Nevertheless the mere presence of indigenous people near the park lends it an aura of profound authenticity which in itself could be termed as a cultural attraction.[435]

3.8 Difference from other conservation areas

Mulu differs from other conservation areas in the region, because there are so many species of flora and fauna to be found here and there some endemic species that cannot be seen in other conservation areas. However, this difference is probably not so great – it is said that Kinabalu has roughly 20 % more species[436] – for the average tourist who has little botanical or zoological knowledge or interest. One of the big differences to other areas is the tropical limestone caves – and connected with one of them: the bats. The four show caves vary from each other so that each is a special attraction in itself. Also in other Malaysian conservation areas visitors can make treks and climbs. The most famous is probably the climb of Mount Kinabalu in Sabah (see "2.3.1: Kinabalu" on page 106), which is climbed by thousands of tourists every year. While the treks up to Gunung Mulu and to the Pinnacles at Gunung Api are unique for their landscape, they are very similar to what can be done in other conservation areas. Nevertheless, each trek (in each conservation area) can be advertised as something unique. Mulu is regarded and advertised as a unique place in Malaysia and has enough attractions that indeed make it distinctive, so that there is no need to

---

434 Ethnic identity in Borneo is not very clear cut and is subject to change. I will not delve further into this topic and simply refer to "Berawans" and "Penans" when talking about the two ethnic groups that live near Mulu. For further information on that issue see Brosius, P.J. 2000 or King, V.T. 2001.
435 For more information on conservation and indigenous people see Colchester, M. 1997.
436 Thorsell, J. 2000.

enhance its uniqueness with the construction of new attractions or the advertisement of new ones.

3.9 Recreation facilities

Mulu does not feature many recreational facilities such as areas for swimming, picnicking or playgrounds. The attractions of Mulu are mostly connected to activities of a relaxing or contemplative nature. At the entrance to Clearwater Cave it is possible to bathe in a pond that is fed with cool water coming from the cave. Around the accommodation in the headquarters there are a few tables where picnics are possible, but they are rarely used. Nevertheless the headquarters' area has the potential for certain recreational facilities. For example near the river would be an ideal area for tourists to sit in the shade (which would have to be provided) and watch the water without having to be in a restaurant but still having the possibility to buy some food or drink (which would be easy for the restaurant to provide).

There are few activities for children except seeing the caves and the other attractions. At the moment there are very few children among the visitors, but that could change in the future when more people want to visit the park. If more children came to the park, it would be possible to specifically design activities for them (i.e. guided trips into the jungle, boat rides, customised adventure caving etc.). The RMR has a swimming pool that serves as a recreation area for adults and children and the large platform on which the resort is built offers opportunities to relax. Initially a golf course was planned near the resort, but the idea was abandoned for ecological reasons. However, most visitors of the RMR do not have the time to relax anyway, because they are there for only one or two nights and are on a tight schedule. A wider range of recreational activities and the advertising them might keep visitors a day or two longer in Mulu, which would enhance their experience and would be ecologically sensible.

3.10 Information centre

Mulu has an information centre which is called 'interpretation centre'. It is conveniently located next to the registration/check in counter. It consists of a large room with a sizable exhibition of different topics related to Mulu. It starts with a historic overview of the expeditions – especially the one of the Royal Geographical Society in 1978[437] – that eventually led to the protection of the area. There are many black and white photographs that lend the expeditions an aura of the distant past when the jungle was impenetrable. Instead of a map, a satel-

---

437 See Anderson, J.A.R., Jermy, A.C. & Cranbrook, G.G.H. 1982.

lite image shows the location of Mulu. Since it is a dim image it is not easy to read it without explanations. A crude map of Sarawak on fake wood shows the location of other protected areas of the state. Since most visitors have access to information that is much more accurate and also aesthetically more appealing, the map looks outdated and uninformative. However, for each park there is a photograph with its typical features, an icon representing the area.[438] There are also a few maps of caves, which show how complex the system is. Unfortunately there are no explanations provided and the maps are difficult to read.

After the section about the caves there is more history of the park, which is redundant and slightly confusing because it is the same information as before but in different words. The show caves are depicted in photographs that give an impression of what the visitors may expect. However, since they are not accompanied by explanations they only depict what looks much better in reality and provides no extra information. There is also a section about the geomorphology of the area (i.e. the Pinnacles) that also lacks explanations. The selection of the pictures looks arbitrary and the quality is with few exceptions quite poor. From landscapes it goes to habitats and landforms. Although 'landscape' and 'landform' differ from each other scientifically, for the lay visitor it is not clear why both expressions are used. It is a pity that scientific information about geology and vegetation in a table are not illustrated with adequate pictures. Indeed there are photographs but they do not correspond with anything brought in a text or table.

From the vegetation formations the visitor is drawn to a section about cave biology with good photographs (although the last photograph depicting "crystal formations" does not belong to biology). The whole section should be integrated into information about the caves (or about flora and fauna). Flora and fauna is a section that features some short but good explanations for pictures. Again somewhat arbitrarily chosen is a text about swiflets, bats, snakes and fish that is not connected to the information before and after. The forest ecosystem is depicted in a diagram but is not accompanied with photographs. Some good examples are found in the sub-section "special relationships" where symbioses are depicted, sadly without further explanations, and thus difficult to understand. Towards the end of the exhibition other attractions and activities are mentioned (i.e. mountain climbing, shooting rapids, education, nature study). Moreover, there is an information board outside the office building as well. A highlight is a three dimensional model of the park, which is well done and concise but which

---

[438] For Gunung Gading a rafflesia is shown, for Batang Ai a ride in a longboat, for Kubah a waterfall, for Bako sandstone formations, for Mulu a cave, for Lambir Hills a waterfall, for Niah its cave and for Similajau a beach.

needs an update. The collection of artefacts without any information about their origin and their significance seems strange. The final item of the exhibit is a model of a caver and his equipment, which is rather interesting.

3.10.1 Results from the survey: not many visitors go to the interpretation centre

Although located conveniently, more than sixty percent of the visitors do not visit the interpretation centre (see figure 78 on page 239). It can therefore be regarded as an inefficient means of distributing information. Group travellers visit it much less often than individual travellers. It is simply not part of their itinerary and for information the group travellers rely on their guides. Most visitors have informed themselves about Mulu before they went there. The majority used a travel guide and the favoured guide was the Lonely Planet book. Many also visited the Sarawak Tourism Board that has offices in Kuching and Miri, some consulted the internet and many used other information, mostly from other people who have been there (see figure 79 on page 240). Very few solely relied on the information provided by the guides. Therefore, the interpretation centre has to provide information that the other media do not provide. The popular Lonely Planet guide book does not mention the interpretation centre, which could be a reason why only few people visit it. They may think that if something is not mentioned in a guide book it is not worth looking at. Even so, more than half of the Lonely Planet readers visited the information centre.

Figure 78: Visit and evaluation of the interpretation centre and its information

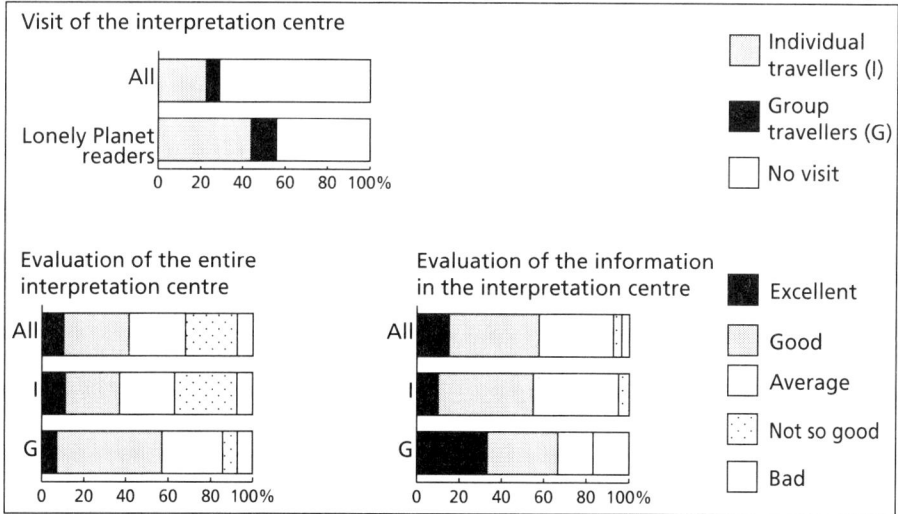

Source: own survey and draft.

Individual travellers were more critical than group travellers in their evaluations of the interpretation centre. It might be because the former tend to visit more such centres and thus are able to compare them. It could also be that the group travellers were accompanied by their guide when visiting the interpretation centre and received additional information. The opinions about the centre are divided. Roughly forty percent find it good or even excellent, whereas a quarter thinks it is average and a third finds it not so good or worse. Interestingly the answers were slightly better when people were asked about the information that is provided in the interpretation centre. I draw the conclusion that the information is good or okay, but that its display is regarded as not good, or less adequate.

Figure 79: Information media used before the visit to Mulu

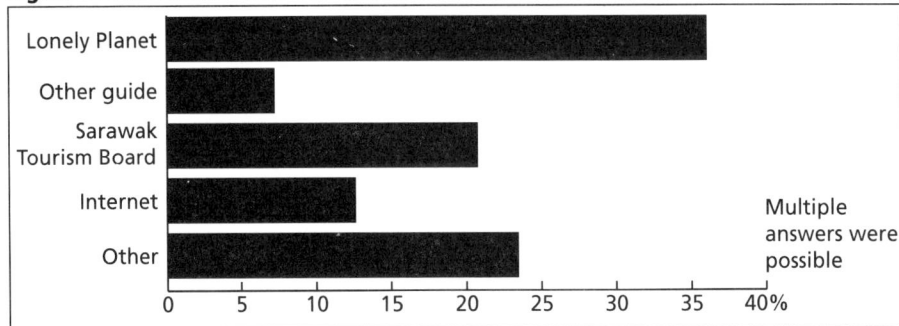

Source: own survey and draft.

If we compare the information given in the interpretation centre with the postulations of Frost[439] (see "5.2.5: Ecotourism in rainforests" on page 73) we get the following results:
1. *What makes a rainforest and the debate over what is, and what is not a rainforest*
   The interpretation centre gives information about what makes the rainforest in Mulu, but there is little information on rainforests in general.
2. *The different types of rainforest and, in particular, the type that this rainforest belongs to*
   The type of rainforest that can be found in Mulu is described rather well, but there are no comparisons with other types of rainforests.
3. *How indigenous people interacted with this rainforest*
   Only the Penans are described, and only as having been in the area a long time, but not what the forest means to them and how they used its resources.
4. *How European colonization or settlement affected this rainforest*
   European colonization did not affect the area around Mulu much, because it was not very well accessible and not of great interest to the colonial powers.[440] Although, the area of Mulu was relatively undisturbed by events of

---

439 Frost, W. 2001, p. 193-204.

colonial history, it would be interesting to have a section giving a short overview of the history of Sarawak.
5. *The major threats today*
There is almost no information about any threats to Mulu. Since logging activities are still a touchy issue with the government, it is not surprising that there is no information concerning logging activities around the park. Any (potential) threats by tourism are also not mentioned.
6. *Plant (and especially tree) varieties*
Plant varieties are explained and there are some examples of interesting species, but there could be more.
7. *Animals (especially birds and insects)*
Although Mulu is advertised as having close to 300 species of birds, there is not much information about them. However, some unique species such as the world's smallest falcon are explained and displayed in photographs. Insects are mentioned but not in great detail.
8. *Special growing conditions associated with this rainforest (i.e. nutrient cycle or the presence of buttressed roots)*
There are some good explanations about nutrient cycles, some are even a little bit too complex for the lay person.
9. *The fragility and resilience of rainforests in general and of this particular rainforest*
The fragility of rainforests is addressed, but there is no reference to resilience.
10. *Any revegetation or scientific research projects in progress*
Since the caves are the major attraction of Mulu, a substantial part of the exhibition is dedicated to exploration of the caves. Most examples are from early expeditions and no specific ongoing research project is mentioned, although there are frequent explorations of the vast cave system.

The interpretation centre in Mulu does not conform very well with Frost's postulations. Therefore, it would be a good idea to pick up some of his ideas, though they do not necessarily all deserve the same attention. Frost forgot to mention how the specific attractions of a park can be related to the rainforest.

---

440 Before the Anglo-Dutch treaty of 1824, which regulated the zones of influence of these two colonial powers, the north of Borneo was nominally controlled by the Brunei court. The treaty itself did not mention Borneo, which left its status somewhat ambiguous. However, the Dutch established treaties with several sultanates in the south and southeast, whereas the British East India Company stressed 'trade not territory' east of the Melaka Straits. After 1840 James Brooke was given control over what later became Sarawak's first division around Kuching, by the *raja muda* (sultan) of Brunei, for suppressing an uprising of several tribes. The Brooke family controlled and extended the area until after the Second World War, when Sarawak became a British crown colony. In 1963, together with Sabah and Labuan it became a part of the Malaysian Federation. (Watson Andaya, B. & Andaya, L.Y. 2001)

3.10.2 Future prospects: more cohesion, better display

The fact that only few people visit the interpretation centre should give cause to think about the exhibition. The closer look which we elaborated above reveals that the exhibition has gradually grown without a proper concept or layout. Of course it is not cheap to make a good exhibit, but the current information could be enhanced along with the display, without great cost. The most important thing is to structure the information better with comprehensible and more in-depth texts that are sequenced in a coordinated way. Good images, maps and graphics are crucial. Another problem is encouraging people to visit the exhibit. The majority of group travellers have a very tight itinerary and not the leisure to dwell on an exhibition if it is not worthwhile. A possibility would be to relocate a part of the interpretation centre to the bat-observation platform. The visitors stay a while there and have nothing to do. An exhibit could even quiet them down in order that they not disturb the animals. Of course the information provided (e.g. with posters, that are protected from moisture and direct light) should include the topic of the bats and their environment. A good display there could "lure" more visitors to the remaining information in the current interpretation centre. A considerable effort in overhauling the exhibition would be worthwhile, because it can raise the ecological awareness of the visitors. Of course much information can be provided by (tour) guides as well, but they cannot really provide graphic information and not all the visitors have a guide whom they can ask questions. In the future a good exhibit can be an attraction in itself and could for example attract teachers who eventually bring their pupils, or tell them to visit Mulu, when they can.

3.11 Proximity to other areas of interest

Mulu is located in a rather remote area of Sarawak bordering on Brunei's most densely forested part. Therefore, in terms of metrical proximity Mulu is far from other areas of interest. However, since most people fly into Mulu, by plane it is rather near to Miri regarding the temporal distance. With the plans of Vision Air Malaysia to connect Mulu with Kota Kinabalu, the national park is on a path leading from Kuching via Miri to Sabah and its own attractions and vice versa. Therefore the remoteness has to be seen relatively. But apart from the Headhunter's trail leading to Limbang there are no areas of interest physically bordering to Mulu, it remains an "attractive island".

3.12 Appeal of the surrounding area

The surrounding area of Mulu does not differ much from the park itself. Figure 63 on page 207 shows areas of a proposed extension of the park and of the adjacent and newly gazetted Gunung Buda National Park which are both deemed pristine enough to be worth protecting. The indistinct borders of Mulu Park are a problem for the park administration, because hunters are sometime unable to distinguish/recognize borders. Most boundaries of the park follow rivers. Today the surrounding area is rapidly changing. Much logging occurs and wide stretches of land are converted to oil palm plantations with a much lower biodiversity. This encroachment inhibits the establishment of buffer zones and alternative hunting grounds for the Penans whose activities are thus focused even more on the park. It also curtails the foraging area of larger mammals and of flying animals such as swiftlets and bats. The government is therefore trying to extend the park into areas that are still in good condition.

4 Summary

Gunung Mulu National Park was chosen as an example of a large Malaysian national park with the potential for increased numbers of visitors. Being a relatively newly gazetted park in a remote area but with outstanding attractions, Mulu has the potential or even the need to change or improve. The awarding World Heritage Site status by the UNESCO in 2000 made the park undoubtedly more attractive for tourists. Therefore, it was the goal of this part of the study to get more information about what the visitors of the park think of their experiences there. While every park is unique, the results of the survey can be used as a reference for other parks.

The biggest problems in Mulu are that in some caves the carrying capacities tend to be reached which disturbs the bats living in them. Moreover, a lot of other animals hide deeper in the forest due to the increasing number of visitors but also because they are still hunted by the Penans. The improved air service means many visitors stay for shorter periods which is detrimental to local revenue generation. The lack of leisure activities does not entice (domestic) visitors to stay longer in the park.

We can conclude that Mulu has a great potential for effective ecotourism but does not use this potential well. An improvement of the access by boat in combination with a better structure of possible activities in the park could change that development, which would bring more revenue into the area. Better interpretation and more and better trained guides could help to heighten the visitors' ecological awareness and let them have more authentic experiences. The introduction of buffer zones in which the Penans are allowed to hunt and log would probably take much of the pressure off the animals in the core area of the park. Moreover, the Penans could – if they are allowed to – use and structure the buffer zone according to their needs and need not be regarded as cultural objects that are part of a conservation area and thus a tourist attraction. Therefore, Mulu could become an important centre for a successful ecotourist area for both individual and group tourists. While backpackers are frequent visitors of conservation areas, they are not specifically catered for in most parks, although there is cheap accommodation available. However, a better management of the individual travellers' needs (more information about treks, better hostels and places to relax) would entice them to stay longer and consequently spend more money in the park.

Conclusion

VII Regionalising conservation areas

1 Conservation areas: a consequence of aggregated actions

A conservation area is a context that is structured by an aggregation of different actors' (or agents') actions. This specific context is regionalised according to people's perception and use or appropriation. This regionalisation does not result in a clearly defined and fixed description of the area. Every person makes this regionalisation in his or her own way, according to his or her needs, desires, fears, hopes, habitus and context. People from the park administration perceive it as an area containing fauna and flora and geomorphological elements that have to be protected against detrimental influences, and as an employer. Tourists see it as a destination, where they expect to have unique or authentic experiences. Local people may perceive it as a restriction of their resource use or as a source of income generation. In this study I have concentrated on the opinions of tourists and of experts who are working in the field of conservation and/or tourism. The needs and views of the local people who are involved in conservation were the subject of interviews. They were not the focus of the study, mainly because of time restrictions, and, initially, for political reasons. Therefore, it would be useful to have additional studies about this angle and their points of view.

In Malaysia, the educational and recreational functions of national parks are regarded as very important, by the authorities. Therefore, tourism in national parks is encouraged, and seen as an income source and as a means of drawing more foreign tourists to Malaysia. Nature has become an important aspect of tourist promotion and image creation. One sees slogans like, 'Malaysia naturally', 'Sabah natur*e*ally' or 'Sarawak – hidden paradise'. Malaysian national parks are depicted as covered by pristine, impenetrable jungles, containing a vast abundance of species, which may be perceived as authentic environments. The intention is to draw tourists to conservation areas, in order to create revenues for the maintenance of the parks. It is also to provide environmental education for tourists. These both have unintended consequences. For example, the revenues gathered are often not enough to cover the park maintenance, which is why the privatisation of infrastructure (i.e. accommodation, restaurants, transport) is being considered. Moreover, the increase of visitors has, according to the opinion of NGOs, sometimes exceeded the carrying capacity of certain places. At some places, e.g. Gunung Mulu and Taman Negara, improved access has caused visitors to stay shorter periods, which increases costs and the impact on the environment.

In the following sections, I want to answer the research questions (see "Aim and research questions" on page 6) according to the results of the individual parts of the study: 2 "Urban Malaysians are discovering conservation areas", p. 247, 3 "The experts' biggest concerns", p. 249, 4 "Types of tourists become forms of tourism", p. 255, 5 "Creating the potential to have authentic experiences", p. 258. In chapter 6 "Important issues of the National Ecotourism Plan", p. 260, the most important issues of the NEP will be addressed. In the last chapter, I make some concluding remarks about theory, methods, and future prospects.

2 Urban Malaysians are discovering conservation areas

What are urban Malaysians' opinions about nature conservation and ecotourism?

Members of the growing urban middle class are potential visitors of conservation areas, because they have the resources to be able to journey to a park. Their needs and desires have to be increasingly taken into consideration by the park management. In the survey, 500 respondents from the Kuala Lumpur area, interviewed at public places, were asked about their opinions about nature conservation and ecology. 'Nature' was usually defined as something that is unspoiled, clean, peaceful and harmonious. Many defined it as the opposite of the city (by older people), or pollution and waste (by younger people), also meaning the opposite of 'changed by humans'. Nature is also considered as something that must be protected, which indicates that the interviewees have an environmental awareness as targeted by the National Ecotourism Plan. Although there is a difference between what people say and what they do, the answers I received indicated, from the point of view of NGOs and the park administration, that, at least the urban population is well informed about environmental issues.

Regarding the respondents' expectations from a visit to a national park, most favour activity over contemplation. The activities they favour include hiking, camping, fishing, and rafting. Many said they just want to get away from the congested cities and have a good time with family or friends in nice surroundings. What they most remember from a visit are special animals and plants. This means that conservation areas do indeed have attractions that are well remembered. However, initial expectations are not always met. Better information before a visit is needed in order to avoid visitors travelling to a park with false expectations. The feasibility of fun and leisure activities available in certain parks should be considered. Three fifths of the interviewees had already been to a conservation area, or what they thought was a conservation area. Besides actual national parks, many non-conservation areas were mentioned, which shows that for the respondents it is more important to be in a *nice* place, than in an *'authentic'* place. It is also a sign that many national parks need a clearer profile to distinguish them from other nature tourism.

The most visited national park is Taman Negara, which may be called the flagship among the Malaysian parks. It is also visited by many foreigners. NGOs say that in the area around the headquarters, the carrying capacity is already exceeded, at least during the peak season. The fact that many Kuala Lumpurians also visited Bako in Sarawak and Kinabalu in Sabah, indicates that mobility is great and that with better access, even more people will come. With this influx, pressure on the environment will increase. Parks that feature a certain leisure infrastructure, a canopy walkway, a beach, a waterfall, picnic areas etc., are more often visited by Malaysians than those lacking these features, which are usually visited only once. This corroborates that 80 % of the respondents have already been to a theme park. Theme parks are located nearer to their places of residence but are also much more expensive. Visits to theme parks are more than double the number of visits to conservation areas. This information can be used as a planning tool for the different parks, because not all parks need to have the same attractions and the same visitor infrastructure. In parks where the number of domestic visitors is already high, the introduction of special leisure or recreational areas could take away some pressure on sensitive areas. The Matang Family Park, adjacent to Kubah National Park, is a good example of this, because the people who want to picnic or bathe in the river, can do so in a controlled environment without compromising the park or its image. The respondents included the lack of picnic or bathing facilities as bad aspects of visited parks, rather than overcrowding. Therefore, a general upgrading of park infrastructure is called for. Experts from the administration have said this will be implemented in the near future.

Ninety percent of the respondents want to have more parks in the future. They do not agree with the argument of those against more parks, that economic development and nature conservation are mutually exclusive. Most urban people do not experience any disadvantage if a park is gazetted somewhere in the countryside. Local people often have to lose much more, though it was generally accepted by the interviewees that they reaped large benefits, as well. This also explains the high rate of acceptance. Regarding their attitudes towards ecology, the respondents do not differ strongly. This can partly be seen as a methodological result, from averaging the values that were attributed to their opinions. I noticed that people over fifty, christians, people with an average education and women are more ecologically minded, whereas those below 20, university students, business people, housewives, muslims and men are more economically minded. We can conclude, that an extension of conservation areas in Malaysia is in the interest of the urban population. They are eager to visit them, if they can satisfy the desire to be active, have fun with their friends and family and to picnic and bathe, for example, in or near a park.

The increasing numbers of domestic visitors, as well as those from other ASEAN countries, is seen as a threat to conservation areas by the park administration. They fear ecological problems, because these visitors are not seen as environmentally conscious enough. It was often mentioned, that the visitors should change their attitudes, but not the park its policies. The protection of the environment is consequently regarded as a given that cannot be compromised. While a lack of environmental consciousness can indeed have detrimental effects on a conservation area, I think that a national park is an area that can change once it has been established. If tourism is an important part of nature conservation, protection strategies should incorporate the changing needs and desires of visitors, to a certain extent. I regard nature conservation as a structuration process that involves all stakeholders who enter the arena of conservation. I propose that park management should adapt to changes within the visitor structure, to a certain degree. However, they should not do this in a passive and reactionary way, but actively. Thus, the desired changes of the environmental consciousness of (domestic) visitors can be addressed, discussed and maybe achieved in the process of the tourists visits. Through an increase of domestic visitors, the local people, who do not have sufficient English language skills, could also be involved better, because they speak the same language.[441]

3 The experts' biggest concerns

> *How do Malaysian experts perceive the tourism-nature conservation nexus?*

The experts who are concerned either with conservation or tourism or both, have been selected from four groups according to their affiliation. Respondents within the administration and the park management form one group, ones working for NGOs another, scientists affiliated with universities a third, and tour operators the forth. The differences within these groups were minimal. The largest differences were within the group of tour operators, who also compete with each other. Between the groups there were different opinions, but I could not discern any great fault lines, probably because in Malaysia it is generally re-

---

441 However, for many Malaysians, Malay is only the second or even third language, although the government emphasises Malay as the national language.

garded as better to find a consensus, than to openly oppose each other, especially on issues in which the government is involved.

All respondents favour an increase in the number, if not the acreage, of conservation areas. They want to protect many different ecosystems and connections between them, rather than only pristine forests or other environments. Today, it takes much less time from the proposition to convert an area into a conservation area, to the actual establishment. This is regarded as a result of better collaboration between the interested parties, better knowledge about the process, and environmentally better educated and more environmentally aware politicians. However, not only are conservation areas easier to establish, it is also easier for foreign companies to invest in or build large tourist resorts. There seems to be a race between conservationists and tourism developers for the best nature spots, which, according to the principles of ecotourism, should be carefully evaluated for environmental risks before any enterprise is started. The interest and need to create revenue from tourism lets the government favour large, mostly foreign owned enterprises, that also promise to boost the local and state economies. According to NGO respondents these have a great potential for ecotourism, although they rarely work that way. Therefore, the government should invest more in small local tourist operations.

The privatisation of infrastructure is also a development that has reached Malaysian conservation areas. The government favours privatization, so that, with their limited manpower, they can better look after core tasks, if the park administration does not have to manage accommodation and restaurants too. Moreover, private companies are seen as having better skills and knowledge to provide for specific tourists' needs. While both are regarded as true by the respondents, the park administration wants to maintain control of the private enterprises. This was initially regarded as an undue restriction of their activities. NGOs and scientists warn about the incompatible interests of conservation and tourism, and insist that these enterprises have to be carefully monitored. In areas where privatisation was introduced some years ago, exponents from both the private sector and the park management state that they now work well together, after two seasons of struggling. For tourists it can be confusing to distinguish between park employees and those from restaurants or lodges. Therefore, private enterprises have started to train their staff in conservation matters, so that they can at least give the tourists some information about the environment. For the private companies, the control of the park management can be problematic if there are restaurants or hotels just outside the park, and outside the jurisdiction of the park management, that do not have the same restrictions. The proliferation of businesses outside the control of park authorities can become a problem, especially regarding the carrying capacity of the area. Cooperative management, between the park authorities, the political authorities who are responsible for the area outside the park, as well as all the concerned private companies, should be aimed at.

In most cases, it is not possible to establish a national park in Malaysia without tourist facilities, and tourism is not seen as a detriment to conservation. The exceptions are strict nature reserves, which are generally small areas protected for their use as water catchment areas. A national park is regarded as a means of income generation as well as an educational tool. Since almost no parks are financially self-sufficient, with the exception of Kinabalu Park and possibly Taman Negara, income generation is an important topic, and the raise of entrance fees is frequently discussed. It is not considered a problem for westerners to have to pay more, but it could deter Malaysians and citizens of other Asian countries. There is a debate about whether there should be a differentiated price system, with cheaper fees for domestic tourists. This leaves the problem of how much should be paid by Asian visitors. Since the park's educational function is regarded as especially important for domestic visitors, they should not be excluded by high fees.

In Sarawak, and now also in Sabah, there are great hopes of the possible royalties from patents on pharmaceutical substances which are extracted from plants from conservation areas. Huge amounts of money can be made from medicines, and there are appropriate laws that force pharmaceutical companies to share their revenues with the respective state. It is difficult, however, to prove whether a substance was extracted from a plant in a certain area and whether it is the crucial agent of a new medication.

The share of revenues from privatised tourist enterprises that flows to the state via taxes, increases with the number of guests and with the amount they are paying (and leaving in the state). Therefore, the administration is interested in having private luxury accommodation in a park. This is detrimental to the educational aspect whose aim it is, to give people from the Malaysian middle class access to conservation areas. Moreover, it neglects the fact that also low budget travellers spend a lot of money in an area, because they generally stay longer and their money does leak less from the area. A mixture of all means of income generation, coupled with a certain decentralisation which allows the parks to better see and change what they spend and what they earn, could improve the financial situation of the parks. Moreover, it must be decided whether each, all or any parks should be self-sufficient, or whether their function as a general attraction to entice tourists to come to Malaysia, should be seen as an investment by the government.

Poaching is an unresolved problem, which cannot be controlled with the current manpower in the parks. While the hunting practices of indigenous people, who are allowed to hunt in conservation areas, pose some problems, the illegal hunt for wild meat (which is generally prohibited) is the bigger threat to parks. Sarawak has loosened restrictions that prohibited the selling of wild meat. They now allow hunters to kill and sell up to ten animals from the wild (which still does not include protected areas), per month. This has lessened the pressure on respective wildlife populations and has kept more hunters away from conservation areas. Illegal plant collection, of sandalwood, orchids, *nepenthes* or *rafflesia*, is more difficult to prevent. The markets for these products are abroad, and the plants can be easily hidden. The prevention of this illegal collection only works with the help of the local people, who apprehend or accuse culprits. This, again, functions only if they perceive the park as an asset for themselves which they want to protect. Biopiracy is regarded as a big threat for the potential financial loss it can cause. Results of official research projects that lead to a new medication or a new crop variety can be easily traced back to a specific plant or region. Patents from extracts of plants collected illegally and smuggled clandestinely out of the country are much more difficult to trace. Although biopiracy is unjust and unfair, it probably does not pose a big threat to the biodiversity of a conservation area, because only very few species can be taken out at a time.

The participation of local people is regarded as important by all respondents. Locals are rarely involved from the beginning of a project. They react to the establishment of a conservation area in their vicinity, and make claims in order to benefit economically or to be allowed to continue using certain resources from the area. Participation is often viewed as a means of creating alternative uses of newly protected resources. Their possible desire to keep their traditional way to support their livelihood and to continue using the resources they have used before, is usually not regarded as an option by the authorities. Therefore, the local people do not really participate in the process of gazetting a park, at least not directly. Often NGOs assume advocacy for them on critical issues. Therefore, on a participation scale from 'actively consulting' to 'transferring authority and responsibility'[442], Malaysian nature conservation is still very near its starting point. A better inclusion of the local people in the decision making process of nature conservation is called for, in order to avoid conflicts.

Usually, the people concerned, lack adequate knowledge to benefit from tourism, almost the only resource that is accessible for them except for a job as park employee. This is why they are considered to need training and protection from outside competition. NGOs often state that the local people are lured by

---

442 Borrini-Feyerabend, G. 1997, p. 17 in Soliva, R. 2002, p.74.

the benefits they can get from tourism, in order to have them consent to, or at least not to oppose, a conservation or tourist project. The possible benefits of tourism not only depend on adequate knowledge which can be achieved with proper training, but also from how parks are designed and set up. For instance, the access road to Bako Park stops at Kampung Bako, where visitors have to hire local boatmen to drive them to the park. An example where people were excluded, is Mulu: air access that is controlled by large national and international companies, is being improved, and access by boat is neglected.

The respondents were mainly referring to skills that are needed for contact with foreign visitors. However, if the domestic tourist sector is growing, it is worthwhile to train local people who do not speak English, to guide domestic tourists, for example, before they have adequate language skills to work with foreigners.

Some people, such as the Penan, not only lack the knowledge for tourism related tasks, but often do not know how to deal with severe changes that affect their livelihood. This is because they are not used to the concepts of land ownership or paid work, which are common knowledge to other ethnic groups. The Swiss environmentalist Bruno Manser, visited them, and subsequently stayed with them for many years. He wanted to learn from an 'authentic' people, and tried to help them when their territory was threatened by logging companies. He confronted the logging companies, and later on the government, head-on, and caused a great stir in Sarawak, resulting in his being declared *persona non grata*. After he left Malaysia and continued his campaign in Europe, he illegally entered Sarawak several times in order to call attention to the Penans' problems. On his last visit, he went missing in the jungle near the Indonesian border, and is now officially declared dead. My respondents unanimously said that he chose the wrong approach to help his friends. The respondents within the administration perceived him as an adventurer who meddled inappropriately with internal affairs that were none of his business. Others admitted that he had raised an important issue, and while his approach may have been wrong, what he did was, in a way, remarkable.

Opinions about the loss of rainforests and living space for indigenous peoples are still controversial. NGOs have gained better access to the authorities and have therefore more influence. They are able to increase their authoritative resources, in order to argue about allocative resources, such as land. Their advocacy for indigenous people, and nature conservation, has become an important factor in the discussion. However, there are limits to their influence. They often have to tread lightly in order not to antagonize the government. This is especially important, when vital development issues, like the discussion about the

Bakun dam in Sarawak, clash with the needs of indigenous people. Nevertheless, there is a discourse going on, in which NGOs, and increasingly the indigenous people, participate, and which they can try to structure according to their needs and wishes.

It is a challenge for the experts, that the tourists who visit a conservation area have become more heterogeneous. In the past, they were mostly nature lovers who had an environmental awareness and had similar needs. Today many visitors have different needs and some knowledge about conservation and ecology. Since the park administration's task is primarily to protect the environment, they think that some tourists need to change their attitudes, and not that the parks have to be adapted or restructured. This might not be feasible, because the situation has changed and probably cannot be entirely reversed. While education of visitors, even before their visits, is crucial, the fact that parks are increasingly advertised as tourist destinations, and thus reach more and different kinds of people, calls for certain adaptations.

Guides are seen as the best means for information and interpretation. However, there are not enough, especially with tourist numbers increasing, and they are often not well trained. Local people often lack the necessary (language) skills. According to the respondents, students do not regard working as guides in a national park as something from which they could benefit. A good system of (private) guides could help to avoid misunderstandings and conflicts that are detrimental to the park and the experience of the visitors. For this they would need good and organised training opportunities which they often do not have. Although guides are regarded as important "tools" for the dissemination of information, they are not the only options. Each park has an interpretation centre which can provide relevant information, especially for (individual) travellers who cannot or do not want to hire a guide. The centres often lack the resources needed to create good exhibits and therefore they are either not visited or not regarded as informative. Another possibility that is rarely used, is track-side information that gives information on the spot, where certain aspects of the visited ecosystem can be seen, heard or felt. This is difficult and costly, as signs would have to be protected from wind and weather. Besides the information in the parks, there is a need for better information before people book a journey to a park. This would insure that visitors would not arrive at a park with false expectations. However, most tourist offices want to promote conservation areas, and are reluctant to provide information that could deter people from going there. It would be better, however, for the potential visitors if they would not go somewhere where they cannot experience what they want.

Malaysia still struggles with its image, which is not well defined for the whole country. Sarawak's image is defined by its logging practices, which according to some respondents have improved considerably and were exaggerated in the first place. Others claim that the logging companies are still clearing areas that are too large, because of loopholes in the law. Sabah has the problem of not having an image at all, because it is not well known abroad. Besides this fuzzy image, tourist promoters do not seem to know what tourists want, and therefore cannot promote properly. NGOs also say that the needs and ideas of the visited are not considered, which is why some tourist sites do not work as well as they should or could. I do not think that a survey of tourists' expectations before they visit Malaysia, alone would yield useful results. Evaluations should be conducted after the visit of existing attractions and sites in, order to get a better picture of what tourists want. Further surveys on the local peoples' perceptions of tourists and tourism could complete that picture. Results from the experts' discourse suggest that nature conservation is working rather well in Malaysia without great conflicts or viciously opposing interests.

4 Types of tourists become forms of tourism

> *What are the needs of different groups of tourists (i.e. individual and group travellers and domestic and foreign travellers) and how can they be balanced in conservation areas?*

For analytical and statistical reasons, we often define groups of tourists that can be differentiated, according to one or more criteria. I used the categories 'individual traveller' and 'group traveller' for the study I conducted with over 80 tourists in Gunung Mulu National Park. These categories were restricted to the visit to Mulu, which means that group travellers could become individual travellers after their visit or vice versa. The more possibilities and the more experience (a form of authoritative resources) tourists have, the more they are able to change the way they travel. For example some backpackers of the 1970's or 80's are still often individual travellers, because they have experience in that form of travel. Occasionally, however, they book a tour or even an all-inclusive arrangement. On the other hand, experienced mass tourists occasionally try to travel independently for a part of their journey. This may be because their children do it, but also because travel guidebooks became more comprehensive and detailed. The standardisation of tourism infrastructure might allow them to travel to destinations which were until recently considered as remote and inaccessible, for ordinary tourists. Therefore, it makes better sense to speak of tourist forms, meaning forms of travel that tourists engage in for a specific period, rather than tourist types. The latter suggests that people can be classified according to their tourist behaviour and that their habitus is consistent with that type. I do not want to deny the importance of the habitus for the decision about how and to which destinations people travel. I do not, however, think that people acquire a 'mass-tourist habitus' or an 'ecotourist habitus', it is rather the other way round. People with certain habitus tend to engage in certain forms of tourism, although that can change if the context changes. For the study in Mulu, this means that the needs of people who are engaged in a specific form of tourism should be tied to the forms of tourism and not to the types of tourists.

Since Mulu became a World Heritage Site in 2000, it has become much better known and can now count on more visitors than before. It is easily accessible by air, albeit with an old aircraft which makes the flight from Miri an adventure. It takes the better part of a day to reach the remote national park by boat, and there is no fixed schedule, which makes a trip difficult to plan. Moreover, the flight is even cheaper than the boat ride, which requires the tourist to change boats, because the big river boats cannot enter the smaller tributaries. Because of the uncertain schedule of flights and also because it is easier to arrange transport for more than one or two people, groups usually travel by boat. Regardless of the means of transport or the form of tourism, most evaluated their transportation as good. The boat ride was even said to be excellent, by 50 % of the boat riders. Therefore, the river transport deserves more attention. There are efforts underway to improve air access, but none to create a regular boat service. This would on the one hand enable people to have an adventurous access to the park. It is planned that the old planes be exchanged for newer ones, which will make air access less adventurous. On the other hand, if people make the longer journey with the boat, they are likely to stay longer in the park. They will incur lower costs and have more time to appreciate conservation efforts, along with Mulu's attractions. Although the high biodiversity can be regarded as a great attraction of the park, fauna and flora are not the main reasons why people visit it. Group travellers came more because of 'nature' than individual travellers, who mostly came in order to go trekking. Moreover, except for the bats who fly out of the world's biggest cave mouth by the millions, animals are rarely seen. Because Mulu is understaffed, there are almost no guided tours to watch animals or view special plants. Mulu's variety of attractions is great. Most people come because of the four show caves that are extraordinary, or to make a trek. It is often difficult, especially for individual travellers to book a trek, because they have to find the people to accompany them and an available guide, themselves. Therefore, many of them who would rather like to stay longer in the park, leave earlier, because they could not go on a trek for the lack of opportunity. The length of stay does not correlate positively with the number of visited attractions. It is almost the opposite. This is because a trek takes a few days and is counted as one attraction, whereas the four show caves can be visited within one day, but are counted as four separate attractions. This is not the only reason why individual travellers, particularly, do not visit as many attractions as group visitors, although they stay longer. For one thing, it is the uncertainty of organising a trek which often keeps them from walking to a cave. Another reason could be that they are not interested in visiting 'touristic' attractions.

The maintenance of infrastructure, especially in the caves, is quite costly, which is why the park management wants to raise the rather low entrance fees. Although most respondents want to keep fees as low as they are, the majority found them average or low. Individual travellers found them slightly higher than did group travellers. The intent of the Sarawak government, to raise entrance fees from RM 3 to RM 10 (without camera fee), was suspended after protests by Malaysians.

Mulu offers all sorts of accommodations for visitor from the basic hostel to the four star Royal Mulu Resort (RMR). Although the majority of individual travellers stay in the park headquarters' hostel, some also stayed in the RMR. While there is cheap and rather expensive accommodation, there are not too many rooms in the middle range. According to the survey, individual travellers are more critical about the staff and prices, whereas group travellers were more concerned about cleanliness and infrastructure. In general, the headquarters' rooms were rated worse than those of the RMR (which is to be expected, with the difference in price). This suggests that accommodation, as well as restaurants, have to be improved but necessarily made more luxurious. With the planned privatisation, these things probably will improve, but mostly there will be an upgrade. Therefore, it will become more expensive, instead of adapting to more appropriate, local, standards.

There are no cultural sights for visitors, except for a Penan village where the inhabitants sell some handicrafts. Mulu does not have a great potential for cultural activities, because the area is not densely populated. Nevertheless, there should be a bottom-up approach, starting with the visited regarding any cultural activities. Otherwise exploitation can quickly result from efforts coming top-down.

Mulu does not have many recreation facilities either, except for the swimming pool at the RMR, and a natural pond near a cave entrance. However, the area of the headquarters has a great potential for tourists to relax and enjoy themselves, just by being there. Although there are already mountain bike trails and rocks for climbing outside the park, these possibilities are rarely used. I do not think that Mulu needs a lot of recreational attractions, but with a little input, and better coordination, with restaurants, for example, it could become a destination where tourists could see the attractions as quickly as possible, and while "idle" time away between the visit of attractions comfortably.

Although the interpretation centre is conveniently located next to the park office, it was only visited by 30 % of the respondents, most of whom were individual travellers. Since the centre gets a good review in the Lonely Planet guide book, the rate of its visitors who use this travel guide book is more than 50 %. This is an indicator of the increasingly important role of these books. Although the average rating of the centre is mostly good, there are also people who consider it not so good or even bad. Individual travellers are more critical than group travellers, who probably received additional explanations by their guide, or are not as used to visiting exhibits and museums, as individual travellers. I found the exhibit interesting but arbitrary. With a few improvements, it could be converted into something good. The problem is, that not many people visit it. Therefore, it would be better to move information and interpretation to the place where the tourists are. One might move it to the viewing platform from which the bats can be seen flying out of the cave, and where tourists wait for about an hour, as a rule. While every park is a unique conservation area, many observations made by the visitors in Mulu also apply to other national parks. As the visitor structure becomes increasingly heterogeneous, emphasis should be put on the improvement of interpretation, as well as on recreational possibilities. The latter not only satisfy the needs of domestic tourists, but may also cause visitors to extend their stays, which would bring more revenue to the park, decrease costs, be more sustainable and give the authorities the chance to build up ecological awareness on site.

5 Creating the potential to have authentic experiences

> *How can an increasing number of tourists be guided through a park with limited personnel, without causing harm to the environment? Can authenticity be constructed or staged in a way that enhances the experiences of the visitors without compromising nature conservation?*

Tropical rainforests with their seeming inviolateness, can be regarded as authentic from different actors' perspectives. Their high biodiversity can serve as indicator for authenticity. The fact that some of them are protected, and that this protection is enforced, can be interpreted as a sign of authenticity. Moreover, we have to ask whether authenticity is what tourists seek in national parks. For many western tourists, the tropical rainforest is something special, and they want to see it in its undisturbed splendour. For many domestic visitors, a national park is merely a nice place to be outdoors. Therefore, the 'jungle' can also be a nice backdrop in front of which visitors may enjoy themselves. Especially in the age of the tourist gaze where people are well acquainted with pictures of rainforests, it is important to be able to actually see the image in reality. As we have discussed in the introduction, gazing is not everything, experiencing is important too. Experiences that tourists want to make are based on images that they create of these experiences, before they actually make them. Therefore, visiting a conservation area can be regarded as a mixture between seeing and experiencing something that corresponds with the images in the tourists heads, and to contribute to the conservation of nature. Tourists want to realise this mixture at a specific locale. Thus, we can conceive of a specific national park that is visited by tourists on the one hand, as a mere setting in which the tourists' desires can and should be satisfied. On the other hand, the parks are not interchangeable, because they have distinct features. Therefore, even if we regard the Malaysian national parks as a 'foil' on which the tourists' wishes are projected, this foil with its ecosystem is firmly localised. In the strictest sense it cannot be regarded as a non-place that has no local reference.[443] However, for many experiences (and gazes) that tourists want to make, it does not matter where exactly they make it. From a constructivistic point of view, any national park, or conservation area, has to be regarded as a social construction. The people who are professionally engaged in nature conservation, perceive their parks in a different way. For them, the parks are much more distinct 'individuals' and less foils on which to project something. This difference has to be borne in mind by those who construct and structure a park for visitors. It therefore has to be their aim to let the tourists make their experiences without compromising the protection of the environment and to let them make their experiences in a way that heightens their ecological awareness.

Tourists expect a certain safeness of their experiences which includes protection from harm, as well as, that they can make experiences that correspond, if not exactly then in essence, with what they have in mind. They also want to make new experiences that go beyond what they actually expected. Paradoxically, they often expect to experience or see something unexpected. If the tourists consequently visit a national park, the expected and unexpected need to be in a

---

443 The newly opened Masoala rainforest ecosystem in the Zurich zoo is located in a huge hall in order to keep the temperature and humidity constantly at a tropical level. It is an example of a non-place, because the hall could be located anywhere, even though there are strong references to the Madagascar Masoala region, because its plants and animals were imported from there.

balance, which, unfortunately for the management, is different for each visitor. However, if the unexpected or adventurous occurs when a certain safeness is expected, it can be detrimental to the over all experience and consequently to the park's image. This kind of adverse experience could include a lack of transportation or accommodation, inadequate or unhygienic accommodation, or not being able to see what was expected. Therefore, in situations where safeness is expected by most tourists, as well as in places or situations where the park management deems it necessary to convey certain messages or meanings, elements of non-places can be very helpful. Upon arrival, for example, it should be clear how to get to the accommodation, which forms have to be filled in and what can be experienced when, where and at which price, etc. While the architecture of the accommodation can be uncommon to a certain degree (i.e. traditional), from the point of view of the visitors, the way the rooms can be used should be self explanatory. Moreover, it should be clear which paths lead to which attraction, and whether they cost something. One ought to be able to read and understand interpretation in an exhibit without the help of park employees. On the other hand, there is much room for small adventures in the forest and around attractions as well as in the realm of foods and customs. In summary, national parks in Malaysia are not non-places. If visitor intensive parts of parks would make more or better use of elements of non-places that tourists are used to, it could reduce financial and environmental costs, and could enhance the probability for tourists to make what they perceive as authentic experiences.

6 Important issues of the National Ecotourism Plan

In this chapter I want to address issues of the National Ecotourism Plan (NEP) that arose during this study and that were either controversial or very important.[444] The experts regarded the plan as a good tool, although according to respondents within the administration, it lacks precision in the assessment of carrying capacity. Moreover, the NGOs often argue that many politicians do not have sufficient background to be able to implement the plan adequately. Therefore, the risk remains that they make decisions that are detrimental to the environment. Regarding this problem, scientists have had good experiences with organised field trips to 'problem areas' with politicians. Some of the scientists argued that the NEP is not making strict enough rules for the tourist industry that, according to them, has to be forced to act in an environmentally friendly

---

[444] The NEP addresses tourism within Malaysia and does not focus on the sustainability of the transport means that are used by the tourists.

way. Nobody is really happy with the label 'ecotourism', and many think it will disappear in the near future.

Regarding *carrying capacity* (2)[445] there seems to be no clear understanding about where and when they are exceeded. Because it is difficult to formulate general criteria, NGO respondents argue that for each conservation and ecotourism area, individual assessments should be made. A closer collaboration between the park authorities and NGOs could solve this problem, if the research can be funded. This could be achieved, for example, with a raise of the entrance fees. After, or better during such an assessment, it is important to include all stakeholders in park resources, in order to prevent misunderstandings and opposition.

There are almost no studies about what *ecotourists expect* (3), when they come to Malaysia (or any other Southeast Asian country), which makes it difficult to plan sites accordingly. On the one hand, the unclear definition of 'ecotourist' does not make it easy to develop criteria for a survey. Tour promoters seem to have a rather clear understanding about what ecotourists want, which, according to NGOs and scientists is not based on adequate (scientific) knowledge. Moreover, it may not be an adequate approach to look for ecotourists as tourists with a distinct profile or even a habitus that defines them as ecotourists. Tourists increasingly tend to change their attitudes and desires during their journey, according to their social contexts, their daily wishes and the opportunities presented to them. Tourists who travel in an ecologically unsustainable way for one week, may book a tour that complies with ecotourism's requirements for the next. Therefore, it would be better to more clearly define criteria for ecotourism, in specific areas, and subsequently ask potential tourists whether they would like to use such an offer or not. In addition they can be asked about their experiences, after they have visited a site. I do not think that ecotourists, whether they can be called ecotourists before they actually use an ecotourist product or not, have a clear understanding of ecotourism sites in general. Rather, they can discuss how a specific site is set up. Contextualised qualitative studies regarding selected sites could offer great insights about the issue. The results of this study's quantitative and qualitative aspects could serve as a stepping stone from which such a survey could be launched.

Besides the lack of information about the desires of (eco)tourists, there is insufficient knowledge about the numbers and expenditures of tourists and different kinds of activities. The needs and expenditures of individual travellers seem to be under reported, which is why promotion does not address this group

---

445 The numbers in brackets refer to the number of the main issues of the National Ecotourism Plan (see figure 16 on page 90).

much. Surveys taking the different forms (not types) of tourism into account could provide much better planning tools. From my interviews, I gathered the impression that while promoters claim to be interested in all tourists, they would rather discourage individual travellers, or backpackers, because their lifestyles do not always conform with Malaysian social values. Although it may be true that certain backpackers behave in a way that is regarded as unacceptable by the visited, it would be more helpful if their needs would be better understood, in order to provide them with adequate information. In the long run the (mostly young) backpackers turn out to be "ordinary" tourists who may come back and spend more money. Therefore, this tourist segment should not be neglected.

Although some indigenous people can make *use of park resources* (8), there is a tendency to create alternatives for them, in order to stop any extraction of plants or animals from the conservation area. Some practices of local people can be harmful to the ecosystem, such as poison fishing, or excessive logging. Other local practices, like hunting protected species or using firearms, may harm tourism. On the other hand, other local customs, like subsistence plant collection or hunting with traditional weapons, could be incorporated into park management plans. Unresolved land claims pose a threat to conservation, because the needs of different stakeholders cannot be well coordinated. It could be feasible to introduce biosphere reservations that could incorporate the traditions of the local people as a basic element of a reservation and not as a more or less tolerated activity that is regarded as detrimental to conservation.[446] Such a biosphere reservation only works well if all stakeholders are involved from the beginning. This especially applies to the protection of core areas from poaching which does not work without the help of local residents.

Ecotourism is often regarded as a *niche tourism for small scale enterprises* (10, 37) that do not generate much tax revenue. Consequently, Malaysian tourism promotion still concentrates on large scale projects. While it is difficult to convert mass tourism into ecotourism, it is not impossible. More and better statistics could give better information about revenue generation (including leakages) of ecotourism enterprises, and thus make it possible to assess it better. With better information about the long term, financial, ecological and social advantages of ecotourism, and the will to forego short term investments that favour unsustainable mass tourism operations, the government could gain better control over tourist development. In this way, they would be better able to create a consistent image of Malaysia and its conservation areas.

---

446 Culmsee shows how a biosphere reservation can be an instrument for development with the example of the Arganeraie reservation in Morocco (Culmsee, H. 2003).

Reliable information is crucial for ecotourism, and enhances the possibility for tourists to have authentic experiences (11, 20). Although the conservation areas have interpretation centres and a number of knowledgeable guides, the information provided could be better. One problem is the accessibility of information for tourists. Booking offices, tour operators and guidebook publishers should be provided with information for their consumers, in order to avoid misunderstandings and false expectations. The interpretation centres in the parks, although they are often arranged with great care, are not visited by many people. Probably because more and more tourists are used to good museums, they are not enticed by the often small, low budget exhibits. Others would rather see and experience ecological interrelations in the "authentic" environment. Therefore, the possibility for tourists to engage interpreters for short periods as well as self-explanatory track-side interpretation should be increased and better organised. With such improved interpretation, more tourists could be informed about the principles of ecotourism and their ecological awareness could be heightened.

The NEP complains about mass tourism increasingly encroaching upon ecotourism sites, which is perceived as a threat to the environment. As mentioned above, mass tourism and ecotourism are not necessarily mutually exclusive. However, since most mass tourism is not organised in an ecological way, it can pose a threat to conservation areas. If those involved continue to reinforce the difference between these forms of tourism, little will change. There should be a greater concentration on and consideration of small-scale operations that enable local people to benefit from tourism. The potential of bigger enterprises (with good economies of scale) to decrease their environmental impact, should also not be neglected.

Small scale operations often lack adequate *information* to process the increasing flow of visitors into conservation areas (27). Larger tourist companies could handle bookings, transport etc. much better. However, these enterprises often lack knowledge about environmentally and socially friendly tourism and should therefore be consulted and/or controlled by agencies (e.g. the government or NGOs) that can provide this knowledge. They should also try to engage local people, primarily, and train them, in order to build their capacities and not only rely on outside people. Local small scale operations, should be supported or subsidised until they can compete with mass tourism operations or find a niche in which to operate. A constant subsidising of tourism operations, excluding the park management, should be avoided, because it creates dependencies and can inhibit competition and the development of new ideas.

The widening gap between *manpower needs and supply* (28, 31) can probably not be closed using only local people. One expert stated that with better job descriptions and incentives, productivity could be increased considerably. If the influx of outsiders could be limited to people who were only to work temporarily in conservation areas the possibility of driving out local people until they have adequate skills, can be diminished. So far, work in national parks is not regarded as an interesting job, as it is in many western countries. The knowledge gained during a season of helping out in a park could be beneficial for many environmentally or tourist related studies and occupations. No matter who is working in a park, adequate and constant training is very important, in order to be able to adequately react to changes in visitors' behaviours and needs.

Images of destinations (30) cannot be fully controlled by those who create or promote them. Nevertheless, a concise promotion that pays attention to environmental issues, could prevent false expectations of visitors. One problem with promotion may be that promoters generally want to entice people to visit a destination and not deter them, in order to avoid a glut on the carrying capacity. A park should therefore neither be promoted as an eco-theme park nor as luxury resort. The possibility of limiting access to a park should be incorporated into management plans and should also be communicated to visitors. Besides the entrance fee, or costs for accommodation or activities, the limitation of guests is the most efficient way to control impacts on the environment which are related to the number of visitors. In contrast to the price as a regulation measure, a limitation of the number of visitors is not socially unfair.

7 Final remarks on theory, methods and future prospects

Towards the end of this study some remarks are indicated about the usefulness of the theoretical framework that was chosen. The theory of structuration, which was mainly used, makes us perceive nature conservation first as a process and second as a result of intended and unintended consequences of different actors' (or stakeholders') actions. For example, Gunung Mulu National Park is shaped by Sarawak state law that allows protection of areas from many kinds of resource use. The internationally renowned labels 'national park' (or IUCN category II) and 'World Heritage Site' (awarded by UNESCO), further strengthen its protection. People who work for the park administration are concerned with the protection of species and the environment. The park is a means for them to be employed and have an income. Some of the local residents perceive the park as a (new) regulation that prohibits them from using the forest's resources the way they did before its establishment. If they follow the regulations they also reproduce them, if they act against them, and are caught, there may be consequences. If this happens, the area may become restructured as a 'contested terrain'. Tour operators perceive the park as an asset with which they can generate income. If they can lead tours to the area, they also reproduce the rules. If they boycott it which some do, because of the unreliable air transport, they may structure the park as place with bad accessibility. Tourists change the environment of the park with their mere presence, and with the infrastructure that is necessary to satisfy their needs and desires. Easy access by air, chosen by a majority of tourists, impacts the local boat men, and has changed the image of the park from one of a remote area, to an easily accessible one. Thus, the shape of the social construction 'Gunung Mulu National Park' is reproduced and changed with each action that enters its 'arena'. Every actor perceives this construction in a different way, and incorporates this perception into his or her actions. An important aspect of the theory is power relations. Every action also incorporates power, when certain resources are used, according or against rules. However, some actors have much more power than others. The government that decides whether a park is established has more allocative and authoritative resources at its disposal than indigenous people or a single tourist. Nevertheless, aggregated actions of actors with little power amount to an important structuring force. Bruno Manser tried to encourage this power, but failed, for the most part, although the discourse about rainforests in Sarawak had a lasting effect on the image of Sarawak with western tourists. The view through the lens of structuration theory also makes clear that conservation is, although it is meant to endure, neither a stable or a static state, and that it is not determined by an unalterable system. However, in my studies I discovered that for some people nature conservation makes that impression.

My recommendations, based on the interpretation of the results of the single studies, can also be seen as a part of shaping or structuring nature conservation in Malaysia. The variety of actors and factors, which play a role in nature conservation, led me to use a triangulation of methods. This is not necessarily a consequence of using the theory of structuration, but one way of implementing it. In this study I used a triangulation of methods in order to grasp the issue 'ecotourism and nature conservation in Malaysia', from different angles. In fact, I conducted three studies, (half-)standardised interviews with 500 Kuala Lumpurians, 82 (half-)standardised interviews with tourists of the Gunung Mulu National Park, and 25 focused expert interviews in all parts of Malaysia. These, along with (participant) observations, helped me to get more information in less time about the contexts in which the single studies were embedded. While each single study produced coherent results, one cannot a priori expect the same from the combination of the three single studies. Indeed, it is not feasible to compare the opinions of an expert in a longer interview, with answers given in a standardised interview. This was also not my intention. Rather, with my method I could ascertain that (potential) domestic tourists have, indeed, different hopes and desires about visiting a national park than foreigners. I also found that there are fewer differences regarding their estimations of the importance of nature conservation. Moreover, the study showed that within the pool of experts, there is an abundance of knowledge that, if well combined and aggregated, could help to set up more efficient parks, and nature conservation. As a result of these deliberations, I will use the triangulation of methods in future studies again. Triangulation allows one to view issues from different angles and to relate results from one study to another.

The concept of 'habitus' and 'social field', taken from Bourdieu's theory of social practice, were useful for the explanation of different forms of tourism. I did not, however, use these concepts for the empirical studies. It would be interesting, but not easy, to make a study of certain tourist's habitus and the social fields they move in.

The field I am moving in or through is the one of social geography which is concerned about how social processes manifest themselves spatially, and how actors subsequently regionalise their living space (or their Lebenswelt). Because ecotourism is a concept that is widely discussed, although not well defined, and which is applied to nature conservation, images are created for tourists that suggest that tourism can be beneficial for nature conservation. Malaysian national parks are constantly newly regionalised and structured, although they remain the same, spatially. The introduction of the concept of non-places served to cast a new light on national parks and to be able view them in a different light.

Of course I could only analyse specific topics within the vast field of ecotourism and nature conservation. For studies starting from this point, I suggest taking a closer look at the needs, wishes, opinions and problems of the visited who live near or in conservation areas. Additional qualitative studies about the different forms of tourism, and their combination and interrelation, would be useful.

VIII Index and Bibliography

Index of authors

A
Ackermann, A. & Müller, K. E. (eds.) 2002. *43*
Ahrens, D. 2001. *49*
Anderson, J.A.R., Jermy, A.C. & Cranbrook, G.G.H. 1982. *237*
Asia Pacific Solidarity 1993. *230*
Augé, M. 1995. *46, 48, 49, 164*
Azahari, B.O. 2001. *146, 228*

B
Backhaus, N. & Keller, S.A. 2001. *161, 234*
Backhaus, N. & Kollmair, M. 2001. *76*
Backhaus, N. 1999. *22*
Badaruddin, M. 2002. *80, 89, 149*
Baysan, S.K. 2001. *69*
Beck, U. 1986. *22*
Bieger, T. & Laesser, C. 2002. *28, 40, 42*
Black, R. 1999. *220*
Blamey, R.K. 2001. *53, 54*
Bormann, R. 2000. *49*
Borrini-Feyerabend, G. 1997. *85, 252*
Bossart S. 2003. *76*
Bossart, S. 2003. *75, 76*
Bourdieu, P. 1977. *20*
Bourdieu, P. 1999. *21*
Brilli, A. 1997. *25*
Brosius, P.J. 2000. *153, 218, 236*
Bruner, E. 1994. *44*
Bryant, C.G.A. & Jary, D. 1991. *15, 17*
Buckley, R. 2001. *69, 70*
Budowsky, G. 1970. *76*
Bundesamt für Statistik Schweiz 2002. *4, 31*

C
Ceballos-Lascuráin, H. 1996. *53, 66, 70*
Chin, C.L.M. & Bennett, E.L. 2000. *83*
Chin, C.L.M., Moore, S.A., Wallington, T.J. & Dowling, R.K. 2000. *69, 70*
Chrismond, S.P. 2001. *216*
Cohen, E. 1988. *44*
Colchester, M. 1997. *236*
Consumers' Association of Penang 1999. *137*
Cook, S.D. et al. 1992. *62*
Corner, E.J.H. and Beaman, J.H. 1996. *108*
Craib, I. 1992. *15, 16*
Cranbrook, G.G.-H., Earl of 2000. *103*
Crichton, M. 1999. *43*
Crouch, H. 1996. *149*
Culmsee, H. 2003. *262*

D
DeLyser, D. 1999. *44*
Department of Forestry of Sarawak 2000. *100, 101, 103, 104, 105, 106, 114, 133, 134*
Department of Forestry of Sarawak 2001. *100, 204*
Department of Forestry Peninsular Malaysia 2000. *96, 114, 133, 134*
Department of Statistics Malaysia 2001. *116, 120, 123*
Department of Wildlife and National Parks Malaysia 2002. *97*
Dörfler, T., Graefe, O. & Müller-Mahn, D. 2003. *20*
Douglas, I. 1999. *83*

E
Eagles, P.F.J., McCool, S.F. & Haynes, C.D. 2002. *2, 3, 8, 67, 68, 70, 73*
Eaton, P. 2000. *153*
Ecotourism Society 2002. *59*
Elsrud, T. 2001. *35, 36, 37*

F
Firth, T. & Hing, N. 1999. *38*
Fischer Weltalmanach 2001. *150*
Fischer Weltalmanach 2002. *2*
Frankenberg, P., Lauer, W. & Rheker, J.R. 1990. *205*
Frost, W. 2001. *73, 240*

G
Gäth, P. 1999. *37*
Geisel, S. 2002. *27*
Ghimire, K.B. 2001a. *39*
Ghimire, K.B. 2001b. *39*
Giddens, A. 1976. *16*
Giddens, A. 1991. *15, 22*
Giddens, A. 1992. *15*
Giddens, A. 1993. *15*
Giddens, A. 1995. *14, 15, 18*
Giddens, A. 1999. *20*
Giddens, A. 2000. *20*
Golley, F. 1983. *76*
Gomez, E.T. and Jomo, K.S. 1997. *149*
Grütter, K. & Plüss, C. 1996. *18*

H
Hampton, M.P. 1998. *37*
Hawkins, D.E. & Lamoureux, K. 2001. *59*
Herbers, K. 1991. *25*
Hitchcock, M. & Jay, S. 1998. *46, 67, 150*
Honey, M. 1999. *53*
Huber, A. 1999. *126*
Hupke, K.-D. 2000. *76*
Hutton, W. 1998. *45*

I
Immigration Department of Malaysia 2001/ 2002. *6*
INSAN, Institute for Social Analysis 1994. *151*
Institute for Development Studies 1996. *110*
Ioannides, D. & Debbagge, K. J. 1998. *41*
IUCN 1994. *2, 94, 116, 129*
IUCN, 1974. *76*

J
Jenkins, D.V., de Silva, G.S., Wells, D.R. and Phillipps, A. 1996. *107*
Jenkins, R. 1993. *2, 19, 20, 28*

K
Kamphues, M. 1998. *138*
Keller, U., Backhaus, N. & Elsasser, H. 2002. *30*
Khaidir, A. 1994. *153*
Kiefl, W. 1997. *28, 30*
King, V.T. 1992. *47*
King, V.T. 1993. *47, 207*
King, V.T. 2001. *236*
Kollmair, M. & Backhaus, N. forthcoming. *73*
Korte, H. 2001. *172*
Krais, B. & Gebauer, G. 2002. *18, 19, 20, 21*
Küpfer, I. 2000. *81*
Kurte, B. 2002. *52, 53, 54*

L
Laarman, J.G. & Durst, P.B. 1993. *62*
Laman, T. 2002. *99*
Lamnek, S. 1995. *173*
Lamprecht, H. 1984. *76*
Lash, S. & Urry, J. 1994. *25, 28, 31, 32, 41*
Lawai Anak Kumpang 2001. *226*
Le Monde diplomatique 2003. *29*
Leach, M., Mearns, R. & Scoones, I. 1999. *21*
Lee Tain Choi, D. 1996. *107*
Lee, B.T. & Bahrin T.S. 1998. *46*
Lee, B.T. & Bahrin, T.S. 1998. *153*
Liew, F.S.P. 1996. *107*
Lim Chan Koon 2000. *103*
Lim, G.L. 1999. *80*
Lindberg, K. 2001. *67*
Lude, A. 2001. *75*
Luger, K. 1995. *32*
Lutterjohann, M., Homann, E., Homann, K. & Kuster, R. 1998. *112, 131, 215*

M
MacCannell, D. 1989. *43, 44*
Magick River, A. 2002. *137*
Malaysian Nature Society 2000. *137*
Manser, B. 1999. *189*
Markwell, K.W. 1997. *34*
Masing, J.J. 1999. *51*

May, J. 1996. *44*
Meethan, K. 2001. *18*
Meredith, M. & Woolridge, J. 1992. *208*
Merriam-Webster 2002. *77*
Mohamed, I.A. 2001. *101*
Moscardo, G. & Woods, B. 1998. *75, 152*
Myers, N. 1983. *76*

N
North, D.C. 1990. *21*

O
Oppermann, M. 1992. *35*
Orams, M.B. 2001. *54*

P
Parker, T. 1993. *62*
Peet, R. 1998. *43*
Perkins, H.C. & Thorns, D.C. 2001. *34*
Phillips, N. & Hardy, C. 2002. *173*
Plüss, C. 1999. *18*

R
Regis, P. 1996. *107*
Reichertz, J. 2000. *10*
Relph, 1976. *43*
Richards, P.W. 1973. *76*
Ritzer, G. 1998. *41*
Ritzer, J. & Liska, A. 1997. *18*
Road Atlas of Malaysia 1996. *122*
Rojek, C. 2000. *22, 23, 24*
Rowthorn, C., Andrew, D., Hellander, P. & Lindenmayer, C. 1999. *112, 131, 215*
Rowthorn, C., Benson, S., Kerr, R. & Niven, C. 2001. *84, 226*
Rüegge, B. 2003. *46*

S
Sabah Parks 2000. *107, 108, 109, 111, 113, 114, 133, 134*
Saifuddin, B.S. 2001. *103, 118, 134, 141*
Sanggin, S.E., Noweg, G.T., Abdul, R.A. & Mersat, N.I. 2000. *153, 230*
Sarawak Tourism Board 199?. *215*
Scheyvens, R. 2002. *37, 38*
Schiemann, G. 1996. *125*
Schulze, H. & Suratman, S. 1999. *185*
Schumann, S. 2000. *146*
Schurian-Bremecker, C. 2001. *24*
Seckelmann, A. 2002. *39*
Selengut, S. 1995. *51*
Siebers, W. 1991. *26*
Sirakaya, E. 1999. *54*
Smart, B. 1999. *31*
Soliva, R. 2002. *2, 184, 252*
Sontag 1979. *31*
Swerdlow, J.L. 2000. *182*

T

Taman Negara Resort n.a. *95*
Tan Chin Siang 1999. *212*
The Ecotourism Society, 1991. *53*
Thorsell, J. 2000. *208*, *215*, *236*
Thrift, N. 1996. *9*
Torres, R. 2002. *27*, *40*, *41*
Tourism Authority of Thailand 2002. *139*
Tourism Malaysia 2002. *149*
Tourism Malaysia 2003. *29*, *39*
Treibel, A. 2000. *172*
Trojanow, I. 2002. *36*

U

UNEP, W.C.M.C. 1992. *93*, *94*, *95*, *97*, *99*, *103*, *112*, *129*, *149*
UNESCO 1978. *76*
UNESCO 2000. *106*, *208*
Uriely, N., Yonay, Y. & Simchai, D. 2002. *35*
Urry, J. 2002. *18*, *33*
Urry, J., 2002. *24*

V

Vision Air 2001. *214*
Vorlaufer, K. 1996. *32*, *35*, *45*

W

Watson Andaya, B. & Andaya, L.Y. 2001. *117*, *241*
Watson Andaya, B. and Andaya, L.Y. 2001. *119*, *149*, *162*
WCED 1987. *57*
Weaver, D.B. 2001. *56*, *57*, *58*
Werlen, B. 1995. *9*, *15*
Werlen, B. 1997. *9*
Werlen, B. 1999. *14*
Werlen, B. 2000. *9*
Whitmore T.C. 1993. *76*
Whitmore, T.C. 1998. *76*

Wight, P.A. 2001. *62*, *63*
Wittenberg, R. and Cramer, H. 2000. *160*
Wöhler, K. 2001. *66*
Wöhler, K. 2003. *34*, *50*
Wolfe, T. 1990. *19*
Wong, K.M. & Phillipps, A. 1996. *45*, *106*
Wong, M. 2002. *101*
World Conservation Monitoring Centre & IUCN 1998. *2*, *3*, *4*, *98*
World Conservation Monitoring Centre 2002. *4*, *5*, *104*, *107*, *208*
World Tourism Organisation 2001a. *51*, *62*, *63*, *65*
World Tourism Organisation 2001b. *51*, *59*, *62*, *64*, *66*
World Tourism Organisation 2002a. *51*, *59*, *62*, *64*, *66*
World Tourism Organisation 2002b. *51*, *59*, *62*, *64*, *66*
World Tourism Organisation 2002c. *51*, *59*, *62*, *63*, *65*
World Tourism Organisation 2002d. *51*, *62*, *64*, *65*
World Tourism Organisation 2002e. *51*, *54*, *62*
World Tourism Organisation 2003. *29*
WRI et al. 1985. *76*
WTO News, 1997/98. *62*
WTO/UNEP 1992. *11*, *211*
WWF Malaysia 1996. *6*, *59*, *86*, *88*, *89*, *90*, *92*, *135*, *194*
WWF Malaysia and Cubitt, G. 1998. *93*, *97*, *98*, *99*, *102*, *108*, *110*

Z

Ziffer, K. 1989. *53*

Bibliography

Ahrens, D. 2001. 'Grenzen der Enträumlichung – Weltstädte, Cyberspace und transnationale Räume in der globalisierten Moderne'. Opladen: Leske + Budrich.

Anderson, J.A.R., Jermy, A.C. & Cranbrook, G.G.-H., the Earl of 1982. 'Gunung Mulu National Park – A Management and Development Plan'. London: Royal Geographical Society.

Asia Pacific Solidarity 1993. 'Berawans' Struggle in Mulu Park' (http://nativenet.uthscsa.edu/archive/nl/9309/0083.html, 20. August 2002).

Augé, M. 1995. 'Non-Places – Introduction to an anthropology of supermodernity'. Stanford: Stanford University Press.

Azahari, B.O. 2001. 'The Perception of Visitors of the New Entrance Fees to National Parks and Wildlife Centres'. Hornbill.

Backhaus, N. 1998. 'Globalization and Marine Resource Use in Bali' in King, V.T. (ed.) Environmental Challenges in South-East Asia, Singapore: Curzon, p. 169–192.

--- 1999. 'Zugänge zur Globalisierung – Konzepte, Prozesse, Visionen' (Schriftenreihe Anthropogeographie, Vol. 17). Zürich: Geographisches Institut der Universität Zürich.

Backhaus, N. & Keller, S.A. 2001. 'Streetfood und Stadtkultur – Hawker in Telok Bahang/Malaysia'. Asiatische Studien/Etudes Asiatiques 55, p. 577-610.

Backhaus, N. & Kollmair, M. 2001. 'Heilige Institutionen? – Regelungen von Nutzungsansprüchen an Ressourcen von Nationalparks'. Geographica Helvetica 56, p. 57-69.

Badaruddin, M. 2002. 'The Development of Ecotourism in Malaysia – Is it Really Sustainable?' Community Based Ecotourism in Southeast Asia. Chiang Mai/Thailand.

Baysan, S.K. 2001. 'Perceptions of the Environmental Impacts of Tourism: a Comparative Study of the Attitudes of German, Russian and Turkish Tourists in Kemer, Antalya'. Tourism Geographies 3, p. 218-235.

Beck, U. 1986. 'Risikogesellschaft – Auf dem Weg in eine andere Moderne'. Frankfurt am Main: Suhrkamp.

Beck, U., Giddens, A. & Lash, S. 1994. 'Reflexive Modernization - Politics, Tradition and Aesthetics in the Modern Social Order'. Cambridge: Polity Press.

Bieger, T. & Laesser, C. 2002. 'Tourismustrends auf dem Prüfstand – Quantitativer Einbruch und struktureller Wandel der Nachfrage' Neue Zürcher Zeitung. Zürich.

Black, R. 1999. 'Ecotour Guides – Performing a Vital Role in the Ecotourism Experience' World Ecotourism Conference. Kota Kinabalu, Malaysia.

Blamey, R.K. 2001. 'Principles of Ecotourism' in Weaver, D.B. (ed.) The Encyclopedia of Ecotourism, New York: CABI, p. 5-22.

Bormann, R. 2000. 'Von Nicht-Orten, Hyperräumen und Zitadellen der Konsumkultur: Eine sozialtheoretische Reise durch postfordistische Landschaften'. Tourismus Journal 4, p. 215-234.

Borrini-Feyerabend, G. (ed.) 1997. 'Beyond Fences – Seeking Social Sustainability in Conservation'. Gland: IUCN.

Bortz, J. 1999. 'Statistik für Sozialwissenschaftler'. Berlin: Springer.

Bossart, S. 2003. 'Regenwaldschutz in den Medien – Eine Inhaltsanalyse in Schweizer Tageszeitungen'. Diplomarbeit Zürich: Universität Zürich.

Brilli, A. 1997. 'Als Reisen eine Kunst war – Vom Beginn des modernen Tourismus: Die 'Grand Tour''. Berlin: Wagenbach.

Brosius, P.J. 2000. 'Endangered Forest, Endangered People: Environmentalist Representations of Indigenous Knowledge' in Ellen, R., Parkes, P. and Bicker, A. (eds.) Indigenous Environmental Knowledge and its Transformations – Critical Anthropological Perspectives, Amsterdam: Harwood Academic Publications, p. 293-317.

Bryant, C.G.A. & Jary, D. (eds.) 1991. 'Giddens' Theory of Structuration – A Critical Appreciation'. London: Routledge.

--- 1991. 'Introduction: Coming to Terms with Anthony Giddens' in Bryant, C.G.A. and Jary, D. (eds.) Giddens' Theory of Structuration – A Critical Appreciation, London: Routledge, p. 1-31.

Buckley, R. 2001. 'Environmental Impacts' in Weaver, D.B. (ed.) The Encyclopedia of Ecotourism, New York: CABI, p. 379-394.

Bundesamt für Statistik Schweiz 2002. 'Tourismus weltweit': BfS (http://www.statistik.admin.ch, 31. May 2002).

--- 2002. 'Umweltstatistik Schweiz Nr. 12: Ferienreisen'. Neuchâtel.

Ceballos-Lascuráin, H. 1996. 'Tourism, Ecotourism and Protected Areas'. Gland: IUCN.

Chin, C.L.M. & Bennett, E.L. 2000. 'Beside the beaten Track – Effects of Increased Accessibility on Wildlife and Patterns of Hunting in Sarawak' in Leigh, M. (ed.) Borneo 2000. Kuching.

Chin, C.L.M., Moore, S.A., Wallington, T.J. & Dowling, R.K. 2000. 'Ecotourism in Bako National Park, Borneo – Visitors' Perspectives on Environmental Impacts and their Management'. Journal of Sustainable Tourism 8, p. 20-35.

Chrismond, S.P. 2001. 'The Importance of the Bats to Visitors at Deer Cave, Mulu National Park, Sarawak, Malaysia'. Hornbill.

Cohen, E. 1988. 'Authenticity and Commoditization in Tourism'. Annals of Tourism Research 15, p. 371-386.

Consumers' Association of Penang (CAP) 1999. 'Comments on the Detailed Environmental Impact Assessment Study for the Proposed Development of the Sungai Selangor Dam in Hulu Selangor' (http://www.xlibris.de/magickriver/doecap.htm, 31. May 2002).

Colchester, M. 1997. 'Salvaging Nature – Indigenous Peoples and Protected Areas' in Ghimire, K.B. and Pimbert, M.P. (eds.) Social Change and Conservation, London: Earthscan, p. 97-130.

Corner, E.J.H. & Beaman, J.H. 1996. 'The Plant Life of Kinabalu – An Introduction' in Wong, K.M. and Phillipps, A. (eds.) Kinabalu – Summit of Borneo, Kota Kinabalu: The Sabah Society/Sabah Parks, p. 101-150.

Craib, I. 1992. 'Anthony Giddens'. London: Routledge.

Cranbrook, G.G.-H., Earl of 2000. '40,000 years of Man & Biodiversity in Borneo: An Archaeozoological Perspective' in Leigh, M. (ed.) 6th Biennal Borneo Research Conference. Kuching/Sarawak: Institute of East Asian Studies.

Crichton, M. 1999. 'Timeline'. New York: Ballantine.

Crouch, H. 1996. 'Government & Society in Malaysia'. St. Leonards NSW: Allen & Unwin.

Culmsee, H. 2003. 'Das UNESCO-Biosphärenreservatkonzept als Instrument der Entwicklungszusammenarbeit' in Kaiser, M. (ed.) Weltwissen – Entwicklungszusammenarbeit in der Weltgesellschaft, Bielefeld: Transcript, p. 163-182.

Dahles, H. 2002. 'The Politics of Tour Guiding – Image Management in Indonesia'. Annals of Tourism Research 29, p. 783-800.

DeLyser, D. 1999. 'Authenticity on the Ground: Engaging the Past in a California Ghost Town'. Annals of the Association of American Geographers 89, p. 602-632.

Department of Forestry of Sarawak 2000. 'Visitor Statistics'. Kuching.

--- 2001. 'Visitor Statistics to the National Parks in 2000': Department of Forestry of Sarawak (http://www.forestry.sarawak.gov.my/forweb/np/about/ff/np-vis.htm, 12. September 2002).

Department of Forestry Peninsular Malaysia 2000. 'Visitor Statistics'. Kuala Lumpur.

Department of Statistics Malaysia 2001. 'Key Summary Statistics by State, Malaysia 2000' (http://www.statistics.gov.my/English/KeyesumStats.htm, 14. February 2002).

Department of Wildlife and National Parks Malaysia 2002. 'Taman Negara Fest' (http://www.wildlife.gov.my, 7. August 2002).

Dörfler, T., Graefe, O. & Müller-Mahn, D. 2003. 'Habitus und Feld – Anregungen für eine Neuorientierung der geographischen Entwicklungsforschung auf der Grundlage von Bourdieus "Theorie der Praxis"'. Geographica Helvetica 58, p. 11-23.

Douglas, I. 1999. 'Sediment – A Major River Management Issue' Rivers '99 – Towards Sustainable Development. Pulau Pinang: Universiti Sains Malaysia.

Eagles, P.F.J., McCool, S.F. & Haynes, C.D. 2002. 'Sustainable Tourism in Protected Areas – Guidelines for Planning and Management' (Best Practice Protected Area Guidelines Seiries, Vol. 8). Gland: IUCN.

Eaton, P. 2000. 'Land Tenure, Local Communities and Protected Areas – A Borneo Perspektive' in Leigh, M. (ed.) 6th Biennal Borneo Research Conference. Kuching/Sarawak: Institute of East Asian Studies.

Ecotourism Society 2002. 'Québec Declaration on Ecotourism': travelmole (http://www.travelmole.com/cgi-bin/item.cgi?id=81853, 17. December 2002).

Elsrud, T. 2001. 'Risk Creation in Traveling – Backpacker Adventure Narration'. Annals of Tourism Research 28, p. 597-617.

Firth, T. & Hing, N. 1999. 'Backpacker Hostels and their Guests: Attitudes and Behaviours Relating to Sustainable Tourism'. Tourism Management 20, p. 252-254.

Fischer Weltalmanach 2001. 'Der Fischer Weltalmanach 2002'. Frankfurt am Main: Fischer Taschenbuch Verlag.
Frankenberg, P., Lauer, W. & Rheker, J.R. 1990. 'Das Klimatabellenbuch'. Braunschweig: Westermann.
Frost, W. 2001. 'Rainforests' in Weaver, D.B. (ed.) The Encyclopedia of Ecotourism, New York: CABI, p. 193-204.
Gäth, P. 1999. 'Ökonomische Effekte des Trekkingtourismus im Langtang Nationalpark, Nepal', Diplomarbeit Zürich: Universität Zürich.
Garland, A. 1997. 'The Beach'. London: Penguin.
Geisel, S. 2002. 'McDonald's Village' 1520). Zürich: Vontobel-Stiftung.
Ghimire, K.B. 2001. 'The Growth of National and Regional Tourism in Developing Contries: An Overview' in Ghimire, K.B. (ed.) The Native Tourist, London: Earthscan, p. 1-29.
--- 2001. 'Regional Tourism and South-South Economic Cooperation'. The Geographical Journal 167, p. 99-110.
Giddens, A. 1991. 'Modernity and Self Identity – Self and Society in the Late Modern Age'. Cambridge: Polity.
--- 1992. 'The Consequences of Modernity'. Cambridge.
--- 1993. 'Sociology'. Cambridge: Polity.
--- 1995. 'Die Konstitution der Gesellschaft – Grundzüge einer Theorie der Strukturierung' (Theorie und Gesellschaft, Vol. 1). Frankfurt/New York: Campus.
--- 1996. 'Konsequenzen der Moderne'. Frankfurt am Main: Suhrkamp.
--- 1999. 'Der dritte Weg – Die Erneuerung der sozialen Demokratie' (Edition Zweite Moderne) Frankfurt am Main: Suhrkamp.
--- 2000. 'The Third Way and its Critics'. Cambridge: Polity.
Gomez, E.T. & Jomo, K.S. 1997. 'Malaysia's Political Economy – Politics, Patronage and Profits'. Cambridge: Cambridge University Press.
Grütter, K. & Plüss, C. 1996. 'Herrliche Aussichten – Frauen im Tourismus' (Tourismus & Entwicklung, Vol. Zürich: Rotpunktverlag.
Hampton, M.P. 1998. 'Backpacker Tourism and Economic Development'. Annals of Tourism Research 25, p. 639-660.
Hawkins, D.E. & Lamoureux, K. 2001. 'Global Growth and Magnitude of Ecotourism' in Weaver, D.B. (ed.) The Encyclopedia of Ecotourism, New York: CABI, p. 63-72.

Herbers, K. 1991. 'Unterwegs zu heiligen Stätten – Pilgerfahrten' in Bausinger, H., Beyrer, K. and Korff, G. (eds.) Reisekultur – Von der Pilgerfahrt zum modernen Tourismus, München: Beck, p. 23-31.
Hitchcock, M. & Jay, S. 1998. 'Eco-tourism and Environmental Change in Indonesia, Malaysia and Thailand' in King, V. (ed.) Environmental Challenges in South-East Asia, Richmond: Curzon, p. 305-316.
Huber, A. 1999. 'Heimat in der Postmoderne' (Soziographie), Zürich: Seismo.
Hutton, W. 1998. 'Sarawak' (Insight Pocket Guides, Vol. Singapore: APA Publications.
Immigration Department of Malaysia 2003. 'Malaysia Tourist Arrivals 2002' (http://www.tourismmalaysia.gov.my/statistic/2001b.htm, 2. April 2003).
INSAN, Institute for Social Analysis 1994. 'Logging Against the Natives of Sarawak'. Petaling Jaya: INSAN.
Institute for Development Studies 1996. 'Sabah Tourism Masterplan – Executive Summary'. Kota Kinabalu: The State Government of Sabah.
IUCN 1994. 'Guidelines for Protected Area Management Categories'. Gland: IUCN.
Jenkins, D.V., de Silva, G.S., Wells, D.R. & Phillipps, A. 1996. 'An Annotated Checklist of the Birds of Kinabalu Park' in Wong, K.M. and Phillipps, A. (eds.) Kinabalu – Summit of Borneo, Kota Kinabalu: The Sabah Society/Sabah Parks, p. 397-438.
Jenkins, G. 2001. 'Heritage, Conservation and Tourism in a Malaysian City: Georgetown under Threat?' EUROSEAS. London.
Jenkins, R. 1993. 'Pierre Bourdieu'. London: Routledge.
Kamphues, M. 1998. 'Soziokulturelle Perspektiven zum Tourismus in Malaysia – Am Beispiel Longbeach auf den Perhentianinseln'. Diplomarbeit Zürich: Universität Zürich.
Keller, U., Backhaus, N. & Elsasser, H. 2002. 'Indischer Tourismus in der Schweiz'. Tourismus Journal 6, p. 383-396.
Khaidir, A. 1994. 'Save the Penans'. Kuala Lumpur: Berita Publishing Sdn. Bhd.
Kiefl, W. 1997. 'Wo du nicht bist, dort ist das Glück'. Tourismus Journal 1, p. 207-224.
King, V.T. 1992. 'Tourism and Culture in Malaysia, with Reference to Borneo' in King, V.T. (ed.) Tourism in Borneo – Issues and Perspectives: Borneo Research Council, p. 29-44.
--- 1993. 'The Peoples of Borneo'. Oxford: Blackwell.

--- 2001. 'A Question of Identity: Names, Societies, and Ethnic Groups in Interior Kalimantan and Brunei Darussalam'. Sojourn – Journal of Social Issues in Southeast Asia 16, p. 1-36.
Kollmair, M. & Backhaus, N. forthcoming. 'Environmental Entitlements in the Use of Resources in National Parks'. Environmental Management.
Korte, H. 2001. 'Soziologie im Nebenfach: Eine Einführung'. Konstanz: UVK Verlagsgesellschaft.
Krais, B. & Gebauer, G. 2002. 'Habitus'. Bielefeld: Transcript.
Küpfer, I. 2000. 'Die regionalwirtschaftliche Bedeutung des Nationalparktourismus: untersucht am Beispiel des Schweizerischen Nationalparks'. Liestal: Lüdin.
Kurte, B. 2002. 'Der Ökotourismus-Begriff – Seine Interpretation im internationalen Bereich' (Materialien zur Fremdenverkehrsgeographie, Vol. 59). Trier: Geographische Gesellschaft Trier.
Laman, T. 2002. 'Proboscis Monkeys'. National Geographic 202, p. 100-117.
Lamnek, S. 1995. 'Qualitative Sozialforschung; Bd. 2 Methoden und Techniken'. Weinheim: Beltz.
Lash, S. & Urry, J. 1994. 'Economies of Signs and Space'. London: Sage.
Lawai Anak Kumpang 2001. 'The Satisfaction of visitors with adventure caving at Mulu National Park, Malaysia'. Hornbill.
Leach, M., Mearns, R. & Scoones, I. 1999. 'Environmental Entitlements – Dynamics and Institutions in Community-Based Natural Resource Management'. World Development 27, p. 225-247.
Lee Boon Thong & Bahrin, T.S. 1998. 'Modernizing Influences and Traditional Villages in Sarawak: The Need for a Paradigm Shift in Development Strategies' in James, V.U. (ed.) Capacity Building in Development Countries – Human and Environmental Dimension, Westport CT: Praeger Publishers, p. 144-153.
Lee Tain Choi, D. 1996. 'Geology of Kinabalu' in Wong, K.M. and Phillipps, A. (eds.) Kinabalu – Summit of Borneo, Kota Kinabalu: The Sabah Society/Sabah Parks, p. 19-29.
Le Monde diplomatique 2003. 'Atlas der Globalisierung'. Berlin: taz Verlags- und Betriebs GmbH.
Liew, F.S.P. 1996. 'Kinabalu Park: Past, Present and Future' in Wong, K.M. and Phillipps, A. (eds.) Kinabalu – Summit of Borneo, Kota Kinabalu: The Sabah Society/Sabah Parks, p. 455-473.
Lim Chan Koon 2000. 'Humans and Swiftlets – Centuries of Affiliation' in Leigh, M. (ed.) 6th Biennal Borneo Research Conference. Kuching/Sarawak: Institute of East Asian Studies.
Lindberg, K. 2001. 'Economic Impacts' in Weaver, D.B. (ed.) The Encyclopedia of Ecotourism, New York: CABI, p. 363-377.
Luger, K. 1995. 'Kulturen im Veränderungsstress – Kulturtheoretische Überlegungen zur Tourismusdebatte' in Luger, K. and Inmann, K. (eds.) Verreiste Berge – Kultur und Tourismus im Hochgebirge, Innsbruck: StudienVerlag, p. 19-42.
Lutterjohann, M., Homann, E., Homann, K. & Kuster, R. 1998. 'Malaysia mit Singapur und Brunei' (Reise Know-How), Bielefeld: Reise Know-How Verlag.
MacCannell, D. 1989. 'The Tourist – A New Theory of the Leisure Class'. Berkeley, Los Angeles, London: University of California Press.
Magick River, A. 2002. 'Unforseen Technical Difficulties – Delay Completion of Dam by at least 6 Months' (http://www.xlibris.de/magickriver/bulletin.htm, 31. May 2002).
Malaysian Nature Society 2000. 'Firefly Study - the effects of the Sungai Selangor Dam on the fireflies and their habitat' (http://www.mns.org.my/article.php?sid=81, 31. May 2002).
--- 2002. 'Gunung Ledang Baseline Inventory' (http://www.mns.org.my/article.php?sid=154, 31. May 2002).
Manser, B. 1999. 'Sarawak (Malaysia) – Die andere Sicht'. Tong Tana, p. 2-8.
Markwell, K.W. 1997. 'Dimensions of Photography in a Nature-Based Tour'. Annals of Tourism Research 24, p. 131-155.
Masing, J.J. 1999. 'Supporting Ecotourism Development at the Regional Level of Government – An Overview of the Sarawak Experience and Future Directions of Growth' World Ecotourism Conference. Kota Kinabalu, Malaysia.
Meethan, K. 2001. 'Tourism in Global Society – Place, Culture, Consumption'. Basingstoke: Palgrave.
Meredith, M. & Woolridge, J. 1992. 'Giant Caves of Borneo'. Kuala Lumpur: Tropical Press Sdn. Bhd.

Merriam-Webster 2002. 'Collegiate Dictionary' (http://www.m-w.com/cgi-bin/dictionary, 3. April 2003).
Meyer, Ü. 2002. 'Warum in aller Welt reisen wir in alle Welt?' Quattro – Beilage "Willisauer Bote".
Ministry of Science Environment and Technology Malaysia 1998. 'Malaysia's National Policy on Biological Diversity'. Kuala Lumpur: Ministry of Science, Environment and Technology.
Mohamed, I.A. 2001. 'Rafflesia of Gunung Gading National Park, Lundu, Malaysia'. Hornbill.
Moscardo, G. & Woods, B. 1998. 'Managing Tourism in the Wet Tropics World Heritage Area' in Laws, E., Faulkner, B. and Moscardo, G. (eds.) Embracing and Managing Change in Tourism, London: Routledge, p. 307-323.
Müller-Böker, U. 1996. 'Erlebnis- und Ökotourismus in Nepal – Das Beispiel des Chitwan-Nationalparks'. Geographische Rundschau 48, p. 174-179.
Murphy, L. 2001. 'Exploring Social Interactions of Backpackers'. Annals of Tourism Research 28, p. 50-67.
North, D.C. 1990. 'Institutions, Institutional Change and Economic Performance'. Cambridge/Melbourne: Cambridge University Press.
Oppermann, M. 1992. 'Tourismus in Malaysia' (Sozialwissenschaftliche Studien zu internationalen Problemen, Vol. 177). Saarbrücken: Breitenbach.
Orams, M.B. 2001. 'Types of Ecotourism' in Weaver, D.B. (ed.) The Encyclopediea of Ecotourism, New York: CABI, p. 23-36.
Peet, R. 1998. 'Modern Geographical Thought'. Oxford: Blackwell.
Periplus Editions n.a. 'Sarawak & Kuching'. Singapore: Periplus.
Perkins, H.C. & Thorns, D.C. 2001. 'Gazing or Performing? – Reflections on Urry's Tourist Gaze in the Context of Contemporary Experience in the Antipodes'. International Sociology 16, p. 185-204.
Phillips, N. & Hardy, C. 2002. 'Discourse Analysis – Investigating Processes of Social Construction' (Qualitative Research Methods, Vol. 50), London: Sage.
Plüss, C. 1999. 'Ferienglück aus Kinderhänden – Kinderarbeit im Tourismus' (Reihe Tourismus & Entwicklung, Vol. Zürich: Rotpunktverlag.
Regis, P. 1996. 'The People and Folklore of Kinabalu' in Wong, K.M. and Phillipps, A. (eds.) Kinabalu – Summit of Borneo, Kota Kinabalu: The Sabah Society/Sabah Parks, p. 31-39.
Reichertz, J. 2000. 'Zur Gültigkeit Qualitativer Sozialforschung': Forum Qualitative Sozialforschung (http://qualitative-research.net/fqs/fqs-d/2-00inhalt-d.htm, 30. Aug. 2000).
Road Atlas of Malaysia 1996. (Globetrotter Travel Atlas, Vol. London: New Holland.
Robertson, R. 1995. 'Glocalization: Time-Space and Homogeneity-Heterogeneity' in Featherstone, M., Lash, S. and Robertson, R. (eds.) Global Modernities, London: Sage, p. 25-44.
Rojek, C. 2000. 'Leisure and Culture'. London: Macmillan.
Rowthorn, C., Andrew, D., Hellander, P. & Lindenmayer, C. 1999. 'Malaysia, Singapore & Brunei – From beach Resorts to Borneo rainforests'. Singapore: lonely planet.
Rowthorn, C., Benson, S., Kerr, R. & Niven, C. 2001. 'Malaysia, Singapore & Brunei'. Melbourne/Oakland/London/Paris: lonely planet.
Rüegge, B. 2003. 'Borneo im Mediendiskurs'. Diplomarbeit Zürich: Universität Zürich.
Sabah Parks 2000. 'Visitor Statistics'. Kota Kinabalu.
Saifuddin, B.S. 2001. 'Why do Visitors Go to Matang Wildlife Centre?' Hornbill.
Sanggin, S.E., Noweg, G.T., Abdul, R.A. & Mersat, N.I. 2000. 'Impact of Tourism on Longhouse Communities in Sarawak' in Leigh, M. (ed.) 6th Biennal Borneo Research Conference. Kuching/Sarawak: Institute of East Asian Studies.
Sarawak Tourism Board 199? 'Sarawak – The Hidden Paradise of Borneo'. Kuching.
Scheyvens, R. 2002. 'Backpacker Tourism and Third World Development'. Annals of Tourism Research 29, p. 144-164.
Schiemann, G. (ed.) 1996. 'Was ist Natur? – Klassische Texte zur Naturphilosophie'. München: Deutscher Taschenbuch Verlag.
Schulze, H. & Suratman, S. 1999. 'Villagers in Transition – Case Studies from Sabah'. Kota Kinabalu: Universiti Malaysia Sabah.
Schumann, S. 2000. 'Repräsentative Umfrage' (Lehr- und Handbücher der Politikwissenschaft), München/Wien: Oldenbourg.
Schurian-Bremecker, C. 2001. '"Anpirschen, beobachten, abwarten, schiessen" – Fotografieren als touristische Verhaltensweise' in Köck, C. (ed.) Reisebilder – Produktion

und Reproduktion touristischer Wahrnehmung, Münster, Berlin, München, New York: Waxmann, p. 199-208.
--- 2002. 'Der Mann mit dem Stiefel – Fotografie und touristisches Verhalten' in Bakkes, M., Goethe, T., Günther, S. and Magg, R. (eds.) Im Handgepäck Rassismus – Beiträge zu Tourismus und Kultur, Freiburg: iz3w, p. 175-190.
Seckelmann, A. 2002. 'Domestic tourism – A Chance for Regional Development in Turkey?' Tourism Management 23, p. 85-92.
Selengut, S. 1995. 'Protected Areas and the Tourism Industry' in McNeely, J.A. (ed.) Expanding Partnership in Conservation, Gland: IUCN, p. 127-133.
Siebers, W. 1991. 'Ungleiche Lehrfahrten – Kavaliere und Gelehrte' in Bausinger, H., Beyrer, K. and Korff, G. (eds.) Reisekultur – Von der Pilgerfahrt zum modernen Tourismus, München: Beck, p. 47-57.
Smart, B. 1999. 'Facing Modernity'. London: Sage.
Soliva, R. 2002. 'Der Naturschutz in Nepal – eine akteurorientierte Untersuchung aus der Sicht der Politischen Ökolgie' (Kultur, Gesellschaft, Umwelt/Culture, Society, Environment, Vol. 5). Münster: Lit.
Swerdlow, J.L. 2000. 'Nature's Rx'. National Geographic 197, p. 98-117.
Taman Negara Resort n.a. 'Taman Negara Resort: National Park Pahang Darul Makmur'. Kuala Lumpur.
Tan Chin Siang 1999. 'Air Accessibility crucial in further promotion of Mulu National Park' New Straits Times. Kuala Lumpur.
Thorsell, J. 2000. 'Gunung Mulu National Park – World Heritage Nomination – IUCN Technical Evaluation'. Gland: IUCN.
Thrift, N. 1996. 'Spacial Formations'. London: Sage.
Torres, R. 2002. 'Cancun's tourism development from a Fordist spectrum of analysis'. Tourist Studies 2, p. 87-116.
Tourism Authority of Thailand 2002. 'Tourism Statistics' (http://www.tat.or.th/stat/index.html, 31. May 2002).
Tourism Malaysia 2002. 'Malaysia – Truly Asia' (http://www.tourism.gov.my/, 14. June 2002).
--- 2003. 'Malaysia – Truly Asia' (http://www.tourism.gov.my/, 28. May 2003).
Treibel, A. 2000. 'Einführung in soziologische Theorien der Gegenwart'. Opladen: Leske + Budrich.

Trojanow, I. 2002. 'Augen zu und Geldbeutel festhalten – Beobachtungen im Reich der neuen Alternativtouristen' Neue Zürcher Zeitung. Zürich.
UNEP, W.C.M.C. 1992. 'Protected Areas of Malaysia': UNEP (http://www.wcmc.org.uk:80/protected_areas/data/sample/0277v.htm, 28. February 2002).
UNESCO 1998. 'Convention concerning the protection of the World cultural and natural heritage': UNESCO (http://www.unesco.org, 12. December 2001).
--- 2000. 'World Heritage Committee Inscribes 61 New Sites on World Heritage List': UNESCO (http://www.unesco.org/whc/nwhc/pages/news/main2.htm, 14. December 2000).
Uriely, N., Yonay, Y. & Simchai, D. 2002. 'Backpacking Experiences – A Type and Form Analysis'. Annals of Tourism Research 29, p. 520-538.
Urry, J. 2002. 'The Tourist Gaze'. London: Sage.
Vision Air 2001. 'Mulu Visitors double – Second air Link to Mulu has Travel Trade Breathing Easier': Vision Air (http://www.visionair.com.my/, 12. September 2002).
Vorlaufer, K. 1996. 'Tourismus in Entwicklungsländern: Möglichkeiten und Grenzen einer nachhaltigen Entwicklung durch Fremdenverkehr'. Darmstadt: Wissenschaftliche Buchgesellschaft.
Watson Andaya, B. & Andaya, L.Y. 2001. 'A History of Malaysia'. Hampshire: Palgrave.
Weaver, D.B. 2001. 'Ecotourism in the Context of Other Tourism Types' in Weaver, D.B. (ed.) The Encyclopedia of Ecotourism, New York: CABI, p. 73-83.
Werlen, B. 1995. 'Sozialgeographie alltäglicher Regionalisierungen 1: Zur Ontologie von Gesellschaft und Raum' 116). Stuttgart: Franz Steiner Verlag.
--- 1997. 'Sozialgeographie alltäglicher Regionalisierungen 2: Globalisierung, Region, und Regionalisierung' (Erdkundliches Wissen, Vol. 119). Stuttgart: Franz Steiner.
--- 1999. 'Handlungszentrierte Sozialgeographie. Replik auf die Kritiken' in Meusburger, P. (ed.) Handlungszentrierte Sozialgeographie – Benno Werlens Entwurf in kritischer Diskussion, Stuttgart: Franz Steiner Verlag.

--- 1999. 'Regionalism and Political Society' in Embree, L. (ed.) Schutzian Social Science, Dordrecht: Kluwer, p. 1-22.
--- 2000. 'Sozialgeographie'. Bern: Haupt UTB.
Wight, P.A. 2001. 'Ecotourists – Not a Homogenous Market Segment' in Weaver, D.B. (ed.) The Encyclopedia of Ecotourism, New York: CABI, p. 37-62.
Wittenberg, R. & Cramer, H. 2000. 'Datenanalyse mit SPSS für Windows'. Stuttgart: Lucius & Lucius.
Wöhler, K. 2001. 'Tourismus und Nachhaltigkeit'. Das Parlament – Aus Politik und Zeitgeschichte B 47, p. 40-46.
--- 2003. 'Topographie des Erlebens – Zur Verortung touristischer Erlebniswelten' Materialien zur angewandten Tourismuswissenschaft, Neue Folge. Lüneburg: Universität Lüneburg.
Wolfe, T. 1990. 'The Bonfire of the Vanities'. New York: Bantam.
Wong, K.M. & Phillipps, A. (eds.) 1996. 'Kinabalu – Summit of Borneo'. Kota Kinabalu: The Sabah Society/Sabah Parks.
Wong, M. 2002. 'Rafflesias of Malaysia'. Malaysian Naturalist 55, p. 20-27.
World Conservation Monitoring Centre 2002. 'Protected areas of Malaysia': WCMC (http://www.unep-wcmc.org, 30. July 2002).
World Conservation Monitoring Centre & IUCN 1998. '1997 United Nations List of Protected Areas'. Gland: IUCN.
World Tourism Organisation 2001. 'The British Ecotourism Market'. Madrid: Market Intelligence and Promotion Section, Sustainable Development of Tourism Section.
--- 2001. 'The German Ecotourism Market'. Madrid: Market Intelligence and Promotion Section, Sustainable Development of Tourism Section.
--- 2002. 'The Canadian Ecotourism Market'. Madrid: Market Intelligence and Promotion Section, Sustainable Development of Tourism Section.
--- 2002. 'The French Ecotourism Market'. Madrid: Market Intelligence and Promotion Section, Sustainable Development of Tourism Section.
--- 2002. 'The Italian Ecotourism Market'. Madrid: Market Intelligence and Promotion Section, Sustainable Development of Tourism Section.
--- 2002. 'The Spanish Ecotourism Market'. Madrid: Market Intelligence and Promotion Section, Sustainable Development of Tourism Section.
--- 2002. 'The U.S. Ecotourism Market'. Madrid: Market Intelligence and Promotion Section, Sustainable Development of Tourism Section.
WTO/UNEP 1992. 'Guidelines: Development of National Parks and Protected Areas for Tourism' (Tourism and the Environment – UNEP-IE/PAC Technical Report, Vol. 13). Madrid: World Tourism Organisation & United Nations Environment Programme.
WWF Malaysia 1996. 'National Ecotourism Plan Malaysia'. Petaling Jaya.
WWF Malaysia & Cubitt, G. 1998. 'The National Parks and other Wild Places of Malaysia'. Singapore: New Holland.

Kultur, Gesellschaft, Umwelt

Schriften zur Südasien- und Südostasien-Forschung
Culture, Society, Environment – South Asian and South East Asian Studies

Herausgegeben von Ulrike Müller-Böker und Samuel Wälty

Band 1   Samuel Wälty
         Kintamani. Dorf, Land und Rituale
         Entwicklung und institutioneller Wandel in einer Bergregion auf Bali
         (1997, 352 S., DM 54.–, ISBN 3-8258-3264-3)

Band 2   Helmut Buchholt
         Zwischen Macht und Ohnmacht
         Die chinesische Minderheit in Südostasien
         (1998, 337 S., DM 54.–, ISBN 3-8258-3593-6)

Band 3   Michael Kollmair
         Futterbäume in Nepal
         Traditionelles Wissen, Stellenwert in kleinbäuerlichen Betrieben
         und räumliche Verteilung
         (1999, 186 S., DM 49.80, ISBN 3-8258-4698-9)

Band 4   Thomas Meier
         Mini Hydropower for Rural Development
         A New Market-Oriented Approach to Maximize Electrification Benefits
         With Special Focus on Indonesia
         (2001, 311 S., DM 49.80, ISBN 3-8258-5560-0)

Band 5   Reto Soliva
         Der Naturschutz in Nepal
         Eine akteurorientierte Untersuchung aus der Sicht
         der Politischen Ökologie
         (2002, 468 S., Euro 35.90, ISBN 3-8258-6154-6)

Band 6   Norman Backhaus
         Tourism and Nature Conservation in Malaysian National Parks
         (2005, 288 S., Euro 28.90, ISBN 3-8258-9037-6)

--- 1999. 'Regionalism and Political Society' in Embree, L. (ed.) Schutzian Social Science, Dordrecht: Kluwer, p. 1-22.
--- 2000. 'Sozialgeographie'. Bern: Haupt UTB.
Wight, P.A. 2001. 'Ecotourists – Not a Homogenous Market Segment' in Weaver, D.B. (ed.) The Encyclopedia of Ecotourism, New York: CABI, p. 37-62.
Wittenberg, R. & Cramer, H. 2000. 'Datenanalyse mit SPSS für Windows'. Stuttgart: Lucius & Lucius.
Wöhler, K. 2001. 'Tourismus und Nachhaltigkeit'. Das Parlament – Aus Politik und Zeitgeschichte B 47, p. 40-46.
--- 2003. 'Topographie des Erlebens – Zur Verortung touristischer Erlebniswelten' Materialien zur angewandten Tourismuswissenschaft, Neue Folge. Lüneburg: Universität Lüneburg.
Wolfe, T. 1990. 'The Bonfire of the Vanities'. New York: Bantam.
Wong, K.M. & Phillipps, A. (eds.) 1996. 'Kinabalu – Summit of Borneo'. Kota Kinabalu: The Sabah Society/Sabah Parks.
Wong, M. 2002. 'Rafflesias of Malaysia'. Malaysian Naturalist 55, p. 20-27.
World Conservation Monitoring Centre 2002. 'Protected areas of Malaysia': WCMC (http://www.unep-wcmc.org, 30. July 2002).
World Conservation Monitoring Centre & IUCN 1998. '1997 United Nations List of Protected Areas'. Gland: IUCN.
World Tourism Organisation 2001. 'The British Ecotourism Market'. Madrid: Market Intelligence and Promotion Section, Sustainable Development of Tourism Section.
--- 2001. 'The German Ecotourism Market'. Madrid: Market Intelligence and Promotion Section, Sustainable Development of Tourism Section.
--- 2002. 'The Canadian Ecotourism Market'. Madrid: Market Intelligence and Promotion Section, Sustainable Development of Tourism Section.
--- 2002. 'The French Ecotourism Market'. Madrid: Market Intelligence and Promotion Section, Sustainable Development of Tourism Section.
--- 2002. 'The Italian Ecotourism Market'. Madrid: Market Intelligence and Promotion Section, Sustainable Development of Tourism Section.
--- 2002. 'The Spanish Ecotourism Market'. Madrid: Market Intelligence and Promotion Section, Sustainable Development of Tourism Section.
--- 2002. 'The U.S. Ecotourism Market'. Madrid: Market Intelligence and Promotion Section, Sustainable Development of Tourism Section.
WTO/UNEP 1992. 'Guidelines: Development of National Parks and Protected Areas for Tourism' (Tourism and the Environment – UNEP-IE/PAC Technical Report, Vol. 13). Madrid: World Tourism Organisation & United Nations Environment Programme.
WWF Malaysia 1996. 'National Ecotourism Plan Malaysia'. Petaling Jaya.
WWF Malaysia & Cubitt, G. 1998. 'The National Parks and other Wild Places of Malaysia'. Singapore: New Holland.

Kultur, Gesellschaft, Umwelt

Schriften zur Südasien- und Südostasien-Forschung
Culture, Society, Environment – South Asian and South East Asian Studies

Herausgegeben von Ulrike Müller-Böker und Samuel Wälty

Band 1   Samuel Wälty
Kintamani. Dorf, Land und Rituale
Entwicklung und institutioneller Wandel in einer Bergregion auf Bali
(1997, 352 S., DM 54.–, ISBN 3-8258-3264-3)

Band 2   Helmut Buchholt
Zwischen Macht und Ohnmacht
Die chinesische Minderheit in Südostasien
(1998, 337 S., DM 54.–, ISBN 3-8258-3593-6)

Band 3   Michael Kollmair
Futterbäume in Nepal
Traditionelles Wissen, Stellenwert in kleinbäuerlichen Betrieben
und räumliche Verteilung
(1999, 186 S., DM 49.80, ISBN 3-8258-4698-9)

Band 4   Thomas Meier
Mini Hydropower for Rural Development
A New Market-Oriented Approach to Maximize Electrification Benefits
With Special Focus on Indonesia
(2001, 311 S., DM 49.80, ISBN 3-8258-5560-0)

Band 5   Reto Soliva
Der Naturschutz in Nepal
Eine akteurorientierte Untersuchung aus der Sicht
der Politischen Ökologie
(2002, 468 S., Euro 35.90, ISBN 3-8258-6154-6)

Band 6   Norman Backhaus
Tourism and Nature Conservation in Malaysian National Parks
(2005, 288 S., Euro 28.90, ISBN 3-8258-9037-6)